BET 3753

SHAKESPEARE SURVEY

ADVISORY BOARD

1 Shakespeare and his Stage
2 Shakespearian Production
3 The Man and the Writer
4 Interpretation
5 Textual Criticism
6 The Histories
7 Style and Language
8 The Comedies
9 *Hamlet*
10 The Roman Plays
11 The Last Plays (with an index to *Surveys 1–10*)
12 The Elizabethan Theatre
13 *King Lear*
14 Shakespeare and his Contemporaries
15 The Poems and Music
16 Shakespeare in the Modern World
17 Shakespeare in his Own Age
18 Shakespeare Then Till Now
19 *Macbeth*
20 Shakespearian and Other Tragedy
21 *Othello* (with an index to *Surveys 11–20*)
22 Aspects of Shakespearian Comedy
23 Shakespeare's Language
24 Shakespeare: Theatre Poet
25 Shakespeare's Problem Plays
26 Shakespeare's Jacobean Tragedies
27 Shakespeare's Early Tragedies
28 Shakespeare and the Ideas of his Time
29 Shakespeare's Last Plays
30 *Henry IV* to *Hamlet*
31 Shakespeare and the Classical World (with an index to *Surveys 21–30*)
32 The Middle Comedies
33 *King Lear*
32 Characterization in Shakespeare
35 Shakespeare in the Nineteenth Century
36 Shakespeare in the Twentieth Century

SHAKESPEARE SURVEY

AN ANNUAL SURVEY OF
SHAKESPEARIAN STUDY AND PRODUCTION

36

EDITED BY
STANLEY WELLS

CAMBRIDGE UNIVERSITY PRESS

CAMBRIDGE
LONDON NEW YORK NEW ROCHELLE
MELBOURNE SYDNEY

Published by the Press Syndicate of the University of Cambridge
The Pitt Building, Trumpington Street, Cambridge CB2 IRP
32 East 57th Street, New York, NY 10022, USA
296 Beaconsfield Parade, Middle Park, Melbourne 3206, Australia

First published 1983

Shakespeare Survey was first published in 1948. For the first
eighteen volumes it was edited by Allardyce Nicoll.
Kenneth Muir edited volumes 19–33

Printed in Great Britain
by the University Press, Cambridge

Library of Congress catalogue card number: 49–1639

British Library Cataloguing in Publication Data
Shakespeare Survey
36
1. Shakespeare, William – Societies, periodicals, etc.
I. Wells, Stanley
822.3'3 PR2885
ISBN 0 521 25636 4

EDITOR'S NOTE

The first eight articles in this volume (except for Philip Brockbank's) were delivered to the International Shakespeare Conference at Stratford-upon-Avon in August 1982. The theme of the next volume will be 'Shakespeare's Earlier Comedies' (up to and including *The Merchant of Venice*). Volume 38 will have the same theme as the Conference in 1984, 'Shakespeare and History'; submissions should reach the Editor at 40 Walton Crescent, Oxford OX1 2JQ, by 1 September 1984 at the latest. Volume 39, with a deadline of 1 September 1985, will be concerned particularly with Shakespeare on film and television. Many articles are considered before the deadline, so those that arrive earlier have a greater chance of acceptance. Please either enclose return postage (overseas, in International Reply Coupons) or send a non-returnable xerox. A style sheet is available on request. All articles submitted are read by the Editor and by one or more members of the Advisory Board, whose indispensable assistance the Editor gratefully acknowledges.

With this volume we extend our thanks to our retiring reviewers – Roger Warren, Harriett Hawkins, and Gāmini Salgādo – and welcome their successors. George Walton Williams is withdrawing after six years of service: MacDonald P. Jackson, of the University of Auckland, New Zealand, will fill his place.

In attempting to survey the ever-increasing bulk of Shakespeare publications our reviewers have inevitably to exercise some selection. Review copies of books should be addressed to the Editor, as above. We are also very pleased to receive offprints of articles, which help to draw our reviewers' attention to relevant material.

S.W.W.

CONTRIBUTORS

RALPH BERRY, *Professor of English, University of Ottawa*

PETER BILTON, *Lecturer in English, University of Oslo*

PHILIP BROCKBANK, *Professor of English Language and Literature and Director of the Shakespeare Institute, University of Birmingham*

ALAN C. DESSEN, *Professor of English, University of North Carolina*

JULIET DUSINBERRE, *Fellow of Girton College, Cambridge*

PHILIP EDWARDS, *Professor of English Literature, University of Liverpool*

ANN FRIDÉN, *University of Gothenburg*

BRIAN GIBBONS, *Professor of English, University of Leeds*

JOHN JOWETT, *Assistant Editor, Shakespeare Department, Oxford University Press*

ALEXANDER LEGGATT, *Professor of English, University of Toronto*

JILL L. LEVENSON, *Associate Professor of English, University of Toronto*

LU GU-SUN, *Professor of English, Fudan University, Shanghai*

LOIS POTTER, *Lecturer in English, University of Leicester*

WILLEM SCHRICKX, *Professor of English and American Literature, University of Ghent*

NICHOLAS SHRIMPTON, *Fellow of Lady Margaret Hall and Lecturer in English, University of Oxford*

SUSAN SNYDER, *Professor of English, Swarthmore College, Pennsylvania*

WOLE SOYINKA, *Professor of Dramatic Arts, University of Ife*

MICHAEL TAYLOR, *Professor of English, University of New Brunswick*

GEORGE WALTON WILLIAMS, *Professor of English, Duke University, North Carolina*

CONTENTS

List of Plates   *page* ix

Shakespeare and the Living Dramatist *by* WOLE SOYINKA   1

Blood and Wine: Tragic Ritual from Aeschylus to Soyinka *by* PHILIP BROCKBANK   11

Hamlet Andante/*Hamlet* Allegro: Tom Stoppard's Two Versions *by* JILL L. LEVENSON   21

Auden, Shakespeare, and the Defence of Poetry *by* SUSAN SNYDER   29

Graves on Lovers, and Shakespeare at a Lovers' Funeral *by* PETER BILTON   39

Tragic Balance in *Hamlet by* PHILIP EDWARDS   43

Hamlet Across Space and Time *by* LU GU-SUN   53

Shakespeare's Scripts and the Modern Director *by* ALAN C. DESSEN   57

'He Shall Live a Man Forbid': Ingmar Bergman's *Macbeth by* ANN FRIDÉN   65

Komisarjevsky at Stratford-upon-Avon *by* RALPH BERRY   73

Troilus and Cressida and the Definition of Beauty *by* JULIET DUSINBERRE   85

The Pastoral Reckoning in *Cymbeline by* MICHAEL TAYLOR   97

New Created Creatures: Ralph Crane and the Stage Directions in *The Tempest by* JOHN JOWETT   107

Arden of Faversham by ALEXANDER LEGGATT   121

'Pickleherring' and English Actors in Germany *by* WILLEM SCHRICKX   135

Shakespeare Performances in Stratford-upon-Avon and London, 1981–2 *by* NICHOLAS SHRIMPTON   149

The Year's Contributions to Shakespearian Study:

    1   Critical Studies *reviewed by* BRIAN GIBBONS   157

    2   Shakespeare's Life, Times and Stage *reviewed by* LOIS POTTER   172

    3   Textual Studies *reviewed by* GEORGE WALTON WILLIAMS   181

Index   197

PLATES

BETWEEN PAGES 72 AND 73

IA   Ingmar Bergman's production of *Macbeth*, at the Gothenburg City Theatre, 1948.
[Reproduced by courtesy of the Teaterhistoriska museet, Gothenburg; Photo: G. Cassirer]

B   Bergman's *Macbeth*, 1948: the opening of the production's third act.
[Reproduced by courtesy of the Teaterhistoriska museet, Gothenburg; Photo: G. Cassirer]

IIA   Komisarjevsky's production of *King Lear*, act 1, scene 1; Shakespeare Memorial Theatre, 1936.
[Reproduced by courtesy of the Shakespeare Centre Library, Stratford-upon-Avon]

B   The first scene of the Induction in Komisarjevsky's *Taming of the Shrew*, Shakespeare Memorial Theatre, 1939.
[Reproduced by courtesy of the Shakespeare Centre Library, Stratford-upon-Avon]

BETWEEN PAGES 156 AND 157

IIIA   *All's Well That Ends Well*, Royal Shakespeare Theatre, 1981. The Countess (Peggy Ashcroft) and Lavache (Geoffrey Hutchings).
[Photo: Nobby Clark]

B   *All's Well That Ends Well*, Royal Shakespeare Theatre, 1981. Parolles (Stephen Moore) and Bertram (Mike Gwilym).
[Photo: Nobby Clark]

IVA   *All's Well That Ends Well*, Royal Shakespeare Theatre, 1981. The King of France (John Franklyn-Robbins) gives Bertram to Helena (Harriet Walter).
[Photo: Nobby Clark]

B   *All's Well That Ends Well*, Royal Shakespeare Theatre, 1981. Bertram and Diana (Cheryl Campbell).
[Photo: Nobby Clark]

VA   *Macbeth*, Royal Shakespeare Theatre, 1982. Macbeth (Bob Peck) and his wife (Sara Kestelman) at the end of the banquet scene.
[Photo: Holte Photographics]

B   *Much Ado About Nothing*, Royal Shakespeare Theatre, 1982. Act 1, scene 1: left, Beatrice (Sinead Cusack) questions the Messenger; centre, Edward Jewesbury as Leonato.
[Photo: Joe Cocks]

VIA   *Much Ado About Nothing*, Royal Shakespeare Theatre, 1982. 'Lady Beatrice, have you wept all this while?'; Derek Jacobi as Benedick.
[Photo: Joe Cocks]

B *Much Ado About Nothing*, Royal Shakespeare Theatre, 1982. John Carlisle as Don John (left) with Borachio (Ken Bones).
[*Photo: Joe Cocks*]

VIIA *King Lear*, Royal Shakespeare Theatre, 1982. Lear (Michael Gambon), the Fool (Antony Sher), and Edgar disguised as Poor Tom (Jonathan Hyde).
[*Photo: Holte Photographics*]

B *King Lear*, Royal Shakespeare Theatre, 1982. Act 4, scene 6: Edgar watches the reunion of Gloucester (David Waller) and Lear.
[*Photo: Joe Cocks*]

VIIIA *1 Henry IV*, Barbican Theatre, 1982. Left, Joss Ackland as Falstaff.
[*Photo: Chris Davies*]

B *2 Henry IV*, Barbican Theatre, 1982. Miriam Karlin as Mistress Quickly, Gemma Jones as Doll Tearsheet, and Joss Ackland as Falstaff (act 2, scene 4).
[*Photo: Chris Davies*]

IXA *The Tempest*, Royal Shakespeare Theatre, 1982. Act 1, scene 2: Prospero (Derek Jacobi) and Miranda (Alice Krige), with Ariel (Mark Rylance) on the ship behind them, and Ferdinand (Michael Maloney) in foreground.
[*Photo: Joe Cocks*]

B *The Tempest*, Royal Shakespeare Theatre, 1982. One of the goddesses in the masque, act 4, scene 1.
[*Photo: Joe Cocks*]

XA *Hamlet*, Donmar Warehouse Theatre, 1982. Anton Lesser as Hamlet.
[*Photo: Sophie Baker*]

B *Hamlet*, Donmar Warehouse Theatre, 1982. Hamlet with Gertrude (Susan Engel), act 3, scene 4.
[*Photo: Sophie Baker*]

SHAKESPEARE AND THE LIVING DRAMATIST

WOLE SOYINKA

Your statement is an impudently ignorant one to make. . . . Do you really mean no one should or could write about or speak about a war because one has not stood on the battlefield . . .? Was Shakespeare at Actium or Philippi . . .?[1]

That tart response from Sean O'Casey to Yeats will be familiar to many. O'Casey is not of course a 'living' dramatist, but I am certain that no one here expects a coroner's interpretation of that expression. O'Casey could have picked no worthier defender of his arguments; the universal puzzle of Shakespeare's evocative power often leads to speculations – in various degrees of whimsy – about his real identity. That is only another way of questing after the unrecorded things he actually did in real life – especially in the area of travel. If Shakespeare was never at Actium or Philippi contemporaneously with the events which he dramatized on these sites, he must have stood on their ruins or visited their living replicas in his wanderings – preferably press-ganged into one of those notorious merchant ships while he was hanging around the theatres, waiting to audition for a small role. Is it any wonder that the Middle Eastern poets and dramatists claim that he must, at the very least, have been a sometime visitor to North Africa and the Arabian peninsula? How else, for instance, could he have encountered the legend of Majnun Layla which he transformed – albeit without acknowledgement – into *Romeo and Juliet*? And so Ali Ahmad Ba-Kathir (who died in 1969), an Indonesian-born poet who became a naturalized Egyptian, restored to his adopted race what belonged to Arab literature in the first place – he translated *Romeo and Juliet* into Arabic free verse.

One interesting poser for Ahmad Ba-Kathir arose from the fact that, in the legend of Majnun's love for Layla, there was no history of family feuds; not only that, Arabic custom prevents a Romeo-style declamation of love even into the empty expanse of the desert – this is bringing dishonour to the girl and ruining the name and reputation of her family. The fate of an Orlando caught in the act of hanging love-sick verses on tamarind trees is better left unimagined – still, such are the impieties to be expected when a gifted Arab like Shakespeare loses his roots among the English infidels!

The difficulties encountered by Arab dramatists as a result of the opposing nature of much of the conventions and mores of Arabic culture, not to mention the actual intervention of language for these poets and dramatists, heighten the phenomenon of the fascination of Shakespeare for Arab-speaking authors, both those who turned naturally to classical (i.e. literary) Arabic and others, like Gibran at the turn of the century, and the contemporary dramatist Tawfik-al-Hakim who have revolutionized the concept of Arabic literature with their adoption and enrichment of colloquial Arabic.

But I should make it quite clear that I am not about to speak on Arabic writers or their adaptations, about whom I have only very superficial knowledge. The phenomenal hold of Shakespeare on modern European and American dramatists and directors is however not merely well-known but accepted as natural.

---

[1] Quoted in *Sean O'Casey: A Collection of Critical Essays*, ed. Thomas Kilroy (Englewood Cliffs, N.J., 1975), p. 115.

The ideological interrogatories which a Marxist play-wright like Brecht injects into his versions of Shake-speare, such as *Coriolanus*, are normal developments in European literary and dramatic sensibilities – Shake-speare is over-ample fodder for the creative browser. Indeed, the search for a moral anchor among the literary-inclined leads sooner or later to the vast arena of unresolved moral questions in his works and sometimes life. Thus, for Edward Bond, it was not enough that Shakespeare's *Lear* should be re-worked through some ideological framework, how-ever vague and ultimately cosseting. Clearly Bond's interest in *Lear* was only a temporary holding device for his real subject, William Shakespeare himself, whom Bond sees – despite some rather 'nice' dis-claimers – as a petit-bourgeois Lear: 'Shakespeare's plays show this need for sanity and its political expression, justice. But how did he live? His be-haviour as a property-owner made him closer to Goneril than Lear.' The explanation for this bizarre claim is that 'He supported and benefited from the Goneril-society – with its prisons, workhouses, whip-ping, starvation, mutilation, pulpit-hysteria and all the rest of it.' Like me? And you? Introductions and Prefaces are not of course the most helpful clues to an author's intentions or even thoughts, not even in the case of Bernard Shaw. The basic declarations of intent by Bond are valid enough: 'I wrote *Bingo* because I think the contradictions in Shakespeare's life are similar to the contradictions in us', complemented, for our purpose, by: 'Part of the play is about the relationship between any writer and his society.' That that relationship, in the case of Shakespeare, is closer to Goneril's than Lear's carries for me, I must confess, the air of one of those paradoxes which all writers – especially those with a poetic bent – like to indulge in from time to time. Artfulness is indeed a stock-in-trade of the self-conscious moralist; from Edward Bond we are instructed, in similar vein, that 'Shake-speare created Lear, who is the most radical of all society critics.' Well, Shakespeare's countryman should *know*, I suppose; so on that note I shall return to Shakespeare's distant cousins and demand, like Hamlet: 'What's Hecuba to him, or he to Hecuba?'

Among other statistical and factual details of this fascination is this: between about 1899 and 1950, some sixteen plays of Shakespeare had been translated and/or adapted by Arab poets and dramatists. They include plays as diverse as *Hamlet*, the ever-popular *Julius Caesar*, *The Merchant of Venice*, *Pericles*, *A Midsummer Night's Dream*, *King Richard III* and – need I add? – *Antony and Cleopatra*. There will have been others by now because even the government of the United Arab Republic, fed up with the number of embarrassingly inaccurate and inelegant translations, set up a committee to produce a scrupulous and complete translation of Shakespeare's works. So much for statistics, for much of which as well as for other details I am indebted to an essay by Professor Bushrui, formerly of the University of Ibadan, and to Dr Kole Omotoso, of my own University and department.

But the Arab world was not content to adopt or 'reclaim' Shakespeare's works. M. M. Badawi, in an article in *Cairo Studies* (1964) titled 'Shakespeare and the Arab World', states that the matter goes much further. Apparently it was not simply that Shake-speare stumbled on to an Arab shore during his unpublicized peregrinations; he was in fact an Arab. His real name, cleansed of its anglicized corruption, was Shayk al-Subair, which everyone knows of course is as dune-bred an Arabic name as any English poet can hope for.

Well, on our side, that is, in our own black Africa, we know that Julius Nyerere did translate *Julius Caesar* into Kishwahili and I believe there has been one recent adaptation of another of Shakespeare's plays – I think it was *The Taming of the Shrew* – into a little-known language, also in East Africa. But I have yet to hear of any claims that Shakespeare was a suspected progeny of a Zulu or Fulani herdsman or an Ashanti farmer. A young Ghanaian cineast did adapt *Macbeth* for the cinema, setting it in Northern, pastoral Ghana, but I believe the matter was taken no further.

Well, there are the historical causes. The experience of colonized North Africa has been one of a cultural struggle between French and English cultures – beginning with their educational systems – wherein the literature is always centrally placed. Then there is the history of Arabic literature itself on which the Islamic culture placed a number of constraints from which the European culture became not merely a liberating but, in certain aspects, even a revolutionary force. At the heart of that literary culture – the European that is – stood Shakespeare, with his limitless universal themes, themes which were congenial to the Arabic epic – or narrative – tradition, promoting the romance of lyrical language for its own sake, as a tool of elegant discourse, formalized social relations and pious conduct. Arabic is the conscious vehicle of Islamic piety. The English language, even of King James's Bible, is not tied to any kind of piety; the Shakespearian use of it, however, makes it the very homeland of moral beings – we can see why the Arab poet felt an instant affinity with this language. It should be emphasized that modern, colloquial Arabic is so distinct from the classical that it makes a practitioner of both virtually bilingual – it was this classical form that was considered for a long time the only poetic vehicle fit to bear the colossal weight of Shakespeare, only this language could map the moral contours of the minds of tragic and romantic heroes and heroines, and their judges.

Earlier, in listing the plays which have been transformed by the pen of Arab dramatists, I gave a special kind of note to *Antony and Cleopatra*. Much of course is correctly made of the universality of Shakespeare's plays; here, I find myself more concerned with a somewhat less usual particularity, one with which, I am convinced, the Arabic, and most especially the North African, poet simply could not fail to identify. How could he? O'Casey makes a case for the art of the dramatist by reminding us that the greatest poetic illusionist of all, Shakespeare, did not require physical participation in the battles of Actium or Philippi; to the North African dramatist, especially if he is also a poet, *Antony and Cleopatra* must appear to belie O'Casey. Shakespeare, it seems, must have sailed up the Nile and kicked up sands in the shadow of the pyramids to have etched the conflict of Egypt and Rome on such a realistic canvas, evoking tones, textures, smells, and even tastes which were so alien to the wintry climes of Europe. This is a theme with which I find myself in more than a little sympathy.

Some years ago, I watched a production of *Antony and Cleopatra* at the Aldwych, by the Royal Shakespeare Company – and winced throughout the entire night. We all have our prejudices of course, but some of these prejudices are the result of experience. Perhaps

the RSC knew that it had a problem in persuading even an English audience to accept any interpretation of Cleopatra by an English actress – so the actress sent up the whole thing – a sort of 'Look at me, we both know that this Cleopatra is not a character for real'. The production was very much of that order – a sort of variation of the play-within-a-play, only, this time, it was a director's critique-within-a-play – this Cleopatra was 'neither fish nor flesh; a man knew not where to have her'. If there was one female character that Shakespeare knew damned well where to have, it was Cleopatra. Come to think of it, I recall that my mind continually drifted off to a not too dissimilar occasion – this was the erotic, gastronomic orgy so sumptuously designed by the director of the film of Henry Fielding's *Tom Jones*. But at least that actress was trying her hardest, only I could not help superimposing on her performance the face and body of the actress Anna Magnani, one of the few European actresses of my knowledge who are truly endowed with a natural presence of erotic vulgarity. Shakespeare foresaw the problem, mind you:

> Saucy lictors
> Will catch at us like strumpets, and scald rhymers
> Ballad us out o' tune; the quick comedians
> Extemporally will stage us, and present
> Our Alexandrian revels; Antony
> Shall be brought drunken forth, and I shall see
> Some squeaking Cleopatra boy my greatness
> I' th' posture of a whore.   (5.2.213–20)

The other side of the balance sheet however is an ironic one. The near-unanimous opinion of the Arabic critics themselves on the translations and adaptations of their 'compatriot' Shayk al-Subair's masterpieces is that they were, in the main, the work of 'scald rhymers' who 'ballad him out of tune'. But I am not qualified to pronounce upon that, knowing no Arabic beyond 'Salaam ailekum', a benediction which we must pronounce on Shakespeare's motions in his grave if what those critics say is true. The special fascination of Arabic literature with Shakespeare however, mends all, at least for those of us who are safe from a direct encounter with the early consequences.

Quite apart from language and colonial history, other theories have been offered, theories closer to the content of literature. For instance, it is claimed – as one of the reasons for endowing Shakespeare with Arab paternity – that only an Arab could have understood or depicted a Jew so 'convincingly' as in *The Merchant of Venice*. Similarly, the focus is sometimes placed on *Othello* – the Moor's dignity even in folly has been held up as convincing proof that no European could have fleshed out this specific psychology of a jealousy complicated by racial insecurity but a man from beneath the skin – an Arab at the very least. This of course would have to account for the unpredictability of a full-blooded Arab who suddenly turns against his kind in the portrait of Aaron in *Titus Andronicus*, reducing the representative of that race to unprecedented depths of savagery and inhuman perversion. No, I find that my judgement inclines to giving most of the credit to *Antony and Cleopatra* for the full conquest of the Arab poet-dramatist, and the reasons lie of course with that universally seductive property of the best dramatic literature – a poetic ease on the ear which, in this case, has been drawn to the service of a specific terrain. Throughout his career, this terrain held great fascination for William Shakespeare. I do not speak here of an inert geographical terrain, but of the opposing and contradictory in human nature. It is not entirely by accident that the physical terrain in *Antony and Cleopatra* was the meeting point of the Orient and the Occident – for Shakespeare, these had come to represent more than the mercantile or adventurers' stomping-ground; they are absorbed into geographical equivalents of the turbulences which the poet observed in human nature, that playground, and warring-ground of 'humours', of performance and intent, will and emotion: Angelo is the unfinished paradigm in *Measure for Measure*. The transfer by Shakespeare, obsessed apothecary, of the unstable mixture called humanity into the Elizabethan (i.e. European) exotic crucible of the Middle East was inescapable – the signs are littered in images throughout his entire corpus, and the Arab world acknowledged itself as the greatest beneficiary even when its dramatists held up the same models through opposing viewpoints.

Ahmad Shaqui, the poet laureate of Egypt who was hailed 'the Prince of Poets' and 'Poet of Princes' by his own peers is often credited with introducing poetry into Arabic drama. Was it just a coincidence that the play in question was *Masra' Kliyupatra* (The Fall or Death of Cleopatra), and that it was inspired unequivocally by Shakespeare's own *Antony and Cleopatra*? It is true that he used material both from Egyptian and Arab-Islamic history but he did set out, according to our sources, to rewrite Shakespeare's own play. Fired by the Egyptian struggle for independence from the British, he recreates Cleopatra as a woman torn between her love of her country and her love for a man. In the end she commits suicide. For Shaqui, Shakespeare's Cleopatra was unacceptably unpatriotic, even a traitress, since she appeared ready to sacrifice her country on the altar of love. The emendations are predictable; they are of the same political and historically conscious order as, for example, the reversal of relationships which takes place when the theme of Caliban and Ariel is handled by anyone from the colonial or slavery experience, most notably in the West Indies. The case of the Arab world is however very different, owing its primary response not simply to politics or history, but to an order of visceral participation in the humane drama of its politics and history.

When one examines the majority of Shakespeare's plays very closely, there really is not much overt respect paid to 'local colour'. If anything, the colour is not infrequently borrowed from elsewhere to establish a climate of relationships, emotions or conflicts: 'Her bed is India; there she lies, a pearl' (*Troilus and Cressida*, 1.1.99). Where we encounter a localized immediacy we are wafted instantly away on a metaphoric bark to nowhere:

> Between our Ilium and where she resides
> Let it be call'd the wild and wand'ring flood;
> Ourself the merchant, and this sailing Pandar
> Our doubtful hope, our convoy, and our bark.
>
> (1.1.100–3)

Nestor finds Achilles' brains as barren as the banks of Libya while Ulysses considers it kinder fate that he parch in Afric's sun than be withered by the arrogance in Achilles' eye. Beyond two or three boastful and mutual admiration lines from Ulysses to Hector in act 4, scene 5, however, it is remarkable that in a war no less celebrated, no less legendary than Antony's scrap with Caesar, very little of the terrain of struggle is actually conveyed in Shakespeare's lines. I do not suggest that we miss it; on the contrary. The absent hills, moats, turrets and physical *belonging* all pass unnoticed thanks to the clamour of *machismo*, the conflicts of pride, the debates of honour and schemes of war. The atmosphere is replete, nothing appears missing. In *Coriolanus* we experience the city state as a corporate entity against which one man is ranged, while the Rome of *Julius Caesar* could be anywhere, and the arguments of both, unchanged.

Compare these examples with the other remarkable exception, *Macbeth*:

Duncan.
  This castle hath a pleasant seat, the air
  Nimbly and sweetly recommends itself
  Unto our gentle senses.
Banquo.   This guest of summer,
  The temple-haunting martlet, does approve
  By his lov'd mansionry that the heaven's breath
  Smells wooingly here; no jutty, frieze,
  Buttress, nor coign of vantage, but this bird
  Hath made her pendent bed and procreant cradle.
  Where they most breed and haunt, I have observ'd,
  The air is delicate.   (1.6.1–10)

Shakespeare, drawing local colour into the service of fatal irony. The colours of *Antony and Cleopatra* belong however to a different segment of the spectrum and are applied on a more liberal canvas – after all, the whole world is up for grabs. But note that even where we encounter no more than what may be called a roll-call of names, there has been prior fleshing-out, so that the discomfiture of Octavius Caesar at the rallying of former mutual enemies behind Antony is real and problematic. It is historical personages that are summoned centre stage of the tapestry of events, not mere exotic names and shadowy figures from legend:

      He hath given his empire
  Up to a whore, who now are levying
  The kings o' th' earth for war. He hath assembled
  Bocchus, the king of Libya; Archelaus
  Of Cappadocia; Philadelphos, king
  Of Paphlagonia; the Thracian king Adallas;
  King Manchus of Arabia; King of Pont;
  Herod of Jewry; Mithradates, king
  Of Comagene; Polemon and Amyntas,

  The kings of Mede and Lycaonia, with a
  More larger list of sceptres.   (3.6.66–76)

The prior setting for what would otherwise be a mere catalogue of titles is contributive to the emergence of real figures from a mere bas-relief. For this is Caesar caught in a domestic dilemma involving his sister, using the arguments of war to get it into her head that she is neither an Emperor's wife nor an ambassador but, quite ordinarily – a rejected woman. Caesar's passion is both that of a contemned protector of a weak woman, and a contender for empire on a larger-than-historic scale. And these empires become accessible, reduced to a human scale because of what Antony has done with the accumulated panoply of power: 'He hath given his empire / Up to a whore...' The whore? Cleopatra. Her other names – queen, whore, gipsy, Egyptian dish, the serpent of old Nile, ribaldered nag of Egypt, etc., one whose every act, whose every caprice, every clownish or imperious gesture confirms that she deserves every one of these accolades and more. And thus the kingdoms and empires which she draws into her fatal net through Antony partake of this same personal quality and expand our realistic conception and dimension of the drama being waged for possession of the world. Not without cause does Octavius Caesar envision, when the scale of war turns firmly in his favour: 'The time of universal peace is near.'

Shakespeare's enlargements of the ridiculous through sublime prisms are deft and varied; the process happens at bewildering speed, resolving seeming improbabilities through the credible chimeric qualities of the tragic heroine of the piece. Who can quarrel with the steely patriotism of Cleopatra even in defeat? Confronted with the stark choice between death and humiliation:

      Rather a ditch in Egypt
  Be gentle grave unto me! Rather on Nilus' mud
  Lay me stark nak'd, and let the water-flies
  Blow me into abhorring! Rather make
  My country's high pyramides my gibbet,
  And hang me up in chains!   (5.2.57–62)

Ahmad Shaqui, poet and patriot, had most of his work already cut out for him; there really is not much left to do in mending whatever else appears to contradict this poise of nationalist dignity. Even the repulsive imagery has been turned to good account; the worst is evoked, and embraced – if that should be the only choice. How much more those other passages of contrasting physical evocation, those sumptuous, festal passages upon which Shakespeare has poured such haunting sensuousness. Have they not driven later poets and dramatists – notably T. S. Eliot – to an ambiguous relationship with their own literary heritage?

> The silken tackle
> Swell with the touches of those flower-soft hands
> That yarely frame the office. From the barge
> A strange invisible perfume hits the sense
> Of the adjacent wharfs. The city cast
> Her people out upon her; and Antony,
> Enthron'd i' th' market place, did sit alone,
> Whistling to th' air; which, but for vacancy,
> Had gone to gaze on Cleopatra too,
> And made a gap in nature.   (2.2.213–22)

Does the palate tend to cloy a little? Possibly. But by now Egypt, whom all, including Octavius Caesar, have made us identify with Cleopatra totally, is quickly manoeuvred towards our reassurance that we are still in command of our faculties of judgement, then acquitted absolutely. Admittedly the foreman of the jury is none other than a prejudiced Enobarbus, but we know him also for a blunt-spoken soldier. Most importantly, that habitual juxtaposition of harsh lingual rigour with lines of ineradicable sublimity leaves no room for doubt that an objective assessment has been fairly concluded. In short, the advocate acknowledges faults, but witness how he phrases the extenuating circumstances:

> Age cannot wither her, nor custom stale
> Her infinite variety. Other women cloy
> The appetites they feed, but she makes hungry
> Where most she satisfies; for vilest things
> Become themselves in her, that the holy priests
> Bless her when she is riggish.   (2.2.239–44)

That Cleopatra should match, in her final hours, the dignified poise of humility with a final thought (and abandonment) of defiance against the jealous gods is, in my view, both dramatically expected and aesthetically satisfying:

> No more but e'en a woman, and commanded
> By such poor passion as the maid that milks
> And does the meanest chares. It were for me
> To throw my sceptre at the injurious gods;
> To tell them that this world did equal theirs
> Till they had stol'n our jewel.   (4.15.73–8)

But the awesomeness of the lines that follow can only be fully absorbed by an Egyptian, or one steeped in the esoteric cults of Egypt and allied religions, including Islam. Cleopatra is speaking figuratively here of the house of death, and then again, she is not. She is evoking the deeper mysteries of the cult of Isis and the nether kingdoms of an other-existence, and it spreads an eerie quality over the final tableau – unlike any comparable end in all of Shakespeare.

The following recites like any article of faith in the Resurrection:

I have believed in Allah, and his angels, and His books, and His messengers, and the Last Day and the decree of its good and evil from Allah-ta'alla, and in the Rising after death.

                          (*Islamic Book of the Dead*)

But the Arabic script that transcribes this *ayat* from the Hadith is composed like a high-prowed gondola with a crew of ritualized (hierographically speaking) rowers.[2] What Islam in fact opposes in the 'Kafir' cults of Osiris and Isis have merely been transposed from their elaborate structures with all their sacrificial rites to a mystic opacity of liturgical language – in the Islamic exegesis of death, the kinship remains blatant. Their neighbours the pagan Greeks, who borrowed from them much of their cults and religions in any case, would have no difficulty in identifying the Osiris-prowed Hadithic boat of death with Charon's canoe, scything through the River Styx. Islamic injunctions, prayers and invocations on the theme of death more than compensate the exhortations to practical meagreness by their endless liturgy and lyrical wealth of going, and the aftermath of dissolution.

Cleopatra, whom we have watched throned as Isis, imbues the approach of death with a measured

---

[2] A marvellously preserved carving of the Egyptian 'Boat of the Dead' in the Pushkin Museum, Moscow, demonstrates most glaringly the relationship of the transcription to the funerary craft.

ritualism that is suffused with the palpable shadowiness of the crypt. Not just her contemporary worshippers at the shrines of Isis and Osiris, but their descendants, born into the counter-claims of Islamic religion, would therefore share more than a mere metaphor of language with Cleopatra's demand: 'Then is it sin / To rush into the secret house of death ...?' We can hear its echo in the following lines also from the *Islamic Book of the Dead*:

> It is said that every day the
>   graves call out five times:
> I am the house of isolation. . . .
> I am the house of darkness. . . .
> I am the house of earth. . . .
> I am the house of the questioning
>   of Munkar and Nakir . . .

I know of no parallel echo in the Christian offices of the dead. Arabic 'classical' poetry is however full of it, and of Shakespeare's sonnets, the ones which seem to attract the finest 'classical' poets among the Arabs seem to share this preoccupation with the imagery of death as a place of physical habitation. Sometimes they are outright translations but more often they are original compositions inspired by a specific sonnet of Shakespeare. And we find a consistency in the emphasis given to one part of Shakespeare's variations on the theme of love as against the main theme itself. Comparatively underplayed is the defiant sentiment:

> Not marble nor the gilded monuments
> Of princes shall outlive this pow'rful rhyme;
> But you shall shine more bright in these contents
> Than unswept stone, besmear'd with sluttish time.
>
> (Sonnet 55)

The humanistic verses of Omar Khayyám are considered worse than irreverent – they are termed heretical and subversive; nor does the graveyard humour of an Andrew Marvell hold much appeal for the True Islamic poet:

> The grave's a fine and private place
> But none, I think, do there embrace.
>
> ('To His Coy Mistress')

No, it is essentially the grave as a place, an abode in time, that taxes the poetic genius of Shakespeare's adapters, not as a spur to the demands of love,

presented as an end which is worse for overtaking its victim loveless, against which is held the imperishable products of the Muse or the talisman of immortality in love's offspring. Elias Abu Shabbakah's 'The Song of Death' is aptly titled, though it derives from Shakespeare's Sonnet 71, 'No longer Mourn for me when I am Dead'. The contrast, despite the opening abnegation, is revealing:

> My will, which I want you to remember, is to forget me when I am dead. And, if memories move you one day and your affection chooses to remind you of me, take the guitar of my inspiration into the dark night and go to my tomb in silence, and tap the guitar once; for it will let you hear a moaning sigh such as mine.

The unearthly moisture of suicide, the aspic's trail of slime on fig-leaves transports us to this totally alien earth, and I mean alien, not from the view of Shakespeare's culture alone. This is yet another world opening inwards from the mundane one into which we have already been inducted by some of the most unnerving imageries in poetic drama: a yoking of approaching bodily corruption with the essence-draining paradox of birth and infancy closes the fatal cycle of the union of opposites that began with the aspic's slime:

> Peace, peace !
> Dost thou not see my baby at my breast
> That sucks the nurse asleep ?   (5.2.306–8)

In this dark ceremonial, the crown which Cleopatra dons becomes not just a prop for composing herself for death as befits a queen, nor her robe the final cover for a soon-to-be-hollowed vessel, but ritual transformation steps towards the mystic moment of transition:

> Give me my robe, put on my crown; I have
> Immortal longings in me. . . .
> I am fire and air; my other elements
> I give to baser life. So, have you done?
> Come then, and take the last warmth of my lips.
> Farewell, kind Charmian. Iras, long farewell.
> Have I the aspic in my lips? Dost fall?
> If thou and nature can so gently part,
> The stroke of death is as a lover's pinch,
> Which hurts and is desired.   (5.2.278–9, 287–94)

7

Iras has now preceded, and in that calm recital of Cleopatra,

> The stroke of death is as a lover's pinch,
> Which hurts and is desired

is heard the reprise and conclusion of that death aria which we have earlier descried. It commenced in the penultimate act, 'The crown o' th' earth doth melt. . . .' (4.15.63), and winds into the awesome darkness at the Osiric passage:

> Then is it sin
> To rush into the secret house of death
> Ere death dare come to us?   (4.15.80–2)

In sustaining its threnody through one more Act, despite the triumphant boots of Caesar and entourage, punctured by the country yokel humour of the aspic-hawking Clown, it becomes clear that our playwright has already inscribed *Finis* on the actual historic conflicts of power and passion. The crown of the earth has melted, and there is nothing left remarkable beneath the visiting moon. But in this setting, is that all? Beyond it? And beneath earth itself? The spectral power of Shakespeare's poetry remains to lead us into the 'other side' of the veil whose precedent reality, which is now seen as merely contingent, gives awesome splendour to the finale of an otherwise butterfly queen. The rest of *Antony and Cleopatra* is our excursion into that world, one which lies more innocently on the Egyptian reality of that time than on the most stoical, self-submissive will in the inherent or explicit theologies of Shakespeare's other drama:

> I am dying, Egypt, dying; only
> I here importune death awhile, until
> Of many thousand kisses the poor last
> I lay upon thy lips.   (4.15.18–21)

Contrast this with the death of the genuine Moor whose folly was of a more excusable circumstance than Antony's:

> I kissed thee ere I killed thee. No way but this –
> Killing myself, to die upon a kiss.
>
>   (*Othello*, 5.2.362–3)

One dirge-master is understandably Shayk al-Subair, the other William Shakespeare. Here most noticeably, the cadences of death in Shakespeare's tragic figures are as crucial to his poetry as his celebration of life, even when the celebrants are flawed and their own worst enemy of life. It is difficult to underestimate this property as one which the Egyptian dramatists identified in their own world, for in *Antony and Cleopatra* Shakespeare's sensuous powers climaxed to evoke not merely the humanity of actors of a particular history, but the glimpsed after-world whose liturgy of resolution imbued them with their unearthly calm at the hour of death.

There are other minor but no less critical touches to the realistic evocation of a credible Egypt even within its very mythology. One need only examine the comparative sociologies of Shakespeare's stock characters – the Soothsayer for instance. In *Julius Caesar*, he simply comes off the street like a disembodied voice, and sinks back into urban anonymity once his dramatic role is fulfilled. Cassandra in *Troilus and Cressida* is a hysterical weirdo who, if anything, mars her cause with a melodramatic manner of revelations. Is she a member of the household? We do not really experience her – all these are not pejorative remarks, merely contrastive for a point of view. The Soothsayer in *Antony and Cleopatra* is an individual, a solid, recognizable persona. He follows Antony to Rome as his personal soothsayer and emerges more in the role of a shrewd psychologist than a mere mumbo-jumboist digging in eagles' entrails and seeing portents in the clouds. His analysis of Antony's psyche is as detachedly clinical as Antony's own lecture on the scientific achievements of his adopted home, which he delivers as a cool, observant voyager to a curious stay-at-home:

> Thus do they, sir: they take the flow o' th' Nile
> By certain scales i' th' pyramid; they know
> By th' height, the lowness, or the mean, if dearth
> Or foison follow. The higher Nilus swells
> The more it promises; as it ebbs, the seedsman
> Upon the slime and ooze scatters his grain,
> And shortly comes to harvest.   (2.7.17–23)

This mixture of clinical information on human beings and the cultivated soil alike makes the earth of Egypt dominate Rome and take over the half-way house Misenum, making one suspect that Shayk al-Subair cannot wait to get back to his own soil where his genius for this story resides. He compromises by transferring a touch of Egypt to the no man's land of Pompey's ship in Misenum. Between Enobarbus and Antony – with a little help from Lepidus – the essence of Egypt continues to haunt the concourse of Rome, the Mediterranean and its buccaneers. Does Shakespeare lavish any such comparative care in preserving the smells, sounds, and allied definitions of a yearned-for home? We are not speaking now of rhetoric, even of the pathetic kind old John of Gaunt expends in *Richard II*:

> This royal throne of kings, this scept'red isle,
> This earth of majesty, this seat of Mars,
> This other Eden, demi-paradise,
> This fortress built by Nature for herself
> Against infection and the hand of war,
> This happy breed of men, this little world,
> This precious stone set in the silver sea . . .
>
> (2.1.40–6)

nor of the philosophical, disinterested speculations on land and Nature in *As You Like It*. No! To a people to whom land, fertile land, is both worship and life, an Egypt of Shakespeare's *Antony and Cleopatra* cannot be served by such rhetoric or abstract morality. And like morality, even so those qualities that grace (or disgrace) humanity cannot be rendered in the abstract but must be invested in characters and the affective community – we need only contrast the following with Portia's peroration on the quality of mercy:

> For his bounty,
> There was no winter in it; an autumn 'twas
> That grew the more by reaping. His delights
> Were dolphin-like: they show'd his back above
> The element they liv'd in. In his livery
> Walk'd crowns and crownets; realms and islands were
> As plates dropp'd from his pocket. (5.2.86–92)

This, then, is the soul we recognize in Antony, so generous in giving that he loses all judgement. His rejection of pettiness over the defection of Enobarbus, his agonizing concern for the safety of his followers after defeat – these small redeeming features approve his humanity and contribute to a suspicion that our judgement of him may be lacking in that generosity which was his one redeeming grace. And what proud Egyptian, especially a poet, will fully resist the anti-chauvinist fervour of a one-third shareholder of the world, one who – no matter the motivation – declaims, both in word and deed:

> Let Rome in Tiber melt, and the wide arch
> Of the rang'd empire fall! Here is my space.
> Kingdoms are clay; our dungy earth alike
> Feeds beast as man. (1.1.33–6)

'Here is my space.' John of Gaunt's rhetorical flourish does not do half as much for the Englishman as Antony the Roman does, in that brief speech, for the land-proud Egyptian. The conqueror is himself conquered by the land in the person of her capricious Queen, the same land whose foulest ditch she would rather inhabit, upon whose highest gibbet she would rather hang, than be taken to grace the triumphal march of a conqueror (albeit a new one) in Rome. 'Here is my space' – it is at once a hint that the land has doomed him, and a taste of the largeness of a man whose bountifulness – as we come to know this – imbues our space with a heroic grandeur, even when events are trivialized by the humane weaknesses of our kind.

Only Shakespeare could contract the pomp and panoply of love and royalty into a gastronomic experience, yet unfailingly elevate both into a veritable apotheosis without a sense of the ridiculous or the inflated. Enobarbus, in Rome, unerringly predicts that Antony 'will to his Egyptian dish again'. The Egyptian dish herself boasts 'I was / A morsel for a monarch' without a hint of self-mockery, indeed with pride and womanly preening. When things go sour,

> I found you as a morsel cold upon
> Dead Caesar's trencher. (3.13.116–17)

Food, wine, violence, sexuality and putrefaction – both qualitatively and in sheer quantity – this is a different landscape of human activities from the more familiar settings of Shakespeare's. A moist land and visceral responses. The transitions from the physical to the metaphysical are unforced, and this is in no small measure due to the magnitude of extremes with which the human vehicles are imbued. Is it not through the same lips of the lustful gipsy, tripping credibly because it is made the active response of any jealous woman, that we are led into the self-apotheosis of an irrepressible pair?

Eternity was in our lips and eyes,
Bliss in our brows' bent, none our parts so poor
But was a race of heaven. (I.3.35–7)

With such a subject, is it any wonder that Shayk al-Subair reveals again and again that he cannot wait to escape home from the land of a 'holy, cold, and still conversation'? In *Antony and Cleopatra*, Shakespeare's borrowed imageries finally come home to roost. That the *terra firma* of his choice happens to be Egypt may be an accident – it could easily have been India. It was nearly the Caribbean but Shakespeare chose there to employ stage effects, deliberately, and thus denied his island that specific dimension of richness which comes from a physical and human identity. Moreover, in *The Tempest* Shakespeare is concerned not with history, but with enchantment. By contrast, Alexandria (or Tripoli in this case) is the home of that tantalizing glimpse of the topography of Achilles' frazzled brains, it is the demythologized context of Othello's romantic yarns, the source of all those secret potions of love or death-like sleep from *Romeo and Juliet* to *A Midsummer Night's Dream*, the destination or port-of-call of those rich argosies that billow through the pages of *The Merchant of Venice*, and even the unseen crusader ship of Shakespeare's history plays.

Only if Ahmad Ba-Kathir, Ahmad Shaqui, Khali Mutran, Gibran and a host of others had failed to recognize this, would the history of this relationship have been astonishing. Their fascination with Shakespeare is not in the least surprising after all; the scepticism of some of their fellow-poets and dramatists about Shakespeare's claim to an English ancestry is simply a passionate compliment to those qualities in Shakespeare, a few of which we have touched upon, but above all the paradox of timelessness and history, a realism evoked – simultaneously - of time, place and people – with which he has infused *Antony and Cleopatra* more deeply than any of his plays except perhaps *Macbeth* – which is a horse of an entirely different colour.

Sean O'Casey may be proved only partially right – I return to his rhetorical question, regarding whose answer there is nothing rhetorical in the stance of Shakespeare's Arab co-practitioners in the field of drama. The Shayk was born too early for Philippi, or

indeed for the battle of the Nile, but the Nile did course through his veins. Personally, I was left with only one problem to resolve – if the Shayk was indeed an Arab, who was his wife? It seemed to me that we could not dispose of one problem without the other – such being the power of documents in our time. Those documents insist that our William was well and truly wived by someone whose name was recorded as Anne Hathaway. Perhaps there were others, but even Othello had imbibed sufficient European influence to content himself with only one wife, so why not his very creator, Shayk al-Subair? Being a monogamist does not therefore destroy the case for Shakespeare's Arabic origin. Well then, I consulted my colleague in Arabic Studies and our assiduousness was rewarded. Anne Hathaway proved to be none other than an English corruption of Hanna Hathawa. The first name stands for 'to dye red'; the second, Hathawa means 'to scatter, to disperse', someone who disseminates. The puzzle was resolved. Shayk al Subair's spouse Hanna Hathawa, a high-coloured lady, came to life in her own right, a little-known theatrical agent whose publicity activities on behalf of her husband will, I hope, provide endless preoccupation for at least a dozen doctoral theses.

In the meantime, one acknowledges with gratitude the subjective relation of other poets and dramatists to the phenomenon of Shakespeare, for even the most esoteric of their claims lead one, invariably, to the productive source itself, and to the gratification of celebrating dramatic poetry anew. That Shakespeare may turn out to be an Arab after all is certainly less alarming a prospect than that he should prove to be Christopher Marlowe. No one has yet begun to ransack the sand-dunes of Arabia, shovelling aside the venerable bones of Bedouins in the hope of disinterring the bones of the author of *Antony and Cleopatra*. By contrast, that talented but junior brother of his genius, the author of *Tamburlaine*, has not been permitted a peaceful sleep in his grave, especially at the hands of yet another group of ex-colonial enthusiasts, this time, the Americans. Happily, for the majority of Shakespeare-lovers, those other secret lives of the Shayk which remain to be uncovered outside *Bingo* or the *Arabian Nights*, will just have to wait, until his tomes have yielded up the last of their treasures.

BLOOD AND WINE:
TRAGIC RITUAL FROM AESCHYLUS TO SOYINKA
PHILIP BROCKBANK

To get good wine, George Herbert tells us, we must trample upon God made flesh; the agony of the press and the vinous delights meet in religious ecstasy: 'Love is that liquor sweet and most divine, / Which my God feels as blood; but I, as wine' ('The Agonie'). Shakespeare is rarely so explicit about the contiguities of cannibalism and the communion service, yet there are in his theatre many equivalent radical insights. What we may take to be remote, pagan and even barbaric rites persist and flourish in complex urban civilizations and in finely tempered urbane communities like that of Herbert's Little Gidding, or that to which Timon supposes himself to belong in the Athens of Apemantus.

Little is to be gained by considering Shakespeare in relation to the theatre of our own time unless we recognize that the continuing traditions of tragedy have primordial as well as literary sources, and that its literary history of some twenty-five hundred years in the western world is, in an anthropological perspective, quite brief. This does not mean that it is the business of criticism and scholarship to return the complexities of civilized theatrical art to the apparent simplicities of its speculative beginnings. Our primordial selves are a present as well as a past reality; we all, as it were, grow from seed, and some of the most powerful dispositions of human consciousness continue to manifest themselves in ways that certainly would not have surprised Aeschylus, and probably would not be wholly strange to the Neanderthals either. If we are to encourage the slow, perplexed growth of a more adequate humanism, the ritual processes still at work in our own societies urgently need to be understood and revalued. Nigeria is

well placed to make a formidable contribution to this understanding, through its cultural history and through its new-made theatre.

The plays of Wole Soyinka are a revelation of the way in which theatre can reach into the heart of a community and make vital, amusing and distressing discoveries about its ordeals and its capacities for life. They therefore invite fresh responses – very much of our own time – to the plays of ancient Athens and of the English Renaissance; the twentieth-century playwright clarifies paradigms of tragic art that span perhaps a hundred generations. It is not merely that Shakespeare and the Greeks have had an influence upon Soyinka; it is rather that influences – currents and flowings-in from the remote past – are by his work made more accessible to us in plays that have gone before. Because there are persisting strains in our nature certain tragic structures are apt to recur, but it does not therefore follow that they are archetypal and unchanging. Tragic art is an instrument for changing human nature, not for impaling it on rigorously conceived necessities. The paradigms on which I shall focus attention are related to the ritual figure of the 'carrier' and to the festivals of Dionysus.

Soyinka's *The Strong Breed* (1966)[1] is about a schoolteacher in an African village who dies in his attempt to save a simple-minded child from becoming the symbolic victim of a festive rite. We may discern in the play three sets of moral imperatives, each of which makes a distinctive contribution to its theatrical structure and to the expressiveness of its language.

---

[1] I have quoted throughout from Wole Soyinka, *Collected Plays*, 2 vols. (Oxford, 1973).

Two sets relate to differing versions of the carrier ritual. In Yoruba culture the tradition by which a specially selected figure 'carries' away the evils of the community takes a variety of forms, and Soyinka here distinguishes between the ritual practice of the hero's home village, where for many years his father was 'carrier', and the different but related practice of the village where he is a newcomer, working in its school and living with a nurse who is the chief's daughter. Both forms of the ritual are expiatory, but the one honours the carrier who bears away the village's afflictions, while the other, for comparable ritual ends, humiliates him. In the several visionary retrospects of the play we find that the old man, year after year obeying the imperatives of his community, carrying the ritual boat to the water, is allowed enough strength and clarity of purpose to perfect with dignity what Soyinka elsewhere calls 'the monstrous cycle of regeneration'. He knows, and the village knows, that one day he will not return from the ceremony but will die in the performance of it, but in the meantime he performs his role with pride. 'I have taken down each year's evils for over twenty years,' he tells his son Eman (whose name means 'saviour'), 'I hoped you would follow me.' But Eman has left his father's domain and when, caught in a human predicament, he comes to offer himself as carrier, it is to a community with significantly different practices. The host village afflicts its stranger-carrier with ritual beatings and abuse, driving him out. Because Eman does not endure his ordeal acceptingly, he fails to satisfy the ritual imperatives of the host community, and the headman, Jaguna, is contemptuous of a carrier who lacks the manly virtues: 'He had not even gone through one compound before he bolted. Did he think he was taken round the people to be blessed? A woman, that is all he is.' Oroge, the assistant master of ceremonies, responds more perceptively: 'He would let himself be stoned until he dropped dead.' The answer to Jaguna's question 'What made him run?' is to be sought not in Oroge's glance at the 'unhinged' mind of the unprepared carrier but in the third set of human and ritual imperatives dramatized actively in the play's present, and retrospectively in its flashbacks. Eman, in refusing to submit to a certain kind of humiliation, knowingly brings about his own death.

He flees for his life, but also for all life; he makes from the rite, and he makes a human get-away. Many complexities attend the ambiguities of Eman's flight in the play, but the human imperatives are readily outlined. At the start of the play Eman cannot bring himself either to take Sunma, the chief's daughter, away with him or to leave her behind at the festival. He stays, and offers himself as carrier, in order to save Ifada, the idiot, from being frightened to death. In the course of the play we learn that he fled his father's village years ago, because there he had found the solemnities of the circumcision ritual corrupted by a lecherous tutor. Eman in the play's last phase goes to his death in an act of fidelity to his father, in the role of carrier, towards the life-sustaining river of death, into the trap which Jaguna has prepared for him. He is in flight from the ritual, but in an unexpectedly human way, he honours it – he dies to save the child.

From Jaguna's point of view the ritual is a failure because both the carrier and his communal hunters, lacking virtue, were womanish and craven: 'I am sick to the heart of the cowardice I have seen tonight.' But in the play's human perspectives we can see that Jaguna's own priestly role is contaminated. He is provoked into malice both by his daughter's association with Eman and by Eman's challenge to the custom of enlisting a stranger: 'A village which cannot produce its own carrier contains no men.' The community, infected by its chief's malice, generates ferocities and revulsions of its own until it finally recoils from the climax of its own ritual excitement – Eman hanged from a tree. 'But did you see them?' asks Jaguna, 'One and all they looked up at the man and words died in their throats.' 'It was no common sight,' says Oroge, referring not merely to the spectacle of the hanged man (words dead in his throat) but to the villagers' response. 'Women could not have behaved so shamefully,' says Jaguna, 'One by one they crept off like sick dogs. Not one could raise a curse!' Eman's sacrifice of himself (it is made to feel like that) belongs to neither of the old ritual patterns. His death, however lyrically conveyed as he runs to keep pace with his dead father, is finally an atrocity that shames the community – 'they crept off like sick dogs'. At the end of the play the moral energies of the community seem exhausted and the acting out of the old ritual has brought it to a stop. The victim has moved humanity a step forward, for the ugly victimization of Eman, the enlightened school-teacher trying to save an imbecile child, works ironically in the manner of a carrier ritual; the sick dogs will in time be ready for a fresh start.

In the opening chorus of the *Agamemnon* of Aeschylus the story is told of the king's submission to pressures and pieties requiring him to sacrifice his daughter, Iphigenia, to prosper 'a war waged to avenge a woman'. This is not a seasonal rite but an occasional one, and Iphigenia, although a sacrifice, is not precisely a carrier; she is not bearing away the evils of the society or carrying messages of appeasement to the gods. While his ships are rotting and his soldiers starving, Agamemnon is told by Calchas that the wind will change only if he offers his own daughter to Artemis, the daughter of Zeus. Aeschylus recovers the pathos and ceremony of the event but he shouts too, in pained and ironical protest against the inhuman outrage enacted by priest and king (*Agamemnon*, 217–54).[2] In this play, as in Soyinka's, there is an apparent conflict of human and ritual imperatives. Without in any way diminishing the heroic stature of Agamemnon, and fully exploiting the imaginative potency of the old stories, Aeschylus exposes the values of which the stories are an expression – the pieties, commitments to war, revenge and sacrifice – to severe sceptical analysis.

The analysis is not of the discursive kind; it works through poetry, using all the resources of the language, upon our sympathetic imaginations and upon the obscurities of our verbal awareness. As in the plays of Shakespeare (and Soyinka) the language makes covert connections between one range of values and another, and between the fabulous event and the ordinariness of human experience. Thus Agamemnon's readiness to give his daughter to the war is still vivid to the audience's memory when the chorus later tells of the trading of men for dust at the quayside as the Greek dead are sent back from Troy (*Agamemnon*, 432–55). Through a series of exquisitely painful equivocations war is compared with a gold-merchant. Ares, bartering the bodies of men for gold, holds his balance in the poised spears of the battlefield and scrupulously offers the Greeks value for money.

From Ilium he sends back those who have passed through his refining fire – a heavy weight of precious dust for the price of a man, and at home the women marvel at their jars of gold, their urns of dust – 'How skilled in battle! Fallen nobly in the carnage!' Moving against the tide of acquiescent eloquence is a protesting undertow: 'grief charged with resentment spreads stealthily against the sons of Atreus.' The earlier responses to the grand sacrifice of Iphigenia are generalized in all their instability. Sacrifice is ubiquitous in war, and the tragic poet both commemorates and repudiates it.

Neither kings nor gods are exempt from the playwright's imaginative and ethical scrutiny, for the poet knows that the gods and sanctities of human piety and government are the creation of the human imagination. From the old values re-created and freshly imagined, Aeschylus assists in the making of those new, transmuted values that were in process of being embodied, however imperfectly, in the laws and customs of a new city-culture. Thus the series of plays which begins with a tale of human sacrifice ends with a joyous invocation to the presiding goddess of the city of Athens. But, while it ends upon a festive note, the tragic festival of the theatre leaves us as conscious of the destructive as of the creative potencies of human consciousness. Thus the Trojan war, belonging then as now to the distant past, belongs also to Aeschylus' time and to our own; the play endeavours to see the last of an all-too-present condition. The passage of the trilogy from sacrificial song to civic rejoicing is, in Soyinka's phrase, its 'threnodic essence'.

In the plays of Euripides the ritual affirmation is exposed to a more intimate (but not more profound) human inspection. In *Iphigenia at Aulis* Euripides gives us not only the threnodic essence of Iphigenia's sacrifice, but also its human comedy. We are brought close to the personal, familial, political and theocratic roles of Agamemnon, who is shocked by the deed of sacrifice but also drawn to it. Iphigenia herself voices the antinomies of tragic response – recoiling from the cruelty and arbitrariness of premature death:

---

[2] References to Aeschylus are to the Loeb edition, ed. H. W. Smyth, 2 vols. (1946).

Below, there's nothing: he's mad who prays to die.
Even base living profits more than noble death;

(1250–2)[3]

yet attracted, under the pressure of necessity, by its apparently sublime significance (1368–1401, 1420). For an analogous attraction and repulsion we could go to Shakespeare's *Measure for Measure* (from 'I will encounter darkness as a bride' to 'Ay, but to die, and go we know not where', 3.1.85, 119) but more directly, to a choice of tragic victims in the plays of Soyinka – Eman, for example, in *The Strong Breed*, or Elesin in *The Death of the King's Horseman* (1975). Iphigenia is snatched from the altar by Artemis, Elesin snatched from his suicide dance, at once willingly and unwillingly, by Pilkings, the District Officer. Both get-aways are evasions of the tragic festival. In Soyinka's play the Praise Singer is denied his natural and communal role when the son is impelled to die in his father's place: 'this young shoot has poured its sap into the parent stalk, and we know this is not the way of life. Our world is tumbling in the void of strangers, Elesin.' But Soyinka gives to his theatre audience the tragic catharsis that the District Officer denies the villagers watching the death-dance. Elesin strangles himself in a *coup de théâtre*, his bride closes his eyes, and the playwright contrives his own valedictory dirge. The *Iphigenia at Aulis* reaches a differently equivocal crisis; she whom the gods love is carried away to live with the gods (1610–13) leaving Clytemnestra to wonder if report is 'but a sweet lie to heal the broken heart' (1617–18) and the audience to wonder if the play is a tragedy or a melodrama. Euripides' interest in the inhumanity of the death rites persists in the *Iphigenia in Tauris* where Iphigenia on the island of Artemis is required to preside over continuing sacrifices even more arbitrary than her own. Her get-away silences the tragic death music and leaves King Thoas to make the best of 'a doom reversed and a life re-won'.

Unlike Aeschylus, Euripides and Soyinka, Shakespeare seldom deals directly with ritual deaths. Only in *Titus Andronicus* is human sacrifice ('T'appease their groaning shadows that are gone') assimilated into the narrative and there through the juxtaposition of Roman and Gothic rites, it is associated with bar-

barism, the state from which Rome arose and into which it declined. In Shakespeare's more mature tragedies, the several traditions that converge from Greek and Latin theatre, from the Christian Church and from the literature of the Bible, find more oblique expression. But in this ample perspective it may be said of all Shakespeare's tragedies that they have a 'threnodic form' which sings out about the 'dying-into-life' process, and a dissenting form which cries out against it. Thus in *Romeo and Juliet* a poignantly lyrical death, of some redemptive significance to the community, is also a disgraceful outrage brought about by human malignancies and inadequacies. In *Julius Caesar* and in *Othello* the heroes preside like priests over acts of butchery which they represent to themselves and to the gods as sacrifices, before taking their own lives in acts of tragic suicide. In relating Shakespeare's tragic forms to Soyinka's, however, I take the very different instances of *King Lear* and *Antony and Cleopatra*.

King Lear may still come back to us in the form of an old tale, told by the fireside: 'There was once a king and he had three daughters. One day, grown old and tired, he divided his kingdom into three parts and called his daughters to him. "Which of you," he asked, "loves me most?" . . .' The old tale, before Shakespeare lays hands on it, moves to a consolatory outcome: 'The youngest daughter defeated her sisters in battle and gave the kingdom back to her father. He reigned over it for the last happy years of his life, and when he died, the daughter that had truly loved him reigned in his place.' Shakespeare's tale says: 'But her sisters defeated her in battle and they cast the king and his youngest daughter into prison. The youngest daughter was hanged and the king died of age, pain and grief.' Keeping these folk-story simplicities in mind, it is possible to see the fundamental nature of Shakespeare's defiance of one range of his audience's expectations. The old *Leir* might have been reshaped into a Last Play, a melodrama, with the formal solace of song and masque. But in *King Lear* Shakespeare

---

[3] References to Euripides are to the Loeb edition, ed. A. S. Way, 4 vols. (1919). The translation of these lines is from D. J. Conacher, *Euripidean Drama* (Toronto and London, 1967), p. 259.

plots the deaths of king and daughter and leaves the kingdom desolate. Why? The question is capable of many answers,[4] but it is apt to reopen it with other tragic rituals in mind.

In the Iphigenia story the king's daughter 'dies' in order that his armies may in time prevail against Troy, and the king himself dies in the feuds attending the city's advance towards a better understanding of divine justice. In *The Strong Breed* the Old Man and his son die in order that the life of the village (i.e. pagan) community should, in a variety of senses, be renewed. Christian rituals celebrate 'the Lamb of God that taketh away the sins of the world', and Christ, by this metaphor, was the greatest and last of the carriers. Audiences of Shakespeare's play then (and even now) would be familiar with an earlier carrier, in the fifty-third chapter of Isaiah:

Surely he hath borne our griefs and carried our sorrows. . . . But he was wounded for our transgressions, he was bruised for our iniquities. . . . He was oppressed, and he was afflicted, yet he opened not his mouth; he is brought as a lamb to the slaughter, and as a sheep before her shearers is dumb, so he openeth not his mouth. He was taken from prison and from judgement . . . cut off out of the land of the living.

There is no allusion to Isaiah in *King Lear* but a reading of the prophet alongside the play creates tantalizing prospects for our moral and aesthetic sensibilities, and this passage is a reminder of the transcendent moral status that, in one tradition of human understanding, we allow to the unprotesting victims we beat up. In the play's first scene the exalted response is that which the old ritual figure – the sheep before the shearer – once elicited: 'What can you say . . .? Nothing, my lord. . . . Nothing? . . . Nothing.' Shakespeare's intervention in the old story recovers the values at work in the old Hebraic and Christian carrier rite, but not without qualification. Cordelia is brought to judgement again in the last scene, and the play's structure first admits and then denies the solace of its ritual. The triumphant cry 'Come, let's away to prison' affords to Shakespeare's audience something of the satisfying exaltation that Soyinka's village communities look for in their carrier rites, an effect that might be played more poignantly if Lear, to

'take upon's the mystery of things', literally carried Cordelia off in his arms. The interlude that follows is made out of another set of traditional ritual confidences, as Edgar prevails over Edmund in trial by combat. But the evils of the kingdom have not been carried away. '*Enter Lear with Cordelia in his arms*' says the stage direction. The carrier has come back. There is no transcendent exaltation, no snatching away of a Cordelia loved by the gods. The atrocity is more conspicuous than the sacrifice, the play's dissenting form prevails over its threnodic form.

The figure in Isaiah is said to 'bear the sins of many'. Shakespeare's assimilation of the ritual compels us to keep watch over the disintegration of the king and his kingdom. The old kingdom from which Lear abdicates was sustained by certain allegiances, appropriately associated with the old feudal order, still kept up in the play by the best of its survivors – Kent, Edgar, the Fool, and (with a difference) Gloucester and Albany. The division of the kingdom entails its dissolution, but Lear in the storm finds that the old kingdom was divided before he divided it. There were (and are) communities of the oppressors and of the oppressed, of the rich and the poor, the torturers and the tortured, the protected and the exposed, the masters and the servants, the knaves and the fools, and the governed and the ungoverned. They are not stable communities either – they shift about, collapse and destroy each other; and a man's history can take him into many communities. So it is with Lear's history, which is of his exposure to the arrogances and distresses of the multiple community, within the largest community of all – that of human mortality. It is not a history of exposure only, however, but of inward assimilation. Lear takes his kingdom into his inmost consciousness and Shakespeare through him takes it into ours.

In the ritual of the theatre the audience is required to go through what Lear goes through, and the progressive destruction of the old king and his 'own kingdom' exposes us to fresh insights into our common humanity and mortality. One instance of the oblique immediacy of Shakespeare's theatrical art will

---

4 I have attempted some answers in 'Upon Such Sacrifices . . .', British Academy Annual Shakespeare Lecture, 1976.

serve to suggest the ways in which the play creates a new relationship between the king's consciousness of his power and his recognition of weakness. At the start of the play Lear, at his most absolute, threatens Kent with an imaginary bow and arrow: 'The bow is bent and drawn; make from the shaft!' (1.1.142). Much later, when the king himself has been exposed to 'feel what wretches feel', we meet that bow and arrow again.[5] Lear, who 'lacks soldiers', imagines himself as the warrior-king again, pressing conscripts into his army. 'That fellow,' he says, catching sight of Edgar, 'handles his bow like a crow-keeper; draw me a clothier's yard' (4.6.87). Lear presumably draws his imagined bow again, in proud full stretch. Then his memory fails him and he looks helplessly at his left hand, pointing like an arrow, and at his right, held inexplicably in space. The straying mind finds reason first for the arrow-hand – 'Look, look, a mouse!', and his voice drops to a whisper as he wanders between the two auditory senses of the word 'peace' before he can explain the other hand: 'Peace, peace; this piece of toasted cheese will do't.' As he feeds the mouse, the oscillations between terror and solicitude start up again. The player-king may even choose to crush the mouse with his gauntlet as it falls into the cheese-trap – 'There's my gauntlet; I'll prove it on a giant.' In the phantasmagoria of Lear's consciousness life is paying a forfeit to the warrior's power.

An analogous account of tragic processes, large and small, might be given of Soyinka's *The Road* and of his *Madmen and Specialists*. Other modes of tragedy, however, invite a different account. When the National Theatre in 1972 commissioned from Soyinka a new version of *The Bacchae* of Euripides, it was in the fully realized expectation that the distance between ancient Greece and modern Nigeria would be readily diminished; the resulting play still belongs to ancient Athens, to the Yoruba, and to us. The story is told again virtually unchanged, and its commanding metaphors are retained, with much the same significance for our understanding of society and consciousness. Dionysos is welcomed to Thebes in human form, but repression is soon seen at work in the community, as the king jails the revellers, and in Pentheus' own psyche as he attempts to shut up the god himself; he is unable to control the instinctual life because it takes

precisely the violent animal character he attributes to it – symbolized by the escaping bull. Euripides' play, beginning with serene and joyful song and dance in honour of Dionysos, ends in savage horror under the dominion of the same god, and the king is lynched in festive frenzy by the woman who bore him. Soyinka keeps the plot with a more muted opening movement. In both versions certain life-delighting and life-sustaining impulses turn sour and self-destructive. Both Euripides and Soyinka honour the old stories and the old pieties while exposing them to fresh experiential tests of their validity, and both put authority, order and regiment upon trial. But Soyinka's Nigerian play shows that the old turbulent energies, delights and excitements, instinctual aspirations and malignancies have assumed new disguises, put on new masks. The scourging scene, the sack-cloth and ashes, the chorus of slaves, and many other episodes and images, extend the play's scope into Christian and socialist references and values. More strikingly, moreover, the human perspective changes. The play gets even closer than Euripides to the pathos and absurdity of human ordinariness, while at the same time being sophisticated and knowing in its treatment of the old Greek, Christian and African rituals.

When Tiresias, in Soyinka's version, picks himself up from the procession of revellers who are featuring him in what is meant to be a symbolic scourging of the old dispensation, covered in weals, he cries out in protest: 'Can't you bastards ever tell the difference between ritual and reality?' The theatre is neither ritual nor reality, but it is in a position to make a spectacle of both. It can also make a spectacle of itself (a trick Soyinka might have learned from Shakespeare) and set traps for its audience, including the academics in it, who can easily be tricked into talking like Tiresias ('I found that significant', says Tiresias to Kadmos, who has just said 'foreskin' when he meant to say 'fawnskin'; 'when you start on significance', says Kadmos, 'you lose me'). Throughout the play the tragic ritual is put under severe comic pressure. Some of the comedy comes from life picking itself up again (like Tiresias) when the ritual knocks it down.

---

[5] I owe this observation to conversation with Dr A. C. Charity of the University of York.

But some of it is inhuman, meant to amuse the gods rather than men, and if we enjoy it, the explanation is to be found in the kind of all-seeing aloofness which the theatre enables us to share with Dionysos.

The Bacchae of Soyinka is not in itself a particularly Shakespearian play, but it inherits from Euripides a myth and structure that clarify, without oversimplifying, the antinomies of energy and order that reach a high point of tragic and comic conflict in a number of Shakespeare's plays. When, for example, the blood-and-ale-intoxicated followers of Jack Cade process through the London streets with the heads of Lord Say and Cromer upon poles, we cannot precisely say that Dionysos is avenged upon Pentheus, but we can see that the energies of anarchy have been liberated in a community whose government has lapsed into oppressive disarray. The procession that scourges Tiresias in Soyinka's first scene moves through the afflicted landscape of a slave state, with crucified figures 'mostly in the skeletal stage' and green vines clinging to the charred ruins of the temple of Semele. It is not from Euripides (though it would not have been wholly unfamiliar to him), but from the Nigerian civil war, shadowed by Golgotha. Dionysos waits, relaxed 'as becomes divine self-assurance' in the ruins. The priests who intone a liturgy as they lead the revellers are the first tragedians, the first singers of goat-songs, trying to make harmony and rhythm (Aristotle's *melopeia*) out of what is in danger of becoming a suddenly ugly event. When Dionysos, an amused witness on stage, intervenes to save Tiresias from rough handling with the words, 'Sing death of the Old Year, and – welcome the new – god', we the off-stage audience recognize a seasonal rite; we too have read *The Golden Bough*. Dionysos, with the playwright's connivance, is out to save the song, the 'threnodic form' of the rite and the play.

The ritual form meets its dissenting challenge, however, both from the old Euripidean sources and from some new ones. 'Which of us is victim this year?' a herdsman asks, and is told, 'That old man of the king's household. The one who looks after the dogs.' The slave-leader's indignation (which has no counterpart in Euripides) is met by peasant fortitude: 'Suppose the old man dies?' – 'We all have to die sometime' – 'Flogged to death? In the name of some

unspeakable rites?' – 'Someone must cleanse the new year of the rot of the old or, the world will die.' The slave-leader persists – 'Why us? Why always us?' – but the herdsman points to the crosses to remind him that 'The palace does not need the yearly Feast of Eleusis to deal with rebellious slaves.' The routine victims of the repressive, warring society are, by the wit of the play, related to its ritual victims.

In Shakespeare's *Henry IV* the Dionysiac figure of Falstaff is not a god, but an idol of the theatre, and his celebrants at the Boar's Head are without a liturgy; if we look for a ritual in the play we must make what we can of the scenes staged by 'the harlotry players' in anticipation of the king's repudiation of the flesh. The play, however, sets up its own set of relationships between life-delight, wine-delight, the readiness to die and the readiness to kill. As the nobles come 'like sacrifices in their trim', the expendables are tossed to 'fill a pit as well as better'.

Soyinka's theatrical analysis of the political dynamics of the play's community is not of a naively predictable kind. It is the slave leader who proves to be most excited by the apparition of the god, his sensitivity to the plight of others makes him the more vulnerable to the 'god of seven paths: oil, wine, blood, spring, rain, / Sap and sperm', and his revolutionary energies are diverted into destructive festive fury. The violence here, as in *Julius Caesar* where the crowd moves from 'O piteous spectacle!' to 'tear him to pieces' when it meets the poet Cinna, is generated out of human fellowship and humane indignation.

The play's divine comedy is more active in its early movements than in the last. Dionysos not only energizes the revolution, he also confronts old age and priestly celibacy with desolating insights into the inadequacy of human wisdom:

Poor Tiresias, poor neither-nor, eternally tantalized psychic intermediary, poor agent of the gods through whom everything passes but nothing touches, what happened to you in the crowd, dressed and powdered by the hands of ecstatic women. . . . You poor starved votary at the altar of the soul, what deep hunger unassuaged by a thousand lifelong surrogates drove you to this extreme self-sacrifice. Don't lie to a god Tiresias.

Tiresias makes his confession. At first he claims political motives for playing the victim's role; it was touch and go with Thebes: 'if one more slave had been killed at the cleansing rites, or sacrificed to that insatiable altar of nation-building . . .' the state would have gone to pieces. But the god doesn't believe the politician; he looks for different flagellant impulses and finds them – those lashes did begin something, he feels 'a small crack in the dead crust' of his soul, and at the god's invitation he begins to dance. It would be possible to find many more such instances in the play of tragic ritual under comic inspection – a god's eye view of the pretensions of men – as when Kadmos grumbles about being an administrator: 'An administrator Tiresias! Then an old-age pensioner on the court list. I who slew the dragon and bred a race of warriors from his teeth.' The comedy is addressed to a sophisticated audience that knows about the classics, but also to any Yoruba leader who until quite recently might have been the theme of fables.

Soyinka's play glances too at an aspect of Dionysos that is not conspicuous in Euripides' version – his role at weddings. The action is broken in upon by two nuptials, in which Dionysos offers Pentheus a glimpse of 'the past and future legends of Dionysos'. In the first, a feast breaks up in disorder as the groom makes off with the wine-girl under the spell of Dionysos and the influence of drink; in the second, Dionysos is manifest in the figure of Christ at the feast of Cana, turning the water into wine. The large point made in the fable about the contrary potentials of Dionysos – violent and tranquil – is thus repeated in the familiar sacrament and festival of marriage. Dionysos is a perennial and ubiquitous presence, assuming many forms.

This is a necessary reflection as we look again from Soyinka to Shakespeare. While there are no sustained processional pagan rituals in Shakespeare's plays, and nothing directly equivalent to *The Bacchae*, there are sacrifices, lynchings, dances, drunken parties and other manifestations of the savage divinity. And there are figures to keep Dionysos and Falstaff company (Autolycus among them), with others to challenge their destructive skills, like Prince Hal, Prince John and Octavius Caesar. In *Antony and Cleopatra*, the Romans 'dance . . . the Egyptian Bacchanals' and drink themselves into a stupor:

Come, let's all take hands,
Till that the conquering wine hath steep'd our sense
In soft and delicate Lethe. (2.7.104–6)

But the play does not invite us, as *The Bacchae* does, to revalue the cult of Dionysos, Shakespeare's 'monarch of the vine, / Plumpy Bacchus with pink eyne!' The old wisdoms that are exposed to scrutiny have a more complex presence in its theatre, and our humanity is differently discomposed and reordered. Like the *Bacchae* plays, the action of *Antony and Cleopatra* is bounded by the comprehensive and inescapable catastrophic process by which we are all born, flourish and die, and the poet articulates that elemental cycle through which life reverts to the slime which breeds it ('let the water-flies / Blow me into abhorring') and then starts up again with the help of erotic agriculture ('he ploughed her and she cropped').

That way of putting it does not account for the scale of the play, however. Unlike Euripides and Soyinka in their Bacchic plays, Shakespeare is looking for his agons not in the story of a ritual but in the history of an empire. *Antony and Cleopatra* spans the epic space that imperial ambitions opened up between the power and values of Rome on the one hand and Egypt on the other. The play's threnodic form, however, still requires us to perceive that Antony and Cleopatra die because (like Soyinka's Elesin) they are completely caught up in the cycle of regeneration whose law is a perpetual dying-into-life; Cleopatra's 'celerity in dying' is itself an expression of her life-delight. Caesar, the survivor, is, to borrow a phrase from Eliot, 'outside the scheme of generation'; being Fortune's 'nave' and 'knave' he does not go round with the wheel. Pentheus, on the other hand, is impaled on the wheel, a spectacular sacrifice to the cycle whose festive drives he tried to arrest. There are, of course, other perspectives to be constructed for the play. One strain in the Roman view of Antony, for example, looks back through Plutarch to the cult of *sophrosyne* in Greek ethical traditions, and it is apt enough that Caesar's sophronistic regulative virtues should be revalued in a Jacobean court which had its own imperial aspirations. The Egyptian range of energies and insights is less capable of systematic exposition but there was much to respond to it in the taste and culture of the Jacobean court, including the exuberance of Shakespeare's own theatre and poetry.

The continuities of theatre and ritual, however, retain their own distinctive importance – when, for example, Apemantus grieves 'to see so many dip their meat in one man's blood', or Perdita plays as she has 'seen them do / In Whitsun pastorals', or Feeble reflects that 'he that dies this year is quit for the next'. Some valuable explorations of Shakespeare's assimila-

tions of ritual form have found their starting points in Freud, or in Nietszche's *Birth of Tragedy from the Spirit of Music*, but we nevertheless do well to call on the lively analogues, close and distant, that the history of theatre itself affords. Soyinka's *Bacchae* ends:

Tiresias. What is it Kadmos? What is it?

Kadmos. Again blood Tiresias. Nothing but blood.

Tiresias. [*He feels his way nearer the fount. A spray hits him and he holds out a hand, catches some of the fluid and sniffs. Taste it.*]
  No. It's wine.

George Herbert would have understood that.

'HAMLET' ANDANTE / 'HAMLET' ALLEGRO:
TOM STOPPARD'S TWO VERSIONS
JILL L. LEVENSON

With the passage of time, Tom Stoppard's first *Hamle.* begins to look like his *Romeo and Juliet*: an experiment undertaken during a period of energetic theatrical activity in England, and a spirited union of materials from various dramatic and non-dramatic sources. As soon as *Rosencrantz and Guildenstern are Dead* appeared in performance, reviewers and academic commentators recognized its derivation not only from Shakespeare's *Hamlet*, but also from Beckett's *Waiting for Godot*. They have noticed other influences as well: Pirandello, T. S. Eliot, Wilde, Kafka, and Pinter have left theatrical or literary traces, and Ludwig Wittgenstein's late *Investigations* provide philosophical bearings.[1] For the most part, critics describe the composition of Stoppard's play as if it had been neatly prescribed by a recipe: plot and characters from Shakespeare folded into a Beckettian *ambiance*, or vice versa; a dash of concept, echo or tone from the other dramatic or literary sources; and Wittgenstein's philosophy cracked, its language-games separated and used to bind the other ingredients. Yet the texture of *Rosencrantz and Guildenstern are Dead* hardly resembles that of a pudding, or any other confection assembled in a predictable way. Let that be the character note of Stoppard's dramaturgy.

Stoppard and others have often ascribed the original idea for *Rosencrantz and Guildenstern are Dead* to Kenneth Ewing, the playwright's agent. Toward the end of 1963, in an attempt to cheer Stoppard after the rejection of a script, Ewing revealed a long-cherished notion about *Hamlet*. 'Quoting the speech in which Claudius sends Hamlet to England with a sealed message (borne by Rosencrantz and Guildenstern) enjoining the ruler of that country to cut off Hamlet's head, Ewing said that in his opinion the King of England at the time of their arrival might well have been King Lear. And, if so, did they find him raving mad at Dover? Stoppard's spirits rose . . .'[2] 'The possibility appealed to me,' Stoppard later explained in an interview, 'and I began work on a burlesque Shakespeare farce.'[3] By autumn 1964, he had written a bad one:[4] 'in which they got to England, and King Lear was on the throne . . . I mean, the whole thing was unspeakable'.[5]

Although some of the dialogue from the burlesque remains in the final version of *Rosencrantz and Guildenstern are Dead*,[6] Stoppard scrapped the early effort and

---

[1] See, for a representative sampling, Normand Berlin, '*Rosencrantz and Guildenstern Are Dead*: Theater of Criticism', *Modern Drama*, 16 (1973), 269, and *The Secret Cause: A Discussion of Tragedy* (Amherst, 1981), p. 78; C. W. E. Bigsby, *Tom Stoppard*, Writers and Their Work (Harlow, 1976), pp. 11, 15; Robert Brustein, 'Waiting for Hamlet', *The New Republic*, 4 November 1967, pp. 25–6; Richard Corballis, 'Extending the Audience: The Structure of "Rosencrantz and Guildenstern Are Dead"', *Ariel*, 11 (1980), 57–8, n. 7; Felicia Hardison Londré, *Tom Stoppard*, Modern Literature Series (New York, 1981), pp. 34, 38–41; and Kenneth Tynan, 'Profiles: Withdrawing with Style from the Chaos', *New Yorker*, 19 December 1977, pp. 72, 74. In addition, Neil Sammells explores a connection between Stoppard and James Saunders in an unpublished manuscript titled 'Giggling at the Arts: Tom Stoppard and James Saunders'.

[2] Tynan, p. 64.

[3] Tom Stoppard, 'The Writer and the Theatre: The Definite Maybe', *The Author*, 78 (1967), 19.

[4] *Ibid.*

[5] Tom Stoppard (with the Editors of *Theatre Quarterly*), 'Ambushes for the Audience: Towards a High Comedy of Ideas', *Theatre Quarterly*, 4 (1974), 6.   [6] *Ibid.*

began a different play in October 1964:[7] 'the transition from one play to the other was an attempt to find a solution to a practical problem – that if you write a play about Rosencrantz and Guildenstern in England, you can't count on people knowing who they are and how they got there. So one tended to get back into the end of *Hamlet* a bit. But the explanations were always partial and ambiguous, so one went back a bit further into the plot, and as soon as I started doing this I totally lost interest in England. The interesting thing was them at Elsinore.'[8] Stoppard recast this explanation in admitting that he has great difficulty in working out plots, and using *Hamlet* – as he would later use other plays or classical whodunits – relieved the pressure of composition.[9] By April 1965, Stoppard had written two acts of *Rosencrantz and Guildenstern are Dead*. A commission from the Royal Shakespeare Company inspired him to complete a third act, but the play was not actually performed until the Oxford Theatre Group picked it up and presented it, revised, at the Edinburgh Festival in 1966.[10]

Hamlet therefore served as Stoppard's point of departure for this multifarious full-length (and lengthy) play. When asked why, Stoppard answered that he had no other choice for this kind of drama: he considers Shakespeare's tragedy probably 'the most famous play in any language; it is part of a sort of common mythology'; and Rosencrantz and Guildenstern 'are so much more than merely bit players in another famous play. . . . As far as their involvement in Shakespeare's text is concerned they are told very little about what is going on and much of what they are told isn't true. So I see them much more clearly as a couple of bewildered innocents rather than a couple of henchmen . . .'[11] From the beginning, then, Stoppard viewed *Hamlet* as a means for solving practical problems of composition and a familiar text whose interpretation he could share with his audience. When he acknowledges his debt to Beckett, he emphasizes what he calls 'a Beckett joke', meaning a technique which Beckett uses in his novels as well as his plays: 'It appears in various forms but it consists of confident statement followed by immediate refutation by the same voice. It's a constant process of elaborate structure and sudden – and total – dismantlement.'[12] *Rosencrantz and Guildenstern are Dead* thus shares with

Waiting for Godot not only 'the image of two lost souls waiting for something to happen', but Stoppard's idea of Beckett's humorous, dialectical mode of expression.[13]

Stoppard is vague or non-committal about the other components of *Rosencrantz and Guildenstern are Dead*: 'Prufrock and Beckett are the twin syringes of my diet, my arterial system'; 'I really wasn't aware of . . . [Pirandello] as an influence. It would be very difficult to write a play which was totally unlike Beckett, Pirandello and Kafka . . .'[14] As one might expect from these remarks, allusions in *Rosencrantz and Guildenstern are Dead* to writers other than Shakespeare and Beckett tend to be unsustained, superficial, even unintended. Yet there is a third important presence. Although no one has pressed Stoppard about Wittgenstein's influence on *Rosencrantz and Guildenstern are Dead*, striking reflections of ideas and language from the *Philosophical Investigations* suggest that this text was the third major paradigm for Stoppard's.

If Stoppard backs away from discussions of influences, he utterly rejects analyses of his work which announce that they have discovered the correct combination. He describes his method of playwriting with the image that Wittgenstein uses to represent the way one learns a concept: 'convergences of different threads'.[15] That metaphor certainly works

---

[7] Stoppard, 'The Definite Maybe', p. 19.

[8] Stoppard, 'Ambushes for the Audience', p. 6.

[9] *Ibid.* p. 8.

[10] Stoppard, 'The Definite Maybe', pp. 19–20.

[11] 'Tom Stoppard' (interviewed by Giles Gordon), *Transatlantic Review*, 29 (1968), repr. in Joseph F. McCrindle, ed., *Behind the Scenes: Theater and Film Interviews from the 'Transatlantic Review'* (New York, Chicago, and San Francisco, 1971); p. 80.

[12] 'First Interview with Tom Stoppard 12 June 1974', in Ronald Hayman, *Tom Stoppard*, Contemporary Playwrights (London and Totowa, N.J., 1977), p. 7.

[13] 'Tom Stoppard' (interviewed by Giles Gordon), p. 84.

[14] 'First Interview with Tom Stoppard', p. 8; 'Tom Stoppard' (interviewed by Giles Gordon), p. 84.

[15] Compare 'First Interview with Tom Stoppard', p. 4, with Ludwig Wittgenstein, *Philosophical Investigations*, trans. G. E. M. Anscombe (Oxford, 1974), p. 32ᵉ. Subsequent references to Wittgenstein's *Philosophical Investigations* will refer to this edition and appear in the text.

for *Rosencrantz and Guildenstern are Dead*, but it implies a certain opaqueness at the points where threads join. I prefer to think of Stoppard's play as several transparencies stacked on top of one another. The wit which has continually engaged Stoppard's audiences arises not only from his verbal ingenuity but also from the meeting of points – sometimes whole lines – in the transparencies. As a writer, Stoppard is preoccupied with the particular, 'contriving to inject some sort of interest and colour into every line'; and he himself remarks that 'Obviously, the more material you have behind you, the greater the possibilities are in arithmetical progression for cross-reference and compass-point co-ordinates, as it were.'[16] The latter quotation refers to his own plays, but applies to his other sources as well. In *Rosencrantz and Guildenstern are Dead*, Stoppard seems to have borrowed his strategies from at least three important works which vary in chronological or generic terms. As these works – content, form and style – are superimposed upon one another in perpetually shifting combinations, likenesses appear for a moment between generally unlike texts and then disappear with the next configuration.[17] Perhaps *Rosencrantz and Guildenstern are Dead* performs like the theatrical version of a metaphysical conceit: it draws connections which can be seen and heard between unlikely partners, and it does not dwell on any single combination or explain its significance. To support this conclusion in brief compass, I shall cite a number of different instances where Stoppard's play introduces *Hamlet* to *Godot* or Wittgenstein through mutual devices, techniques, ideas and phrases.

In addition to direct quotation – Rosencrantz and Guildenstern speak phrases from *Waiting for Godot*[18] – familiar theatrical or literary conventions link the plays: time dislocated from strictly ordered chronology; a minimally localized scene; address to the audience; play within a play; and shifting from a less poetic to a more poetic idiom in order to indicate some other kind of change. Further, Stoppard's manipulation of language produces many points of convergence. Resonances of *Hamlet* and *Waiting for Godot* sound clearly in the multitudes of puns – both serious and frivolous – which are integral to the basic meaning of *Rosencrantz and Guildenstern are Dead*.[19] Even death submits to wordplay, sometimes with an ontological twist (or if one prefers, ontology submits to wordplay with a morbid twist):

Hamlet. . . . This counsellor
Is now most still, most secret, and most grave,
Who was in life a foolish prating knave.
Come, sir, to draw toward an end with you.

(*Hamlet*, 3.4.215–18)

Estragon [referring to Vladimir's bladder problem]: What do you expect, you always wait till the last moment.
Vladimir (*musingly*): The last moment [. . .] Sometimes I feel it coming all the same. Then I go all queer. [. . .] How shall I say? Relieved and at the same time . . . (*he searches for the word*) . . . appalled. (*With emphasis.*) AP-PALLED. [. . .] Nothing to be done.

(*Waiting for Godot*, p. 8a)

Ros. We take Hamlet to the English king, we hand over the letter – what then?
Guil. There may be something in the letter to keep us going a bit.
Ros. And if not?
Guil. Then that's it – we're finished.
Ros. At a loose end?
Guil. Yes.

(*Rosencrantz and Guildenstern are Dead*, p. 76)[20]

The three plays meet as well in other kinds of wordplay which are also intrinsic to thematic content,

---

16 Stoppard, 'Ambushes for the Audience', p. 6; 'First Interview with Tom Stoppard', p. 3.
17 See Clive James's description of Stoppard's work in 'Count Zero Splits the Infinite: Tom Stoppard's Plays', *Encounter*, 45 (1975), 68–76.
18 See Ruby Cohn, *Modern Shakespeare Offshoots* (Princeton, 1976), p. 216, and 'Tom Stoppard: Light Drama and Dirges in Marriage', in C. W. E. Bigsby, ed., *Contemporary English Drama*, Stratford-upon-Avon Studies, 19 (1981), p. 113.
19 Hersh Zeifman, 'Tomfoolery: Stoppard's Theatrical Puns', *The Yearbook of English Studies*, 9 (1979), p. 205, describes Stoppard's use of puns generally in this way.
20 Reference to *Hamlet* in my text comes from the Arden edition by Harold Jenkins (New York and London, 1982); reference to *Waiting for Godot*, from Beckett's translation of his original French text (New York, 1954); reference to Stoppard's play, from *Rosencrantz and Guildenstern are Dead* (1967). On the pun cited in *Rosencrantz and Guildenstern are Dead*, see Jonathan Bennett, 'Philosophy and Mr Stoppard', *Philosophy*, 50 (1975), 10–11.

such as the exposure of clichés. Similarly integral, the imagery in *Rosencrantz and Guildenstern are Dead* frequently seems to conflate Shakespeare's techniques and devices with Beckett's. Stoppard too depends upon metaphor rather than simile; employs iterative imagery such as animals and games; and makes his images concrete at crucial points to materialize concepts of life and death, as Shakespeare does in the graveyard, for example, and Beckett with Pozzo's discarded bones. In Stoppard's play, the audience witnesses the metaphysical journey which Rosencrantz and Guildenstern pursue on a boat, a journey described coherently in vivid images by Shakespeare's Hamlet and sporadically in familiar ones by Beckett's tramps and Pozzo. The coin-game in *Rosencrantz and Guildenstern are Dead* works as a more exact epitome. Comparable to Hamlet's recorder and Beckett's vaudeville hat routine, it makes tangible abstract notions of play – among other things. Operating on principles shared by Shakespeare and Beckett, Stoppard's metaphors also seem to echo Wittgenstein's at several points: a notable instance, his ratiocinated unicorn, 'A horse with an arrow in its forehead' (p. 15), recalls an image devised for contemplation by Wittgenstein, 'an animal in a picture . . . transfixed by an arrow' (p. 203ᵉ).[21]

Like his models, Stoppard manipulates not only language but philosophy, especially logic. In *Hamlet*, as Joan Larsen Klein has recently demonstrated, Shakespeare plays with familiar sixteenth-century adages, that 'fragmentary collection of human wisdom', frequently distorting them to 'reflect moral values which clearly no longer obtain in Elsinore';[22] in *Waiting for Godot* and *Rosencrantz and Guildenstern are Dead*, the dramatists similarly misuse proverbs to reveal ontological and epistemological confusion. Moreover, the three playwrights all depict their protagonists and other characters applying philosophical tools in order to comprehend uncongenial realities. Consequently, syllogisms occur in each of the plays as part of deductive processes, and empirical evidence gathers as part of inductive ones. But these methods and the laws they have created prove undependable in the courses of dramatic action: the tools of reason frequently break down when applied to divers objects – a ghost, a parable, a coin-game – and each world

remains baffling. Glimpses of truth appear only when logic dissolves into madness (*Hamlet*), frenzy (*Waiting for Godot*), or unquestioning resignation (*Hamlet, Rosencrantz and Guildenstern are Dead*).[23]

The modern plays share with *Hamlet* and Wittgenstein's work preoccupations with specific obstacles to the proper functioning of reason: lapses of memory and the variables of perception. When the philosopher Jonathan Bennett interprets the role of memory in *Rosencrantz and Guildenstern are Dead*, therefore, he also throws light on *Hamlet* and *Waiting for Godot*:

> The point is made that memory is needed for access to the past. . . . Their inability to initiate action stems partly from the lack of memory. For one thing, if one is to act against an assigned scenario, doing so rationally and not in random behavioural spasms, one must have reasons for acting; and reasons require knowledge . . . At a deeper level, there is the fact that to know what you are doing you must know what you have just been doing. . . . At a deeper level still, one cannot make sense of anything at all without memory.[24]

Lack of memory subverts activity, as the Player King declaims and as Hamlet admits in the closet scene; knowledge of the past antecedes comprehension of the

---

[21] Correspondences with Wittgenstein run through Stoppard's text; compare, for example, Wittgenstein, p. viii, with Stoppard, pp. 10 and 60; p. 26ᵉ with p. 9; p. 34ᵉ with p. 28; pp. 123ᵉ–124ᵉ with p. 70.

[22] Joan Larsen Klein, '"What is't to leave betimes?" Proverbs and Logic in *Hamlet*', *Shakespeare Survey 32* (Cambridge, 1979), 163–76; pp. 175, 163.

[23] The two modern plays show interesting correspondences with two ideas presented by Wittgenstein. In the *Investigations* (pp. 157ᵉ–59ᵉ), Wittgenstein methodically considers the question 'How does one judge what time it is?' as a philosophical problem. When Pozzo poses the same question in *Waiting for Godot* (p. 55a), and Rosencrantz and Guildenstern try to decide whether it is night or day (pp. 71–2, 81), reason goes awry and the characters momentarily unhinge themselves from chronology. Describing philosophy, Wittgenstein states: 'A philosophical problem has the form: "I don't know my way about".' (p. 49ᵉ). Beckett and Stoppard seem to give this concept tangibility as their characters try to establish senses of direction: see, for example, *Waiting for Godot*, pp. 55a–55b, and *Rosencrantz and Guildenstern are Dead*, pp. 41–2, 62, 71.   [24] Bennett, pp. 16–17.

present and pursuit of the future.[25] Even more than memory, 'The concept of "seeing" makes a tangled impression', as Wittgenstein contends. 'Well, it is tangled. . . . After all, how completely ragged what we see can appear !' (p. 200^e). According to their various lights, different characters entertain different impressions, for instance of the Ghost in *Hamlet*, the landscape in *Waiting for Godot*, the court in *Rosencrantz and Guildenstern are Dead*. Stoppard makes the point tellingly through other senses when he enacts a problem set by Wittgenstein – '"Is this foot *my* foot?" . . . "Is this sensation *my* sensation?"' (p. 123^e) – in a dialogue between Rosencrantz and Guildenstern at the beginning of act 3 (p. 70).

Overall, Stoppard's *Rosencrantz and Guildenstern are Dead* seems at least in part a response to Wittgenstein's order: 'Review the multiplicity of language-games in the following examples, and in others:

Giving orders, and obeying them –
Describing the appearance of an object, or giving its measurements – . . .
Reporting an event –
Speculating about an event -
Forming and testing a hypothesis – . . .
Play-acting – . . .
Guessing riddles –
Making a joke; telling it –
Solving a problem in practical arithmetic –
Translating from one language into another –
Asking, thanking, cursing, greeting, praying.'

(pp. 11^e–12^e)

For the most part, the examples Stoppard chooses are actions central to *Hamlet* and *Waiting for Godot*, all three plays engaging in language-games which are not only general forms of life in Wittgenstein's sense (p. 11^e), but particular literary and theatrical devices with linguistic, structural and symbolic dimensions. Not in the least haphazard, Stoppard's tour of theatre history and modern philosophy has been organized according to various dialectical principles. As the playwright told Giles Gordon in 1968, Rosencrantz and Guildenstern 'both add up to me in many ways in the sense that they're carrying out a dialogue which I carry out with myself'.[26] Typical of his work, this play offers '*no* single, clear statement . . . What there is, is a

series of conflicting statements made by conflicting characters, and they tend to play a sort of infinite leap-frog. You know, an argument, a refutation, then a rebuttal of the refutation, then a counter-rebuttal . . .'[27] 'What I'm always trying to say is "Firstly, A. Secondly, minus A."'[28] The latter statement echoes Stoppard's definition of Beckett's theatrical dialectic: *Waiting for Godot* 'redefined the minima of theatrical experience. Up to then you had to have X; suddenly you had X minus one.'[29] One detects in Wittgenstein's view of philosophy still another model for Stoppard's method: 'Philosophy simply puts everything before us, and neither explains nor deduces anything. – Since everything lies open to view there is nothing to explain' (p. 50^e). Stoppard's first *Hamlet*, typical of his work, 'is essentially dialectical, but without a final synthesis ever being reached';[30] Shakespeare's *Hamlet* serves as the ideal paradigm for this kind of dialectic: the world's most famous text whose infinite complexities defeat intellectual synthesis.

If *Rosencrantz and Guildenstern are Dead* is Stoppard's *Romeo and Juliet*, *Dogg's Hamlet* is Part 1 of his *Henry IV*: 'The comma that divides *Dogg's Hamlet, Cahoot's Macbeth* also serves to unite two plays which have common elements: the first is hardly a play at all without the second, which cannot be performed without the first.'[31] Written by an established playwright using sources he had employed before, this second *Hamlet* forms part of a play composed as a diptych. In his Preface to the published version, Stoppard himself identifies his sources and analogues; to date, few commentators have attempted to describe their formulation.[32]

---

[25] See Bennett, p. 18. Compare Wittgenstein, p. 231^e with *Rosencrantz and Guildenstern are Dead*, pp. 11, 51, on how we know what remembering is, or what the past is.
[26] 'Tom Stoppard' (interviewed by Giles Gordon), p. 81.
[27] Stoppard, 'Ambushes for the Audience', pp. 6–7.
[28] 'First Interview with Tom Stoppard', p. 10.
[29] Tom Stoppard, 'Something to Declare', *The Sunday Times*, 25 February 1968.   [30] Zeifman, p. 214.
[31] Tom Stoppard, Preface to *Dogg's Hamlet, Cahoot's Macbeth* (London and Boston, 1980), p. 7. References to *Dogg's Hamlet, Cahoot's Macbeth* in my text come from this edition.
[32] However, see Ralph Toucatt's illuminating interpretation of the plays in 'Cross-Cultural Stoppard', *The Three-penny Review*, Spring 1981, pp. 19–20.

Like *Rosencrantz and Guildenstern are Dead*, *Dogg's Hamlet* evolved over a number of years, from 1971 to 1979, but its components remained separate until Stoppard combined them in the full-length play. He devised the first part of *Dogg's Hamlet* as an opening ceremony for the Almost Free Theatre in 1971. A language-game deriving from Wittgenstein's *Philosophical Investigations*, this entertainment performed in approximately twenty-five minutes. 'The [original] title [*Dogg's Our Pet*] is an anagram for Dogg's Troupe, a group of actors operating under the umbrella of Inter-Action whose guiding spirit is Ed Berman, sometimes known as Professor Dogg.'[33] In 1972 Stoppard wrote the second part of *Dogg's Hamlet* – his fifteen-minute version of *Hamlet* for seven actors – for the Fun Art Bus, a double-decker bus serving as another performance space for Inter-Action. According to Berman, 'We both coincidentally misplaced the script for four years ...', but in 1976 Dogg's Troupe played it 'on the grey parapets of the National Theatre'.[34] *Dogg's Hamlet* conflates these two playlets – elaborating the first, barely changing the second – as a prelude to *Cahoot's Macbeth*. Stoppard explains that the latter play, which includes an abbreviated version of *Macbeth*, was inspired by specific events: the situation of artists in Czechoslovakia since Charter 77; and, most immediately, a letter from Pavel Kohout in 1978 which he quotes:

As you know, many Czech theatre-people are not allowed to work in the theatre during the last years. As one of them who cannot live without theatre I was searching for a possibility to do theatre in spite of circumstances. Now I am glad to tell you that in a few days, after eight weeks rehearsals – a Living-Room Theatre is opening, with nothing smaller but Macbeth.

What is LRT? A call-group. Everybody, who wants to have Macbeth at home with two great and forbidden Czech actors, Pavel Landovsky and Vlasta Chramostova, can invite his friends and call us. Five people will come with one suitcase.[35]

By 1976, Stoppard said he 'felt ... sick of flashy mind-projections speaking in long, articulate, witty sentences about the great abstractions'.[36] His changed attitude may account for the intriguing composition of *Dogg's Hamlet*, *Cahoot's Macbeth*, which differs markedly from that of his earlier plays, including *Rosencrantz and Guildenstern are Dead*. In the finished play of 1979, the loose weave allows individual threads to remain discrete; transparencies are not superimposed, but juxtaposed. Stoppard arranges long quotations from some of his favourite writers side by side with long quotations from his own experience, allowing the passages to comment on one another. As a result, he sports his wit with a difference. The later play grows on a single horizontal axis rather than an innumerable series of vertical ones. Connections occur not in continually changing overlays of sources, but through a sequential presentation of allusions. All of the familiar derivative devices appear – from play within a play to puns and syllogisms – but they disperse themselves through the action, often as parts of quotations and therefore in their original contexts. *Dogg's Hamlet*, *Cahoot's Macbeth* offers its genealogy in a less intense fashion than *Rosencrantz and Guildenstern are Dead* had assumed. As a result, it speaks less emphatically to the analytical faculties of its audience.

Stoppard begins *Dogg's Hamlet* where Wittgenstein begins his *Philosophical Investigations*: with the presentation of a primitive language. In order to illustrate Augustine's conception of language, Wittgenstein creates the image of a builder working with blocks, pillars, slabs and beams, and his assistant passing him materials. He establishes that the conception is oversimple, but the necessary point of departure for a study of the phenomena of language. Throughout these pages, as Wittgenstein demonstrates that 'to imagine a language means to imagine a form of life' (p. 8e), the key words blocks, pillars, slabs and beams reappear like a refrain. In different combinations, they show the multiplicity of language, helping to dispel the fog which 'surrounds the working of language' and to

33 Tom Stoppard, note to *Dogg's Our Pet*, in Ed Berman, ed., *Ten of the Best British Short Plays*, Ambiance/Almost Free Playscripts, 3 (1979), p. 80.

34 Ed Berman, 'How Long Is an Ephemeron?', in *Ten of the Best British Short Plays*, p. x.

35 Tom Stoppard, Preface to *Dogg's Hamlet, Cahoot's Macbeth*, p. 8.

36 'Second Interview with Tom Stoppard 20 August 1976', in Hayman, p. 136.

provide 'a clear view of the aim and functioning of the words' (p. 4ᵉ). In the original *Dogg's Our Pet*, Stoppard created a language essentially from Wittgenstein's illustration and five words: plank, slab, block, brick and cube; in *Dogg's Hamlet*, however, he produces a more elaborate primitive language with a much larger vocabulary: 'The appeal to me consisted in the possibility of writing a play which had to teach the audience the language the play was written in.'[37] The published text of *Dogg's Hamlet* gives translations of this language called Dogg in square brackets.

As the action unfolds among a group of schoolboys who speak Dogg, two other kinds of languages intermit briefly: a very concentrated form of contemporary English which a lorry-driver compounds of slang, jargon, colloquialisms, journalese and a touch of self-conscious literary phrasing; and bits and pieces of Shakespeare's *Hamlet* which the boys rehearse for performance. After a series of events and a ceremony articulated in Dogg – the setting is actually an English prep school – '*The lighting changes and there is a trumpet fanfare*', and the same characters perform the fifteen-minute *Hamlet* (p. 31). This version constitutes a tour de force undertaken in the same spirit in which Stoppard wrote a play including a whole symphony orchestra (*Every Good Boy Deserves Favour*) and in which he would gladly produce 'an underwater ballet for dolphins'.[38] It comprises a seventeen-line Prologue, an enactment of *Hamlet* which includes almost all of the characters (even Osric) and events, and an Encore which reprises the whole in thirty-eight lines. Every word comes from the original text, although phrases, lines and passages usually turn out to be composites from different acts and scenes. The effect proves mechanical and comedic in Bergson's sense: a famous record played at the wrong speed; Shakespeare in *Modern Times*.

Dogg's Hamlet ends with a bit of stage business, and *Cahoot's Macbeth* begins in a different setting: '*the living room of a flat. Thunder and lightning. Three* WITCHES *in minimal light*' (p. 47). The adult actors perform this Shakespearian tragedy in an abbreviated version without farcical effect: their production contains neither prologue nor encore; it progresses at a reasonable, unmechanized pace; and considerable portions of Shakespearian verse are spoken. Eliza-bethan English serves as the basic idiom of Stoppard's play, interrupted by passages of modern English and finally by passages of Dogg. The embodiment of repressive political forces in *Cahoot's Macbeth*, an Inspector usually expresses himself in the kind of hyperventilated English heard briefly in *Dogg's Hamlet*; he also frequently echoes Stoppard's own observations of life in Husak's Czechoslovakia as they have appeared in periodicals such as *The New York Review of Books*: '[addressing Pavel Landovsky, who plays Macbeth] Well, well, well, so now you're sweeping floors, eh? I remember you from way back. I remember you when you were a night-watchman in the builder's yard, and before that when you were the trolley porter at the mortuary, and before *that* when you were the button-moulder in *Peer Gynt* . . . Actually, Pavel, you've had a funny sort of career [. . .]' (p. 54).[39] As Stoppard's play closes, the actors manage to perform the end of *Macbeth*, despite the Inspector, by speaking the final passages in Dogg as they build a platform with now familiar slabs, blocks, planks and cubes.

Dogg's Hamlet, Cahoot's Macbeth suggests more explicitly than *Rosencrantz and Guildenstern are Dead* how language-games – in Wittgenstein's sense – may serve as the source and end of dramatic art. The invention of Dogg which Stoppard shares with his audience, like Wittgenstein's illustration of Augustine, places the concept of language in a new context and prepares us to receive fresh impressions of our own language and of Shakespeare's. Within this context, the high-speed performance of *Hamlet* demonstrates how cultural factors effect the communication of a sophisticated joke: the language-game of the fifteen-minute *Hamlet* makes sense only in cultures which value Shakespeare as an artist and witty inventiveness as a mode of expression. *Cahoot's Macbeth* presents a culture which values neither, and a group of

---

[37] Stoppard, Preface to *Dogg's Hamlet, Cahoot's Macbeth*, p. 8.

[38] Stoppard quoted in Jon Bradshaw, 'Tom Stoppard, Nonstop: Word Games with a Hit Playwright', *New York*, 10 January 1977, p. 51.

[39] Compare Tom Stoppard, 'Prague: The Story of the Chartists', *The New York Review of Books*, 4 August 1977, pp. 11–15.

artists who struggle nevertheless to communicate through a brilliant imported work of art, a language-game which is truly a form of life. In the end they succeed by translating Shakespeare into a primitive language. Where freedom does not exist, an intellectual game does not dispel fog but produces it; Stoppard's audience now comprehends the aim and function of the actors' words, but the Inspector has only a momentary glimmer: 'How the hell do I know? But if it's not free expression, I don't know what is!'; and this immediately fades into confusion: 'She's making it up as she goes along' (p. 75).

According to Stoppard, 'No plays are written to be studied and discussed [. . .]':[40] 'Playwrights try to move people, to tears or laughter. To sit in the theatre and mutter, "Ah – Pirandello!" – or "Hm, Kafka..." would be curious indeed [...].'[41] If this view were universal, we would not have Aristotle on Greek tragedy, Samuel Johnson on Shakespeare, or even Stoppard on Stoppard. Contemporary dramatists like Beckett and Bond would not co-operate with scholars to establish their proper niches in theatrical history. Yet Stoppard admits that he does not wish to be 'the Kelloggs of British drama'; he has aimed himself at a particular audience and filled his plays with allusions to engage their minds: 'There is a secret in art, isn't there? and the secret consists of what the artist has secretly and privately done. You will tumble some and not others. The whole process of putting them in, albeit unconsciously, gives Art that...texture, which sensibility tells one is valuable.'[42] In Stoppard's plays, one of the least well-kept secrets is Shakespeare. *Hamlet* – and recently *Macbeth* – have served as means of solving practical dramaturgic problems, as sets of ideas and conventions shared by Stoppard and his audience, consequently as limitless sources of wit and as the ultimate language-games. They have made a substantial contribution, times being what they are.

---

[40] Quoted in Bradshaw, p. 51.
[41] Tom Stoppard, 'Doers and Thinkers: Playwrights and Professors', *TLS*, 13 October 1972.
[42] Stoppard quoted in Mark Amory, 'The Joke's the Thing', *The Sunday Times*, 9 June 1974.

AUDEN, SHAKESPEARE, AND THE DEFENCE OF POETRY

SUSAN SNYDER

One of W. H. Auden's own poems, though it is about another poet, offers two points of departure for an exploration of Auden's use of Shakespeare. In his celebrated elegy on Yeats, he says of the poet's works after his death,

Now he is scattered among a hundred cities
And wholly given over to unfamiliar affections . . .
The words of a dead man
Are modified in the guts of the living.

The second point of departure comes a bit later, the blunt statement that 'poetry makes nothing happen'.[1]

A poet becomes what his readers want to make of him, in their historical situations and individual needs, and the same is true of Shakespeare as read and seen by Auden. In an essay of 1959, he admits cheerfully that Shakespeare critics tell more about themselves than about Shakespeare; 'but', he goes on, 'perhaps this is the great value of drama of the Shakespearian kind, namely, that whatever he may see taking place on stage, its final effect on each spectator is a self-revelation'.[2] The self that Auden brought to this Shakespearian mirror was a poet, and – after 1940 – a Christian. Because there was a tension between these two professions, a fear that poetry is in the religious sense beside the point, the self-revelation that Auden seeks is also a self-justification, a place for his art inside religious values and priorities. Almost all of Auden's work about or based on Shakespeare belongs to the 1940s and 1950s, the period after his conversion when he was still working out its implications. He addressed the plays in introductions, reviews, critical essays; several of these were republished in 1962, in a collection, The Dyer's Hand, which he told Stephen

Spender was all about Christianity and Art.[3] Most important, in the early forties he turned to Shakespeare's own play of art and the artist, The Tempest, and used its figures and situations to construct a long poetic meditation on art's relation to life, The Sea and the Mirror.

Shakespeare the Christian artist: for many of us unconvinced by attempts to read the plays as enactments of doctrine, the idea rings alarm bells. I should say at once that for Auden 'Christian' in this context implies a moral attitude and a certain sense of time, rather than overtly religious subject matter. He does not make the plays into allegories. Still, there are occasions when the words of the dead poet do seem too thoroughly modified in the guts of the living one – I suppose I mean occasions when my Shakespeare diverges radically from Auden's. I had originally planned this paper as a dialogue, with a more equal balance between Shakespeare and Auden; time constraints have dictated instead a concentration on Auden, but enough survives of my first design so that Shakespeare can, here and there, answer back.

The other line I quoted from the Yeats elegy looks back to a preoccupation with the social function of art

---

[1] W. H. Auden, 'In Memory of W. B. Yeats', *Collected Poems*, ed. Edward Mendelson (New York, 1976), p. 197; all Auden poems, after a check with the original publication for possible revisions, have for convenience been cited from this edition, hereafter referred to in the text by page number.

[2] *The Dyer's Hand and Other Essays* (New York, 1962), p. 182.

[3] Humphrey Carpenter, *W. H. Auden: A Biography* (Boston and London, 1981), p. 404.

that predates Auden's conversion. Well before the question took on specifically Christian terms, he had been worrying about what art was *for*. He had participated to some extent in the activist aesthetic of the thirties, seeing poetry as an instrument of social change, the poet as diagnostician and prescriber for a sick society. He was, as Spender has remarked, 'genuinely didactic by nature'.[4] Yet he rejected the propagandist's role as undermining the integrity of art; and in *New Year Letter* he listed among his past poetic crimes adopting 'what I would disown, / The preacher's loose immodest tone' (p. 165). Indeed, even while he and Christopher Isherwood were writing Brechtian didactic drama in the thirties, he had admitted, 'you cannot tell people what to do, you can only tell them parables'.[5] By 1939, when he wrote his elegy on Yeats, Auden had abandoned any belief in poetry as an agent of historical change: 'poetry makes nothing happen'. Even so, he could not retreat into celebrating his own consciousness; Romantic solipsism was not the answer. Auden's conversion was prompted in part by the outbreak of the Second World War, perceived as the final failure of liberal humanism, and by his reading of Kierkegaard, Niebuhr, and Charles Williams. But it also connected directly with this search for a poetic stance and his distrust of the self as centre. A comment by Spender applies as well to his aesthetics as to his religion: 'His problem has always been to shift the center of his dogmatic ways of regarding experience from himself to some objective authority, so that he himself becomes a part of what is judged, and not just the center of his own system.'[6]

In some ways, however, conversion made the poet's work still more difficult to justify. In the context of Kierkegaardian Christianity, art is not serious. Only men's wills are serious, and the only serious thing is how they direct them, toward self-love or love of God and their neighbour.[7] Kierkegaard himself had found an unbridgeable gulf between the aesthetic mode of experience and the religious.[8] On this point, Auden supplies a gloss in his own sketch of the aesthetic impulse. The Poet, he says, values the beautiful and the brave, the *interesting*; his response to the transience of these is to 'transform the real world into an imaginary one which is godlike in its permanence and beauty';

he celebrates Being, but has trouble with Becoming, which resists concentration into the significant moments of poetry.[9] Auden's example of this pure Poet's art is a Greek drama, the *Oedipus*, and indeed he liked to use the historical transition from classical to Christian to interpret Kierkegaard's three categories of being – the aesthetic, the ethical, and the religious. In Auden's scheme, the aesthetic religion reflected in classical Greek literature founders on the gap between power and goodness and on the fact of human mortality, to be succeeded by the ethical religion of the philosophers. But by identifying good with reason – to know the good is to will it – the ethical way fails to confront the real problems of *choice*. What if we don't will to know, or if, knowing, we will to deny the good? Choice is, however, central to the religious state, which has its historical expression in the Christian era. From this point of view, poetry, which is a gratuitous act which in turn 'makes nothing happen', becomes even more irrelevant.

It is here that Auden turns to Shakespeare first, that is, as exemplifying a different art that sets against the Poet of the aesthetic way the Historian. Auden saw

---

4 Stephen Spender, *World Within World* (New York, 1951), p. 270.
5 'Psychology and Art Today', in *The Arts Today*, ed. Geoffrey Grigson (1935), p. 18.
6 Spender, 'W. H. Auden and His Poetry', in *Auden: A Collection of Critical Essays*, ed. Monroe K. Spears (Englewood Cliffs, NJ, 1964); p. 35.
7 Auden, 'Squares and Oblongs', in *Poets at Work*, introd. Charles D. Abbott (New York, 1948); pp. 168–9.
8 For example, in a statement that Auden chose to include in his selections from Kierkegaard and to paraphrase as an epigraph to 'Squares and Oblongs' (1948), Kierkegaard says of the poet, 'The cause of his suffering is that he always wants to be religious and always goes the wrong way about it and remains a poet: consequently he is unhappily in love with God': *The Living Thoughts of Kierkegaard*, ed. W. H. Auden (New York, 1952), pp. 102–3.
9 'The Dyer's Hand: Poetry and the Poetic Process', *Anchor Review*, 2 (1957), 255–62. Compare Kierkegaard, *Living Thoughts*, p. 72: 'If I would imagine a hero who stakes his life, it can very well be concentrated in the moment, but not the business of dying daily, for here the principal point is that it occurs every day. Courage can very well be represented in the moment, but not patience, precisely for the reason that patience strives with time.'

history in classical thought as a form of nature, in that it was cyclical and thus endlessly repetitious. But with Christianity, rooted in the Old Testament's gradual unfolding of God and defined by the unique and consequential event of the Incarnation, history becomes linear and progressive, a significant time in which we choose and are shaped by our choices. On the one hand, then, is Oedipus, whose acts of parricide and incest have no effect on what he essentially is; only their discovery brings a change, and that change is in his status rather than himself. In contrast, Auden points to Macbeth, whose willed actions mould him step by step into a different being.[10] There is another aspect to this Shakespearian paradigm, as well, for man in history is dual: 'while in the first world there is no essential difference between man and other creatures of nature, in the second man is unique as a conscious creature who is changed by his acts and at the same time as a physical being subject to the necessities of nature.' Christian art, then, must express not only man's I, maker of history, but his Me, biologically bound to nature's drives and repetitions. This expression Auden finds in Shakespeare's mixture of modes; in *Macbeth* the comic earthiness of the Porter amid the tense elevation of regicide reminds us of 'this creaturely framework within which [man's] freedom of will operates'.[11]

If this were in fact a dialogue, Shakespeare would very likely agree on his 'gift of double focus'[12] and assent to the centrality of choice and consequence in his tragic actions. But he might well protest when Auden sought, as he occasionally does, to fit tragic experience into strictly moral categories. In Auden's more extreme statements, Shakespeare's tragic heroes are sinners who bring suffering on themselves,[13] suffering which is 'defiantly insisted upon by the hero himself so that, instead of making him better, it makes him worse and when he dies he is not reconciled to the law but defiant, that is, damned'.[14] This may work for the criminal hero; Auden's primary choice of *Macbeth* is no accident. But he can turn even Romeo and Juliet into criminals: their suicides ensure their damnation, says Auden, not as external judgement but as internal necessity, for suicide is 'a failure to love, a proof of selfishness'.[15] And Lear, who *is* made better by suffering, is therefore denied the status of tragic hero

altogether.[16] Apparently Auden hears in Shakespeare no paradoxical counter-voice asserting a self stretched and deepened by tragic events themselves. There is also an *absence* of speech he does not attend to sufficiently, an ultimate silence at the conjunction of character and circumstance where choice is born – what Dame Helen Gardner has called tragic mystery.[17] Oddly enough, Shakespeare could have enlisted in his support Kierkegaard himself, who saw that 'truly tragic guilt' has about it an 'ambiguous innocence', and that the tragic effect disappears when the playwright tips the balance of action and suffering too much toward the individual will.[18]

Auden's appropriation of Shakespearian tragedy as a model for the art of Becoming rather than the art of Being may strike us as over-schematic and reductive.[19] *The Tempest* invited him to a more complex creative engagement. Given his doubts about the efficacy of art, the play's terms are attractively problematic. A magician whose art was initially self-serving and inward-turned finally renounces his magic, but not before he has by its means offered the possibility of

---

10 'The Dyer's Hand', pp. 258–64.   11 *Ibid.* p. 266.
12 'So, hidden in his [the artist's] hocus-pocus, / There lies the gift of double focus' (*New Year Letter*, p. 176).
13 *The Dyer's Hand*, p. 176.
14 Introduction to *The Portable Greek Reader* (New York, 1948), p. 24.
15 Introduction to *Romeo and Juliet*, Laurel edn. (New York 1958), p. 38.   16 *Greek Reader*, p. 24.
17 'Tragic Mysteries', in *Shakespeare, Pattern of Excelling Nature*, ed. David Bevington and Jay L. Halio (Newark, Del., 1978), pp. 88–94.
18 Kierkegaard, *Living Thoughts*, p. 58.
19 Auden's perspective seems to have been fundamentally anti-tragic, or more precisely supra-tragic. He acknowledged that suffering can be a tragic fact, as it is not necessarily just or in proportion to the magnitude of sin, but it must be accepted 'as an occasion for grace or as a process of purgation' (*The Dyer's Hand*, p. 175). Tragedy is subsumed in carnival laughter, which Auden calls 'simultaneously a protest and an acceptance' (*Forewords and Afterwords*, ed. Edward Mendelson (New York 1973), p. 471). The comic stance suited not only Auden's temperament but his religion, as the only possible address to a deeply ironic, if not absurd, relation between divine reality and human provisionality and contradiction. If the religious way could find any expression in verbal art, he believed, it was through comic indirection.

regeneration to others; his brother, the one most in need of regeneration, resists it, and ends the play in stubborn silence; restive in different ways under Prospero's control are the inhuman agent of art, Ariel, and the all-too-human Caliban, creatureliness itself. Auden was, I think, drawn especially by a certain open-ended quality of the play.[20] Both Ariel and Caliban are left at the end with no fixed address, and Prospero himself, after shedding his magician's robes, abandons even the actor's magical dominance to assert his human dependence on the audience and ask their mercy. The *Tempest* Epilogue suggests that Shakespeare himself may see a Kierkegaardian gulf between art and authentic religious experience. Furthermore, even that human reality of the audience is called into question at one high moment of the play proper, when Prospero likens it to one of his magic spectacles:

> And like the baseless fabric of this vision,
> The cloud-capp'd tow'rs, the gorgeous palaces,
> The solemn temples, the great globe itself,
> Yea, all which it inherit, shall dissolve,
> And like this insubstantial pageant faded
> Leave not a rack behind. We are such stuff
> As dreams are made on; and our little life
> Is rounded with a sleep. (4.1.151–8)[21]

The Sea and the Mirror takes up where Shakespeare left off *The Tempest*, both as story and as concluded performance. In Part I, Prospero reflects on his past and his future while saying goodbye to Ariel; in Part II the other characters declare their newly discovered selves in a variety of lyric forms from ballad to sestina and villanelle; in Part III, Caliban addresses the audience in a most unexpected style derived from – of all people – Henry James. The whole opens with the Stage Manager talking to the critics. One version of the problem of art emerges at once, when he presents it as a circus, an illusion that denies difficulty and death.

> The aged catch their breath,
> For the nonchalant couple go
> Waltzing across the tightrope
> As if there were no death
> Or hope of falling down;
> The wounded cry as the clown
> Doubles his meaning, and O
> How the dear little children laugh

> When the drums roll and the lovely
> Lady is sawn in half.

Even art that really addresses the Flesh and the Devil stands apart from the choices that define us.

> We are wet with sympathy now;
> Thanks for the evening; but how
> Shall we satisfy when we meet,
> Between Shall-I and I-Will,
> The lion's mouth whose hunger
> No metaphors can fill?

> Well, who in his own backyard
> Has not opened his heart to the smiling
> Secret he cannot quote?
> Which goes to show that the Bard
> Was sober when he wrote
> That this world of fact we love
> Is unsubstantial stuff:
> All the rest is silence
> On the other side of the wall;
> And the silence ripeness,
> And the ripeness all. (p. 311)

I shall return to this Shakespearian pastiche, in which *Hamlet* and *Lear* suddenly join *The Tempest*. For now, what matters is that art stops short of ultimate reality; the smiling secret cannot be quoted.

Prospero explains to Ariel that his past magic was a mode of false power that sought to evade human limitation:

> When I woke into my life, a sobbing dwarf
> Whom giants served only as they pleased, I was not
>   what I seemed;
>   Beyond their busy backs I made a magic
> To ride away from a father's imperfect justice,
>   Take vengeance on the Romans for their grammar,
> Usurp the popular earth and blot for ever
>   The gross insult of being a mere one among many:
> Now, Ariel, I am that I am, your late and lonely
>   master,
>   Who knows now what magic is; – the power to
>   enchant
> That comes from disillusion. (pp. 312–13)

---

20 Gerald Nelson, *Changes of Heart: A Study of the Poetry of W. H. Auden*, Perspectives in Criticism, 21 (Berkeley and Los Angeles, 1969), p. 22.

21 Shakespeare's plays are quoted from *The Riverside Shakespeare*, ed. G. Blakemore Evans (Boston, 1974), omitting square brackets.

In this *now* is the real awakening into life. After dreaming of an immense journey, conducted with all the romantic accoutrements of a fairy tale or an espionage thriller, Prospero finds in old age that the journey really exists and he must take it

> alone and on foot, without a cent in my pocket,
> Through a universe where time is not foreshortened,
> No animals talk, and there is neither floating nor
> flying. (p. 315)

The existential journey truly *is* tremendous – Auden borrows for it Kierkegaard's phrase, 'sailing alone, out over seventy thousand fathoms' – but it must take place in that silence we have heard of from the Stage Manager, beyond the adjusting, harmonizing patterns of art.

> Can I learn to suffer
> Without saying something ironic or funny
> On suffering? I never suspected the way of truth
> Was a way of silence where affectionate chat
> Is but a robbers' ambush and even good music
> In shocking taste. (p. 316)

But this Prospero, like Shakespeare's, has seen another potential in the imagination, for those who renounce the temptation to remake reality. He says to Ariel,

> we have only to learn to sit still and give no
> orders,
> To make you offer us your echo and your mirror;
> We have only to believe you, then you dare not lie;
> To ask for nothing, and at once from your calm
> eyes,
> With their lucid proof of apprehension and disorder,
> All we are not stares back at what we are.

Mirrors offer, by reflection and framing, a truth we cannot see without them. 'No one but you', continues Prospero to Ariel,

> had sufficient audacity and eyesight
> To find those clearings where the shy humiliations
> Gambol on sunny afternoons, the waterhole to which
> The scarred rogue sorrow comes quietly in the small
> hours;
> And no one but you is reliably informative on hell.
> (p. 313)

The opposition of magic and mirror for different kinds of art recurs in Auden's writings of the forties. For example, one review begins,

Art, as the late Professor R. G. Collingwood pointed out, is not magic, i.e., a means by which the artist ommunicates or arouses his feelings in others, but a mirror in which they may become conscious of what their own feelings really are: its proper effect, in fact, is disenchanting.[22]

Magic-art creates a substitute world, dispelling disturbing emotions (like little Prospero's helpless rage) in wish fulfilment – or, even more dangerously, compelling the emotions that the authorities think desirable.[23] The mirror, on the other hand, reflects what wish excludes: 'the problematic, the painful, the disorderly, the ugly'.[24] There is, of course, more involved here than a simple camera-like recording of the actual. Poetry, the art of naming, is not just a means of saying but a means of *knowing*.[25] In an essay of 1948, Auden quotes E. M. Forster: 'How can I know what I think till I see what I say?'[26] Language, the poet's medium, a racial rather than a personal property, is for Auden a separate force that conditions and shapes his vision, as he experiments with its resources of meaning and responds to the demands of form.[27] Here, too, Shakespeare provides the exemplar. Auden called him 'the purest poet who ever lived; that is to say, he explored all life through a single

---

[22] 'The Poet of the Encirclement', *New Republic*, 25 October 1943, p. 579.

[23] Auden feared that postwar upheavals might offer large rewards for state-sponsored 'magicians' who would use their talents to manipulate the masses. He insisted again, in 1948, 'Magic, black or white, is not art; for magic is a means of ruling children and all who cannot rule themselves, one kind of fraud or force, while art, like all kinds of truth, is one of the pleasures of free men' ('Henry James and the Artist in America', *Harper's*, July 1948, p. 39).

[24] *The Dyer's Hand*, p. 338.

[25] Compare a late poem entitled 'I am Not a Camera', which opens, 'To call our sight Vision / implies that, to us, / all objects are subjects. / What we have not named / or beheld as a symbol / escapes our notice' (p. 630).

[26] 'Squares and Oblongs', p. 174.

[27] 'Psychology and Art Today', p. 11.

medium, that of language. . . . The dyer's hand was completely immersed in what it worked in.'[28]

The poet's ordering functions in the mirror effect as well as in his address to and concretizing of many-sided reality.

By significant details [mirror-poetry] shows us that our present state is neither as virtuous nor as secure as we thought, and by the lucid pattern into which it unifies these details, its assertion that order is *possible*, it faces us with the command to make it *actual*.[29]

A command, unlike a magic spell, can be resisted; we have to assent to it. If magic-art is akin to Kierkegaard's aesthetic way, mirror-art relates to the ethical, in bringing about knowledge without operating on the will. The reader himself must make the move from possible to actual, Shall-I to I-Will.

In a notebook Auden was using while he planned and wrote *The Sea and the Mirror*, he left a list of characters from *The Tempest*, following each with associations with other Shakespearian figures. Opposite Ariel there are two, Puck and Lear's Fool. In this suggestive pairing, the agent of art subsumes both the playful spirit and the oblique teller of unpalatable truths. Auden has suggested elsewhere that the Fool stands for the sense of reality Lear has repressed.[30] Puck and Lear's Fool come together again in a later definition of poetry: it is a game, Auden acknowledges, but 'a game of knowledge, a bringing to consciousness, by naming them, of emotions and their hidden relationships'.[31] This is perhaps why, even as he goes into silence, Prospero can ask for Ariel's song to accompany him.

Part II, 'The Supporting Cast, Sotto Voce', displays both the impact of Prospero's mirror-art and its limitations. He himself has been cautious in his assessment:

The extravagant children, who lately swaggered
Out of the sea like gods, have, I think, been soundly
 hunted
By their own devils into their human selves. . . .
 Alonso's heaviness
Is lost; and weak Sebastian will be patient
In future with his slothful conscience – after all, it pays.
 (p. 314)

In a later critical essay Auden complains that *The Tempest* doesn't end like the other romances, in 'a

blaze of forgiveness and love', that Alonso's repentance alone seems real, while that of the others 'is more the prudent promise of the punished and the frightened, "I won't do it again. It doesn't pay," than any change of heart.'[32] In his poem this perceived defect becomes irony or doubt – has Prospero slipped back into the old coercive magic? Prospero also recognizes the enchantments that still dazzle Ferdinand and Miranda, their eyes 'big and blue with love', but a love untested as yet by mundane dailiness.

Will Ferdinand be as fond of a Miranda
Familiar as a stocking? Will a Miranda who is
 No longer a silly little lovesick goose,
When Ferdinand and his brave world are her profes-
 sion,
 Go into raptures over existing at all?
 (p. 314)

Now, in the lyric monologues of the supporting cast, there are similar hints that the achieved self-clarifications may be partial or precarious. Alonso's voice is the surest, as we might expect. He even alludes to one of the less problematic romance endings when he declares himself

 rejoicing in a new love,
 A new peace, having heard the solemn
 Music strike and seen the statue move
 To forgive our illusion.   (p. 322)

Auden's notebook character list links Alonso with Henry IV, and the situation of his lyric is indeed reminiscent of Henry: a dying king advising his son and successor. He warns Ferdinand against the extremes that threaten the human city. On the one hand

---

[28] 'The Dyer's Hand' (review of Mark Van Doren's *Shakespeare*), *The Nation*, 21 October 1939, pp. 444–5. The image of the dyer's hand, oddly turned from Shakespeare's deprecating use of it in Sonnet 111, apparently expressed something central in Auden's idea of true poetry. He used the title not only for this review but for a long meditation on poetry published in 1957, and yet again for the major collection of his critical pieces in 1962.

[29] 'The Poet of the Encirclement', p. 579.

[30] *The Dyer's Hand*, p. 126.

[31] 'Squares and Oblongs', p. 173.

[32] *The Dyer's Hand*, pp. 128–9.

is the sea of immediate sensation, on the other the desert of pure abstract pattern,

> As in his left ear the siren sings
> Meltingly of water and a night
> Where all flesh had peace, and on his right
> The efreet offers a brilliant void
> Where his mind could be perfectly clear
> And all his limitations destroyed.   (p. 321)

Tempting as they are, the one swallows up and the other desiccates; both are wildernesses. Only in between is the human city, the realm of choice and determinate action. We remember Auden's insistence that art must address both historical and natural man; here the task of life turns out to be the same.

Ferdinand may need the reminder about the sea, for in his own sonnet intimations of transcendent relatedness emerge only with difficulty from his physical delight in Miranda. Miranda herself is still half a child, eluding fairy-tale ogres and making circle-dances. The jester, much altered from his Shakespearian original, looks down from the chill of his larger vision, where jokes are born in existential terror, to long for his lost childhood security:

> Green acres far below,
> And the red roof where I
> Was Little Trinculo.   (p. 324)

And through it all we hear the voice of Antonio, whose resistance threatens to shatter Prospero's mirror, as in Shakespeare's play the intractability of Caliban cuts short the wedding masque. After each lyric Antonio comes in with a mocking, reductive refrain that tends to go for the weak spot in the achieved self-knowledge. 'Hot Ferdinand', 'Tense Trinculo' – his adjectives probe the lover's intoxication of the senses, the jester's anxiety. Indeed, he begins and ends the whole section, an isolated voice framing a group.

> Yes, Brother Prospero, your grouping could
> Not be more effective: given a few
> Incomplete objects and a nice warm day,
> What a lot a little music can do.   (p. 317)

It is the grouping, the relatedness, that he resists as much as the self-clarifying. We recall that Prospero's

old magic was an escape from 'the gross insult of being a mere one among many'; Antonio still cannot swallow that insult.

> Your all is partial, Prospero;
>   My will is all my own:
> Your need to love shall never know
> Me: I am I, Antonio,
>   By choice myself alone.   (p. 318)

In Auden's notebook, Antonio was paired with Iago; and another Shakespearian egocentric speaks in these lines, as well – 'Richard loves Richard, that is, I am I.' Antonio saw the same pageant that Alonso did, heard the same words, but felt no heart-sorrow. Asserting will and choice, he thus forcibly circumscribes the game of art and its powers.

Auden's comments on *The Tempest* outside *The Sea and the Mirror* suggest a certain ambivalence about Prospero. He could use the name as a symbol of truth in art,[33] but he was disturbed by Prospero's detached arrogance. 'One might excuse him if he included himself in his cynical scepticism but he never does; it never occurs to him that he, too, might have erred and be in need of pardon.'[34] This recalls Spender's observation about Auden himself, that he needed to shift his centre to some other authority so that he himself became part of what was judged. The Prospero of *The Sea and the Mirror* is in part a corrective portrait, for he does view himself sceptically, as well as the others, and he knows his need for pardon. But Auden's reservations were particularly about Prospero with Caliban: however brutal and corrupt Caliban is, he says, 'we cannot help feeling that Prospero is largely responsible for his corruption, and that, in the debate between them, Caliban has the best of the argument'.[35] Whether or not this is true of Shakespeare's play, certainly in Auden's poem the relation to Caliban that Prospero expresses in his own monologue is only partly realized, and Caliban does finally have the best of the argument, a brilliant 'last word' that is longer than the other two parts together. Moreover, he is allowed to take over as the heart of his message the recognition that Shakespeare had given to Prospero: 'this thing of darkness I / Acknowledge mine.'

---

[33] *Ibid.* pp. 337–8.   [34] *Ibid.* p. 129.
[35] *Ibid.*

Auden's Caliban embodies our natural drives and repetitions, the creaturely embarrassment of fallen flesh, and is associated with the sea of immediate sensation that Alonso has talked of earlier. But Caliban as discourser, speaking in elegant Jamesian convolutions, obviously takes in far more than Caliban as subject. He speaks in turn for the audience, for Shakespeare, for himself and Ariel together, and through these masks fairly certainly for Auden himself. Auden once played Caliban in a school production of *The Tempest*, a part his biographer tells us he wanted very badly.[36] In *The Sea and the Mirror* he seems to be playing it again, with even greater gusto. Caliban's speech is a complicated *tour de force* that defies summary, but the thread that runs through it is the relation of Caliban and Ariel, sea and mirror. The situation itself, a character speaking to the audience after the play is over, takes up the mode of the *Tempest* Epilogue to force a confrontation between art and life; and Caliban goes on to voice the audience's unease at the confrontation they have just experienced *in* the play. They came for magic, but got something more disturbing. That clumsy Caliban reality, both brutish and silly, that they wanted to leave at the theatre door, has intruded into the 'high strangeness' of art. Speaking for them, Caliban rebukes Shakespeare for spoiling the pleasant party, bringing this impossible bumpkin into the urbane salon of the Muse:

She foresaw what He would do to the conversation, lying in wait for its vision of private love or public justice to warm to an Egyptian brilliance and then with some fishlike odour or *bruit insolite* snatching the visionaries back tongue-tied and blushing to the here and now; she foresaw what He would do to the arrangements, breaking, by a refusal to keep in step, the excellent order of the dancing ring, and ruining supper by knocking over the loaded appetising tray –

even making, 'horror unspeakable, a pass at her virgin self' (p. 327). Antonio, as an observer of Prospero's art, could refuse to join the circle-dance; Caliban, as an element within the artist's vision, puts the dance itself in disarray. The audience which wants a 'perfectly tidiable case of disorder' gets instead 'a mortal, face-slapping insult' (p. 330). And why, they worry, was Ariel not neatly disposed of at the end of the play,

but rather perhaps let loose among *them*? His visionary patterns threaten the unexamined compromises and evasions of their daily living: 'We want no Ariel here, breaking down our picket fences in the name of fraternity, seducing our wives in the name of romance, and robbing us of our sacred pecuniary deposits in the name of justice' (p. 331). The enchanted other-world has become a mirror, and all they are not stares back at what they are.

The answer of Shakespeare, whose voice Caliban takes next, is that Ariel when not manipulated to serve escapist magic will reflect Caliban. Some day, he tells an aspiring young poet, your happy partnership with Ariel will cease to fascinate, grow strained. Tired of giving orders, you will gaze into his eyes and find

not what you had always expected to see, a conqueror smiling at a conqueror, both promising mountains and marvels, but a gibbering, fist-clenched creature with which you are all too unfamiliar, for this is the first time that you have met the only subject that you have, who is not a dream amenable to magic but the all too solid flesh you must acknowledge as your own.

(p. 333)

This predicted evolution of the artist recalls Prospero's in Part I, but Auden is still engaged in his corrective portrait. Elsewhere he inveighs against a kind of 'manicheism' in *The Tempest*, which in the inevitable conflict of Nature and Spirit put all the blame on Caliban, on Nature, instead of on both Caliban and Prospero;[37] and indeed, Prospero's monologue in *The Sea and the Mirror* has recognized Caliban only as 'my impervious disgrace' (p. 314). But in his triumphant last word Caliban knows that the artist must find a much closer relationship with his 'thing of darkness', his 'subject' in two senses of the word. Here Caliban speaks for himself:

And if I had, as I consider, a good deal to put up with from you, I must own that, after all, I am not just the person I would have chosen for a life companion myself; so the only chance, which in any case is slim enough, of my getting a tolerably new master and you a tolerably new man, lies in our both learning, if possible and as soon as possible, to forgive and forget

---

36 Carpenter, p. 41.   37 *The Dyer's Hand*, p. 130.

the past, and to keep our respective hopes for the future, within moderate, very moderate, limits.

(p. 334)

In the relationship that is the 'only chance', the very disjunction between Ariel and Caliban - imagined possibility and dishevelled actuality - encourages growth by a kind of reciprocal humiliation. The task of art again merges into the task of life. As Alonso has told Ferdinand in Part II,

> The Way of Justice is a tightrope
> Where no prince is safe for one instant
> Unless he trust his embarrassment.   (p. 321)

Alonso found his own condition in the mirror of art, and now at the end of Caliban's discourse the constituents of that art, Ariel and Caliban *speaking as one*, offer something like a tightrope to the audience as the authentic journey of life. Neither one of them will do by himself as a guide for the journey. Though the masses cry after Calibanic immediacy, and the intellectual elite long for Ariel's constructions of pure mind, these paradises are in fact only versions of Alonso's sea and desert: one disallows choice in biological necessity, the other in endlessly entertained possibility.[38] The way between is as difficult as Prospero's voyage out over seventy thousand fathoms, and there is no waltzing across this void in the circus-illusions of art.

Artist and human pilgrim will stumble, freeze, perhaps fall off. And it is in fact on this very clumsiness that Ariel and Caliban finally rest Auden's carefully limited case for art. Though they do recall the tightrope metaphor,[39] they concentrate on another image for life: 'the greatest grandest opera rendered by a very provincial touring company indeed' (p. 340). When we, the inept performers, become aware of the ludicrous gap between conception and creaturely execution, we can then recognize that, as the badly done opera is to life, so our lives are to divine truth. Life and art come to final adjustment with reference to 'that Wholly Other Life from which we

are separated by an essential emphatic gulf of which our contrived fissures of mirror and proscenium arch - we understand them at last - are feebly figurative signs' (p. 340). The end of *The Sea and the Mirror* thus circles back to the Stage Manager's beginning, with its intimation of a real life elsewhere.

> All the rest is silence
> On the other side of the wall;
> And the silence ripeness,
> And the ripeness all.

Art still cannot go beyond the wall; but the art of disjunctions and gaps, of Ariel and Caliban irreconcilable but bound together, can impress on us forcibly that there *is* a wall, and another side.

I don't know to what extent Auden is claiming Shakespeare's collaboration in his final Christian vision. But if Shakespeare wanted to have his own last word, to resist for his own works this framing in transcendent absolutes, he could do so by reclaiming some of the words Auden has borrowed from him. Hamlet's 'the rest is silence' is an end, not a beginning; by putting it 'on the other side of the wall' and equating it with 'ripeness' in *King Lear*, Auden makes Edgar's 'ripeness is all' refer not to rounding out our human life in awareness and acceptance, but to completion in a truth beyond this world. Yet even Prospero's speech reducing our world to an insubstantial pageant does not end with a transcendent reality in capital letters, but rather in a silence more non-committal, and - again - more mysterious. 'Our little life / Is rounded with a sleep.'

---

38 The 'alternative routes, the facile glad-handed highway or the virtuous averted track' (p. 339) recall aspects of Part II: Trinculo's nostalgia for the secure red roof and green acres of childhood, Gonzalo's over-intellectualizing that 'by speculation froze / Vision into an idea, / Irony into a joke, / Till I stood convicted of / Doubt and insufficient love' (p. 320).

39 The human condition is described as 'neither cosy nor playful, but swaying out on the ultimate wind-whipped cornice that overhangs the unabiding void' (p. 340).

GRAVES ON LOVERS, AND SHAKESPEARE AT A LOVERS' FUNERAL

PETER BILTON

In the Foreword to his *Collected Poems 1965*, Robert Graves wrote that his 'main theme was always the practical impossibility, transcended only by a belief in miracle, of absolute love continuing between man and woman'.[1]

Certainly a large proportion of Graves's poetry is about love; and the range of experience is wide. At one end are humorous or disgusted encounters with sex, and at the other triumphant claims that the miracle he allows for has come about, in the love between himself and embodiments of his Muse or Goddess.

Somewhere in the realistic or even disillusioned area is the popular anthology selection 'The Thieves'.[2] It is short enough to be quoted in its entirety:

> Lovers in the act dispense
> With such meum-tuum sense
> As might warningly reveal
> What they must not pick or steal,
> And their nostrum is to say:
> 'I and you are both away.'
>
> After, when they disentwine
> You from me and yours from mine,
> Neither can be certain who
> Was that I whose mine was you.
> To the act again they go
> More completely not to know.
>
> Theft is theft and raid is raid
> Though reciprocally made.
> Lovers, the conclusion is
> Doubled sighs and jealousies
> In a single heart that grieves
> For lost honour among thieves.

Presumably anthologists select this poem not only on merit or to save space, but because they see it as representative: in its tone of voice, direct attack on the subject, logic, compression, and verbal wit, it shows us the Metaphysical Graves.

John Donne was a kindred spirit also in the variety of his responses to love. Donne was what Graves calls a 'dedicated' or 'Muse' poet, yet he wavered, Graves tells us, in his allegiance: 'He persuaded himself, at times, of his love's absoluteness; yet, when the flame had died down, declared that the spiritual identity of lovers was an illusion.'[3] This is just what 'The Thieves' declares. On the other hand, Graves also quotes from 'A Valediction', beginning with 'Dull sublunary lovers' and ending with

> Our two souls therefore, which are one,
> Though I must go, endure not yet
> A breach, but an expansión,
> Like gold to airy thinness beat.

This vision of two souls as one is described by Graves as a glimpse that Donne allows himself 'of what absolute love can mean'.[4]

Shakespeare is also numbered among Graves's 'dedicated' poets. That Graves is familiar with Shakespeare may go without saying, but he said so himself, remarking for instance that 'Shakespeare is now a museum exhibit, not for home reading as when I was a boy'.[5] It seems safe to assume that Graves would find

---

[1] 1965; second of two unnumbered pages.
[2] *Collected Poems 1965*, p. 156.
[3] 'The Personal Muse', in *Oxford Addresses on Poetry* (1962); p. 71.   [4] *Ibid.* p. 73.
[5] 'The Word 'Báraka'', in *Oxford Addresses on Poetry*; p. 105.

his avowed main theme running through Shakespeare's love poetry no less than through Donne's, and would see Shakespeare, like himself, running the gamut from disgust to apotheosis. He does not, however, merely vibrate in sympathy: a wry poem called 'Beauty in Trouble'[6] ends with the question 'But would you to the marriage of true minds / Admit impediment?', turning one of Shakespeare's strongest affirmations of the constancy of love to an ironic purpose. (Note for future reference that Graves elsewhere refers to 'Beauty in Trouble' as a 'satire'.[7])

The suggestion that I want to go on to make is that 'The Thieves' is a response to 'The Phoenix and the Turtle',[8] which is widely regarded as Shakespeare's most 'Metaphysical' poem, and which both celebrates a miraculous absolute love and grieves for its passing. To my mind, Graves's poem is a rejoinder to it, almost in the sense in which Raleigh's and Donne's were rejoinders to Marlowe's. To point out similarities between the two poems, I must in what follows repeatedly cross from one to the other and back again.

There are clear resemblances in music and rhythm. Whereas Shakespeare has quatrains rhyming ABBA and tercets rhyming AAA, Graves's six-line stanzas rhyme in couplets; but the poems have numerous rhymes in common: dispense–sense and commence–hence; say–away and lay–obey; go–know and crow–go; and the word 'mine' as a rhyme word in both poems. More striking, perhaps, than coincidence of rhymes is the similarity between Shakespeare's 'So they lov'd, as love in twain' and Graves's 'After, when they disentwine'. The two poems are virtually identical in rhythm. Apart from occasional feminine endings and one or two other variations in 'The Phoenix and the Turtle', the lines of both poems can all be formally scanned trochee trochee trochee stop, the seven syllables normally encompassing grammatically complete units of phrase or clause. In reading, however, many lines in both poems have the property that W. H. Matchett pointed out with regard to certain lines in 'The Phoenix and the Turtle' of having three rather than four stresses:[9] 'Either was the other's mine' and 'Neither can be certain who', for instance, sound interchangeable in rhythm.

The anthem in 'The Phoenix and the Turtle'

describes the miraculous love affair in the past tense. Before and after, in the directions for the fully-fledged funeral and at the end of the threne, imaginary listeners are addressed directly in imperatives, and conclusions in the threne are tersely declarative: 'Truth and beauty buried be.' Graves's approach and tone of voice are much the same: lovers and their behaviour are first described in general, and then lovers have the didactic conclusion spoken to them directly. Graves's three stanzas function almost as a syllogism, while legal and scholastic terms in 'The Phoenix and the Turtle' contribute to a rational impression conveyed by conciseness and wit.

The similarities between the two poems extend into expression and ideas. In his first stanza, Graves chastises 'Lovers in the act' for dispensing with their sense of meum and tuum, which would otherwise tell them, in Shakespearian phrase, 'What they must not pick or steal'. Shakespeare states that the wondrous union of phoenix and turtle left property (which includes among its meanings a sense of mine and thine) appalled at the confusion of identities, 'That the self was not the same'. Graves's lovers defy the demands of property; Shakespeare's birds transcend them.

The meum and tuum sense *dispensed* with by Graves's lovers is replaced by a nostrum, two singular possessives merging in a plural – which somehow remains a plural. The word 'nostrum' recalls Renaissance quackery. The order of pronouns in the nostrum suggests the selfishness of these lovers' orgasm: 'I and you are both away' could express the disappearance of their individual identities, but put this way it sounds to me more like separation than togetherness. Shakespeare's truer apothecary appears in the capsular formula 'Simple were so well compounded', in which singular subject and plural verb fuse. The phoenix and the turtle, too, are 'away', but in their case in the shared ecstasy of love's martyrdom:

---

[6] *Collected Poems 1965*, p. 195.

[7] 'The Poet in a Valley of Dry Bones', in *Mammon and the Black Goddess* (1965), p. 92.

[8] I quote from F. T. Prince's Arden edition of *The Poems* (1960), pp. 179–83, adding 'the' to the poem's title.

[9] *The Phoenix and the Turtle: Shakespeare's Poem and Chester's 'Loues Martyr'* (The Hague, 1965), pp. 34–5.

'Phoenix and the Turtle fled / In a mutual flame from hence.'

The first four lines of Graves's second stanza run, if I may repeat them, as follows:

> After, when they disentwine
> You from me and yours from mine,
> Neither can be certain who
> Was that I whose mine was you.

This playing with pronouns is very close in manner to at least two of Shakespeare's lines expressing the fusion of the lovers, 'Either was the other's mine' and 'To themselves yet either neither'. Graves is no less apt than Shakespeare was to allow for two meanings in 'mine', or to let the first-person pronoun 'I' do duty for 'eye' the organ of vision, recalling that 'the Turtle saw his right / Flaming in the Phoenix' sight'.

According to Graves, lovers as a result of their confusion return to their love-making 'More completely not to know'. Literally, not to know who they are; but conceivably also – as a critic may conceive – in an ironic counterpart to the married chastity, the abstention from knowledge, of the phoenix and the turtle.

Whereas the latter fled in a *mutual* flame, Graves's lovers *reciprocally* raid each other. Where in Shakespeare the union, justifying the exclamation 'How true a twain / Seemeth this concordant one!', is such that '*Single* nature's *double* name / Neither two nor one was called', the relationship in Graves's poem leads to '*Doubled* sighs and jealousies / In a *single* heart that grieves'. The grief is for 'lost honour among thieves' – lost chastity *and* lost trust. The conclusions to the two poems resemble each other, the one stating that grief for these lost values results from a dishonest approach to love, and the other telling its hearers that truth and beauty are buried and asking them to *sigh* a prayer for the dead birds: but like their fusion in love, their combination of virtues is unlikely to be repeated, since would-be mourners are either true *or* fair.

The implication of 'The Thieves' is that love must be based on respect for one's own and each other's separate individualities. If we see in 'The Phoenix and the Turtle' a celebration of a magnificent example to the contrary, 'The Thieves' appears as its refutation. It is possible to read 'The Thieves' not as rejecting absolute love outright, but as establishing the premises on which such love must be founded. This, however, is contradicted by the comment I have already quoted on Donne and 'A Valediction', where two souls as one are said to provide a glimpse of what absolute love can mean. The simplest reason for the similarities I have pointed to remains that when writing 'The Thieves' Graves was out to reject just such an idea, or ideal, of spiritual union as he saw eulogized in 'The Phoenix and the Turtle'. I noted earlier how 'Beauty in Trouble' undermines a Shakespeare sonnet on the same subject.

Graves has frequently distinguished between 'Muse' poetry and 'Apollonian' poetry. Disclaiming any concern with the latter, he nevertheless concedes that 'at times the satiric left hand of poetry displaces the lyric right hand'.[10] If this applies to 'Beauty in Trouble', it may also be true of 'The Thieves'. I have mentioned qualities there and in Shakespeare's poem that lend them both rational appeal – a characteristic Graves attributes to Apollo. If I go on to add that the three stanzas of Graves's poem total eighteen lines, and Shakespeare's poem of eighteen stanzas is divided into three parts, or that the fused or confused identities of pairs of lovers are at the centres of their respective poems, I lay both works open to the charge that Graves made against his anti-poet Virgil, who 'never consulted the Muse; he only borrowed Apollo's slide-rule'.[11]

A recent article by Roy T. Eriksen shows that 'The Phoenix and the Turtle' *was* designed with the aid of Apollo's slide-rule.[12] Another 'Apollonian' characteristic that Graves may have noticed is that it was 'occasional', made to order for *Loves Martyr*. It would appear possible that he chose to respond to a poem he regarded as 'Apollonian' by writing, perhaps with his satiric left hand, in the mode he saw before him.

In his account of 'The Phoenix and the Turtle', W. H. Matchett interprets it as ultimately a defence of reason rather than an exaltation of the transcendent.

---

[10] Foreword, *Collected Poems 1965*.

[11] 'The Anti-poet', in *Oxford Addresses on Poetry*; p. 49.

[12] '"Un certo amoroso martire": Shakespeare's "The Phoenix and the Turtle" and Giordano Bruno's *De gli eroici furori*', *Spenser Studies*, 2 (1981), 193–215.

One of the arguments on which Matchett bases his case is that in Shakespeare's day the phoenix was often associated, not with immortality through rebirth, but simply with outstanding qualities. The import of Shakespeare's poem by this reasoning becomes that certain unique qualities have definitively died with their owners, and that since the qualities were supra-rational and unnatural (who needs married chastity?), one should not reasonably hope to see them reborn, however magnificent one allows that they were. Sigh a prayer for them (if you think you are true *or* fair), but otherwise leave them in the ground and let reason and property have the last word.

If we accept this, we see 'The Thieves' confirming rather than refuting 'The Phoenix and the Turtle'. Agreement must be as good a reason as disagreement for the sincerest flattery; but there are inherent objections to reading 'The Phoenix and the Turtle' this way, as well as a clear statement from Graves himself that he did not do so. Eriksen's presentation of the significant structure of the poem shows how it gives pride of place at the centre to the mystical union of two in one, with the rest of the poem symmetrically and subordinately ranged around it; and his interpretation allows the phoenix its familiar role of immortal. That Graves for his part linked phoenix and dove with rebirth and transcendent love is shown in his poem 'The Hearth',[13] and by his use and presentation of that poem in 'Intimations of the Black Goddess': 'There is no more ancient emblem of love than the turtle-dove; or of spiritual rebirth than the phoenix. Shakespeare's strange prophetic line *The Phoenix and the turtle fled in a mutual flame from hence* carries a world of meaning.'[14] In 'The Hearth', the worm of love breeds in the embers on the hearth, turns into a chick, and then grows into a fledgling which will hop 'from lap to lap in a ring / Of eager children basking at the blaze'.

But the luckless man who never sat there,
Nor borrowed live coals from the sacred source
To warm a hearth of his own making,
Nor bedded lay under pearl-grey wings
In dutiful content,

How shall he watch at the stroke of midnight
Dove become phoenix, plumed with green and gold?
Or be caught up by jewelled talons
And haled away to a fastness of the hills
Where an unveiled woman, black as Mother Night,
Teaches him a new degree of love
And the tongues and songs of birds?

Dove *becoming* phoenix makes the two birds one, a complete fusion as in Shakespeare, by a metamorphosis not in Ovid.

For these reasons – that Shakespeare's poem is primarily a celebration of a transcendent union, and that Graves saw it that way – I return after these detours to the suggestion that Graves saw in 'The Phoenix and the Turtle' an idea he was in a mood to contradict and a form in which to do so.

In keeping the English poets at his beck and call, as he has said he does,[15] Graves is living up to his own idea of the dedicated poet, who needs to be steeped in the tradition. If a poet's relationship to his predecessors is a relation to museum exhibits, he faces, in Graves's words, 'a difficult dilemma...his home vocabulary cannot bear the full weight of thought and emotion he may want to express; yet the museum vocabulary is so little his own that borrowings from it will look artificial'.[16]

In my opinion, Graves let Shakespeare's poem make its contribution to his debate about love, without borrowing anything from it that looks artificial in his own poem. Shakespeare focuses on a miracle – two into one *will* go – but emphasizes its rarity. Graves, in 'The Thieves' at least, claims that the concept of such a perfect union deludes us: and this is in keeping with what he declared his own main theme to be. But perhaps we should not see them as diametrically opposed after all: Shakespeare's obsequies are for the miraculous exception that proves the rule; Graves's poem expounds a rule to which only a miracle can be the exception; both leave us grieving.

---

[13] *Collected Poems 1965*, p. 374.

[14] 'Intimations of the Black Goddess', in *Mammon and the Black Goddess*; p. 163.

[15] 'The Word "Báraka"', p. 106. [16] *Ibid.* p. 105.

TRAGIC BALANCE IN 'HAMLET'[1]

PHILIP EDWARDS

The breakdown in sympathy for Hamlet – the prince, that is – during the twentieth century seems to me a critical and cultural fact of some importance, and I believe it has inhibited a genuinely tragic response to the play. Yet although the criticism of our time has eroded the tragic quality of *Hamlet*, one can see latent within that criticism the possibilities of a renewal which might bring the play back to us as tragedy. The twentieth-century view of the play developed as an antithesis to the view which prevailed in the nineteenth century. The new view that one envisages emerges as a synthesis of the two earlier views. I shall argue that this emerging view, though necessarily a product of our own times, could restore to *Hamlet* something of the tragic quality that may have belonged to the play in its own day.

The nineteenth-century view, the thesis with which we begin, received its latest and greatest expression in Bradley's *Shakespearean Tragedy* in 1904. It is a vision of a noble and generous youth who for reasons quite mysterious to himself is unable to carry out the sacred duty, imposed by divine authority, of punishing an evil man by death. It is a vision of paralysis and disablement, of ultimate victory bought at a terrible cost.

Against this I would set, rather obviously, G. Wilson Knight's powerful essay of 1930, 'The Embassy of Death' from *The Wheel of Fire*. Knight had important predecessors, of course, and he himself radically revised his account of the play. Nevertheless, the essay is central. Knight portrayed the Denmark of Claudius and Gertrude as a healthy, contented, smoothly-running community. Claudius is clearly an efficient administrator, and he has sensible ideas about

not letting memories of the past impede the promise of the future. Hamlet, by contrast, is a figure of nihilism and death. He has communed with the dead, and been instructed never to let the past be forgotten. As a 'sick soul commanded to heal', he is in fact a poison in the veins of the community. Knight went so far as to say that 'Hamlet is an element of evil in the state of Denmark', 'a living death in the midst of life'. He is an alien at the court, 'inhuman – or superhuman . . . a creature of another world'. Neither side can understand the other.

Claudius murdered his brother, and Hamlet's mission is the punishment of a murderer. Hamlet, Knight admitted, is in the right. And if he had been able to act quickly and cleanly, all might have been well. But which of the two, he asked, Claudius or Hamlet, 'is the embodiment of spiritual good, which of evil? The question of the relative morality of Hamlet and Claudius reflects the ultimate problem of this play.' He gave his own answer: 'A balanced judgement is forced to pronounce ultimately in favour of life as contrasted with death, for optimism and the healthily second-rate, rather than the nihilism of the superman; for [Hamlet] is not, as the plot shows, safe; and he is not safe, primarily because he is right.' So Hamlet is wrong to pursue that which is right. 'Had Hamlet forgotten both the Ghost's commands [that is, to remember the past and avenge the dead] it would have

[1] This article originated in a series of three public lectures delivered at the University of Otago, Dunedin, New Zealand, in 1980. In its present form, it is a slightly modified version of a lecture given at the International Shakespeare Conference at Stratford-upon-Avon in August 1982.

been well, since Claudius is a good king, and the Ghost but a minor spirit.'

Wilson Knight said 'The ghost may or may not have been a "goblin damned"; it certainly was no "spirit of health".' This sentence is the theme of much of the *Hamlet* criticism which followed. A great many critics have found an element of evil in the pact between the Ghost and Hamlet. Harold Goddard, in *The Meaning of Shakespeare* (Chicago, 1951), said of his ideas about *Hamlet* that he had been expounding them to students since the days of the First World War. The Ghost is the spirit of war and a symbol of the devil, corrupting Hamlet with his 'thirst for vengeance' and his instruction to kill. To kill whom? Claudius, a man who could have been shown the error of his ways. 'The King . . . is no villain.' Shakespeare tempted us in the audience to want Claudius's death in order that we should become ashamed of ourselves and realize with Shakespeare that killing was evil. Hamlet loses in the end because he gives in to the Ghost and 'descends to the level of Laertes'.

L. C. Knights's *Approach to Hamlet* of 1960 was uncompromising in its hostility to the Prince and his mission. Hamlet is an immature person lacking 'a ready responsiveness to life' who is pushed by the Ghost to concentrate on death and evil. Shakespeare himself disapproved of revenge. This latter view achieved its most thorough and scholarly expression in Eleanor Prosser's *Hamlet and Revenge* of 1967. Here the ghost's credentials are picked threadbare and Hamlet's identification with the bloodthirsty villains of revenge fiction is complete.

You may well say that, formidable though the battle-line of Wilson Knight, Goddard, Knights and Prosser may be, I am representing only one trend of mid-twentieth-century criticism. What of C. S. Lewis and Maynard Mack, and many others who cannot be said to share these views? It is more than a trend I am isolating; it is the common currency of *Hamlet* criticism to deplore, not Hamlet's failure to carry out his mission, but the mission itself. Although there are no beginnings in *Hamlet* criticism, I trace the movement back to the extraordinary lines of Mallarmé, in his essay of 1896 on Hamlet and Fortinbras which Joyce brought to our attention in *Ulysses*, and his more extended view in *Crayonné au*

Théâtre (1886).[2] Hamlet is the solitary, 'étranger à tous lieux où il poind'. He walks about, we remember, 'lisant au livre de lui-même'; he denies others by looking at them, and even without willing it spreads death about him. 'The black presence of the doubter causes this poison.'[3]

Many contemporary critics, unable to deny the damning evidence of Prosser but uneasy that the prevailing hostility towards Hamlet tends to make too little of Claudius's crime, have sought to restore a tragic balance to the play by stressing Hamlet's struggle to make a bad deed good. This is associated with the very widespread 'contamination' theory which we find in Maynard Mack. 'The act required of him, though retributive justice, is one that necessarily involves the doer in the general guilt.'[4] A searching and sensitive expression of this view is in Nigel Alexander's *Poison, Play and Duel* (1967). The proof of the King's guilt does not solve Hamlet's problem. 'The question remains, how does one deal with such a man without becoming like him?' (p. 125).

The idea that Hamlet's problem is somehow to punish Claudius and yet transcend the sheer human violence and vindictiveness which such punishment entails goes back to 1839 and the once famous but now forgotten 'conscience' theory of Hermann Ulrici.[5] 'It cannot', he said, 'be an entirely innocent and heavenly spirit that would wander on earth to demand a son to *avenge* his death.' Hamlet has to try to convert the 'external action' of revenge 'into one that is *internal, free, and truly moral*'. The will to the deed must not be a matter of external pressure, it must become 'voluntarily his own'. Ideally this cannot be unless the 'moral necessity' of the deed can be seen to be 'the substance of the divine order of the universe'. Ulrici argues, very interestingly, that Hamlet actually forces the issue of the sympathy of divine power and arrogates to himself the role of providence. Here again he anticipates much modern criticism. I cannot think,

---

[2] Martin Scofield discusses these views in *The Ghosts of 'Hamlet'* (1980), pp. 25–6.
[3] Mallarmé, *Oeuvres complètes* (Paris, 1945), pp. 300–2, 1564.
[4] 'The World of *Hamlet*' (1952), reprinted in *'Hamlet': A Casebook*, ed. J. Jump (1968), pp. 86–121.
[5] Ulrici, *Shakespeare's Dramatic Art*, trans. L. D. Schmitz (1876), vol. 1, pp. 86–121.

however, that the neo-Ulricians have in fact rescued the play of *Hamlet* from being the rather dismal story of blight which it is in great danger of becoming.

At this point, I should like to summarize the four closely-related areas in which the mid twentieth century most strongly diverged from earlier opinion. The first is the authority of the Ghost; whether he is an authorized emissary of heaven, or just the spirit of an aggrieved king, or, at the extreme, a false spirit from hell. The second area is the morality of his injunction – namely, to exact vengeance for murder; the morality, therefore, of Hamlet's quest to kill Claudius. The third area is the moral and indeed material condition of Denmark and its court under Claudius. The fourth concerns Hamlet himself, how we judge his actions and behaviour generally; what we think of him as a man.

I personally cannot see a way forward in any discussion of *Hamlet* that does not take as a point of departure that it is a religious play. Bradley refused to call it this, but he acknowledged that the religious element in the play gave it a distinctive tone among Shakespeare's tragedies. Middleton Murry thought that Hamlet's fear of damnation was of tremendous and unrecognized potency in the play. I agree. What Keats said of *King Lear* would have fitted *Hamlet* better: 'the fierce dispute / Betwixt damnation and impassioned clay'. George Herbert spoke of himself as

> A wonder tortur'd in the space
> Betwixt this world and that of grace.
>
> ('Affliction', IV)

With characteristic reductiveness Hamlet asks 'What should such fellows as I do, crawling between earth and heaven?' The setting of a play which never moves from Elsinore is earth, heaven and hell.

> O all you host of heaven! O earth! what else?
> And shall I couple hell?　　　　(1.5.92–3)

When Hamlet says he is prompted to his revenge by heaven and hell, he means he is involved in the whole supernatural world of good and evil and their eternal warfare.

Hamlet when we first meet him is in a state of despair. He longs for death, and would take his own life if suicide were not forbidden by divine decree. It is at this moment that Horatio and Marcellus burst in on

him with news of an apparition, seemingly a visitant from beyond the grave in the likeness of his dead father. C. S. Lewis said 'The appearance of the spectre means a breaking down of the walls of the world.'[6] Of this equivocal figure, in the 'questionable shape' of his father, Hamlet passionately demands, 'What should we do?', a question which expands from the specific to become a general appeal for guidance, for a direction and a purpose in one's life. The Ghost's response indicates that the doings of a corrupt mortal world are integrated within an eternal world. What Gertrude has done will be taken care of: 'Leave her to heaven.' But Claudius for his crime is not to be permitted to continue among men and enjoy his booty of crown and queen: 'Bear it not.' What is unendurable to heaven is not to be endured by men. Evil is not ineradicable, and heaven may appoint an agent of its justice to pluck it out – Hamlet. Hamlet's reaction to this communication is like a conversion or a baptism. He ostentatiously wipes away all previous values, and dedicates himself as a new man.

> And thy commandment all alone shall live
> Within the book and volume of my brain,
> Unmixed with baser matter.　　　(1.5.102–4)

'As a stranger give it welcome', he says to Horatio about the visitation. He identifies himself with the stranger. He becomes a stranger by adopting the garb of madness.[7] Like Bunyan's Christian, he considers himself a pilgrim and a stranger in his own city of Vanity Fair or Elsinore.

The French Marxist critic Lucien Goldmann scarcely mentioned Shakespeare in his 1955 study of Racine and Pascal, *The Hidden God*. But I found in it much food for thought about *Hamlet*. His theory of tragedy, for which he gives credit to the early work of Lukács, is based on the notion of Pascal that man has to wager that God exists, for he is a hidden God whose presence is not indisputably known and whose voice is not unequivocally heard. The tragic hero longs for clear directives to govern his action; he longs for

---

[6] Lewis, 'Hamlet, the Prince or the Poem?', *Proceedings of the British Academy*, 28 (1942), 139–54; p. 148.

[7] I owe this point to Hiram Haydn, *The Counter-Renaissance* (New York, 1950), p. 626.

absolutes, for an existence which he can value as authentic and uncompromising. But the God to whom he looks, in whose existence he dares to believe, whom he longs to obey, is shrouded and hidden; his voice distorted and scarcely audible, his guidance and his requirements never clearly discernible. The world in which the hero lives, which he would contract out of if he could, is our own accustomed world with our ordinary values. Conspicuously, it is a world never ruled by absolutes, but by perpetual compromise, adjustment and expediency. In this world the hero demands justice, honesty, truth. In his vain efforts to live out what he perceives as the ideals of a higher order in a world which finds his conduct scandalous, offensive, and insane, lies tragedy.

The critical element in this tragic structure is the notion that God is neither absent nor obviously present. If God is dead, or if God is clearly known, the tragedy (Goldmann says) cannot exist. The special irony of the tragic hero's position is that the difficulty of trying to live out what God wants is compounded by the difficulty of *knowing* what God wants, or even whether He exists.

Hamlet seems to be precisely in the position which Goldmann postulates for the tragic hero. From the very first he insists on absolutes – 'I know not seems'. The voice he hears gives him his mission, which he rapidly expands into a cleansing of the world, a setting right of disjointed time. As the scourge and minister of heaven, he wilfully seeks his own salvation by flailing others with his tongue for their moral inadequacies and redirecting their lives as he moves forward to a killing which will re-baptize the state of Denmark.

What the scholarship of this century has taught us is that the status of the voice which Hamlet hears is from first to last uncertain. The ambiguity of the Ghost is of fundamental importance. Shakespeare uses the great perplexity of his age about the origin and status of ghosts to indicate the treacherousness of a sense of communion with a higher world. Hamlet's own sense of this treacherousness seems nearly always underestimated. It is at the very end of act 2, at the conclusion of the 'rogue and peasant slave' soliloquy, that Hamlet openly expresses his fear that 'the spirit that I have seen may be a devil'. But it is on his next appearance, in 'To be or not to be', that he most fully

and profoundly expresses a much wider scepticism. He is once again in the despair of act 1, again longing for the oblivion of death. Since that time he has been given a mission, which he eagerly seized as being heaven-sent, to renovate the world by a single act. Now he rejects such a possibility. The alternative courses which Hamlet sets before himself in the first five lines of the soliloquy, asking himself which of them is the greater nobleness, are: to continue to endure the antagonisms of existence, or to escape from them is the greater nobleness, are: to continue to The only opposition which the individual can make against the mischances of existence is to take his life. No other act can end the sea of troubles. No other act can improve the condition of the world or the condition of its victims. By implication, the deed of revenge, as a creative act bringing earth nearer to heaven, is of no avail.[8] Whether Hamlet kills the King or not, Denmark will continue to be as it is, a place of suffering ruled by fortune. If there is a nobleness in continuing to live, it is a nobleness of suffering, not a nobleness of reforming and transforming the world. This is exactly the view on the alternative of living or taking one's life put by Schopenhauer in his essay 'On Suicide'.[9] Since no human act can improve the world and all acts contribute to its continued beastliness, Schopenhauer said that the only argument against suicide as a praiseworthy course must be that continued suffering is praiseworthy in itself.

If Hamlet rejects, at least as a means of saving mankind, the killing of the King, he refuses the alternative course through fear of damnation. The soliloquy which begins as a debate on nobleness ends in a contest of cowardliness. What is one most afraid of, the possibility of damnation for taking one's life, or the certainty of suffering on earth? It is conscience, the implanted sense of right and wrong, which makes us too cowardly to embrace a course which reason tells us is noble. And it is this same conscience, this worrying

---

[8] Compare A. J. A. Waldock, *'Hamlet': A Study in Critical Method* (Cambridge, 1931), p. 87: 'The feeling that vengeance (or anything) is worth while presupposes an active belief in life. Hamlet ... has almost lost that belief.'

[9] *Essays and Aphorisms*, ed. R. J. Hollingdale (Harmondsworth, 1970), pp. 77–9.

about the consequences of things and the way they look in the eye of eternity, which inhibits other 'enterprises of great pitch and moment' so that they 'lose the name of action'.

Although it is only by inference and by implication, the killing of the King is twice referred to in this great soliloquy. In the later reference we gather that Hamlet has not proceeded with revenge because his conscience cannot convince him that the act is good; in the earlier that, whether the act is good or bad, it cannot change the world. To call Hamlet's mood in 'To be or not to be' a pocket of pessimism, or to speak of his doubts about the Ghost as transient, is to mistake the man whom Shakespeare has drawn. As the play progresses, different surfaces of this many-faceted character catch the light, but the make-up of the whole remains much the same; there is much less 'development' in Hamlet than is often supposed.

Doubts or no doubts, he takes his revenge. Buoyed up by the success of the ruse of the play and determined on action, he decides to spare the King as he prays, but moments later, finding him in the ignominious position of eavesdropper in Gertrude's closet, he kills him, and discovers it is Polonius he has struck. By this misdeed, he triggers off a new cycle of vengeance. By unwittingly killing Polonius, Hamlet unwittingly takes his own life.

The progress from this point to the final chance-medley is complex and intricate. I argued in a lecture in 1980[10] that the less complex version of the latter part of the play in the Folio may well represent Shakespeare's own decision to replace both the defiance of the 'hoist with his own petar' speech and the self-recrimination of 'How all occasions do inform against me' with a silence as regards Hamlet's inner thoughts which is as challenging and mysterious as the silence that lies between acts 1 and 2. If I am right, tremendous weight is thrown forward on to the account of what has been going on in his mind which he gives to Horatio on his return from the sea-voyage; an account most significantly expanded in the Folio.

In recognizing 'a divinity that shapes our ends, / Rough-hew them how we will', Hamlet recognizes, with a clear and conscious modification of his earlier sense of his own freedom and power, that he is subject to the control of a higher power which redirects him

when his own blunders have impeded his progress. The recognition is Hamlet's; not necessarily Shakespeare's; not necessarily ours. He continues with an all-important speech, the full version of which is found only in the Folio.

Does it not, think thee, stand me now upon –
He that hath killed my king and whored my mother,
Popped in between th' election and my hopes,
Thrown out his angle for my proper life,
And with such cozenage – is't not perfect conscience
To quit him with this arm? And is't not to be damned
To let this canker of our nature come
In further evil?   (5.2.63–70)

To have this demand for assurance coming from Hamlet at this point in the play is extraordinary. Such anxiety can only be a measure of much perplexity. Once again, the theme is conscience and damnation. Conscience formerly made great enterprises lose the name of action; now it is conscience to raise one's arm against Claudius. Damnation formerly lay in wait for Hamlet if he took his own life, or killed the king at the behest of a devil-ghost. Now it would be his meed if he failed to stop a cancerous growth in human nature by allowing Claudius to go on living.

Hamlet says 'the interim is mine', in which to carry out what he sees as a holy resolve. But of course it isn't. The interim belongs to Claudius and Laertes. It is too late for Hamlet to act on his conviction. The first time, too much in fancied control of the world's destiny, he killed the wrong man; the second time he kills the King indeed, but not until he has his own death-wound.

There can be no question about the extent of Hamlet's failure. Quite apart from his responsibility for the deaths of Polonius, Ophelia and his school-fellows, there is the simple, inescapable fact that the attempt to rid Denmark of its villain-king has left the country in a worse state than it was at the outset. The foreigner Fortinbras, whose threat to the kingdom opens the play, takes it over at the end without firing a single shot. Fortinbras is success as Hamlet is failure.

---

[10] Given at the International Association of University Professors of English meeting at Aberdeen, August, 1980. The material will be presented in my forthcoming edition of *Hamlet* for Cambridge University Press.

Nor should we take much comfort from Hamlet's own development. Even if we think of his persistent cruelty to Ophelia and his overbearing self-righteousness towards Gertrude as passing stages in his emotional history, we yet face some awkward moments towards the end of the play. Any suggestion that the Hamlet who returns from the voyage is in some state of sanctity has to be resisted. Here again, there is a victory for the criticism of the twentieth century. There has been an anti-Hamlet lobby in every generation but it has become so strong that it is impossible for anyone who to any degree 'believes in' Hamlet to sentimentalize him.

There can be no question about the extent of Hamlet's failure. But tragedy must surely ask about the extent of his success. I have been looking at Hamlet as a somewhat fitfully inspired missionary. It is time to turn to the problem which has so engaged the criticism of the twentieth century, the quality of the mission itself. What do we say about the moral standing of the 'court party'? About the values which Hamlet seeks to reimpose on Denmark? And above all about the ethics of wishing to kill Claudius?

'There is nothing either good or bad but thinking makes it so.' What *is* Denmark like? If we don't see sin and crime at Elsinore we are not likely to feel that Hamlet's despair is anything but an illness, or his mission to cleanse the world other than obsession and delusion. I should like to quote a typical modern attempt to abstain from black-and-white answers to this question, by Michael Long, in *The Unnatural Scene* (1976). In portraying Denmark, says Dr Long, Shakespeare shows 'no ruthless desire to track down viciousness'. No, it is 'a lucid presentation of very ordinary human failings as they prove catastrophically inept in the face of difficult moral demand. . . . The real "crime" in which all these characters are involved is that of participating without protest in a social normality which is hostile to the most essential needs of consciousness' (p. 140). We see the strong influence here of both Wilson Knight and L. C. Knights. I should also like to cite John Bayley's praise for Gertrude in *Shakespeare and Tragedy* (1981); he speaks of the 'innocence' in the play, which 'extends to Gertrude's marriage to Claudius, and his relations with her' (pp. 173–4).

This levelling of the score, as regards moral judgement, between Hamlet and those to whom he is opposed is characteristic of our century and our eagerness to see both sides of the question. We know too much to believe in villains and heroes. And even if we feel uneasy with this moral levelling as applied to the play of *Hamlet*, it is very hard not to feel more uneasy at the severity and sharpness of Hamlet's moral distinctions, at the stridency of his insistence on the beauty of his father's life and the ugliness of his uncle's. Everyone feels something excessive in his disgust at his mother's remarriage, in his charge of incest, and in his savage denunciation of his uncle as a usurper.

The question of the moral distinctions in the play seems to me of the very first importance in considering how far the criticism of our day may have blurred the tragic issue as it was presented to Shakespeare's audience. I agree entirely with Wilson Knight's words: 'The question of the relative morality of Hamlet and Claudius reflects the ultimate problem of this play.'

Three times during the course of the play Shakespeare brings the story of Cain and Abel to our minds.[11] There is the mention of 'the first corse' in 1.2; 'the primal eldest curse . . . A brother's murder' in 3.3; and 'Cain's jawbone, that did the first murder' in 5.1. *Hamlet* is the story of two royal brothers, a kingdom and a queen, given to us as a reflection of the primordial disintegration of the human family in that first murder which resulted from and betokened man's separation from God. In his book *Violence and the Sacred*, René Girard describes how the dissolution of cultural order comes about from the blurring of recognized distinctions and differences, and argues that the basic mythical presentation of this cultural dissolution is in terms of the rivalry of brothers, in fratricidal conflict over something they cannot share – a throne, a woman. The result of cultural dissolution, the 'sacrificial crisis' as Girard terms it, is that violence can no longer be contained, and overflows in the unending cycle of the vendetta.

The obliteration of differences and distinctions is what chiefly worries Hamlet; that Gertrude cannot

---

11 Compare Rosalie Colie, *Shakespeare's Living Art* (Princeton, 1974), p. 230.

distinguish between the two brothers, between Cain and Abel. 'Look here upon this picture, and on this!'

This was your husband. Look you now what follows. Here is your husband. Have you eyes?

(3.4.53, 63–4)

It is abundantly clear that Claudius seduced Gertrude in the old king's lifetime.[12] It is the thought that this complaisant woman was accustomed to sleep with either of two brothers which gives special force to the idea of 'incest'. The fierce refusal to accept the undiscriminating hospitality of Gertrude's loins is where the tragedy begins. Centuries later, the need to accept the undiscriminating hospitality of Molly Bloom's loins is where Joyce's *Ulysses* ends. In between lies the Romantic revolution during which Byron presented Cain as a much misunderstood figure.

'He that hath killed my king and whored my mother.' Here is plain speaking!

A murderer and a villain,
A slave that is not twentieth part the tithe
Of your precedent lord, a vice of kings,
A cutpurse of the empire and the rule,
That from a shelf the precious diadem stole
And put it in his pocket – (3.4.96–101)

Here is a forthright recognition of distinctions!

The sense of distinction which Hamlet apprehends to be weakening has now disappeared, as I think my quotations from Wilson Knight, Michael Long, and John Bayley show. I could adduce many, many more, including those at the edges which tell what a poor fish the old king was, probably an alcoholic and possibly impotent. But, as I say, we are all in this. We can't possibly share Hamlet's sense of values. Hyperion to a satyr? A man's a man for a' that. But nor could Shakespeare necessarily or unequivocally share Hamlet's sense of values. It is in the moment of the weakening and questioning of distinctions that he writes his play. What Shakespeare could not do was to repudiate Hamlet's sense of values. We, having gone right down the road that Shakespeare was on, have turned the corner, and can't see the place where the play happened, the place where blurring has just begun, and might *perhaps* be stopped.

To restore to his mother her sense of difference, to eliminate the man who obliterates distinctions and dares, by murder, to claim the protection of the divinity that hedges a king, to restore to Denmark its beauteous majesty – this is the mission of Hamlet, who, in doing this, can see himself as the scourge and minister of heaven itself. In a scheme of things in which the distinctions between persons are ratified by heaven, the killing of Claudius is as far removed from the brutal poisoning of the former king as can be. It would belong in an area of sacredness which is totally foreign to us. An act of cleansing and not one of pollution, it would have the sanctity of a sacrificial offering.[13]

That there can be a distinction between a violence which purifies, and is acceptable, and all other forms of violence, which are outlawed, must seem to us the most dangerous concept possible. Only among terrorist circles are differences of kind among acts of violence accepted. We don't accept capital punishment if only because as Saul Bellow's hero put it, 'Nobody's hands are clean enough to throw the switch'.[14] But, difficult though it is for us, unless we can see *some* sense in an idea of authorized violence, there can be little hope of recapturing the tragic sense of the play *Hamlet*. Oddly enough, the nineteenth century, which had its own scruples about capital punishment, seems to have had too little doubt about divinely-sanctioned violence in *Hamlet* (apart from Ulrici and his followers of course) and to that extent *they* diminished the tragic balance of the play. Claudius ought to be killed, they felt: it was some terrible paralysis which prevented Hamlet from doing the deed. G. K. Chesterton saw the way things were going and in an essay of 1923 leapt to the defence of the older view. We could no longer apprehend the play, he claimed, because we had ceased to believe in

---

12 Unless the Ghost is a liar of course; and he doesn't lie about the murder. See 1.5.42–6, 55–7. Also J. D. Wilson, *What Happens in Hamlet*, 3rd edn (Cambridge, 1951), pp. 292–4.

13 See the opening chapter of René Girard's *Violence and the Sacred* (1972; English trans. 1977), on the distinction between legitimate and illegal violence in primitive society.

14 Bellow, *The Dean's December* (New York, 1982), p. 180.

punishment, and had substituted pity in its stead. 'The sort of duty that Hamlet shirked is exactly the sort of duty that we are all shirking; that of dethroning injustice and vindicating truth.'[15]

This disarming simplicity has as little to do with what we find in the play of *Hamlet* as has the opposing view that the execution of Claudius is too horrid even to contemplate. The only person who holds a simple view about punishing Claudius is the Ghost. 'Howsomever thou pursues this act, / Taint not thy mind'. This revenge he asks for is a straightforward business, demanding courage and will, like meeting the challenge of old Fortinbras, all those years ago.[16] But for Hamlet nothing is simple or straightforward. His rage to re-establish the world of distinctions and sanctions which he fears is disappearing never quite certainly finds either its divine justification or its true way of proceeding. Throughout the play, to everyone, his language is teasing, riddling, punning, looking two ways at once, never directly serious or directly jesting. In almost everything he says, he reveals his incapacity for or refusal of single vision and single valuation. Hamlet's commitment to killing the king wavers constantly; he tries out the avenger's script, he clearly prefers to chasten his mother, and (for me most significantly) at the second visitation actually fears that the Ghost's presence may convert his 'stern effects' and substitute tears for blood. Because of the impossibility of total conviction, great enterprises lose the name of action. But ''tis not so above. *There* is no shuffling.' Is there a line of communication from that higher region where uncertainty doesn't reign, authorizing conduct which, though it seems terrible, brings the values of heaven into a corrupt Denmark? The play of *Hamlet* takes place within the possibility that there is – in the symbol of the Ghost. Neither positive that there is, nor positive that there is not.

I have for several years suggested to my students that the central dilemma in *Hamlet* is that which Kierkegaard describes, concerning Abraham and the intended sacrifice of Isaac, in his work *Fear and Trembling*. Abraham believed that he had heard God and in obedience was prepared to murder his beloved son. This indeed is faith. It is the idea of the wager again – betting that there is a God – and that trusting in what we hear enables us to fulfil a demand of the

absolute, although we outgo the laws of worldly ethics.

Kierkegaard tries out many scenarios for the intense but skeletal drama provided in Genesis. What would Isaac say when he heard Abraham's explanation of his extraordinary conduct towards him? 'So you were prepared to kill me because a voice told you to?' And so on. There *can* be no certainty. Isaac was not killed, but Abraham was ready and willing to kill him. Either he was a murderer, or he was an obedient child of God. Faith, says Kierkegaard, is 'a paradox which is capable of transforming a murder into a holy act well-pleasing to God'. But, he asks, 'If the individual had misunderstood the deity – what can save him?'

The *mistaken* conviction of the individual that he can be above the universally accepted ethics of society, Kierkegaard calls the 'demoniacal'. He speaks of 'the knight of faith who in the solitude of the universe never hears any human voice, but walks alone with his dreadful responsibility'. Dreadful, because he may be eternally lost, for following the demoniac and not the divine. Either way, he seems mad to the world; at the very least, the world 'denounces as presumption his wanting to play providence by his actions'.[17]

The literary criticism of the past fifty years, with its challenge to the conduct of Hamlet and the authority of the Ghost, has unintentionally moved the play right into that point of terrible balance described by Kierkegaard. Is Hamlet's sense of mission divine or demoniac? A former pupil of mine objected to my use of Kierkegaard concerning a play written when theology was dominated by Luther. It was Wittenberg Hamlet was studying at. William Tyndale, who visited Luther at Wittenberg, will do just as well.

FAITH, is the believing of God's promises, and a sure trust in the goodness and truth of GOD; which faith justified Abraham, and was the mother of all his good works which he afterwards did. Good works are

---

15 Chesterton, *Fancies versus Fads* (1923), p. 33.
16 On the 'absurdly simplified command' of the Ghost, see G. K. Hunter, 'The Heroism of Hamlet', in '*Hamlet*', Stratford-upon-Avon Studies, 5, ed. J. R. Brown and B. Harris (1963), p. 104, and John Masefield, *William Shakespeare* (1911), p. 161.
17 Kierkegaard, *Fear and Trembling*, trans. W. Lowrie (New York, 1941), pp. 64, 71, 90, 95.

works of God's commandment, wrought in faith . . . Jacob robbed Laban his uncle; Moses robbed the Egyptians; and Abraham is about to slay and burn his own son; and all are holy works, because they are wrought in faith at God's commandment. To steal, rob, and murder, are no holy works before worldly people; but unto them that have their trust in God they are holy, when God commandeth them. Holy works of man's imaginations receive their reward here, as Christ testifieth, Matt. vi.

'Holy works of man's imaginations' are what Kierkegaard would call 'demoniac' activity. Stephen Greenblatt, whose *Renaissance Self-Fashioning* directed me towards Tyndale, stresses the violence with which, in the Reformation debates, each side accused the other of creating God in their imaginations. I quote from Tyndale again.

These are they which Jude in his epistle called dreamers, which deceive themselves with their own fantasies. For what other thing is their imagination, which they call faith, than a dreaming of the faith, and an opinion of their own imagination wrought without the grace of God?[18]

Both Horatio and Hamlet understood what Tyndale meant by 'imagination'. 'He waxes desperate with imagination', says Horatio; that is, with self-created ideas of what the Ghost is. And Hamlet fears that if he can't confirm the Ghost's story, 'my imaginations are as foul / As Vulcan's stithy', that is, that he has been building his views of heaven's decrees on a mental image and not on truth.

The practical effects of Hamlet's purifying violence are disastrous. Claudius sought to protect his kingdom and did it efficiently against the attacks of both Fortinbras and Laertes. Hamlet comes in, an alienated, savage, destructive force, and Denmark passes into foreign hands. Against the tangible misery which he causes have to be set the intangible values of salvation and damnation which govern his entire conduct – values which are not only intangible but unverifiable, and may belong in the end to men's imagination.

It has been my contention that the tragic value of the play *Hamlet* has become enfeebled through two successive, antithetical waves of criticism, and that the possibility of renewing that tragic value lies not in

trying to refute or wipe away mid twentieth-century criticism but in acknowledging it, absorbing it and moving on from it with reinforcement from the nineteenth-century criticism it had tried to replace. I should make it clear that so far as I am concerned the twentieth-century critic (who, of course, like Yeats's Fisherman is 'a man who does not exist') has not only refused to follow the old-fashioned custom of identifying with Hamlet, he has positively rejected him. In Nietzschean terms, the twentieth century has completely upset the equilibrium of Apollo and Dionysus by putting all the weight on the Apollonian side. The maintenance of social order takes precedence of all else, and Hamlet is a disturbing nuisance wrecking the social fabric by trying to bring back the past. 'Claudius is a good king, and the Ghost but a minor spirit.' The all-important question for me is, what *kind* of sympathy do we need to find for Hamlet in order to restore an equilibrium which I believe could have been Elizabethan, but which I think you will not easily find in nineteenth- or twentieth-century criticism?

Doubts about the Ghost, doubts about the ethics of revenge, doubts about the nastiness of Claudius, and doubts about the niceness of Hamlet, are a legacy of modern times which we need to hold fast to. But when the doubts become positive scepticism, we are as lost as we were when we supposed that the Ghost was guaranteed, that revenge was good, that Hamlet was noble and Claudius a rotter.

Shakespeare, it may be said, looked at the past not only nostalgically but sentimentally. Yet those of his heroes who try to restore or even preserve the past, and oppose the future, Richard II, Brutus, Coriolanus, have an ineffectuality and a woodenness about them which betoken a grim historical realism on Shakespeare's part. It is in *Hamlet* above all of Shakespeare's plays that I find superbly and movingly presented an openness towards both past and future in which the possibility of restoration is balanced against the futility of trying. And this is not entirely because of the unbelievable interest of the mind which contemplates the task of bringing back the majesty of beauteous Denmark. It is also because of the great transcendental

---

[18] Tyndale, *Doctrinal Treatises*, Parker Society (1848), pp. 407, 53.

hypothesis which is the framework of the play, and the context in which past and future are seen. The sense of an order of distinction among people which is ratified in heaven, the sense that there is a communication between heaven and earth, the sense that there *can* be a cleansing act of violence which is both a punishment and a liberation, these are as powerfully present in the play as is the conviction that these things do not exist. Hamlet's groping attempt to make a higher truth active in a fallen world fails hopelessly. But just suppose we can entertain the *possibility* that he was within reach of a higher truth. 'What should we do?' he asks the Ghost. And of Horatio he asks, 'Is't not to be damned to let this canker of our nature come in further evil?' Wilson Knight, in that brilliant early essay of his, recognized the alien and inhuman prophet that Hamlet essentially is. And he repudiated him. Hamlet vexed and troubled the world and failed to change it for the better. But he continues, or he ought to continue, to vex and trouble us with the suspicion, and the fear, that although he never got there, he may have been after something worth having. It is not faith we need to understand *Hamlet*, but doubt about our own scepticism. We need just enough questioning to keep alive the openness of Hamlet's question to Horatio. 'Is't not to be damned to let this canker of our nature come in further evil?' And to be able to respond also to that other remark of his:

> There are more things in heaven and earth, Horatio,
> Than are dreamt of in your philosophy.

HAMLET ACROSS SPACE AND TIME

LU GU-SUN

The never-waning interest in *Hamlet* has, since the beginning of the twentieth century, spilled over to fields of intellectual endeavour beyond that of literary criticism, causing Hamlet to be interpreted more variously than before – in the light of Freudian psychology or of existentialist philosophy, for instance – with the result that 'Hamletology' has practically become a multidiscipline research challenge. Likewise, throughout the lay world reader and audience response continues to be enthusiastic, a credit to Ben Jonson's prophetic tribute that Shakespeare 'was not of an age, but for all time'. It is true that Hamlet's forte does not lie in an unswerving resolve or in a single-minded and vigorous execution of it, so much so that Hamlet, in Bradley's opinion,[1] is not entitled to the giant stature that Shakespeare's later tragic heroes such as Othello have customarily been accorded. However, it is precisely here, if anywhere, that resides the durable Hamlet motif – neither 'all virtue'[2] nor 'all vice'[3] simplistically, being at once 'the Nemean lion' and a 'muddy-mettled' and 'pigeon-livered' 'John-a-dreams' – a motif, in short, of the three-dimensional man of flesh and blood rather than of a *dramatis persona*. As a result, a modern man, be he an agnostic, a disillusioned cynic, a probing thinker (metaphysical or otherwise), or an ordinary person grappling with day-to-day stressful situations in life, still feels, as Coleridge did, 'a smack of Hamlet' in him.

Such enthusiasm about *Hamlet* in China is of relatively recent origin. The first translation of *Hamlet*, which appeared in 1903, was based on the Lambs' *Tales from Shakespeare*. To tailor it to the Chinese palate for the then current story-telling stereotypes, the translation carried a somewhat melodramatic title,

Bao Da Chu Hanlide Sha Shu, which upon back translation into English, means 'Hamlet Revenges by Slaying his Uncle'. In 1904 the Commercial Press published a translation from the same source by Lin Shu, a well-known writer and translator. As elegance was considered one of the chief virtues in translation as well as in original writing, Lin Shu's version, like his other translations, was in classical Chinese that only the adequately educated could read and, again, the matter-of-fact title of the original was changed to a more refined if less pertinent rendering: *Guei Zhao*[4] – literally 'The Ghost's Edict' in English. A translation of the full text of *Hamlet* into plebeianized modern vernacular Chinese did not appear until two years after the May 4th Students' Movement of 1919 when the left-wing poet and playwright Tian Han – author of the words of the present People's Republic of China national anthem – set himself to the task.

---

[1] *Shakespearean Tragedy*, 1904.

[2] See, for instance, Peter Alexander's *Hamlet, Father and Son* (1955).

[3] See, for instance, Salvador de Madariaga's *On Hamlet* (1948) and Rebecca West's *The Court and the Castle* (1957).

[4] To maintain balanced uniformity Lin Shu's translations of the *Tales* all bear titles composed of two Chinese characters for each, e.g. *Zhu Qing* (*The Forging of Love*) for *Romeo and Juliet*, *Hei Mao* (*A Black Who Is Blind*) for *Othello*, *Rou Quan* (*The Human Flesh Credit Bond*) for *The Merchant of Venice*, and *Nu Bian* (*Daughters Turning Against Their Father*) for *King Lear*. Although such titles are often deficient in accuracy in conveying the true meaning of the play, they have the advantage of being terse and catchy synopses which helped transplant Shakespeare into Chinese soil. Incidentally, some of Lin Shu's titles were to persist in currency for a long time to come.

It is no accident that vigorous work should have begun to be undertaken in real earnest about that time to introduce Shakespeare and, for that matter, other major foreign masters to the Chinese reading public. The first decade of the century witnessed an accelerated popular awakening and a massive democratic revolution of gathering momentum which led to the downfall in 1912 of the last imperial court in Chinese history. Free from the feudal yoke and in a general climate of challenging old institutions, many people, young intellectuals especially, found themselves keenly responsive to new ideas such as humanity, equality and freedom espoused in foreign literature. Against this background it is but small wonder that Hamlet, with his fiery protests against corruption and injustice and with his impassioned affirmation of human dignity, could evoke widespread empathy and arouse increasing enthusiasm in Chinese readers and later – in the early 1940s, for instance, when China was critically in the thick of her War of Resistance – with the theatre-going public as well. On the other hand, for the disadvantaged majority of the population the traditional Chinese value system and psychic pattern remained largely unchanged despite the impact of foreign thought. Chinese civilization, it is generally observed, is characteristically homogeneous, capable through intrinsic processes of assimilating and eventually incorporating alien influences. Therefore, to some of the early Chinese readers and critics of Hamlet the surface theme of the play – the murder of a king revenged by his dutiful prince and the violent death of the usurper together with his sometime sister now his queen – was aesthetically welcome, being conveniently in compliance with the Confucian ethical code demanding filial piety, unquestioning allegiance to the monarch, and constant chastity, and with Buddhist tenets of karma. In this context it is not difficult to explain why and how a Renaissance tragedy of considerable scope and depth like Hamlet could be easily naturalized when adapted to the Sichuan opera, one of China's 300-odd local operatic varieties. To tickle the fancy of an indigenous provincial audience, the adaptation, just as its title 'Murder of a Brother and Taking a Sister-in-Law to Wife' might suggest, dramatized what is morally objectionable in the original and smacked in large measure of a didactic stage production of an authentic Chinese brand.

Apart from the appeal held out by the ideas of Hamlet, no matter how they are interpreted or misinterpreted, certain other factors account for the ready Chinese acceptance of the play. In the first place, whether swayed by some universally valid, mysterious laws governing dramatic composition at the time or by mere accident, Shakespeare when he wrote Hamlet and major Chinese playwrights contemporaneous with him are surprisingly alike in having often drawn liberally on predecessors for the stories of their works. I checked a list of titles of Chinese poetic dramas popular during the sixteenth and seventeenth centuries and found at least thirty-two in the repertoire either having titles identical with their prototypes or traceable to an earlier period. For instance, Tang Xianzu, by far the most influential dramatist of sixteenth-century China, who, incidentally, died in the same year as Shakespeare, based his representative work Mudan Ting – The Peony Pavilion – upon an earlier vernacular story-telling script, not only taking over the plot, the heroine's name, etc., but also quoting verbatim at several places. Secondly, the imperial theme, an austere atmosphere of regal dignity, the image of warriors and, last but not least, the Ghost as a medium of the disclosure of foul play in Hamlet are all familiar features of the Chinese stage. Interestingly, the nightmarish experience of hell recounted by the Ghost in Hamlet is strikingly similar in detail to what the heroine of Mudan Ting went through after death, the only difference lying in the fact that hell in the Chinese play, acted out at adequate length instead of being verbally related as second-hand information, is meant more as a sober parody of the mundane world – a discovered country, if you like, from whose bourn travellers can return – than a nebulous purgatory in the Christian sense. Thirdly, as Shakespeare's plays, Hamlet included, are generally unfettered by the three unities or other rigorous neoclassical dictates, they usually employ conventions almost as elastic as those of a traditional Chinese theatrical performance wherein a few steps taken on stage could mean scores of miles traversed along with a suggestion of a lapse of time. As a result, Chinese audiences invariably find themselves more comfortably at home with Shakespeare than with, say, the Greek tragic masters. Fourthly, such Shakespearian theatrical techniques as occasional comic relief and the frequent use of asides and soliloquies have happily coincided with institutionalized Chinese dramatic techniques and hence have helped to enhance a sense of affinity.

In post-1949 China, except for a ten-year break from 1966 to 1976, translations and studies of Shakespeare have continued to flourish. My own incomplete statistics show that, besides studies in individual plays, articles printed by various academic journals and newspapers which are related to Shakespeare, Shakespearian criticism, Shakespeare's time, his works, and his influence on posterity have added up to well over one hundred and fifty. Of *Hamlet* at least five different translations have been added to the pre-1949 three, two of these five being attempts at a poetic rendering, and more than fifty monographs on *Hamlet* have been published. In 1978 the first Chinese translation of a Complete Shakespeare came out, although the bulk of the monumental work had previously been done by a dedicated translator, Zhu Shenghao, back in the 1930s. Other recent highlights of Shakespearian studies and performances in China include the Old Vic visit in 1979, the 1981 exhibition 'Shakespeare's Time' in Peking, and more recently the publication of an anthology of Shakespeare criticism edited by Professor Yang Zhouhan of Peking University, the founding of a China Shakespeare Society with headquarters in the lake-side city of Hangzhou, the initiation of a specialized Shakespeare Library at Fudan University, Shanghai, and the successful production of *Romeo and Juliet* in Lhasa in the Tibetan language and by Tibetan actors and actresses, which fact, hopefully, suffices to dispel sadly uninformed and biased doubts that Shakespearian performances 'are limited by the old Chinese etiquette: for example, a man may not touch the hand of a woman'.[5]

But how to assure the continued relevance of Shakespeare and of his most enigmatic character, Hamlet, remains a major task Chinese students of Shakespeare have yet to tackle. For all the new opportunities brought about by the advance of science and technology, the twentieth century is rife with problems hitherto unknown to man. One problem typical of our own time is a manifest antithesis between what is heroic and a constant emphasis on the deceptive and futile aspects of life and, resultantly, on a sense of alienation. Serious literature, therefore, seems to move farther and farther away from action, from heroic action in particular, to identity-seeking (though often in vain), to intellectuality; protagonists from heroes to anti-heroes – unheroic heroes who always personify, one way or another, the discrepancy between actual performance and illusory promise.

Under these circumstances *Hamlet* criticism apparently needs to break new ground. One suggestion I have in mind is, if critical emphasis has so far been gradually shifted, as Harold Jenkins observed in his essay '*Hamlet* Then till Now',[6] from the 'character' of Hamlet the man on to the 'theme' or 'idea' of *Hamlet* the play, from the Prince's 'inability to act' onto his 'inability to affirm', may it as well be proposed that we of the present day focus on Hamlet's 'relationships' or on his 'inability to identify'? In Hamlet's 'commutual' relations, for instance, respectively with Claudius, Polonius, Laertes, Rosencrantz, Guildenstern, Gertrude, and Ophelia, what is he or she to Hamlet, or Hamlet to him or her? To Hamlet, as interpretations across a wide critical spectrum often differ, he or she can be many things except an *alter ego*. The Ghost, Hyperion as he was, is but an other-worldly vision. So far as this-worldly identifiability is concerned, Horatio and Young Fortinbras, being intellectual and/or moral equals, are closest to what Hamlet may opt for. However, Horatio frequently appears as spokesman for the playwright comparable in function with the chorus in some of Shakespeare's plays and is therefore far too detached to be able to hold his own beside the Prince, while Young Fortinbras is only a broadbrush (if not altogether anaemic) token presence throughout the play. Thus, failure to identify is found underlying much of Hamlet's predicament and melancholia, which can presumably be epitomized by his own words: 'Now I am alone' and 'man delights not me; no, nor woman neither'.

---

[5] See the entry *China* in F. E. Halliday's *A Shakespeare Companion 1564–1964* (Harmondsworth, 1964).

[6] See *Aspects of Hamlet*, ed. Kenneth Muir and Stanley Wells (Cambridge, 1979), pp. 16–27.

Again, why for instance does Hamlet speak of his mother in such venomous resentment as is expressed in the following sibilant lines:

> O, most wicked speed, to post
> With such dexterity to incestuous sheets!
>
> (1.2.156–7)

Is it his mother's lust alone that Hamlet so spitefully loathes? Or is the passage a vehement outburst on the part of a frustrated Oedipus in private? Not quite in either case. For elsewhere Hamlet has been heard remarking largely to the same effect but in a different vein, in cynical irony this time, and without alluding to lust:

> Thrift, thrift, Horatio! the funeral bak'd-meats
> Did coldly furnish forth the marriage tables.
>
> (1.2.180–1)

Apparently it is this 'most wicked speed' more than anything else that sets Hamlet's teeth grinding, the speed with which his mother has so readily and flippantly identified herself with a new man who in turn has so dubiously and impatiently identified himself with the State of Denmark. The wickedness of the speed is made all the more poignant by the fact that Hamlet should have found identification virtually impossible ever since he was bereft of his dear father.

Unable to identify and without a reassuring sense of belonging, Hamlet is perpetually at a loss where he stands in relation to others at Elsinore and what, ultimately, he is. That accounts for the fuzzy streaks rather than clear-cut facets in his character. Ophelia deplores a mind 'o'erthrown' – 'the courtier's, soldier's, scholar's'. But Hamlet, having something of everything, is not quite anything all over: too proud to mix with thoroughbred politicians like Polonius accustomed to Byzantine-style intrigues or with subordinate courtiers like Rosencrantz and Guildenstern (not to mention Osric the 'waterfly'), too meditative to qualify as a soldier who draws his sword precipitously upon the slightest provocation, too unscholarly to be carried away by sanguine impulses and to let himself go.

Assuming that the 'relationships' approach or the 'inability to identify' approach is by and large viable, *Hamlet* could cease to be 'a religious drama',[7] revenge or whatever otherwise smacks of the bizarre could be played down, metaphysical queries could be subdued as being incidental or secondary, and the Prince could change from the one character of the play as Shaftesbury saw him to be[8] to the pivotal character reliant upon the rest of the cast for realistic cogence. Should the actors and actresses be preoccupied not with how to elevate an audience with the sublime and the grandiloquent (Shakespeare's poetry aside, of course) but with how to act out the 'commutual' relations in unadorned candour while letting whatever philosophy is contained therein sink in, would they be guilty of an aesthetic anticlimax? As a person interested to see Hamlet always and everywhere alive, I think they could thereby claim to be embarking on a commendable new experiment in 'holding a mirror up to nature' – man's nature as it is revealed in the interaction among men. After all, times have changed. Murder is not a routine of life; revenge is rapidly becoming a dated anachronism; heroes are few and far between; a ghost is harder to come by; only relationships – various and ubiquitous in a modern man's milieu – remain agelessly and universally real.

---

[7] A. C. Bradley, *Shakespearean Tragedy* (1904).

[8] *Soliloquy, or Advice to an Author* (1710).

SHAKESPEARE'S SCRIPTS AND THE MODERN DIRECTOR

ALAN C. DESSEN

The twentieth-century interpreter of Shakespeare's plays faces significant problems. Perhaps most basic is the simple fact that the dialogue and stage directions are not directed at *us*. Thus, as R. B. McKerrow noted shrewdly over fifty years ago, Shakespeare's original manuscript of *Hamlet* or *King Lear* 'would not have been written with any thought of the press. It was not intended for the study, or for the minute discussion of students three hundred years away in the future. It was not a literary document at all.' Rather, as McKerrow argues, that original manuscript 'was merely the substance, or rather the bare bones, of a performance on the stage, intended to be interpreted by actors skilled in their craft, who would have no difficulty in reading it as it was meant to be read'.[1] Those manuscripts, then, were not literary texts but theatrical scripts, written to be interpreted and performed by Elizabethan theatrical professionals who shared with both author and spectator a common language that included not only the words themselves but also stage conventions, emblematic costumes and properties, and an overall logic of presentation that today we may no longer recognize or appreciate.

This gap between then and now – sometimes obvious, sometimes invisible – has important implications for editors, critics, teachers, and general readers, but my focus in this essay is upon the relationship between those original Elizabethan playscripts and today's theatrical professional epitomized by the modern director. Thus, anyone, amateur or professional, setting out to produce a Shakespeare play must immediately make many practical decisions about the acting script: for example, will every scene and character be included, much less every line and phrase? Will Elizabethan slang or hard words be modernized? Few directors present the plays with virtually uncut texts, as in some recent National Theatre productions. Rather, faced with passages that appear to create difficulties for the actor or audience, most cut the Gordian knot by omitting such problematic material from their productions. Such cuts sometimes amount only to a deft shaving of archaic words or difficult mythological allusions. At the other extreme lies the kind of radical surgery epitomized by a recent production of *Julius Caesar* (Stratford Festival Canada, 1978) that dispensed entirely with the Roman plebeians (my current favourite for the unkindest cut of all).

My experience in recent years with both seeing plays and interviewing directors has revealed at least three different rationales behind such cutting or reshaping of a Shakespearian script.[2] First, most decisions to omit Shakespeare's words or characters might best be classified as *pragmatic* or *ad hoc*, for the director (unlike the editor, critic, or teacher) must confront such practical matters as personnel, budget, running time, and, last but definitely not least, obscurity. Consider the many problems to be faced in

[1] 'The Elizabethan Printer and Dramatic Manuscripts', *The Library*, IV, 12 (1931), 253–75; p. 266.

[2] For two suggestive treatments of similar problems, each with a perspective different from this essay, see Stanley Wells, 'Shakespeare's Text on the Modern Stage', *Shakespeare-Jahrbuch 1967* (West), 175–93; and Bernard Beckerman, 'The Flowers of Fancy, the Jerks of Invention, or, Directorial Approaches to Shakespeare', in *Shakespeare 1971*, ed. Clifford Leech and J. M. R. Margeson (Toronto and Buffalo, 1972).

mounting a production of one of the history plays. Especially to American audiences, these scripts seem to be long, unwieldy chains of episodes, densely populated with Yorks, Gloucesters, Worcesters, and worse, not to mention innumerable royal Henrys, Richards, and Edwards. To avoid confusion and obfuscation, many directors feel impelled to cut various lords or telescope parts together. Even with the doubling of parts (a practice some directors shun), the personnel demands of such a play can strain a company that lacks the resources of the Royal Shakespeare Company or Stratford Festival Canada, hence the tendency to omit moments that involve less than central characters and seem peripheral to the modern eye. Thus, just about every Shakespeare play has at least one scene that is as often omitted as included: how many veteran playgoers expect to see Ventidius in *Antony and Cleopatra*, or the children of Clarence in *Richard III*, or the carriers, Gadshill, and the chamberlain in *1 Henry IV*? The introduction of one or more intervals, moreover, to a script originally written for 'through' performance can add significantly to the running time, change the rhythm of the show, and lead to cuts. Most obvious, changes in language and culture have made some lines and passages so dense or opaque today that their meaning may be available only to an occasional scholar in the audience. To cite but one of many, many examples, the last four productions of *King Lear* I have seen (including the 1982 production at Stratford) have omitted most or all of Kent's lines describing the 'smiling rogues' who 'Like rats oft bite the holy cords atwain / Which are too intrinse t'unloose' (2.2.68–70).[3] Presumably, the combination of difficult syntax with such phrases as 'halcyon beaks' and 'every gale and vary of their masters' creates a passage deemed beyond the ken of the modern auditor.

The logic behind such pragmatic cutting has been spelled out in a description provided by Tom Markus of how he prepared *2 Henry IV* for the Colorado Shakespeare Festival. In his view, 'play doctoring is necessary as a result of the differences in the knowledge and beliefs of a contemporary audience from those of one in Shakespeare's era'. Included among his guide-lines for such 'play doctoring' are: 'shorten each scene as much as possible . . . eliminate everything that might confuse an audience . . . cut all characters who are unnecessary to the scene . . . cut all scenes which do not advance the story . . . cut or change all words that are archaic or obscure.'[4] Here, in extreme form, is the rationale for cutting Shakespeare's scripts in order to bring them more in line with the idiom and expectations of the 1980s.

For various pragmatic reasons, then, many minor characters, obscure allusions, and syntactically difficult passages do not find their way into modern productions. My favourite example comes from a virtually uncut production of *Othello* (Stratford Festival Canada, 1979). Here, Othello's famous speech building to his suicide was *not* interrupted by the brief lines from Lodovico and Gratiano, so that 'I took by th'throat the circumcisèd dog / And smote him – thus' was, in this production, immediately followed by

> I kissed thee ere I killed thee. No way but this,
> Killing myself, to die upon a kiss. (5.2.358–9)

When I asked the director (Frances Hyland) why this change in Shakespeare's rhythm, she noted that her production was to end with a series of matinees for high school students and that she and the actors were afraid of losing this magnificent scene when Lodovico, in front of 2,000 teenagers, exclaimed: 'O bloody period!'

Beneath the pragmatic argument thereby lies the assumption that various passages or moments have limited value or pose insurmountable difficulties for the modern actor or spectator. In the jargon of the trade: 'it doesn't work'. As one highly knowledgeable theatrical professional proposed the argument to me: 95 per cent of Shakespeare's images, allusions, and conventions do translate well to modern stages and audiences, but, to avoid mystification and frustration, directors and actors should be able to adjust the remaining 5 per cent. In the spirit of modern consumerism, however, some comparison shopping is recommended, for, surprisingly, material cut as unplayable in one production can turn up as a successful

---

[3] Quotations are from *The Complete Pelican Shakespeare*, general editor Alfred Harbage (Baltimore, 1969).

[4] 'Preparing the Text: *The History of Henry the Fourth, Part Two*', *On-Stage Studies*, the Colorado Shakespeare Festival, Number 4 (1980), 53–67; pp. 58, 62.

part of another. A striking example is to be found in the Royal Shakespeare Company production of the *Henry VI* trilogy (1977–8). Aware of the many negative judgements about these plays, the director, Terry Hands, decided 'not to do even our own usual reshaping of a few corners and reorganizing the occasional speech' but chose rather 'just to put it all very crudely, very naively down on the stage – everything that was there, warts and all, in the hope that one or two of them would turn out to be beauty spots. There was something to learn.'[5] From this naive, crude approach without reshaping or reorganizing (albeit with some lines cut) emerged a stunning production that was both a great success at the box office and a revelation to students of the history plays.

In an interview, Hands cites several instances where 'warts' he was tempted to cut turned out to be beauty spots. For example, he notes a moment in the quarto of *3 Henry VI* where young Clifford is directed to enter with an arrow in his neck (2.6.0). According to Hands, 'the first reaction round the table when we were reading was, well, that's funny. And then somebody said, "Well, let's try it with an arrow in his neck and see what happens." The first image was that it would be ridiculous, and in fact it isn't; it's amazing when you actually see it. It's so unexpected, it's so bizarre, that that moment has been following us all through the play.'[6] Premature surgery to remove a supposed wart may leave a scar, an emptiness, a diminished thing.

Let me turn to a better-known script. Within a week in August, 1979, I saw two quite different productions of *1 Henry IV*, one in Stratford, Ontario, the other in Highpoint, North Carolina, both of them heavily cut. Thus, both directors omitted 2.1 and 4.4 (standard cuts); the director at the North Carolina Shakespeare Festival (Louis Rackoff) also cut Francis the drawer and some other sizeable chunks; at Stratford, Peter Moss omitted Vernon's description of Hal (4.1), Hal's disposition of the day's honours in the final scene, and just about all of Hotspur's pre-battle speeches, including all of the 'time of life is short' passage (5.2.81 ff.).

Let me focus, however, upon a moment pared down in both productions, Prince Hal's rescue of his father from Douglas at Shrewsbury. First, consider the Prince's speech as written by Shakespeare:

> Hold up thy head, vile Scot, or thou art like
> Never to hold it up again. The spirits
> Of valiant Shirley, Stafford, Blunt are in my arms.
> It is the Prince of Wales that threatens thee,
> Who never promiseth but he means to pay.
>
> (5.4.38–42)

In North Carolina, all these lines were gone; Hal entered, saw his father fighting with Douglas, and attacked. In Ontario, Richard Monette spoke the first line and a half and then rescued his father. One can understand how all or most of these lines might drop out in rehearsal as impediments to the flow of the action or violations of plausibility. After all, from a 'realistic' point of view, would a son, seeing his father in danger, go through five blank verse lines before coming to the rescue? In response to my query, moreover, the director in Canada told me that the line starting 'It is the Prince of Wales...' was, in his terms, a 'white gloves' passage with a formal or prissy ring to it out of keeping with the scene and with Hal's character. So in both productions the lines disappeared, and few spectators were aware of their absence.

What then can be said on behalf of these five lines? Throughout the play, a wide range of figures, including Falstaff, the King, and the rebels, are associated with not paying their debts and not keeping their promises. In contrast, Prince Hal does honour his debts and promises, whether those made in his early soliloquy (where he vows to 'pay the debt I never promisèd') or in his reply to Falstaff in the major tavern scene ('I do, I will') or in the interview with his father (where he vows, among other things, to force Hotspur to 'exchange / His glorious deeds for my indignities'). Here, just before his climactic fight with Hotspur, the Prince appears as a vengeful warrior, visibly bloodied (5.4.1), who embodies in his arms 'the spirits' of those who have already fallen (Shirley, Stafford, Blunt). But in this speech he describes

---

[5] Quoted in Homer D. Swander, 'The Rediscovery of *Henry VI*', *Shakespeare Quarterly*, 29 (1978), 146–63; p. 149. [6] *Ibid.* p. 151.

himself not as Hal or Prince Henry or the Prince but as 'the Prince of Wales', the Crown Prince, the heir to Henry IV, the role that epitomizes the debt he never promised; and he further characterizes that Prince of Wales as one who, unlike almost everyone else in the play, 'never promiseth but he means to pay'. Both in action (this rescue of his father) and in metaphor, Hal here fulfils a role, a debt, a promise that is central to the final movement of Part 1 (and of Part 2 as well). To cut these lines is then to achieve a modest gain in the flow of the battle and to avoid what might or might not be a 'white gloves' passage, but at the cost of losing a major signpost that should be pointing both the actor and the spectator toward some distinctive meanings embodied in Hal's emergence as the Prince of Wales and eventually as Henry V. Indeed, for anyone interested in the imagistic or metaphorical potential of the final movement of this play, these lines could be considered indispensable.

As a student of the plays, I often find myself debating with theatrical professionals about such cuts and decisions. At the same time, as a playgoer with an average attention span who has heard many tales about the plight of the director I cannot help being sympathetic to the 'real world' problems that have been described to me. To move to more sensitive ground, however, a second and, for me, more insidious basis for cutting or reshaping Shakespeare's scripts can be described as *conceptual*, wherein passages or stage directions or even entire scenes are omitted because their presence would contradict or jar with the director's interpretation. In presenting their analyses, critics and lecturers can silently ignore any such offending passages, but to achieve a selective vision of a play in the theatre a director must either cut the script or bury the words under stage business or audience laughter.

Some conceptual cuts have achieved considerable notoriety (for example, Peter Brook's omission from his production of *King Lear* of Edmund's repentance and the servants' reaction to the blinding of Gloucester); others are much subtler, only becoming blatant when a director's concept conflicts with the interpretation assumed by the playgoer. Thus, the director of an *All's Well* at the Oregon Shakespearean Festival in 1975 opted for a sunny

rather than a dark comedy and therefore wanted a Bertram that an audience would not find culpable or obnoxious. Shakespeare, however, did not always cooperate. For example, when Helena rejoins Bertram for the first time after the enforced marriage, he comments to Parolles: 'Here comes my clog' (2.5.52) – a distinctly unpleasant line that conveys exactly how he feels about her. That line, which would have jarred with this production's concept of Bertram, was omitted. A few years later (1979), the director of an Oregon *A Midsummer Night's Dream* introduced an element of menace into his fairy world, including an Oberon who at times seemed eerie, even Satanic. Although the director denied any such rationale when I sounded him out, I found it revealing that he chose to cut Oberon's speech to Puck that begins 'But we are spirits of another sort' (3.2.388–95) in which the fairy king clearly distinguishes himself from those 'damnèd spirits' that 'must for aye consort with black-browed night'. An attentive auditor might have had difficulty reconciling this speech, if it had been included, with the on-stage presentation of a menacing Oberon and fairy world.

Consider also two recent productions at the Stratford Festival Canada, both directed by Robin Phillips. The much-acclaimed *As You Like It* (1977–8) featured Maggie Smith and Brian Bedford as Rosalind and Jaques. Remember that at key points Shakespeare's Jaques is put down or bested by Rosalind and Orlando. So in 3.2 Jaques tells Orlando 'I was seeking for a fool when I found you'; Orlando responds: 'He is drowned in the brook. Look but in and you shall see him.' Jaques then falls or seems to fall into the trap: 'There I shall see mine own figure', setting up Orlando's rejoinder: 'Which I take to be either a fool or a cipher' (ll. 272–7). In this production, however, Jack Wetherall's Orlando apparently could not be (or was not allowed to be) a match for Brian Bedford's Jaques, so these lines were gone (along with part of Shakespeare's strategy). Similarly, in his production of *The Winter's Tale* (1978) Phillips cut parts of the final scene so that, among other things, Paulina was not married to Camillo. Granted, the marvellous, crusty, iron-willed Paulina provided by Martha Henry would never have subjected herself to Leontes' will in such a marriage disposition, but that in turn means that the actor's and the director's conception of a major figure is in conflict with the facts supplied by Shakespeare who did set up such a marriage for his Paulina as part of the final ordering, just as he set up Orlando's put-down of Jaques, Bertram's snide reference to Helena, and Oberon's clear announcement that 'we are spirits of another sort'. Such changes, small and large, represent a reshaping of the evidence, a detective's rewriting of the clues to conform to his solution.

Such conceptual cuts are most likely to occur when a passage comes in conflict with the prevailing interpretation of a given play or character. For example, I have seen at least four productions of *The Merchant of Venice* (including Jonathan Miller directing Olivier) that omitted Shylock's telling aside in his first scene that, if he once can catch Antonio 'upon the hip', he will then 'feed fat the ancient grudge [he] bear[s] him' (1.3.42–3). Shakespeare's Shylock has pitted himself against Antonio from the outset, but those directors who prefer their own cause-and-effect sequence (wherein, for example, Shylock's revenge is occasioned by Jessica's elopement) choose to omit this passage. Equivalent changes are made in the tragedies to sustain a romantic or heroic posture that a full text would qualify or undercut. Thus, I have never seen a Romeo arrive at the tomb carrying a mattock and a crow of iron (as called for by the dialogue and the first quarto stage direction); rather, Shakespeare's image of his hero is almost always adjusted to conform to something more romantic, less troubling. Again, most stage versions of *Othello* (with the National Theatre in 1980 being a notable exception) omit some, many, or even all of Othello's eavesdropping lines as he watches Iago and Cassio (for example, 'O, I see that nose of yours, but not that dog I shall throw it to', 4.1.140–1) and almost invariably cut the tragic hero's brief appearance to view what he thinks to be the murder of Cassio (5.1).[7] Both the eavesdropping and the cheering on of a murder in the dark underscore the ugly, shameful, degraded side of Othello, a side that some actors and directors would prefer to suppress (Salvini, for one, found the eavesdropping scene 'not in accord with Othello's character'[8]). But if an actor or director must make significant changes in the script to sustain a desired romantic or heroic image (the last

scene of *Coriolanus* is another good example), what has happened to the process of interpretation? Indeed, as Stanley Wells asks, 'where does the borderline come between interpretation and fresh creation?'[9] There is a large gap between the good quarto of *Romeo and Juliet* and *West Side Story*, but, along that spectrum, at what point do production and interpretation turn into rewriting, even translation? In the words of Falstaff, 'a question to be asked'.

My final category is the hardest to characterize or define but is potentially the most interesting for the scholar. These are what I term *conventional* cuts or changes wherein a director, wittingly or unwittingly, makes alterations to remove a disparity between the original logic of presentation (what was shared then by dramatist, actor, and spectator) and what seems to make sense to us today. The problem of staging Gloucester's attempted suicide at Dover Cliff is a classic example, but other less obvious changes or omissions can be equally revealing.

Consider first modern lighting effects, particularly in Elizabethan scenes of night and darkness. For playgoers today, going to the theatre means sitting in a darkened auditorium watching actors perform in a lighted space, but such was not the case at the Globe where, presumably, actors and spectators shared the same light that varied only when the sun moved behind a cloud. To denote night and darkness Shakespeare thereby had to call upon conventional signals (for example torches, lanterns, candles, costume, appropriate acting). In contrast, except for outdoor matinees the modern director can draw upon many sophisticated lighting effects that no one, myself included, expects to be relinquished. But the moment that modern lighting brings verisimilar darkness to an Elizabethan scene, something distinctive has been

---

[7] In his account of John Dexter's 1964 production for the National Theatre starring Sir Laurence Olivier, Kenneth Tynan notes that 'Othello's brief and dramatically pointless appearance is cut, in accordance with sound theatrical custom' (*'Othello': The National Theatre Production*, 1966, p. 11). For a revealing discussion of cuts and alterations in this production, see Wells, 'Shakespeare's Text on the Modern Stage', pp. 183–7.

[8] Cited in the Variorum edition, ed. Horace Howard Furness (Philadelphia, 1886), p. 237.

[9] 'Shakespeare's Text on the Modern Stage', p. 189.

changed. Thus, the modern director uses lighting to establish stage darkness and then has the actors enter carrying torches or groping in the dark or unable to see something of importance; he thereby starts with a verisimilar stage night as a justification for confusion in the dark. But the King's Men used dialogue, torches, nightgowns, groping in the dark, and failures in 'seeing' – all presented in full light – to establish the illusion of darkness for a spectator who, presumably, would infer night from such signals and stage behaviour. For us, the lighting technician supplies night and then the actors perform accordingly; for them, the actors provided the signals and then the audience co-operated in supplying the darkness. For us, one figure fails to see another *because* the stage is dark; for them, one figure failed to see another and therefore the stage was *assumed* to be dark. In the age of Shakespeare, a greater burden thereby lay upon the dramatist, the actor, and the spectator, for only through such imaginative participation could the illusion be sustained. Remember the choric injunctions from *Henry V*: 'let us.../ On your imaginary forces work'; 'Piece out our imperfections with your thoughts'; 'eke out our performance with your mind' (Prologue, ll. 17–18, 23; 3.0.35).

Given the availability of superior modern technology, one may ask, why worry about the original conventions? For one thing, as Lee Mitchell has pointed out, Shakespeare's 'imaginary darkness' had some distinct advantages, for 'no matter how deep the imaginary gloom, the audience could always see the performer quite clearly'. As Mitchell notes, 'many scenes of imaginary darkness actually depend upon daylight visibility for their full effect'.[10] Consider the murder of Banquo where, by the end of the scene, the theatrical darkness is often so deep today that a spectator cannot make out what is happening. Indeed, I recently saw one production in which I *think* that the third murderer's function was to help Fleance escape, but, because the stage was so dark, I could not be sure. But in a Jacobean production no such doubt could have existed for a viewer. Moreover, the scene enacts a murder but also enacts an escape that, as revealed by the dialogue, is accompanied by the putting out of a light: 'Who did strike out the light?' asks the third murderer; 'Was't not the way?' replies the first

(3.3.19). Thus, the original spectator would have recognized that the three murderers end the scene with the body of Banquo in a conventional darkness (the putting out of an on-stage light is one signal for such darkness), but that spectator would also have seen clearly their frustration and failure ('We have lost best half of our affair') represented by their inability to extinguish the light that is Fleance. The killing of Banquo and the putting out of the light help to epitomize what the Macbeths, the creatures of night and darkness, are doing to Scotland (and to themselves), but a director's imposition of a modern verisimilar stage night upon the scene may oversimplify the situation by calling attention away from the failure of the forces of darkness. Many modern productions thereby realize the rich darkness of the murder at the expense of the light of a visible escape.

A second example of the metaphoric advantages of the Elizabethan approach to night and darkness can be found in the last two scenes of *Othello*. I will forgo an exploration of the rich network of images in the final scene linked to 'Put out the light, and then put out the light', but the previous scene, with its violence and aftermath, is complicated enough. Here, as with the murder of Banquo, most directors will provide a deep stage darkness to justify the many allusions to night and to confusion in the dark and thereby make credible for a modern audience the behaviour of Roderigo, Iago, Cassio, Gratiano, and Lodovico. But the spectator watching the scene in 'imaginary darkness' may get a much richer effect, for that spectator would be even more conscious of the manipulative control of Iago, who literally controls the light through much of the scene, and, equally important, the various failures of the other on-stage figures to see and understand what is truly happening. Here as with the murder of Desdemona moments later, darkness is linked to a failure to see, a failure associated not with verisimilar night but with Iago's poison and with a blindness on the part of the observer. As with the earlier eavesdropping, the emphasis here (under Jacobean conventions) can fall upon the gaps or spaces between people, the darkness of misperception, the

---

[10] 'Shakespeare's Lighting Effects', *Speech Monographs*, 15 (1948), 72–84; p. 83.

blindness of inner night, all of which will soon be epitomized tragically in the final scene. Shakespeare has constructed this moment so that his original spectator could imaginatively experience the night but still could see clearly the various groups on stage and, more important, see how they fail to see or understand what is happening. Again, as with the comparable scene in *Macbeth*, verisimilar stage night may satisfy a modern literalism at the expense of some central tragic images and, in effect, may blur the truly insidious darkness.

A related problem for the director wrestling with the original conventions grows out of the imposition upon many Shakespearian scenes by both editors and theatrical professionals of what can be an in-appropriate sense of 'place'. Bernard Beckerman, for one, has demonstrated the fluidity of staging at the Globe and the generalized if not non-existent locales for most scenes,[11] but many current editions still devote considerable space and attention to 'where' an action takes place whether or not the scene itself initiates such a question. Perhaps the most controversy has been generated by act 2 of *King Lear* where within one sequence Kent is left alone, asleep, in the stocks; Edgar enters for a speech of twenty-one lines; and, after his departure, Lear and his group enter to find Kent. Critics and editors have struggled with the apparent anomaly; directors often resort to lighting to black out Kent during Edgar's speech. According to such modern reasoning, the presence of the stocks and the recently completed action involving Oswald, Edmund, Cornwall, and others implies one 'place' (for example, the courtyard of a castle) which is incompatible with a fleeing Edgar who has escaped by means of 'the happy hollow of a tree'. Clearly, most critics, editors, and directors would rather not have Kent and Edgar visible at the same time, but would prefer Edgar's speech to constitute a 'new' scene in a 'new' place – hence the division on the page through scene divisions and some kind of imposed division or break on stage, either through lighting or use of a second acting area or both.

At the Globe, however, the King's Men had no way to black out Kent, nor is there any evidence for a clearing of the stage or any break in the flow of the action. Rather, both the Quarto and the Folio suggest

that Shakespeare chose to have the two figures visible at the same time, not only making no effort to hide the juxtaposition but indeed encouraging a staging that would draw all possible attention to it. The results can be a highly emphatic theatrical effect – what I term theatrical italics – that should tease us into making connections between the two figures. On the open stage, the stocks need not signal a courtyard or any specific locale but could suggest a general sense of imprisonment or bondage, just as Edgar can be a virtuous but beleaguered figure in flight, anywhere. What is important is the juxtaposition, the pairing of these two figures in comparable situations, a juxta-position rich in potential meanings that can easily be blurred by scenic divisions or modern lighting or other supposed 'improvements' that, in fact, impose an anachronistic logic upon a distinctive Shake-spearian effect.

Less often discussed but equally telling is the sequence in act 2 of *As You Like It* where in scene 5 the Duke's banquet is set up on stage (see lines 26–7, 55–6) and then enjoyed in scene 7 with no indication that it is removed for the brief scene 6 (the first appearance of Orlando and Adam in Arden). Both the new Arden and Variorum editors puzzle over the sequence; thus Richard Knowles concludes (p. 109): 'the early setting of the table seems to me thoroughly puzzling; it is totally unnecessary, for the banquet could have been carried on, as banquets usually were, at the beginning of scene 7.' Directors thereby find various ways to eliminate the anomaly. For example, Robin Phillips rearranged the sequence into scene 6, then scene 5, then scene 7, so that the banquet was set up and then enjoyed *after* Orlando's scene with Adam. In contrast, in his recent Royal Shakespeare Company production (1980–1), Terry Hands cut the relevant lines in scene 5 so that the banquet first appeared (silently, with no directions from Amiens) in scene 7.

Almost everyone agrees that Shakespeare did not have to introduce a banquet into the end of scene 5. Yet he did. Although editorial and directorial tastes have muddied the waters, can we not still consider the advantages of having a 'banquet' in full view during

---

[11] See *Shakespeare at the Globe 1599–1609* (New York, 1962), p. 66 and *passim*.

the speeches that constitute scene 6? In particular, how would the highly visible presence of such a meal (again, with no way to black it out at the Globe) affect our reaction to Adam's 'O, I die for food' and Orlando's subsequent string of 'if' clauses: 'If this uncouth forest yield anything savage, I will either be food for it or bring it for food to thee. . . . I will here be with thee presently, and if I bring thee not something to eat, I will give thee leave to die; but if thou diest before I come, thou art a mocker of my labor. . . . thou shalt not die for lack of a dinner if there live anything in this desert.' If the food that Orlando will find in scene 7 is here seen by the audience (present, but symbolically just out of reach), these 'if' clauses carry a different weight. Rather, as with Kent and Edgar (or as with a Bach fugue), meaning and effect often are inseparable from juxtaposition and context, especially in a theatre with great potential for metaphoric and thematic links. To clear the stage in order to maintain a decorous modern sense of place is greatly to simplify the situation and to run the risk of eliminating a rich and potentially meaningful effect, a good insight into the nature of Arden and perhaps the nature of romantic comedy as well, especially since the 'if' clauses here are recapitulated and intensified in scene 7 (see lines 113–26) and then developed at length by Rosalind in act 5. Much virtue in if. And much virtue in the original conventions and the original logic of presentation.

Given my admiration for many directors, I do not wish to sound too negative a note or single out anyone as the villain of this piece. Indeed, if there must be a villain, it would be what Leontes calls the 'wide gap of time' (5.3.154) that separates us from the Elizabethans (along with the tacit assumption that 'modern' equals 'better'). As I understand the situation, behind the directorial changes (and behind much related academic discourse) lies the large and significant issue of trust. Despite the universal lip service (Macbeth calls it 'mouth honour'), how many of us in the theatre or the university really trust Shakespeare's knowhow and skills to the extent that we feel a responsibility to *dis*cover and *re*cover his techniques and meanings? For both the actor and the spectator, a good production should provide a voyage of discovery, a bringing to life of the script (from those dead double columns of many student editions) not available in any other way. To cut from the script the anomalies, the clogs, the supposed warts is to make a smoother voyage but to limit the discoveries. The more arduous path is based upon that trust in Shakespeare. In answer to the director's question 'does it work?' let us oppose Prospero's comment at the first meeting of Miranda and Ferdinand: 'It works' (1.2.494). Such an affirmation, however, requires trust. Thus, if Shakespeare, like Hermione, is to be brought back to life, we must remember what Paulina told Leontes: 'It is required / You do awake your faith.'

'HE SHALL LIVE A MAN FORBID': INGMAR BERGMAN'S 'MACBETH'

ANN FRIDÉN

Although at some times popular, Shakespeare has at others been a rare guest on the Swedish stage. The Second World War stands out as a particularly lean period. During these years only nine of his plays were mounted at major theatres, three of them – *A Midsummer Night's Dream*, and, significantly, *Macbeth* and *Henry V* – not being put on until 1944/5. When *Macbeth* opened at a provincial theatre in November 1944, a Stockholm critic thought it astonishing that this most topical of Shakespeare's plays had not been performed at other theatres. He was not aware, apparently, that the director, Ingmar Bergman, had produced *Macbeth* at a student theatre in Stockholm at the beginning of the war.[1]

All through his career, Bergman has constantly returned to certain classical authors such as Ibsen, Molière and Strindberg, and to some of their works in particular.[2] However, it is equally striking that he has produced very little Shakespeare. An amateur production in 1941 of *A Midsummer Night's Dream* and productions in 1975 and 1979 of *Twelfth Night* are the only works he has directed apart from *Macbeth*. But *Macbeth*, on the other hand, absorbed his attention three times in the same decade – 1940, 1944, and 1948. Bergman has explained that he has done so little Shakespeare because of his admiration for Alf Sjöberg's productions. 'This is Sjöberg's territory. There is no reason for me to take on Shakespeare, because I feel that his direction is congruent with the plays.'[3] But this also implies that his own relation to Shakespeare has been such that he has not felt the urge to produce the plays – except for *Macbeth*.

'UNDER A HAND ACCURS'D': 'MACBETH' 1940

Bergman's first *Macbeth* opened in very special circumstances and would seem to have meant a great deal to him. As a schoolboy he had built highly sophisticated toy theatres where he put on spectacular shows, and he had even planned a toy production of *Macbeth*, which he loved for being such an 'exceedingly glorious and gruesomely bloody' play.[4] When he became the director of a student theatre in Stockholm in 1938 at the age of twenty, it was all still mainly an aesthetic game to him. 'Only very late did I realize that a play might have an intellectual purpose. That I myself had such a purpose with a production of my own came still later', he has confessed.[5]

Bergman was not particularly interested in politics

---

1 This article is based on material intended for a Ph.D. thesis on some twentieth-century Swedish productions of *Macbeth*. I have had access only to press reviews for Bergman's first two productions, but for the one staged in 1948 I have been able to refer to Bergman's prompt-book, the stage manager's script, the designer's scenic model, a large selection of photographs (all this at the Gothenburg Museum for Theatre History), and the script of Anders Ek, the leading actor (in the possession of Mrs Ingrid Ek, Stockholm). I have also interviewed Carl-Johan Ström, the designer (30 May 1981), Ulla Malmström, Second Witch (7 December 1981), and Ingmar Bergman (6 September 1982). Up to now, no account of Bergman's *Macbeths* has made use of this material.
2 See Lise-Lone Marker and Frederick J. Marker, *Ingmar Bergman: Four Decades in the Theater* (Cambridge, 1982).
3 Henrik Sjögren, *Ingmar Bergman på teatern* (Stockholm, 1968), p. 302.
4 Interview, 6 September 1982.
5 Sjögren, *Ingmar Bergman*, p. 295.

or, for that matter, in world affairs, so it is doubtful if his main reason for putting on *Macbeth* was political. But events were to shake him considerably, and the story of *Macbeth* became suddenly very relevant. After one of the last rehearsals, as the actors were walking home through the streets of Stockholm, they learnt that Denmark had just been occupied, and that Norway was at war. It was 9 April 1940.

When *Macbeth* opened on 13 April all the young men at the theatre had been called up but had been granted a few days' leave. This was the first time that the theatre had had press reviews, but it was the experimental staging of the play that attracted most attention. On the podium of a grammar school assembly hall a medieval-type simultaneous stage had been erected. There was no curtain and all the acting areas were in full view: part of a heath with a tree and horizon, a castle with a gate and hall, and a staircase leading to an upper floor with two rooms. The critics commented that there was not much space for moving about, but that that problem had been very cleverly solved. They were also struck by the appropriately mysterious effect of the lighting. There were quite a number of cuts in the text, the number of Scottish lords being reduced in particular, so there was a smaller cast. Bergman himself had to step in and take the part of Duncan. It was not his acting that was applauded, however, but his ingenious staging and intelligent instruction. The actors were given short but fair reviews, but there was no mention of their interpretation and the topicality of the play, which is quite surprising in view of the shattering world events of the week before.

Explaining how this *Macbeth* had changed from being an 'aesthetic game', Bergman wrote:

For a short while we young inexperienced amateurs caught a glimpse of the essence of the theatre. Blood, nerves, appearance, reality, death, and regeneration merged into a strange and wonderful fabric, whose pattern reflected Man's eternal riddles, the immeasurable tragedy and infinite beauty of Life; a burning-glass enlarging, simplifying, but also revealing, gathering the sunbeams into a bright spot, concentrating, scorching.

(*Helsingborgs Dagblad*, 14 November 1944)

'SLEEP NO MORE': 'MACBETH' 1944

Without losing his fascination for the aesthetic, Bergman continued to explore this 'essence of the theatre'. For some years he worked at the Swedish Playwrights' Studio, a meeting-place for those dramatists and actors in the capital who dissociated themselves from the prevailing Swedish policy, i.e. not to offend the Germans. Here he directed the very first production of Kaj Munk's *Niels Ebbesen*, which had been banned in Denmark by the occupying powers. He later admitted that although it was natural for him to belong to this group, he did not at the time fully realize the danger of what he was doing.[6] Moreover, when Bergman decided to put on *Macbeth* once again in the autumn of 1944, he did not hesitate to describe it, in his programme note, explicitly as an 'anti-Nazi' drama. He had just started his career as director of the Helsingborg City Theatre, and in an advance notice he characterized this production as follows: 'mildness, frenzy, thriller, modern people, simplified setting – religious service' (*Helsingborgs Dagblad*, 14 November 1944).

The setting was, in fact, so simplified that the reviewers did not write much about it, but it was said to be concise and effective. The ramp of stairs that connected stage and auditorium was an important acting area. A few published photos show Duncan's camp, the battlefield, and Macbeth's bedchamber. The first was set against a plain, light backdrop with a high wall stage right, while a big tree with the witches crouching beneath was on the left. The chamber contained a fur-covered bed, an arch, and an immense crucifix. Lighting played an important part, and particularly red was used for special effects. The sky was continually black or red, and spotlights cut through the darkness, casting shadows.

The performance started in complete darkness giving particular emphasis to the mournful sounds that came from the three witches, who were portrayed as women mourning their dead on the battlefield. Their parts had been considerably shortened. One of them was given a larger number of lines than the others, and was called a 'Sibyl'. Not only did she prophesy to Macbeth as he walked past, but she

---

[6] *Ibid.* p. 305.

remained in silence on stage for much of the performance, her anguished and wailing voice being heard before the crimes were committed. The unfathomable tragedy of the drama was felt to be concentrated in her.

Ingrid Luterkort, as Lady Macbeth, totally dominated the first part. Her costume, her lips and fingernails were all a deep blood red, and the critics described her as an iron-willed cynic and a sensuous she-cat, with a cold stare and stealthy step. In contrast, the words used of the early Macbeth were 'weak', 'gentle', and 'fragile'. Up to the murder of Duncan the erotic game became the psychological basis of the production, and the crime was planned in or near the marriage-bed.

During the first part the style of acting was felt to be particularly 'modern' – the voices were seldom raised, the verse was spoken quickly as if it were prose. The overall atmosphere was that of a dream-like medieval ballad. Bergman was not satisfied with this, afterwards criticizing himself for his own old desire to 'aestheticize'. The first part, he thought, should have been done 'as a terrible howl, not as a chronicle play in ballad form'. It became too beautiful.[7]

If Bergman's characterization 'mildness' best applied to the first part of the production, his word 'frenzy' better described the second half, which gave the impression of a long nightmare. This was brought out clearly in the description of the change in Macbeth. The actor, Sture Ericson, hinted at continuous inner disintegration on the one hand and displayed the megalomania of the tyrant on the other. He intimidated those around him with hysterical outbursts of arrogance, and fits of anguish were reflected in his white face and staring eyes. The climax of this terror came in act 5, scene 3, which Bergman directed as an orgy of despair with laughing women and shadowy men, ending in a drunken, possessed gavotte with the actors dancing out one by one through a cone of red light, as if in a Danse Macabre.

The red light had already been used symbolically in act 4, scene 1, which was staged not in the witches' house but in Macbeth's chamber. Lady Macbeth slept while Macbeth, half-naked, tossed restlessly beside her. Blood-like streaks surged across the walls as the Sibyl and her sisters emerged at the foot of the bed, a

nightmare or vision of agony for Macbeth. Here, the witches became a psychological reality. Banquo's ghost assumed the same meaning in that he was not shown on stage but seemed to be a hallucination of Macbeth's. This led the critics to write of the King as one already insane. Although the supernatural elements were thus reduced, both by cuts and by other interpretative changes, the reviews were on the whole favourable, as 'the drama was moved into the world of reality without losing anything of the mystery of poetry and dreams' (*Sydsvenska Dagbladet Snällposten*, 20 November 1944).

Bergman's last words to describe his production were 'religious service'. There were several elements in the production that were reminiscent of church, for example the very large crucifix in Macbeth's bedchamber, with an ugly, distorted, and bloody Christ. Lady Macbeth read her husband's letter and invoked possession while standing beneath it, and in the sleepwalking scene some kind of conversion was hinted at. With his back to the crucifix Macbeth questioned the Sibyl about his future. The crucifix represented a possible choice – the Crown of Life instead of the crown of Scotland. But because it was so hideously distorted the figure of Christ might well have served to symbolize the sufferings inflicted by Macbeth and at the same time have been a mirror of his own sufferings.

At least two other scenes were given religious interpretation. The first was the banquet scene which was brightly illuminated and framed by an arch, reminding one of the reviewers of a medieval painting of the Last Supper. The other was the last scene, in which Malcolm's final speech was cut. Here Macbeth's fall was literal – he was wounded on an upper landing, took a few tottering steps and fell, dying. The victors knelt and held up their sword-hilts like crosses against the horizon, 'a new order coloured by the hopes, in 1944, of a non-belligerent country' (*Stockholms-Tidningen*, 20 November 1944).

The critics were extremely cautious when writing of the play's current interest. Most of the daily papers had only very general comments or quotations from the play to show its relevance for the contemporary

---

[7] *Ibid.* p. 298.

audience. Only two of the Stockholm papers (*Svenska Dagbladet* and *Dagens Nyheter*) drew specific parallels to political reality, one quoting Bergman's programme note on *Macbeth* as an anti-Nazi drama, while the other wrote of 'the reality of evil and violence, which, before Hitler's appearance on the scene, we were on the point of idealizing out of existence'.

The most surprising comment came from a reviewer who thought that the production had *not* alluded to contemporary events (*Aftonbladet*, 20 November 1944)! To a certain extent the performance probably invited a comment of this kind. Being obsessed with Man, but not very interested in Society, Bergman had put on a production that did not so much present an anatomy of Nazi tyranny as explore the psychology of a Fascist-like tyrant.

Such a person was Bergman's main interest in his script for the much acclaimed film *Hets* (*Frenzy/Torment*), released in October 1944. A description of Caligula, the film's Latin teacher, seems also to fit Bergman's 1944 Macbeth. He was, on the one hand, an authoritarian and sadistic character, exhibiting a flagrant disregard for the sufferings of others, while on the other hand he proved to be the victim of his own fear and loneliness. His only means of keeping people around him was by rendering them powerless through fear. The attitude towards Caligula is one of both hate and pity, and it is quite conceivable that the portrayal of Macbeth was coloured by the same dichotomy. This would account for a review questioning Bergman's Christian approach on the grounds that war criminals would also be worthy of understanding and compassion (*Scen och Salong*, 12, 1944).

'BLOOD WILL HAVE BLOOD': 'MACBETH'
1948

When Bergman next started to work on *Macbeth*, early in 1948, he was resident director at the Gothenburg City Theatre. Here, the elaborate stage machinery and lighting boards of his toy theatres materialized in full scale, allowing him to develop his aesthetic interests. However, time had moved on, too, and he had now no political intentions whatsoever. In possession of considerable material and artistic resources, his main concern was to use them for 'telling a

cruel story with some kind of objectivity'.[8] Nevertheless, this production was coloured by Bergman's thoughts and reflections on the human condition.

Bergman has very clearly explained his beliefs regarding hell, evil, and the devil.[9] He has always thought of hell as created by man and existing here on earth. For a very long time he believed that there was a virulent evil in man, an evil that did not depend on inheritance or environment, but that could be called original sin. As an expression of this evil power he created in his early drama- and film-texts a person with devilish traits that was, so to speak, 'a spring in the clockwork'. These ideas were very prominent in his work at this time, for example in his film *Fängelse* (*Prison/The Devil's Wanton*), produced in late 1948, in which existential *Angst* and loneliness surround people and religion and the Church are in the service of hell.

In his 1948 production of *Macbeth* Bergman used every device to create an impression of virulent evil and man-made hell. Carl-Johan Ström, his designer, had constructed a permanent set on either side of the proscenium. Stage right there was a huge tree for the witches to climb into. The branches framed the top of the stage opening, and four hanged men dangled from them (see plate I A). Their bodies were replaced with bloody carcasses of oxen during the banquet. Stage left, Ström had erected a tower with an outward staircase. This massive construction was made to seem even heavier and more compact by its dark colours. The heath was simply the open stage stretching over sixty feet to the cyclorama, and there were two decaying, twisted oaks outlined against a bright sky. The impression was surrealistic, with its seemingly endless expanse, strange figures stretching up towards space, and morbid silhouettes. The setting was at once expressive and symbolic, suggesting a barren sterility that forms the background to the void of Macbeth's Scotland.

Macbeth's castle had been built on the elevator stage and contained an upper stage and an inner study that could be closed off by a curtain, painted with pictures copied from the Bayeux Tapestry. Thus each act

---

[8] Interview, 6 September 1982.
[9] *Bergman om Bergman*, eds. Stig Björkman, Torsten Manns and Jonas Sima (Stockholm, 1970), p. 43.

could run on without pause. The main body of the building stood just ten feet inside the proscenium and completely covered the stage opening. It was ten feet high, and with the superstructure being another ten, the final impression was that of a towering and brooding threat. This was emphasized by the fact that there was so little open space surrounding it. In all his work at this time Bergman seems to have had a 'claustrophobic inclination for the cramped space'.[10] The castle, with its heavy horizontals and pillars that in spite of their sturdiness seemed hardly able to support the roof, certainly makes one sense the atmosphere of a prison. Bergman's Macbeth was indeed 'cabin'd, cribb'd, confin'd'.

The colours, various reds, added to the heaviness of this construction. The colour scheme symbolized, of course, all the blood that flows through this drama, but it may have had yet another meaning. In *Cries and Whispers* (1972) Bergman explains that the red of the interior was how he thought of the inside of the soul when he was a child. It was like a moist membrane in different shades of red.[11] In Ström's set dark colours predominated, but there was a bright orange-red pillar next to the witches' tree. Ström had technical problems to solve. Bergman wanted such extremely brilliant white spotlights that part of the set had to be repainted. To Bergman strong, white light, particularly sunlight, is a threat, something frightening and merciless. 'In sunlight I get claustrophobia. My nightmares are always drenched in sunlight.'[12] The use of a wealth of reds and brilliant spots culminated during the banquet, when the only divergent colour was the blue costume of Banquo's ghost, and when Bergman's dramatic lighting plot aimed at the impression of a hangover.

Bergman also availed himself of other means than architecture, colour, and lighting to create a vile atmosphere to surround Macbeth. The crudeness and ill manners of the Scottish court were shown in an interlude between act 1, scene 7 and act 2, scene 1, when a sword-dance was performed by Malcolm and Rosse. They were watched from the stairs by a group of drunken men holding torches and tankards, and, from outside Duncan's door, by the first witch. Bergman's belief that the Church was explicitly in the service of hell was emphasized by one of Banquo's

murderers being dressed as a priest in a black cassock and with a large cross hanging round his neck, and by the porter's equivocator being exchanged for a preacher. Behind this interpretation lay probably Bergman's antagonistic feelings towards his father, a vicar, and particularly his indignation at the pro-German attitude of his father during the war.[13] Finally, and not least important, Bergman gave his production a very definite scenic form. There were three acts, each with a violent last scene: the discovery of the murder of Duncan (act 2, scene 4 was omitted), the killing of the Macduffs, and the final fight. The ruthlessness of the protagonist was thus clearly emphasized.

By making certain cuts in the text, such as the compassionate messenger to Lady Macduff and much of Malcolm's testing of Macduff on good and evil kingship, Bergman allowed little alleviation in the evil atmosphere that he had created. But it is significant that he compensated for his inroads into the text by theatrical means. As the curtain rose for the last act it was on a stage of contrasts. The proscenium still had its dark and looming tree and tower, and behind these was a light and airy arcade with slender pillars and softly rounded arches and two thin and stylized trees with big leaves (see plate I B). Three couples in light and gaily-coloured dresses danced in the arcade. The effect on the audience, still remembering the sword dance and the heavy granite, flaming reds, and barren trees of Scotland, would have been one of surprise. The proscenium setting became a doorway through which the spectators looked into a new, and happier world. However, as the actors started to speak it would also have become clear to the audience that such harmony was not yet for Scotland.

Who or what, then, was the prime mover behind Macbeth's actions, the devilish 'spring in the clock-work'? Everything indicates the witches. The reviewers agreed that they were Fates, determining the

10 Marianne Höök, *Ingmar Bergman* (Stockholm, 1962), p. 61.

11 Maria Bergom-Larsson, *Ingmar Bergman och den borgerliga ideologin* (Stockholm, 1977), p. 12.

12 *Bergman om Bergman*, p. 81.

13 Jörn Donner, 'Three Scenes with Ingmar Bergman' (film interview, 1975).

development of Macbeth. They were on stage for the major part of the performance, to a large extent in or near their tree, where they watched and listened and by their reactions mirrored the drama in front of them. But they also took active part, particularly in the mass scenes.

Bergman had instructed his witches to create their own characters. The first was a cripple, spending the whole performance on her knees, the second had made herself up to look like a drowned woman, dressed in black rags and her face greenish-yellow, while the third was dressed as a whore, in a red wig and a tight, red dress that left one shoulder bare. Her mask was a copy of Lady Macbeth's face, and her heavy chains and the cross-garters on her legs resembled Macbeth's costume, thus establishing the link between the protagonists and the witches. This was also the first time that the relationship between Macbeth's opening line and the witches' 'fair is foul' had been brought out in Swedish. The credit for the new translation at this point must be given to Anders Ek, who played Macbeth and who seems to have studied the original very conscientiously.

After the murder of Banquo the witches took on yet another meaning. In the script of Anders Ek there is a note at the beginning of act 3, scene 4: 'pursued by the Furies', and Ulla Malmström (Second Witch) used the same words in an interview to explain the function of the witches towards the end of the play. Shakespeare's Weird Sisters would seem to have most in common with contemporary belief in witchcraft, but there are certainly classical elements in them as well. There are many different aspects to the Furies, but here they were obviously used as goddesses of vengeance and punishment. During the final battle they squatted on the ground, greedily waiting for the fulfilment of their prophecy, and at the end they fell on Macbeth's severed body, collecting their spoils. Before that, Macbeth had been brought to the brink of insanity, which was also in the power of the Furies.

Finally, there is one more possible interpretation of Bergman's witches. One critic voiced the opinion that in them 'the ugly entrails of the subconscious are turned inside out. They demonstrate all there is of fear, and disgust, and a kind of perverse voluptuousness' (*Expressen*, 15 March 1948). They seem to have been the tangible expression of Bergman's view of original sin.

Ingmar Bergman used his 1948 production to probe into the darkness of Macbeth's soul, finding there a man gradually disintegrating morally. However, his production was not as clear-cut as one might imagine. Anders Ek gave a highly intense performance inspired by the Stanislavski method and had even daubed himself with the blood of a pig for the scene in which Duncan is murdered. His interpretation of Macbeth differed completely from Bergman's, and he would not give way. The difference is apparent even in the acting text. Bergman had chosen Hagberg's translation from 1850, whereas Ek preferred Hallström's from 1928. Almost one-third of Macbeth's part was changed, making it more modern, and also more poetic.

Ek's interpretation was coloured by his very radical political views. Blame was put on feudal society, in which the only possible occupation for Macbeth was that of the warrior, even if this did not suit his nature. Anders Ek did not see Macbeth as a flawless character, but in his script described him as 'unstable, naive, excitable, impressionable, an easily inspired poet with profound sensitivity and enormous imaginative power'. At a certain moment the pressure of circumstances became too great for him, and he chose murder as the easiest way out. But the root of the evil was in the world around him, which had denied him his right to be himself.

Ek's Macbeth had already contemplated murder, but he was optimistic and hoped that things would come his way without his being forced to act. In one way he regretted being persuaded by his wife's incitements, but thought it pleasant to yield and be weak. The main objective of Ek's Macbeth was to win peace and harmony. But – 'I am now two persons'. Such was the effect of the first murder on the murderer. On the one hand, he remained amiable and generous, while on the other, he was tormented by his constant dishonesty. The second murder excited him, and he now acted with feverish, hectic zest. Photographs of the production provide evidence of the change in Macbeth. After the murder of Duncan he donned not only a new costume, but also new facial expressions and gestures, showing hardness, hatred, contempt, and fury, instead of eagerness, love, and hope. The crimes he committed in order to win peace had instead deprived him of it.

An interpretation along these lines would, of course, at times be inconsistent with the rest of the production. The witches – Fates and original sin personified – were hardly to be met in a friendly, encouraging way, and the brooding, threatening stage painted in shades of blood and darkness was not the right background for a tender poet. The reviewers criticized Ek's Hamlet-like interpretation and his hesitant rendering of the lines at the beginning of the performance. But his behaviour at the banquet, his second meeting with the witches, and the final battle were highly thought of, i.e. scenes following the murder of Banquo, when he abandoned his more restrained acting approach to the role.

Karin Kavli, as Lady Macbeth, portrayed a loving wife, strong enough to exercise power over her husband without turning into a monster. She was also the business-like murderess, and the perfect hostess at the banquet, but the critics did not experience any demonic power filling her with 'direst cruelty'. The emphasis was thus put on a normal human being capable of good and evil. During the sleep-walking scene she passed her hand over the open flame of a candle. This dramatic device was found disconcerting by some critics. Others were impressed by her acting. They felt to the very marrow that Lady Macbeth's soul was already in hell.

Distractions of this type caused general complaint among the critics. Certainly, the setting caught the fateful, bloody, and terrible atmosphere, and the multiple acting areas and elevator enabled the director to give the play an excellent rhythm without any dull periods. But 'the eye was so satiated that the ear became distracted' (*Stockholms-Tidningen*, 13 March 1948). Bergman nowadays considers this fair comment. The 1940s were years of experiment, teaching him how to use the possibilities of the theatre. His main interest has gradually switched towards text and actor, and he has willingly confessed that he has at times in the past availed himself of 'gimmicks'.[14]

However, Bergman does not as willingly accept the criticism, generally expressed, that he had read his own experience and view of life into the text instead of listening to it, and he has maintained that he has never deliberately produced a play against the intentions of the author.[15] In this case the two comments are not necessarily incompatible. Most of his visual effects could be legitimately claimed to be found in the text and mood of the play. And, thanks to Anders Ek, the text he offered his audience in 1948 was undoubtedly the most complete Swedish acting version up till then.

Even if both Bergman's professional productions displayed his interest in pictorial composition and lighting and included various theatricalities to emphasize the mood of the play, nevertheless these two *Macbeths* were very different. In Helsingborg in 1944, for example, a simplified setting was a necessity, but in Gothenburg in 1948, there was a well-equipped City Theatre to facilitate an elaborate staging.

Far more important, however, was the change in emphasis of the two productions. In 1944, the audience was given a psychological and to some extent political version of *Macbeth*. The witches were ordinary women, although one had the gift of prophecy, and religion was a positive force in an evil world. 'We must have Faith', wrote Bergman in his programme note at that time. Four years later, the moral issues were more important, and the production focused particularly on the forces of evil. The witches were the Fates and original sin incarnate, and even those who professed themselves to be religious were portrayed as vile. There was little to lighten this spiritual darkness, and although Malcolm's last speech was this time retained, the blocking and lighting of the final scene did not give prominence to the new king.

The reasons for this more sombre outlook may have been both personal and cultural. The revelation after the war of the true nature of the war crimes came as a terrible shock to Bergman.[16] At the same time the pessimism of the Swedish literary school of the 1940s and the influence of the increased importance of Kafka had helped to shape his attitudes.

Thus Ingmar Bergman's *Macbeth*s came at a time when he was exploring primarily the technical and

---

14 Sjögren, *Ingmar Bergman*, p. 314.   15 *Ibid.* p. 293.
16 Donner, 'Three Scenes'.

aesthetic possibilities of the theatre, but the productions also illuminate the problems that preoccupied him at that time, not only his own and not only those of the 1940s. By dwelling on the themes of insomnia and nightmare, blood and murder, evil and damnation, he touched the essence of *Macbeth*. It would seem, however, that theatrical effect dominated to the detriment of poetic quality.

In 1953, on looking back upon his three *Macbeth*s, Bergman concluded that the first and most naive production had been the best. The second was conceived as a psychological 'chamber play', which was a mistake. The third brought out more of the substance of the play, the wild and blood-stained saga, but it went wrong because of a difference in interpretation between himself and the leading actor,

who he now thought had been right (*Stockholms-Tidningen*, 31 December 1953). A fourth Bergman version of *Macbeth* might, in fact, be along the lines once suggested by Anders Ek, though without his political signature. Bergman has recently expressed the opinion that a person confronted by forces with which he cannot cope is no villain, but may well remain innocent even with blood-stained hands.[17] Up to the present, however, there has been no sign of a new production, although Bergman has shown that he likes to return to plays for a fresh interpretation, and although he once said of *Macbeth*: 'The fourth time I think I will make it.'[18]

---

17 Interview, 6 September 1982.
18 Laurence Kitchin, *Mid-Century Drama* (1960), p. 201.

IA *Macbeth*, Gothenburg City Theatre, 1948. Directed by Ingmar Bergman, designed by Carl-Johan Ström.
Act I, scene I: the heath

B *Macbeth*, Act 4, scene 3 (in the production's last act): England

IIA Komisarjevsky's production of *King Lear*, act 1, scene 1; Shakespeare Memorial Theatre, 1936

B The first scene of the Induction in Komisarjevsky's *Taming of the Shrew*, Shakespeare Memorial Theatre, 1939

KOMISARJEVSKY AT
STRATFORD-UPON-AVON

RALPH BERRY

'I am not in the least traditional,' said Theodore Komisarjevsky, in his motto-statement to the press shortly before the opening of his first Stratford production.[1] This was no other than the truth, and Komisarjevsky went on to illustrate it in six remarkable productions at the Shakespeare Memorial Theatre, from 1932 to 1939. They amused, astonished, and outraged. They gave the Theatre what international distinction it possessed during an otherwise lean period. They anticipated much of what has come to be regarded as normal, on today's stage. Even so, Komisarjevsky's seven seasons at Stratford have until recently been thought of as the work of a brilliant prankster, a professional *enfant terrible*. It is time to review as a whole Komisarjevsky's work at Stratford.

To begin with, the Stratford seasons contain almost all of Komisarjevsky's Shakespearian work on the English-speaking stage. His *King Lear* at Oxford in 1927 (with Randle Ayrton as Lear) was a pilot for the Stratford *Lear* of 1936. The notorious *Antony and Cleopatra* (New Theatre, 1936) was his only Shakespearian production of the 1930s in London. There is a late appendix, which I shall deal with in its place. Otherwise, there is nothing of substance; and Komisarjevsky was generally known as a director of modern plays, above all as a master of Chekhov. It is in that capacity that Gielgud praises him highly in his memoirs.[2] When Komisarjevsky came to direct *The Merchant of Venice* at Stratford in 1932, he was a month short of his fiftieth birthday: his reputation was already made, almost entirely outside Shakespeare.

That *Merchant of Venice*, and the productions that followed, saw Komisarjevsky always in the same capacity: he was a guest director. He had no institutional standing, though his annual invitation was recurring after 1934. He was in the first instance invited by the Memorial Theatre's director, W. Bridges-Adams. After Bridges-Adams resigned, in 1934, his successor, Ben Iden Payne, continued to invite Komisarjevsky. However, Sally Beauman states that 'his continuing presence at Stratford was due to the fact that Archie [Sir Archibald Flower, Chairman of the Board of Governors], and not Iden Payne, championed him. Archie appreciated the fact that Komisarjevsky productions attracted publicity and sold tickets.'[3] It is a fascinating alliance, the autocrat and the revolutionary. Later in the 1930s, Sir Archibald must have seen Komisarjevsky as a shield against the criticisms increasingly levelled at the SMT. There, at least, was a symbol of modernity and innovation. And in box-office terms, Komisarjevsky never failed.

If Komisarjevsky's status as guest director remained constant, so did his role. Throughout the decade he remained an *enfant terrible* and foe to the traditional. He gave enormous offence to the traditionalists, few pains being comparable to the violation of a fixed idea. The Stratford theatre records are studded with letters to the local press and reviews from the less wary of critics, which after some wrenchingly reluctant

The research for this paper was made possible by a Leave Fellowship from the Social Sciences and Humanities Research Council of Canada.

[1] Interview, *The Daily Telegraph*, 26 July 1932.
[2] John Gielgud, *Early Stages* (1939), pp. 84–8, 113, 153–4; *An Actor and His Time* (Harmondsworth, 1981), pp. 76–82.
[3] Sally Beauman, *The Royal Shakespeare Company: A History of Ten Decades* (Oxford, 1982), p. 143.

tribute to Komisarjevsky's artistry ask '*But is it Shakespeare?*' The rhetorical identification of Shakespeare, and a certain way of playing him, is a ploy of long standing. As against this order of pain, Komisarjevsky gave great pleasure. Four of his productions were comedies, all were spectacular. How influential they were is now emerging. No less than Peter Brook has acknowledged the ancestry, if not the paternity, of Komisarjevsky: '*Titus Andronicus* was a *show*; it descended in an unbroken line from the work of Komisarjevsky.'[4] There are other parallels between Komisarjevsky's work, and that of the post-war directors.

The new Shakespeare Memorial Theatre, built after the old theatre was destroyed by fire, opened in 1932; and the stage machinery that came with it ravished Komisarjevsky. His sets for *The Merchant of Venice* made delighted use of a chance for extravagant artificiality. Venice was a city of leaning towers and crooked houses, which split down the middle for the Belmont scenes. The pillar topped by the Lion of St Mark's departed stage right, while the Bridge of Sighs exited stage left. From the depths emerged the Belmont loggia, Portia and co. in tableau positions, rather in the style of the old cinema organ. Ivor Brown was reminded of a department store lift, 'First floor, caskets. Second floor, roof garden.'[5] The sliding of Venice to and from the wings grew a little tedious to many spectators, who complained that illusion was wantonly destroyed. But Komisarjevsky wished to sustain the note of unabashed theatricality.[6] And this was necessary, for he was bent on overthrowing the Irving/Benson/Tree model of the play, which still held sway at Stratford, that of *The Merchant of Venice* as a quasi-tragedy. As Komisarjevsky saw it, the play was a romantic comedy.

Hence the opening, a masque of grotesque black and white pierrots to the music of Bach's Toccata and Fugue in D Minor. They were shooed away by Launcelot Gobbo as Harlequin, and the play proper began. The *commedia dell'arte* touches were extended to Old Gobbo, as Pantaloon, and the Prince of Morocco as a golliwog. Komisarjevsky made further use of masks in the court scene: 'I shall try to bring out the power of that scene by having all the senators

of the Doge's court sitting round in a uniform dress, their faces covered by uniform masks. Not a human face will be visible but Portia's, and in the background there will be painted a shadowy ensemble of the court crowd – the sort of people who gloat over sensations in our present-day courts.'[7] The *commedia* had the last word, for 'at the end . . . it is Harlequin Gobbo who makes the final exit, yawning and stretching in relief that his labours are over'.[8] None of your alienated Antonios left alone on stage here.

This was a carnival Venice, the revellers ('fast, bright young people like the crowd we have in London today'[9]) attired in Venetian Renaissance garb with monstrous ruffs, by no means the setting for a major social issue or a human problem *à clef*. The casket scenes were treated with heartless vivacity, Nerissa shamelessly leading on Bassanio with the emphasized rhymes of 'Tell me where is fancy *bred* . . .'. It follows that Shylock could not dominate the production. 'I shall not have a sympathetic Shylock. The point of Shylock is revenge, and revenge can never be sympathetic.'[10] The reviewers took, with some surprise, to the astringent and unsentimentalized Shylock of Randle Ayrton. He seemed to them a Shylock such as the Elizabethans might have perceived, an old rascal who got his deserts.[11]

The reviewers made little, however, of a feature that looked to the future. Komisarjevsky played a virtually uncut text.[12] A few lines in Shylock's

---

[4] *Ibid.* p. 224. Sally Beauman writes of Peter Brook's *Love's Labour's Lost* (1946) as 'the spiritual heir of Komisarjevsky's 1932 *Merchant*' (*ibid.* p. 176).

[5] *The Observer*, 31 July 1932.

[6] Relating his childhood experiences of the Moscow theatre, Komisarjevsky remarked that 'The most unexpected transformations were achieved in full view of the audience' ('From Naturalism to Stage Design', in *Footnotes to the Theatre*, ed. R. D. Charques (1938), p. 80).

[7] Interview, *The Daily Telegraph*, 26 July 1932.

[8] *Birmingham Mail*, 26 July 1932.

[9] Interview, *The Daily Telegraph*, 26 July 1932.   [10] *Ibid.*

[11] See, for example, the review in *The Times*, 26 July 1932, and Ivor Brown's review in *The Weekend Review*, 30 July 1932.

[12] William P. Halstead specifies more substantial cuts, at 1.2.60–70; 1.2.82–9; 3.2.82–96; 3.4.53–6; and 5.1.259–66. *Shakespeare as Spoken: A Collation of 5000 Acting Editions and Promptbooks of Shakespeare*, 12 vols. (Ann Arbor and

court speech, the bagpipe-urine reference, went (presumably a minor Bowdlerization). There are trifling deletions at 2.2.121–6; 3.1.18; 3.2.72; and 5.1.32–3. Otherwise, Komisarjevsky followed the text meticulously. Moreover, he followed the Shakespearian scene order. Since the prompt-book is a palimpsest – it was used originally for the 1929 production at Stratford – one can see through the erasures that he reduced the number of indicated scenes from eighteen to fifteen. This was a fluid, speeded-up version; and Komisarjevsky allowed a single interval only. Of course, he played some tricks with inflections. One reviewer noted that Morocco, upon finding he had chosen the wrong casket, intoned 'O hell! What have we here?' in the manner of a motorist who had burst a tyre.[13] But all the fantastications were created out of a text that was itself untouched. That should be remembered, as we contemplate Komisarjevsky's dream-Venice, with its sprightly and inventive stagecraft, inexhaustible high spirits, and continuous delight in its own artifice. The reviewers, with varying degrees of delight and regret, acknowledged the theatrical virtuosity that had transformed a stereotype. And Komisarjevsky had a mere ten days to rehearse it.[14]

In 1933 Komisarjevsky repeated his *Merchant of Venice*, this time with George Hayes as Shylock and Fabia Drake again a successful Portia. His major production that season, however, was *Macbeth*, with George Hayes and Fabia Drake in the leading roles. This *Macbeth* was an ambitious attempt at universalizing the tragedy. Often, and incorrectly, referred to as a 'modern-dress' *Macbeth*, its impressions came from diverse sources. 'Komisarjevsky has eliminated time, and, so far as the text allows, has eliminated space; he has made the tragedy universal.'[15] While there were medieval shields and swords, the soldiers carried objects like rifles. The main allusion was to the twentieth century: 'Helmets of the German war type, and long military cloaks and uniforms of greenish-grey, form an outfit of marked Teutonic tendency.'[16] And the opening was a clear evocation of the World War:

The play opens in a mysterious twilight, in which three old hags are seen robbing a dead soldier who has been reduced to a skeleton. Against the sky, the mouths of two guns are pointing. The place appears to be a chateau that has been ruined by artillery, and a few broken columns alone are left standing.[17]

Komisarjevsky drew on the imagery of the war here; and throughout stressed that the action took place against a background of war.[18]

The *mise-en-scène* for this dark fable was constructed of aluminium. Scrolls, screens, a platform for the banquet and sleepwalking scenes, stairways, all were of metal. Variety came from adjustment of masses, and the play of light and colour.[19] This futurist, dehumanized setting was an apt metaphor for the action, a metallic nightmare. As Komisarjevsky saw it, the core of *Macbeth* was psychological, not supernatural. He ruthlessly cut the Witches' scenes to the bone: the opening scene consists only of 'A drum! a drum! Macbeth doth come'. But the metamorphosis of the Witches into aged Scottish fortune-tellers – their accents were considered the only Scottish element in the play – gave some offence; it was held to vulgarize the play. Several reviewers regretted the absence of 'Scotland', the traditional milieu of the action. Even so, the loss was a clear transference of 'Scotland' from the literal to the imagination. 'The strange, surreal images . . . show a setting in keeping with Macbeth's hallucinatory imagination rather than with most readers' visualization of the "Heath",

London, 1977–80), vol. 3. Save for the fourth passage (undeleted in the prompt-book), these passages are restored on the verso. I take it that Komisarjevsky decided to restore passages cut from Bridges-Adams's text of 1929. The prompt-books for Komisarjevsky's Stratford productions are listed and described in Charles Shattuck, *The Shakespeare Promptbooks: A Descriptive Catalogue* (Urbana, Illinois, 1965). Here and subsequently I identify each prompt-book by its listing in that work: *The Merchant of Venice* is Shattuck, 120.

13 *Stratford-upon-Avon Herald*, 29 July 1932.
14 Beauman, p. 125.
15 *Sheffield Daily Telegraph*, 24 April 1933.   16 *Ibid.*
17 *Birmingham Post*, 19 April 1933.
18 There was a recurring deployment of soldiery, and the prompt papers contain an elaborate Super plot for twenty-five. Macbeth spoke in staccato tones, oddly suggestive of a machine gun, and appeared to be a soldier under nervous stress.
19 There is a detailed analysis of the sets in *Punch*, 10 May 1933.

"Forres", "Inverness", and other locales given by modern editors.'[20]

Komisarjevsky made, said *The Times*, 'an attempt to relate Shakespeare to an age dominated by psychological conceptions, rationalizing the play's magic and witchcraft and making Banquo's ghost a mere figment of the imagination.'[21] 'Rationalizing' here meant no loss of intensity. 'But the horror that is to be derived from vagueness Mr Komisarjevsky endeavours to realize through expressionist means – for example, amplifiers drumming out incantations which Macbeth's conscience speaks, and shadows projected for bodies.'[22] The apparition of Banquo was a gigantic shadow of Macbeth himself thrown against his castle walls, and Macbeth's second visit to the Witches was transformed into 'a vision or dream in which, as he cries, "Blood will have blood", he seizes their shadows, black and menacing, thrown on the wall above him.'[23] There is a strong impression from the reviews that the very excellence of Komisarjevsky's expressionistic effects tended to diminish the psychological interest which the major actors were capable of communicating. W. A. Darlington, who admired the production, thought that 'The men and women of the play seem to dwindle to a phantasmagoria of shadows blown hither and thither by the wind of evil forces.'[24] That, it seems, was the price to be paid for this original and disturbing production, one that almost obliterated in the minds of its audiences all previous *Macbeth*s. All reviewers testify to the haunting, dreamlike quality of this metallic nightmare's images:

The castles of Inverness and Dunsinane, weird labyrinths built of aluminium, with ever-shifting storm clouds above them and the moonlight shining on their walls, glitter metallically. All movement is abrupt and harsh, matching the wildness of the scene.

> Foul whisperings are abroad: unnatural deeds
> Do breed unnatural troubles.

Lady Macbeth, alone, her taper among the other discarded properties, glides noiselessly down the castle steps, pallid, under a green light, wringing her hands, breathing heavily, and pausing now and then in her descent, while the doctor and the waiting woman, in the centre of the stage, watch her as she circles them and ascends the flight of steps on the other side.[25]

The acting text (Shattuck, 137) was fast, being cut in the interests of speed and concentration of impression. Among the major cuts were the Witches, who actually appeared only in the opening scene, thereafter existing via shadowgraph; act 3, scene 5; many of the longueurs of act 4, scene 2 (though the latter part, with its simplicity and pain, stayed uncut); act 5, scenes 4 and 6 (it is unnecessary to show the English army advancing on Macbeth, and conceptually undesirable for the production to move 'outside' the nightmare's centre); and the Young Siward episode. There was a single act drop (after 'Then 'tis most like / The sovereignty will fall upon Macbeth'). In all, this was a rapid but not vandalized playing text, one which reflected a coherent view of the play.

Its *succès de scandale* features aside, this *Macbeth* was widely recognized as brilliant theatre. Its limitations were felt to be those of the actors, rather than the director. Its most forward-looking virtues were, however, not fully appreciated at the time. Michael Mullin lists three features as cardinal: its use of multiple acting areas, the continuity of action, and its freedom from specific locale or period.[26] Against this it seems scarcely adequate to complain, as one critic did, that martlets nest but infrequently in aluminium.[27] The Johnsonian literalism of English theatre criticism died hard. Still, Komisarjevsky's handling of a major tragedy was too openly magisterial for such objections to weigh heavily.

The cardinal features of *Macbeth* were present in Komisarjevsky's next production, *The Merry Wives of Windsor* (1935). Again, we find the annihilation of time and space, and continuity of action allied to multiple acting areas. Most characteristic of Komisarjevsky was, however, the attack on genre, hence the

---

[20] Michael Mullin, 'Augures and Understood Relations: Theodore Komisarjevsky's *Macbeth*', *Educational Theater Journal*, 26 (1974), 21.

[21] 19 April 1933.   [22] *Ibid*.

[23] *Birmingham Post*, 19 April 1933.

[24] *The Daily Telegraph*, 19 April 1933.

[25] *The Scotsman*, 21 April 1933.

[26] Mullin, p. 23.

[27] *The Manchester Guardian*, 20 April 1933.

attack on tradition and expectation. No Shake-spearian comedy is more firmly anchored in time and location than *The Merry Wives of Windsor*: it is a comedy of Elizabethan bourgeois life in which *Windsor* is a felt presence (as, say, Illyria and Sicily are not, in their plays). Normally, and this holds good even today, it receives a setting of Elizabethan half-timbering peopled with actors whose costumes are no later than Cavalier. Here is Komisarjevsky's Windsor:

For the setting, imagine a series of ice-cream kiosks on a seaside pier each enamelled in a different tint . . . all freshly painted and awaiting their proprietors' names. Imagine tall slender pillars supporting balconies such as these on ornate house-boats, with steps and companion ways of a millionaire's yacht. Then think of a highly decorated birthday cake of many tiers and conjure up the impressions of all the French farces with their multitude of doors and cubby holes that you have ever seen.[28]

Centred upon the old town well, the acting space

was sometimes the open square, sometimes Mistress Ford's parlour, sometimes old Quickly's kitchen, some-times (I fancy) the bar of the Garter, at first very confusing to keep track of location, what with people popping in and out through these numerous doors, and scene following scene with nothing to mark the author's chaptering, but the pattern, once you allowed that it existed, was regular enough in its bizarre boldness, and speed was naturally consistent. For the forest scene the framework of the same set was used skeleton-wise, with a single cut-out oak replacing the well . . .[29]

Komisarjevsky thus created his own convention of acting spaces: it is instructive to follow the reviewer above as he adjusts to the new convention, while dis-carding with some reluctance Shakespeare's 'chapter-ing'. Other reviewers admitted to finding it all puzzling, especially the alternation of indoor and out-door scenes. 'Since the superstructure of a well graces the centre of the stage, this illusion of a living room is sometimes difficult to capture.'[30] Such literalism, with its call for the established mechanisms of illusion, was common to much adverse criticism of Komisar-jevsky. It was no doubt the symptom of a deeper

resistance. 'Those', said the *Birmingham Post*, 'who desire timbered houses and the English trees of Windsor Forest will not merely be disappointed: they will be enraged.'[31] The *enragés* had much else to swallow.

If Windsor went, so did the old-style Falstaff. Roy Byford's Falstaff appeared in a scarlet coat and *jaeger* hat with a bunch of feathers; he reminded reviewers of Franz Josef, especially as depicted in *White Horse Inn*. Though Justice Shallow wore a gown from the Middle Ages, tights were common among the men, and Ford was a villain of Edwardian melodrama. Falstaff's henchmen were Corsican bandits, while the men who took away the buck-basket were American express delivery men. The ladies wore crinolines and low bodices. The elements were heterogeneous, but the main period allusion was to the 1830s and 1840s, with a strong flavour of Viennese light opera. The Windsor of tradition was erased.

Komisarjevsky, as he said, had 'turned *The Merry Wives of Windsor* into farce or musical comedy',[32] much of it with a Victorian inflection. 'Here and there it becomes merely pantomime. And now and again, in the parts most dramatically tense, he makes it a burlesque of melodrama, with the characters hissing "hist" and the orchestra striking sudden chords expressive of apprehension every time the characters take a stealthy step across the stage.'[33] Not simply a romp, all this: Komisarjevsky's conception of the play as musical farce led to the apotheosis of the dance: 'An undercurrent of Viennese music, swelling at times to a major stream, accompanied the performance, and at the end a pas de deux by Anne and her triumphant Fenton was the signal for a jolly dance by the whole company, who in this novel fashion took their several and collective "curtains".'[34] The lyricism of the Fenton–Anne Page passages, and their apotheosis in the final dance, is perhaps the key to the production.

As before, Komisarjevsky's playing text was more

---

[28] *Yorkshire Post*, 20 April 1935.
[29] *Birmingham Mail*, 20 April 1935.
[30] *Birmingham Gazette*, 20 April 1935.
[31] 20 April 1935.
[32] Interview, *Western Daily Mail*, 20 April 1935.
[33] *Birmingham Gazette*, 20 April 1935.
[34] *Birmingham Mail*, 20 April 1935.

respectfully prepared than his reputation would suggest. The prompt-book (Shattuck, 78) reveals a playing version sparingly cut, with cuts clearly aimed at removing obscurity and pushing the action along briskly. Even act 4, scene 1 (William's Latin lesson) is retained. There is only one scene-transposition – in act 4, scene 1 is worked in after scene 4 – which is necessitated by the cutting of the short third scene and the whole of scene 5. (These two scenes contain the obscure German foolery, which Komisarjevsky dispensed with.) The sober judgement of *The Scotsman* was that Komisarjevsky 'superimposed a foreign element upon one of the most English of comedies, and has got away with it'.[35] The prompt-book goes some way to accounting for the trick: Komisarjevsky did not tamper with the play's foundations.

His treatment of the text of *King Lear* was altogether fascinating, and warrants a longer discussion. But first to the features of the production as they impressed the public. The *King Lear* of 1936 (repeated in 1937) was, by general consent, Komisarjevsky's masterpiece. Critic after critic hauled down his colours, and acknowledged that here was no eccentricity or iconoclasm, but a masterly response to a master work. *The Times*, while denying that Komisarjevsky's previous work was Shakespearian save by chance, said: 'This year it is magnificently Shakespearian, taking up rather than flinging out a challenge, joining issue with Lamb and Bradley and all who have maintained with varying degrees of emphasis that *Lear* is too huge for the stage and cannot be acted.'[36] *The Times*'s judgement, 'He succeeds brilliantly', registered the overwhelming majority verdict.

To the challenge of notorious difficulty, Komisarjevsky responded with severe simplicity. He used a single set only:

the whole stage is occupied by stairs, put at different angles, with platforms on which the action takes place; the highest platform is against the skyline, and the great resources of the theatre are used to the full in expressing the phases of the sky – blue, misty, stormy, sinister and gloomy. Thus the elemental quality of the play is suggested throughout, and the placing of the actors high on the stage enhances this quality.[37]

The steps or terraces of his set ascended from the orchestra to over half-way up the cyclorama. The potential of this arrangement was exploited thrillingly in the opening scene, when the apex of the terracing was a golden throne upon a pyramidal stair (see plate IIA). 'When the light first shone on the throned King, trumpeters blew a wild barbaric blast.'[38] The symbolisms of hierarchy blended with the advantages of an unlocalized setting.

On this severely limited set, Komisarjevsky's main technical instrument was lighting. His effects may well have been the most imaginative in the history of the Memorial Theatre. 'The smallest scenes were played in spots circumscribed only by light. For example, the change from the storm-swept heath (which had been indicated by scudding clouds of black on a sky of olive green) by a sudden dimming of lights, leaving a single beam rising from the floor in the centre of the stage. This was the hut.'[39] The concrete simplicity of 'hut' – one critic was reminded of a brazier – illustrates the director's economy of means. All reviewers were taken with the cyclorama sky effects: a serene blue for the opening, flecks of cloud at the end of act 2, dark scurrying clouds for the heath. *The Times* particularly admired the sky, which

by subtle gradations of hue, reflects the deepening intensity of the play. From the pale neutrality that heightens the golden magnificence of the spectacle of Lear dividing his kingdom this vast reflector of mood passes through dun disquiet to dark, tremendous contention, but it remains a reflector and no more, as the lights that break from pale blue to blood red on the ten-tiered stage itself are never more than a powerful reinforcement of the acting.[40]

In Randle Ayrton, Komisarjevsky found an actor who could use the freedom given by the simple stage. Ayrton had played Lear for Komisarjevsky before (the OUDS production of 1927) and focused the play as George Hayes's Macbeth had not. This was an august, Jehovah-like figure (a Blake engraving, thought *The Scotsman*), with the authority to compass the tragic bitterness of the fall.

[35] 18 April 1935.
[36] 21 April 1936.
[37] *Sheffield Telegraph*, 21 April 1936.
[38] *Ibid.*
[39] *Yorkshire Post*, 21 April 1936.
[40] *The Times*, 21 April 1936.

Particularly striking was the opening scene, in which Lear, seated on a golden throne at the top level of the terrace and bathed in a golden light, with the Fool lying lower down, restless and obviously perturbed, suggested a majesty not yet fallen and a King still possessing the capacity for kingship. The subdivision of the kingdom is seen, therefore, as an act of will of one still in full possession of his faculties, accomplished with something of the coolness of a man making a settlement to escape death duties, and not as a rash whim or a decision proceeding from senility . . .[41]

Ayrton's Lear is recognizable to us, over the distance of time. His acting reconciled the traditionalists to Komisarjevsky's technical innovations, and no startlingly new interpretation was offered of the action as a whole. Still, the Knights are interesting: Komisarjevsky made them a Chorus commenting on the futility of the old King's aims. They repeated, in unison, the Fool's songs and sayings. And one reviewer's response, surely, points to the future and Peter Brook's *King Lear*: 'If anything, one rather sympathizes with Goneril and Regan in their objection to these violent guests.'[42] The case for Goneril and Regan is there, germinating. But it was not allowed to develop. This *Lear* was a magnificent title role, set in a production of consummate technical mastery: the timeless, cosmic setting, the command of atmosphere and symbolism, all came together to create a triumph. Let T. C. Kemp describe its qualities:

. . . the significant grouping of characters points the action and brings a miming quality to static knots of players. On different levels the protagonists hurl their challenges. Edgar, Gloucester and Lear, silhouetted against the stormy sky, show the burden of man 'carrying the affliction and the fear'. Heralds on the skyline blow their challenge from the cliff through great trumpets. But nowhere is the studied congregation of characters used so meaningly as in the closing moments of the play when the light dies out in the sky and darkness travels slowly down the steps. Line by line the motionless soldiers fade from view: the light lingers for a moment on the dead Lear and Cordelia. Finally they, too, dissolve into the gloom; the rolling drums die away, and the curtain slowly descends on the darkened stage.[43]

There, if the records of the past can speak at all, was catharsis. Komisarjevsky did it with six rehearsals.[44]

For us, the text of *King Lear* holds a significance that it lacked even a few years ago. Many issues crystallize in the question: a two-text *Lear*, or a conflation? It is natural that we should now turn to the past, and appraise Shakespearians on their disposition towards this question. We cannot expect clear-cut answers. But we may find at least an attitude, a set of the face. Komisarjevsky's address to the question is clear. With variations and some transpositions, he offered what was in essence a Folio-based *Lear*.

In this, Komisarjevsky presumably followed the prescription of Granville-Barker, whose Preface to *King Lear* was first published in 1927. 'On the whole, then – and if he show a courageous discretion – I recommend a producer to found himself on the Folio. For that it does show some at least of Shakespeare's own reshapings I feel sure.'[45] In Komisarjevsky's playing text (Shattuck, 105) one immediately encounters a preference for Folio readings over Quarto. Thus, in the opening scene – line references here are to the Riverside edition – 'richer' becomes 'ponderous' (80), 'Go to, go to' becomes 'How, how, Cordelia?' (94), and 'covered' becomes 'dowered' (204). A test currently much discussed is the form of dialogue between Kent and Lear in act 2, scene 4 ('No.' 'Yes.' 'No, I say'), and Komisarjevsky chooses the F version, declining the conflation. This preference does not, in itself, indicate more than the general sense (literary, as well as theatrical) that F supplies superior readings. And Komisarjevsky is less than submissive to the authority of F, for his transpositions are sometimes quite free. To cite a few, he includes some material from act 4, scene 2 – the dialogue between Edmund and Goneril – in act 1, scene 4.[46] The heath scenes are

[41] *The Scotsman*, 13 June 1936.

[42] *Morning Post*, 21 April 1936.

[43] *Birmingham Post*, 21 April 1936.

[44] J. C. Trewin, *Shakespeare on the English Stage 1900–1964* (1964), p. 169.

[45] Harley Granville-Barker, *Prefaces to Shakespeare*, First Series (1927), p. 229.

[46] Gordon Crosse, in *Shakespearean Playgoing 1890–1952* (1953), p. 97, found this objectionable. But the forward move of the dialogue brings out earlier a latent motivation, for Edmund and Goneril; and Komisarjevsky's fourth act races faster for the displaced material.

reorganized into a single extended scene. After the single interval (on Gloucester's 'Come, come, away', 2.6.104), Part Two opens with Albany's 'O Goneril! / You are not worth' (4.2.29 ff.), continues to Goneril's 'O vain fool' (62), then moves to Regan's 'What might import my sister's letter to [Lord Edmund]?' (4.5.6–7). The next speech, which refers to the blinding (not yet played in this version) is of course cut. But this scene establishes the Regan–Goneril–Edmund intrigue before the blinding. The prompt-book then moves, after the end of act 4, scene 5, to the blinding scene in act 3, scene 7. After this episode and act 4, scene 1 (which I shall return to later), Komisarjevsky, having already dealt with act 4, scene 2 and dispensed with act 4, scene 3, proceeds directly in the scene sequence act 4, scene 5, then act 4, scene 6. The main line of the narration has now been regained, and there are no further transpositions. They constitute, clearly, a highly individual treatment of the material in this great dramatic quarry.

It is, however, in the matter of cuts and passages retained that adherence to F or Q is established. Of the passages found in F but not Q Komisarjevsky retains, for example, 1.2.109–14; 1.2.166–71; 1.4.322–30; and 2.4.140–5. (These are samples, not a complete list.) More crucial are passages found in Q but omitted in F, the most substantial of which is the entire third scene of act 4. Komisarjevsky cut this scene from his playing text; also 1.4.232–4; 2.2.137–41; Edgar's concluding soliloquy in act 3, scene 6; half of the Q passage in 4.2.31–49 (beginning with Albany's 'I fear your disposition'); 4.7.34–7; 5.3.203–21. I should add that Komisarjevsky is not a doctrinaire Folio follower, for he retains the Mock Trial of act 3, scene 6, a passage not found in F but widely felt to play well. Also, for his conclusion Komisarjevsky adopts an ingeniously eclectic plan: of the last four lines ('The weight of this sad time') he assigns the first two to Edgar, the last two to Albany. But the main thesis is clear. Komisarjevsky retains the Folio readings when they are the only ones; he prefers them when they conflict with Q; he at least includes F omissions from the Q text in his own scheme of cuts, though he does not slavishly follow F's omissions. It is, in Granville-Barker's prescription, a production founded upon the Folio.

I have left till last what is to us, though not to Komisarjevsky's contemporaries, the most controversial of textual cruces: the servants' dialogue immediately following the blinding of Gloucester. This passage, absent from the Folio, was notoriously omitted from Peter Brook's *King Lear* of 1962. At the time, this decision was fiercely attacked as an extreme instance of director's licence: 'After such knowledge, what forgiveness?' asked Maynard Mack.[47] Brook did not make his cut on grounds of textual scholarship; nevertheless, the entire thrust of recent scholarship has been, in effect, to support Brook's decision. In preferring not to adopt the model of healing offered by the Q text, Brook – so the argument runs – aligned himself with Shakespeare's own second thoughts.

And also with Komisarjevsky. For he, too, cut the post-blinding dialogue. The prompt-book is explicit about the horrors of the blinding – '[Cornwall] Rushes at Glo. gouges one eye' – and the main text is substantially retained, 'vile jelly' staying. After Cornwall's exit with Regan, at 'Give me your arm', the stage direction states:

2 Serv's pick up 1st Serv body and exit R2
2nd Serv helps Glo to rise and both move C.

No servants' dialogue at all, and no 'flax and whites of eggs'. And no break, for the scene continues with 'Alack, sir, you cannot see your way' in which the Old Man's lines of act 4, scene 1 have been put into the mouth of the second Servant. So Komisarjevsky continues with act 4, scene 1 without a break, Gloucester retaining the important 'I have no way', etc. Komisarjevsky cannot be said to have *confronted* the audience with the fact of the blinding, as Brook did. Instead, he made the act 4, scene 1 passages act as a kind of balm. It is a most original handling of the crux. No one seems to have noticed it at the time: the reviews are uniformly silent on the matter. And Komisarjevsky made no announcement concerning his intentions. Perhaps academics went less frequently to the theatre then than now. Whatever the explanation, the *King Lear* of 1936 anticipated by a quarter of a century Brook's omission of a famous passage. The prompt-book says that Komisarjevsky cut the post-

47 *King Lear in our Time* (Berkeley, 1965), p. 40.

blinding dialogue, and the record says that not a critic croaked.

In the summer of 1936, Komisarjevsky stood at the zenith of his reputation as a Shakespearian director. Did a kind of hubris drive him to his fall in October, the *Antony and Cleopatra* at the New Theatre? This production, which closed after four days, is now remembered largely for Charles Morgan's devastating phonetic transcriptions ('O weederdee degarlano devar' – 'O wither'd is the garland of the war') and James Agate's review-heading: 'ANTON AND CLEOPATROVA: A TRAGEDY BY KOMISPEARE'.[48] Komisarjevsky made an irrecoverable error of judgement in casting Eugenie Leontovich, a Russian comedienne, in the title role; her command of English was strikingly inadequate. And yet, as one reads the sympathetic account in Margaret Lamb's *Antony and Cleopatra on the English Stage*,[49] it is plain that the production was otherwise perfectly defensible. There were excellent actors (led by Donald Wolfit's Antony), and Komisarjevsky's rearrangements of scenes and lines now seem scarcely shocking. The concept of a Cleopatra able to tap the play's rich vein of comedy is familiar: one thinks, for example, of the Cleopatras of Margaret Leighton, Maggie Smith, Janet Suzman. Leontovich herself went on to a successful career in the United States. But to cast her as Cleopatra was the lapse for which Komisarjevsky's critics were waiting. He exposed his flank, and was hit, hard. Gielgud says that Komisarjevsky thought it all 'a splendid joke'.[50] One doubts that so public a fiasco – which included booing on the first night – could be laughed off as easily as Komisarjevsky made it appear. The disillusionment with English theatre, which led to his move to the United States in the latter 1930s, must have been given a strong impulse by the failure of *Antony and Cleopatra*. Komisarjevsky directed no more Shakespeare in London.

He returned to Stratford, however, for the revival of his *King Lear* in 1937, and for the seasons of 1938 and 1939. His last two productions there were *scherzi*, brilliant and showy jests which showed his powers before appreciative audiences. It is as though he recognized the inner limitations of his life-work and the times, and thus the essential decorum of his art. At all events, *The Comedy of Errors*, as *The Times* astutely noted, 'has perhaps a smaller bodyguard of conservative admirers than any other in the canon'.[51] Komisarjevsky chose it for his 1938 production, and lavished upon it all his virtuosity as director and stage designer. One can comprehend its success, in part, from the much-reproduced photograph of the final scene; it is, I suppose, the best-known moment of his entire work.[52] The stage has a haunting, almost hallucinogenic quality. One takes in the toytown set, the twins seated on bollards and gazing intently at each other, the fantastically varied crowd with habiliments ranging from Elizabethan farthingales to U.S. Navy pork-pie caps, the odd angle of the balcony gazer whose body and head extend the line of the 'iron' work. The balcony gazer – it is the Abbess – dominates the frame, and the eye returns always to her. There is some deep law of visual dynamics illustrated here, just as in the Carrollian logic of the production's time-scale: 'the clock in the tower between the two inns every now and again strikes an hour to which the hands of the clock are not pointing. And the hands gallop to overtake the time.'[53] The artificiality of the plot, the quintessentially dreamlike nature of the action for those experiencing it – those were the elements of *The Comedy of Errors* on which Komisarjevsky seized.

On such an occasion, the director together with the company as ensemble reigns supreme. *The Times*, reviewing the production favourably, mentioned no individual actor at all. Other reviewers were

---

[48] Charles Morgan's review is conveniently reprinted in J. L. Styan, *The Shakespeare Revolution* (Cambridge, 1977), pp. 155–6.

[49] New Brunswick, 1980, pp. 127–9.

[50] Gielgud, *An Actor and his Time*, p. 80.

[51] 12 April 1938.

[52] It is conveniently reproduced in, for example, Trewin, facing p. 37; and Crosse, facing p. 97. *Shakespeare Survey 2* (Cambridge, 1949) has a photograph (Plate VII) illustrating a different moment in the same scene.

[53] *Birmingham Gazette*, 13 April 1938. 'Time itself', said the *Sheffield Telegraph* (14 April 1938), 'joined in the sport.' Gāmini Salgādo takes Komisarjevsky's device as the text for his analysis of time, in '"Time's Deformed Hand": Sequence, Consequence, and Inconsequence in *The Comedy of Errors*', *Shakespeare Survey 25* (Cambridge, 1972), 81–91.

less austere. The resemblance of Peggy Livesey's Courtesan to Mae West, for example, did not pass unnoticed. Even the dour Crosse allowed that her interjection 'Oh, well !' into a speech of the Abbess's brought down the house.[54] But only a curmudgeon could have resisted this production.

The curtain rises on a painted stage, an Ephesus of dolls' house quaintness, no element, certainly, of Asia Minor, but proper scene of eternal pantomime and harlequinade. Its citizens appear as puppets and play-boys bound to no especial century, but heirs of a timeless invention. In a moment we are enraptured.[55]

A whole society was created, with policemen, usurers, the bad girl of the town, drunken sailors: the town periodically got into the act. A favourite Komisarjevsky trick was to break up a speech and hand parts around. Take this sample: in Adriana's longish speech, 'May it please your grace' (5.1.136–60), Komisarjevsky redeployed his forces:

Adriana.   By rushing in their houses
Courtesan.   Bearing thence
               Rings
Angelo.   Jewels
4th Merchant.   anything his rage did like.
Adriana.   Once did I . . .

There are numerous reassignments, and a speech of Balthazar's (3.1.85–106) is parcelled out to no fewer than six actors: Balthazar, Tailor, Fourth Merchant, Fifth Merchant, Angelo, and Innkeeper (Shattuck, 26). This joyous collectivization of response found its purest expression in the Victorian glee club moments. 'The closing line of the first Act is repeated as a choral effort. The characters range themselves across the stage and repeat "This jest shall cost him some expense" with authentic Handelian reiteration.'[56] Now operetta, now ballet, this extravaganza astonished even those familiar with Komisarjevsky's methods. The pink bowler hats of the Dromios, and the pink of the Abbess, lodged crazily in the minds of the audience. All resistance was neutralized. 'Great is Komis of the Ephesians,' said Ivor Brown.[57]

The Comedy of Errors must, I think, have been Komisarjevsky's supreme jest, as King Lear was his major claim not to be dismissed as a farceur. He repeated The Comedy of Errors in 1939, and added to it

The Taming of the Shrew. This was marginally less successful, because the comedy itself is less artificial. Still, Komisarjevsky's treatment gained a strategic advantage: 'If the farce has a brutality repugnant to modern taste, Mr Komisarjevsky gives it a brilliant artificiality which makes it not only possible for us to suspend ethical and sociological judgement, but inevitable.'[58] Even the accomplished acting of Alec Clunes (Petruchio) and Vivienne Bennett (Katharina) did not disturb the note of farcical comedy. Besides, Komisarjevsky retained the Induction, and gave great licence to Jay Laurier's Sly thereafter (allowing him, for example, to referee the contest between two of Bianca's suitors, 'Giving his verdict in the approved boxing fashion'[59]); so the frame itself was the determinant of mood. With it went the music of Haydn, Mozart, and Anthony Bernard (the musical director).

For his visual metaphors, Komisarjevsky sought a combination of England and Italy. The opening was pure Warwickshire:

We are in the heart of England, in front of one of those remote taverns which, outside convivial hours, bear a prim, withdrawn aspect. The episode of Christopher Sly's expulsion is well managed, and has the quick thrust and counter-thrust of a good-humoured rustic brawl. There follows a pause, through which we sense the drowsy countryside; and this is broken by the sound of a horn announcing the arrival of the young lord and his fellow huntsmen.[60]

The huntsmen turn out to be a house party (see plate IIB): 'The Lord and his rout are habited as Stuart sportsmen who have gone a-fowling in periwigs and are as dashing as any in the world of Wycherley.'[61] One of the players who follow is Petruchio, whose move into the play world is thus prepared. 'The Padua play', on the other hand, 'is done in the manner of "ingeniouse Italy", with the masks, false noses, and

54 Crosse, p. 95.
55 Ivor Brown, The Observer, 17 April 1938.
56 Birmingham Post, 13 April 1938.
57 The Observer, 17 April 1938.
58 The Times, 4 April 1939.
59 Evesham Journal, 8 April 1939.
60 Richard Clowes, The Sunday Times, 9 April 1939.
61 Ivor Brown, The Observer, 9 April 1939.

piping pantaloonery of the Harlequinade.'[62] All was presented in a riot of 'polychromatic artificiality'.[63]

The *commedia dell'arte* touches harked back to *The Merchant of Venice*, as did the open use of stage machinery. The moving stage provided some happy moments: 'The stage first moves in full view of the audience with Lucentio balancing Eros-like on a bedroom chair, reaching out for a decanter which the laughing Laurier holds to within one teasing inch of Lucentio's fingertips . . . the whole receding from view.'[64] Again, there was a taking passage 'where Petruchio and Katharina march against the moving boards on their way from Pisa to Padua and thus, miraculously, still remain in sight'.[65] Against a constant background of green colonnades, identification of scene was no problem. Komisarjevsky simply employed as compère the leader of the troupe of players, whose duty was to call out 'Padua, a public place' or 'Verona, Petruchio's country house'. He may have derived some satisfaction from spelling matters out, for those of the audience who complained at the puzzling locations of *The Merry Wives of Windsor*. The free and flexible exploitation of stage location was basic to Komisarjevsky's method.

All this was watched, from a sumptuous Jacobean bed, by Sly. And he had the last word, for Komisarjevsky retained, logically, the ending to *A Shrew* (Shattuck, 69). He closed the main play with Petruchio's 'God give you good night' (thus cutting the final couplet), then brought out the Hostess to play out the Epilogue. The production ended with Sly's 'I'll to my wife presently, and I'll tame her too', and after the Hostess's exit he sang the nonsense song 'Doodle-doon' (which had also brought down the interval, at the pregnant 'And let Bianca take her sister's room'). It was, I suppose, as near as Komisarjevsky came to *Twelfth Night* and Feste's 'When that I was'. Sly's song lingered on in the air. It was Komisarjevsky's envoi to Stratford.

'I personally am by no means a pedant where interpretation of a part or of a play on the stage is concerned . . . In the free interpretation of parts or of plays lies the life and soul of the theatre.'[66] Komisarjevsky's enemy, like Brook's, was the Deadly Theatre; and in the 1930s the defendants of the Deadly Theatre were much stronger, numerically and qualitatively, than in the 1960s. Hence Komisarjevsky incurred the opposition of historic forces which were partially successful in blurring his achievement. He was licensed to be a jester, no more. His attack on the general perception was tolerated on the terms of the four comedies he directed in his Stratford years, and strongly resisted in his *Macbeth* (and *Antony and Cleopatra*). Only in *King Lear* did his gifts receive overwhelming applause, for the production of a tragedy. *The Times*'s phrase, 'chartered revolutionary',[67] must have acquired a special meaning for Komisarjevsky. The oxymoron is a reminder of the knife-edge dividing subversion from suppression.

Technically, his work looks forward to the postwar era. The free use of acting space, the refusal to accept the constraints of period or location, the emphasis on continuity of action, all this is familiar to us. Komisarjevsky preferred a single interval, and a rapid forward movement. He was no sort of textual purist, but his prompt-books reveal a considered, sometimes a scholarly, treatment of the text. The last two comedies, especially, show a taste for reassigning speeches, but this I would attribute to his sense of music and rhythmic groupings. Certainly there is very little that a later generation would take exception to: one really cannot grow choleric over reassigning some of Biondello's lines to a new-created Servant. Komisarjevsky's free ways often overlaid a return to the vital essences of the text: thus, in different ways, the uncut *Merchant of Venice*, the Folio-based *King Lear*, the retained Induction and Sly scenes culminating in the ending of *A Shrew*. This was no textual Goth; and his major excisions seem to me well justified in purely theatrical terms.

The prompt-books are at least as sound a guide to Komisarjevsky's work as the reviews. Their stark, algebraic formulations express the values and intentions of the director in coded but unmistakable ways. The reviews, on the other hand, need to be

---

[62] *Ibid.*   [63] Trewin, p. 179.
[64] *Evesham Journal*, 8 April 1939.
[65] *Stratford-upon-Avon Herald*, 7 April 1939.
[66] Komisarjevsky, *Footnotes to the Theatre*, p. 85.
[67] 21 April 1936.

approached with some care. The apparent modernity and clarity of the language mask a set of attitudes which are profoundly ambivalent. There is usually admiration for Komisarjevsky's virtues – his unfailing musical and rhythmic sense, the pictorial quality of his compositions, the volatility and inventiveness of his stagings, his capacity to create a dream world with its own inner coherence and conviction. But there is also a determination to score Komisarjevsky's work as 'only' virtuosity, the effusions of a gifted child who must sometimes be reproved for his own good. It is not easy, at times, to comprehend how intelligent and instructed playgoers can be mortally offended by, say, the 'vulgarity' – it is Crosse's word, among others – of having Macbeth's fortune told by three Scots palmists. (In 1982 the RSC presented a *Macbeth* with three attractive young ladies as Witches; it passed almost without comment. The era of heroic confrontation is clearly over.) One must, I think, postulate a deep-seated antipathy to the new as permeating the English theatre world of the 1930s. The playing of Shakespeare was not to be revolutionized by a Russian émigré. So Komisarjevsky was allowed to succeed, but only on terms. He could re-inflect certain plays, he could revitalize certain comedies, but the playing of Shakespeare on the English stage remained, as it seemed, largely unchanged. Fireworks do not transform landscapes. The School of Komisarjevsky did not exist, and he left no heir in sight. Komisarjevsky had essentially finished with the English stage when the war came; it found him in America, and there he stayed. His work on Shakespeare was all but over.

There was, however, a strange late coda to his work. In the summer of 1950, Komisarjevsky was invited to direct at the Montreal Open Air Playhouse, which is a grassy strip with trees by Beaver Lake on the top of Mont-Royal. A guest director to the last, he accepted, and chose – not *The Tempest*, nothing so portentous – but *Cymbeline*. That gallimaufry of genres was Komisarjevsky's farewell to Shakespeare; at least no army of traditionalists could contest his production. And it went off well. We read[68] of a *Cymbeline* in modern dress, with the British army in khaki and the Romans in black uniform, of Beefeaters parading across the grass, of the strains of 'Sophisticated Lady' accompanying the opening garden party, of two actors exiting to 'We're off to see the Wizard, the Wonderful Wizard of Oz'. The cast did not lack distinction, and the Posthumus of the young Christopher Plummer took the eye. Even the plot made a kind of sense. It sounds like a mellow enough leave-taking, the sprightly and good-humoured gesture of an old master. One wonders what the Montreal audience made of it, as they shivered under the cold July moon. Komisarjevsky ended it all on a note of witty bathos: Cymbeline, King of Britain, brought down the curtain with his patriotic oration, and, there being no curtain to bring down, the actors filed off quietly behind the bushes. His career was like that. 'A great *metteur en scène*', in Gielgud's phrase,[69] finished up exploiting the artificiality of the natural. Let that stand as Komisarjevsky's curtain line, the final paradox of the jester as revolutionary.

---

[68] Herbert Whittaker, *Toronto Globe and Mail*, 20 July 1950.
[69] Cited in Norman Marshall's account of Komisarjevsky's life in *DNB 1951–1960*.

'TROILUS AND CRESSIDA' AND THE DEFINITION OF BEAUTY

JULIET DUSINBERRE

The problem of how to define beauty is central to *Troilus and Cressida*. Shakespeare depicts Helen as incapable of acquiring symbolic stature and this creates in the play questions about the nature of beauty.[1]

In the world of *Troilus and Cressida* beauty is defined by the beautiful woman, whether it be Helen or Cressida. But the idea of Helen as the archetype of beauty seems to have been challenged very early by shifts in perspective. The poet Stesichorus was legendary for a poem defaming Helen, for which the gods blinded him. He recanted and recovered, as Plato records in both *The Republic* and *Phaedrus*. Stesichorus' palinode asserted that the Helen story was a fabrication:

> False, false the tale
> Thou never didst sail in the well-decked ships
> Nor come to the towers of Troy.[2]

Dio Chrysostom, a first-century critic of Homer, declared that Homer was a beggar who told lies for a living and that the Judgement of Paris was an unlikely tale, in the first place because the 'consort of Zeus' would not have required Paris, a mere shepherd, to testify to her beauty, and secondly, because Helen was Aphrodite's sister, and the goddess would not have wished to disgrace her. Dio claims that Helen was lawfully married to Paris: 'If anyone does not accept this account under the influence of the old view, let him know that he is unable to get free of error and distinguish truth from falsehood.'[3] Euripides' version of the story in the play *Helen*, in which Paris abducts a phantom while the real Helen is taken to Egypt by Hermes, finds an echo in the Renaissance in the writings of the art historian, Giovanni Petro Bellori, who believed that the Trojan war was fought for art rather than nature:

---

[1] John Vyvyan, *Shakespeare and Platonic Beauty* (1961), argues Shakespeare's familiarity with Neoplatonic thought. Since Vyvyan's study J. E. Hankins has discussed in *Shakespeare's Derived Imagery* (Lawrence, Kansas, 1967) and *Backgrounds of Shakespeare's Thought* (Hassocks, 1978) the extensive influence on Shakespeare of Pierre de la Primaudaye's *The French Academie*, of which the first three parts were translated into English in 1586, 1594 and 1601 respectively. I. A. Richards's essay, '*Troilus and Cressida* and Plato', in *Speculative Instruments* (1955), pp. 198–213, contributes to an older debate about Plato's influence on the play, which is fully documented in the New Variorum *Troilus and Cressida*, ed. Harold N. Hillebrand and T. W. Baldwin, pp. 391–2 (Ulysses' speech on degree and *Republic* VIII), and pp. 411–15 (Ulysses' 'strange fellow' and Achilles' mirror speech, related to Plato's *First Alcibiades*).

[2] *Phaedrus*, trans. R. Hackforth, in *The Collected Dialogues of Plato*, ed. Edith Hamilton and Huntington Cairns, Bollingen Series, 71 (Princeton, 1961), p. 475. I refer to this edition hereafter as Plato, *Dialogues*.

[3] Dio Chrysostom, 'The Eleventh, or Trojan, Discourse', trans. J. W. Cohoon, 1 (Loeb Library, 1932), pp. 453–4. First translated – before any of the other Discourses – by Filelfo in 1428 and printed at Cremona in 1492, this one Discourse was followed by complete Latin translations of Dio in the mid sixteenth century (1555, 1585, 1604). Thomas Watson's Latin translation, *Helenae Raptus*, published in 1586, of the Greek Colothus' version of the Judgement of Paris (a manuscript discovered at the end of the fifteenth century) contains in the 1731 edition notes which refer to Dio's scepticism about the story.

[4] Vyvyan, *Shakespeare and Platonic Beauty*, p. 164, records both Euripides' version of the Helen myth and the fate of Stesichorus.

Helen was not as beautiful as they pretended, for she was found to have defects and shortcomings, so that it is believed that she never did sail for Troy, but that her statue was taken there in her stead, for whose beauty the Greeks and the Trojans made war for ten years.[5]

In the late Dialogue 'Greater Hippias', Plato focuses on the intellectual dilemma which lies at the heart of the Helen myth.[6] Socrates presses the Sophist Hippias to define beauty, but ruthlessly demolishes each definition that is offered. Whether or not Shakespeare knew this Dialogue, its arguments throw light on the dramatist's preoccupations in *Troilus and Cressida*.

I

When Socrates asks Hippias what beauty is, he replies, as any of the characters in Shakespeare's play might do, that beauty is the beautiful maiden. Socrates refuses to accept the definition because it admits the possibility of comparison. The beautiful maiden is more beautiful than a mare, a lyre or a pot, but 'ugly in comparison with the race of gods'.[7] By the yardstick of heavenly beauty her human beauty is ugliness and therefore cannot embody the essence of the beautiful.

The opening scene of *Troilus and Cressida* sets up a competition between the beauty of Cressida and of Helen. Troilus sighs for 'fair Cressid', Pandarus declares that 'she look'd yesternight fairer than ever I saw her look, or any woman else', and is betrayed by his own tag into placing her in his mind's eye at Helen's side:

An her hair were not somewhat darker than Helen's – well, go to – there were no more comparison between the women. But, for my part, she is my kinswoman; I would not, as they term it, praise her, but I would somebody had heard her talk yesterday, as I did. I would not dispraise your sister Cassandra's wit: but –[8]

Troilus responds with poetic ardour:

O, that her hand,
In whose comparison all whites are ink
Writing their own reproach; to whose soft seizure
The cygnet's down is harsh ...   (1.1.54–7)

It seems as if Troilus, with true gallantry, disdains to compare his lady to another. But does he? The softness

of the cygnet's down is tellingly evoked in Golding's translation of Ovid's *Metamorphoses*, XIII, where Polyphemus praises Galatea in words which recall the contest on Mount Ida:

Of valew more than Apples bee although they were of
    gold. . . .
More soft than butter newly made, or downe of
    Cygnet is.[9]

Troilus, despite the different contours of his imagination, like Pandarus measures Cressida's beauty by Helen's. Pandarus tries to heat the young man's passion with both praise and disparagement of his niece: 'An she were not kin to me, she would be as fair a Friday as Helen is on Sunday.' Troilus protests: 'Say I she is not fair?' and Pandarus retorts in a fit of pique, partly feigned and partly real: 'I do not care whether you do or no. She's a fool to stay behind her father. Let her to the Greeks; and so I'll tell her the next time I see her' (1.1.75–81). This is not all bluff; Pandarus calculates the effect which later in the play Cressida's beauty does have on the Greek camp. In Troy, cheek

---

[5] 'The Idea of the Painter, Sculptor and Architect, Superior to Nature by Selection from Natural Beauties', reprinted in Erwin Panofsky, *Idea: A Concept in Art Theory*, trans. Joseph J. S. Peake (Columbia, 1968), p. 161.

[6] Although Shakespeare might have read Ficino's translations of Plato and Plotinus in a number of editions, it is tempting to see the publication of the Basel *Opera Omnia* of Plato in 1602, with adjacent columns of Latin and Greek, as a spur to the composition of *Troilus and Cressida*, which appears in the Stationers' Register in 1603.

[7] 'Greater Hippias', trans. Benjamin Jowett, in Plato, *Dialogues*, p. 1542.

[8] 1.1.30, 32–4, 41–6. All quotations from Shakespeare are from *William Shakespeare: The Complete Works*, ed. Peter Alexander (1951).

[9] Ovid's *Metamorphoses*, the Arthur Golding Translation, 1567, ed. John Frederick Nims (New York, 1965), p. 344. Shakespeare probably used some lines from *Metamorphoses*, XII, and the first 500 lines of XIII, as a source for the play (Geoffrey Bullough, *Narrative and Dramatic Sources of Shakespeare*, vol. 6 (1977), pp. 151–7). Having read Ovid's account of the Trojan war earlier in Book XIII Shakespeare might naturally have connected Polyphemus' worship of Galatea's beauty with Paris' giving of the apple to Aphrodite and with the goddess's promised reward of the most beautiful woman in the world, Helen of Troy.

by jowl with Helen, she will always be black where beauty is counted fair.

Shakespeare might have known of an early Greek Cressida – very different both from Chaucer's Criseyde and from Henryson's – who was alert to the dangers of comparison. Dio Chrysostom's 'Sixty-First Discourse: Chryseïs',[10] gives substance to the shadowy Homeric figure of Agamemnon's concubine, whom medieval writers sometimes identified with Briseis, beloved of Achilles, when they looked for Criseyde's Homeric ancestry.[11]

When Dio's Chryseïs observed that the fall of Troy was imminent she contemplated the prospect of returning with Agamemnon to the household of Clytemnestra. But the king's propensity to compare her with his wife – 'For he says that she is in no wise inferior in mind to his own wife' – alarmed the concubine:

For Chryseïs knew that such talk breeds envy and jealousy. Then too, she observed Agamemnon's character and saw that he was not stable but arrogant and overbearing, and she calculated what he would do to her, a captive, when he ceased to desire her, seeing that he referred to his wife, queen though she was and the mother of his children, in such disparaging terms. For though foolish women delight in their lovers when they are seen to disparage all other women, those who are sensible discern the true nature of the man who acts or talks that way.[12]

Another Cressida calculates how the successful lover will behave:

That she belov'd knows nought that knows not this:
Men prize the thing ungain'd more than it is.
That she was never yet that ever knew
Love got so sweet as when desire did sue;
Therefore this maxim out of love I teach;
Achievement is command; ungain'd, beseech.

(1.2.280–5)

Dio suggests that the likelihood that Agamemnon's favourable comparisons would turn into unfavourable ones in the course of time, and that his devotion would be translated into tyranny, led Chryseïs to prompt her father to send for her to the Greek camp. Events proved her wisdom, for her successor in Agamemnon's love, Cassandra, another witty

daughter of a priest, was murdered on her return with the king. Pandarus' boast that his niece is wittier than Cassandra may testify to the dramatist's residual memory of an earlier Chryseïs who chose to return to her father rather than suffer comparison with another woman. In the Greek camp it is Cressida who will do the comparing, as Troilus anticipates:

I cannot sing,
Nor heel the high lavolt, nor sweeten talk,
Nor play at subtle games – fair virtues all,
To which the Grecians are most prompt and pregnant.

(4.4.84–7)

In her first scene in the play Cressida teases Pandarus by disparaging her lover: 'There is among the Greeks

---

[10] Shakespeare might also have read Dio's 'Sixty-sixth Discourse: On Reputation', a mordant attack on seekers after fame in which the sequence of images of over-eating, uncurrent coin and beggary anticipate Ulysses' speech 'Time hath, my lord, a wallet at his back, / Wherein he puts alms for oblivion' (3.3.145–6). Dio remarks that Perseus carried in his wallet the Gorgon's head with which to turn men to stone but that 'most men have been turned to stone by just one word, if it is applied to them; besides, there is no need to carry this around, guarding it in a wallet' (v.109). He asserts that 'notoriety-seekers' become 'beggars and no longer would any one of all who formerly were fain to burst their lungs with shouting greet them if he saw them' (v.91). Achilles observes the neglect cast on him by the Greek generals: 'they pass'd by me / As misers do by beggars – neither gave to me / Good word nor look. What, are my deeds forgot?' (3.3.142–4). While Shakespeare might have found such images in other sources the cynical tone of the Discourse brings to mind not only *Troilus and Cressida* but also *Timon of Athens*. Dio recalls in the same Discourse Thersites' deflating jests.

[11] Although the heroine of John Lydgate's *The Hystorye Sege and Dystruccyon of Troye* (1513), is called 'Cryseyde', in Caxton's translation of Raoul Lefevre, *The Recuyell of the Historyes of Troye* (c. 1474), her name is Breseyda. Dares Phrygius, writing in the sixth century, calls her Briseis in *De Excidio Troiae Historiae*, and in Benoît de Sainte-Maure's *Roman de Troie* she is again Briseida (Bullough, vol. 6, pp. 90, 94). Bullough notes that the translation of Benoît's romance into Latin prose by Guido delle Colonne in *Historia Troiana* (1287) 'became the chief medium by which the story of Troilus was disseminated' (vol. 6, p. 90).

[12] Dio, *Discourses*, v.3, 15.

Achilles, a better man than Troilus.' Pandarus explodes: 'Well, well! Why, have you any discretion? Have you any eyes? Do you know what a man is? Is not birth, beauty, good shape, discourse, manhood, learning, gentleness, virtue, youth, liberality, and such like, spice and salt that season a man?' 'Ay,' snaps the Beatrice of the ancient world, 'a minc'd man' (1.2.239–48). Dio's Chryseïs would have felt as sceptical as Socrates of Hector's challenge to the Greeks that:

> He hath a lady wiser, fairer, truer,
> Than ever Greek did couple in his arms.
>
> (1.3.275–6)

When Dio's second speaker admits Chryseïs' prudence but doubts Dio's version of the story, the critic retorts that the real is more worth writing about than the ideal: 'Would you rather hear how they [events] assuredly did take place, or how it would be well for them to have taken place?'[13] Cressida, Diomedes and Thersites are all governed by their regard for the unideal aspects of their world. Cressida has enough of Chryseïs' discernment to realize that in Troy her beauty is the casualty of the comparative mood.

Troilus is obtuse about the threat to beauty implicit in comparisons, but yet quick to deny Socrates' premise that the beautiful maiden is ugly compared with the gods:

> He brought a Grecian queen, whose youth and freshness
> Wrinkles Apollo's, and makes stale the morning.
>
> (2.2.78–9)

Such a claim would have been sacrilege in the ancient world. But one of the radical differences between the *Iliad* and *Troilus and Cressida* lies in Shakespeare's discarding of deities. In Homer the Trojan war is waged as much in heaven as in Troy. In Shakespeare the gods are names but not numina. Men and women have deposed them, so that Helen is more beautiful than Apollo and Agamemnon a 'god in office'. Compared with other plays set in the pagan world – *King Lear*, *Cymbeline*, even *The Winter's Tale* – *Troilus and Cressida* lacks religious dimension.[14] It is as though Shakespeare asked what the significance of beauty

might be once the gods no longer cared about the fate of Troy. The impact of Troilus' comparison is poetic not religious. Socrates might have argued that Troilus, beautiful and appealing though his image is, sacrifices the intellect to the imagination, thus denying beauty immutability. For a man to find a beautiful maiden more beautiful than the gods demonstrates not her beauty, but how little his gods mean to him, a denial of order which looks forward to Ulysses' great speech, and which Hippias, worldly Sophist though he is, never contemplates. In *Troilus and Cressida* beauty translated into the form of the beautiful maiden must, like Helen and Cressida, come to dust.

II

Hippias abandons the beautiful maiden when logic forces him to. But turning triumphantly to his tormentor, he shifts ground, claiming that beauty is distinguished by gold. In *Troilus and Cressida* Greeks and Trojans alike identify Helen's beauty by what it costs.

Troilus, surprisingly enough considering his championing of Helen in the Trojan debate, is the first person in the play to claim that the cost of Helen's beauty is too high. Throwing down his arms he cries:

> Fools on both sides! Helen must needs be fair,
> When with your blood you daily paint her thus.
>
> (1.1.89–90)

Helen's beauty is grotesquely embellished not with vermilion but with blood, like a painted statue.[15] The image contains the two Renaissance themes of Nature improved by Art and yet corrupted by artifice. Troilus' outcry implies what Hector later argues: 'She is not worth what she doth cost / The keeping', but in the debate Troilus forgets his own scepticism, declaring: 'What's aught but as 'tis valued?' (2.2.51–2). According to this argument beauty is defined by what it costs, as Hippias tells Socrates. Yet Troilus had seemed in that first scene to value Helen's

---

13 *Discourses*, v.21.

14 Philip Edwards, *Shakespeare and the Confines of Art* (1968), p. 106, remarks on 'the absolute lack of any sense of non-human guidance'.

15 Arnold Stein, '*Troilus and Cressida*: The Disjunctive Imagination', *ELH*, 36 (1969), 145–67; p. 148.

beauty in Diomed's negative terms as 'a hell of pain and world of charge . . . a costly loss of wealth and friends' (4.1.59, 62):

> For every false drop in her bawdy veins
> A Grecian's life hath sunk; for every scruple
> Of her contaminated carrion weight
> A Troyan hath been slain. (4.1.71–4)

Paris's retort: 'Fair Diomed, you do as chapmen do, / Dispraise the thing that you desire to buy' (4.1.77–8), recalls the lightweight sparring of Shakespeare's comedies[16] and sounds incongruous amidst the carnage of war. Yet Bassanio's rejection of the golden casket at Belmont expresses a Renaissance distrust of beauty adorned by gold, which anticipates the buying and selling metaphor in *Troilus and Cressida*:

> Look on beauty
> And you shall see 'tis purchas'd by the weight,
> Which therein works a miracle in nature,
> Making them lightest that wear most of it;
> So are those crisped snaky golden locks
> Which make such wanton gambols with the wind
> Upon supposed fairness often known
> To be the dowry of a second head –
> The skull that bred them in the sepulchre.
> Thus ornament is but the guiled shore
> To a most dangerous sea; the beauteous scarf
> Veiling an Indian beauty. (3.2.88–99)

The language of gold, weight, light, fair, the Indian beauty and the dangerous sea suggests the eulogy of Cressida which follows Troilus's outburst against the folly of defending Helen's fairness:

> Tell me, Apollo, for thy Daphne's love,
> What Cressid is, what Pandar, and what we?
> Her bed is India; there she lies, a pearl;
> Between our Ilium and where she resides
> Let it be call'd the wild and wand'ring flood;
> Ourself the merchant, and this sailing Pandar
> Our doubtful hope, our convoy, and our bark.
> (1.1.97–103)

Here Cressida is the pearl sought by the merchant across perilous seas. In the Trojan debate Troilus defends Helen's beauty:

> Why, she is a pearl
> Whose price hath launch'd above a thousand ships,
> And turn'd crown'd kings to merchants.
> (2.2.81–3)

For Troilus beauty is defined by cost. To deny Helen's worth is to deny Cressida's, for in the world of Troy both are weighed in the same scale.

Troilus' image identifies a beauty measured by price. There are no gods in the play, but neither is there any royalty, despite a plethora of princes. Majesty has been devalued by merchantry. The pearl of great price, symbol of the spiritual life, is here both literal and secular. The word 'thousand' recurs in the play as part of its inflated currency, the thousand ships sent for Helen haunting Cressida's brag of love:

> But more in Troilus thousand-fold I see
> Than in the glass of Pandar's praise may be.
> (1.2.276–7)[17]

Hundredfold is the Biblical measure of perfection. The inflation of language describes an economy where beauty has proved not priceless but worthless. No one in the play is capable of understanding Juliet's: 'They are but beggars that can count their worth' (2.6.32).

---

[16] Compare *Love's Labour's Lost*, 2.1.15. 'Beauty is bought by judgment of the eye, / Not utt'red by base sale of chapmen's tongues.'

[17] Chaucer uses 'thousand fold' in *Troilus and Criseyde* as a measure of intense feeling: the pain of love (1.546), curiosity (11.142), ardour (111.1540) and fulfilled passion (111.1684). But it is also used more ambiguously in flattery of Troilus by Pandarus (11.1103) and by Helen and the guests at the supper party when Troilus is sick and Pandarus contrives to bring Cressida to his room for him to declare his love (11.1586). It acquires the dubiety it has in Shakespeare's play in Pandarus' prevarication with Criseyde about whether Troilus is in his house on the night on which he has planned for the love affair to be consummated:

> Soone after this, she gan to hym to rowne,
> And axed hym if Troilus were there.
> He swor hire nay, for he was out of towne,
> And seyde, 'Nece, I pose that he were;
> Yow thurste nevere han the more fere;
> For rather than men myghte hym ther aspie,
> Me were levere a thousand fold to dye.' (111.568)

All line references are to *The Works of Geoffrey Chaucer*, ed. F. N. Robinson (Boston, 1933; repr. Oxford, 1957).

The pricing of beauty has forced it into the market-place to be valued, bought, sold, stolen or sullied: 'We turn not back the silks upon the merchant / When we have soil'd them' (2.2.69–70).

III

Having routed gold and the beautiful maiden as definitive of beauty, Socrates proposes to Hippias that beauty is perceived truly by the senses of sight and hearing. He rejects the witness of taste and touch as being rooted in the physical and incapable of ascent to the spiritual.

Troilus argues in the Trojan debate that Helen has been chosen through the consent of the eyes and ears, as all men choose beauty:

> I take to-day a wife, and my election
> Is led on in the conduct of my will;
> My will enkindled by mine eyes and ears,
> Two traded pilots 'twixt the dangerous shores
> Of will and judgment.   (2.2.61–5)

Sight and hearing mediate between 'will', with its Elizabethan sense of sexual drive, and 'judgment', the operation of reason. But the thrust of the passage is to give greater dominance to will:

> How may I avoid,
> Although my will distaste what it elected,
> The wife I chose?   (2.2.65–7)

Troilus' Platonic orthodoxy in recognizing eyes and ears as arbiters of the beautiful is here compromised by the word 'distaste'. In the *Commentary on Plato's Symposium* Ficino reinforces Socrates' distrust of the lower senses:

What need is there of the senses of smell, taste, and touch? Odors, flavors, heat, cold, softness, hardness, and like qualities are the objects of these senses . . . Love regards as its end the enjoyment of beauty; beauty pertains only to the mind, sight, and hearing . . . Desire which arises from the other senses is called, not love, but lust and madness.[18]

Troilus' rhapsody on the softness of Cressida's hand is echoed later in Paris' plea to Helen to unarm Hector with her 'white enchanting fingers' (3.1.144). Accord-ing to both Plato and Ficino the tactile imagination of wallowing in lily beds would demonstrate the local sensuality of lust or madness, as does Troilus' anticipa-tion of the taste of loving:

> Th' imaginary relish is so sweet
> That it enchants my sense; what will it be
> When that the wat'ry palate tastes indeed
> Love's thrice-repured nectar?   (3.2.18–21)

The sweetness of love for Cressida is tainted by its dramatic proximity with Pandarus' saccharine flat-tery of Helen in the preceding scene: 'My sweet queen, my very very sweet queen . . . honey-sweet queen' (3.1.75, 134). Sweetness has gone off in this play, as Thersites observes:

> *Hector.* Good night, sweet Lord Menelaus.
> *Thersites.* Sweet draught! 'Sweet' quoth 'a? Sweet
>   sink, sweet sewer!   (5.1.72–3)

Shakespeare knew as well as Socrates that beauty identified by taste turns swiftly to distaste. But where Socrates relies on the superior senses of sight and hearing, in *Troilus and Cressida* eyes and ears persuade the will of the form of physical beauty, but mislead the judgement about its relation to goodness. Cressida blames the eye for the vacillation of her affections:

> Ah, poor our sex! this fault in us I find,
> The error of our eye directs our mind.
> What error leads must err; O, then conclude,
> Minds sway'd by eyes are full of turpitude.
>   (5.2.107–10)

The false logic almost parodies Socrates' methods of disputation. But Shakespeare refuses to endorse the gendered vision. Troilus, who had boasted of choosing with eyes and ears, is staggered by their false witness:

---

18 *Marsilio Ficino's Commentary on Plato's Symposium*, trans. Sears Reynolds Jayne, The University of Missouri Studies, 19 (Columbia, 1944), 130, translating the Latin text, p. 41: 'Quid olfactu? Quid gustu? Quid tactu opus est? Odores, sapores, calorem, frigus, mollitiem et duritiem, horumque similia sensus isti percipiunt . . . Amor tamquam eius finem fruitionem respicit pul-chritudinis; ista ad mentem, visum, auditum pertinet solum . . . Appetitio vero, quae reliquos sequitur sensus, non amor sed libido rabiesque vocatur.'

Sith yet there is a credence in my heart,
An esperance so obstinately strong,
That doth invert th'attest of eyes and ears;
As if those organs had deceptious functions
Created only to calumniate.   (5.2.118–22)

The eye and ear seemed to promise unity between the good and the beautiful where the judgement is forced to concede disunity.

In the 'Greater Hippias' Plato exposes the dilemma of the two and the one with brilliant if evasive wit. Socrates ties Hippias in knots over the problem of how the double sense of sight and hearing can perceive the single nature of beauty, forcing the Sophist to admit that he himself is two rather than one, and bidding an insouciant farewell to 'the two of you'.[19] Ficino, more concerned to elucidate than to obfuscate, explains Plato's premise in *Philebus* that the good and the beautiful are one, by pointing to the dissolution which attends their disjunction: 'All things are preserved by unity, but perish from disunity . . . Whoever departs from the good falls away from the one too.'[20] Observing a beauty fallen away from goodness, Troilus is confounded by the evidence of disunity where eyes and ears had claimed oneness:

> If there be rule in unity itself,
> This was not she.[21]

Identity cannot survive such division:

> This is, and is not, Cressid.
> Within my soul there doth conduce a fight
> Of this strange nature, that a thing inseparate
> Divides more wider than the sky and earth;
> And yet the spacious breadth of this division
> Admits no orifex for a point as subtle
> As Ariachne's broken woof to enter.[22]

Cressida's recognition of the two and the one parodies Troilus':

> Troilus, farewell! One eye yet looks on thee:
> But with my heart the other eye doth see.
>
>   (5.2.105–6)

Socrates chose eyes and ears as the registers of beauty because he believed that they created a harmony inherent in the beautiful. Cressida divides the organ of sight against itself, one eye looking one way and one

another. The single nature of the beautiful and the good has disintegrated into a grotesque disunity of perception.

The philosopher Plotinus argued that beauty is inevitably fragmented by its embodiment in material form: 'In the degree in which the beauty is diffused by entering into matter, it is so much the weaker than that concentrated in unity.'[23] Plotinus shares Socrates' scepticism about the power of the beautiful maiden to embody beauty itself. Beautiful human beings are no more than the shadows of an eternal and immutable spirit of beauty: 'Whence shone forth the beauty of Helen, battle-sought; or of all those women like in loveliness to Aphrodite; or of Aphrodite herself; or of any human being that has been perfect in beauty?' Lovers of the beautiful, swayed by eyes and ears: 'Undisciplined in discernment of the inward, knowing nothing of it, run after the outer, never understanding that it is the inner which stirs us.' Beauty resides not in the 'concrete object' but 'in soul or mind'.[24]

---

[19] Plato, *Dialogues*, p. 1559.

[20] *Marsilio Ficino: The Philebus Commentary*, trans. Michael J. B. Allen (Berkeley, 1975), pp. 102–3.

[21] Hankins, *Backgrounds of Shakespeare's Thought*, pp. 68–70, discusses Troilus' use of 'unity' in relation to the mathematics of Plato and Macrobius (in *Timaeus*, in Ficino's *Compendium in Timaeum*, and in Macrobius' *Opera*). See also Vyvyan, *Shakespeare and Platonic Beauty*, pp. 169, 197, 199.

[22] It is interesting that Ficino uses the image of the spider's web in his discussion of the difference between reason in human beings and instinct in beasts, in *Five Questions Concerning the Mind*: 'Thus all spiders weave their webs in a similar manner; they neither learn to weave nor become more proficient through practice, no matter how long' (trans. Josephine L. Burroughs, in *The Renaissance Philosophy of Man*, ed. Ernst Cassirer, Paul Oskar Kristeller and others (Chicago, 1948), p. 206). Shakespeare's reference to Ariachne's web in an outburst about the annihilation of reason might have been prompted by Ficino's Latin: 'Omnes arancae similiter texunt telam, neque texere discunt, neque tempore quamius longo in melius texendo proficiunt', where 'arancae' suggests 'Ariachne' (Marsilius Ficinus, *Opera* (Basileae, 1576), vol. 1, p. 680).

[23] *The Enneads*, trans. Stephen MacKenna (1956), p. 422. I am indebted to the very clear discussion of Plotinus' views on beauty in Panofsky, *Idea: A Concept in Art Theory*, pp. 25–32.   [24] *The Enneads*, pp. 423–4.

In *Troilus and Cressida* Shakespeare seems deliberately to have rejected any consciousness of beauty in the mind. Troilus may cry despairingly: 'If beauty have a soul, this is not she', but can resolve despair into a complex pun: 'Farewell, revolted fair!' (5.2.136, 184). In the same spirit of resurgent parody on the part of the dramatist Paris' servant ushers Pandarus into his master's bedroom:

Servant. With him the mortal Venus, the heart-blood of beauty, love's invisible soul –
Pandarus. Who, my cousin, Cressida?
Servant. No, sir, Helen. Could not you find out that by her attributes? (3.1.30–5)

Shakespeare seems to burlesque the whole concept of inner beauty. Yet it is one which is recurrent in his drama as a whole. Viola in *Twelfth Night* bears 'a mind that envy could not but call fair' (2.1.26). She trusts the Sea Captain because she 'will believe thou hast a mind that suits / With this thy fair and outward character' (1.2.50). The play, despite transitory disruptions – 'O, how vile an idol proves this god!' (3.4.349) – celebrates concord between the beautiful and the good, the inner and the outer man, the fair in body and the fair in mind. Even Iago perceives a relation between the two which is inaccessible to Paris and Troilus:

> If Cassio do remain,
> He hath a daily beauty in his life
> That makes me ugly.   (*Othello*, 5.1.18–20)

Shakespeare could have injected such awareness into the world of *Troilus and Cressida*, yet it remains conspicuously absent. Even Hector, the closest to owning a daily beauty in his life, cannot escape the debased values of his own society, its preference for will over judgement, its self-absorption, faded chivalry and domestic poverty:

> Andromache, I am offended with you.
> Upon the love you bear me, get you in.
>   (5.3.77–8)

The lack of religious dimension in the play has turned the worship of beauty as Plato conceived it into idolatry of its material forms.

Plotinus argued that the power to perceive inner beauty behind the outward is dependent on the purity of each man's soul. A man must shape his own nature to accord with the beautiful, just as the sculptor fashions stone according to his Idea of beauty: 'When you know you have become this perfect work, when you are self-gathered in the purity of your being, nothing now remaining . . . can shatter that inner unity.'[25] Beauty and identity are here one and the same, singleness of spirit defining the single nature of the beautiful. The fragmentation of identity everywhere apparent in *Troilus and Cressida*, which reaches its apotheosis in Troilus' recognition of a Cressida divided against herself,[26] is part of the dramatist's complex vision of the disintegration created by war. Ironically the defence of beauty in the Trojan retention of Helen, and its pursuit by the Greeks, creates a savagery and moral deformity which blinds men and women to the true nature of beauty itself. The eye which in other plays discerns the unity of the beautiful and the good can in this play only see the beautiful through the obscuring mists of its own imperfections.

The mirror into which a man looks in order to know himself, a favourite Renaissance image culled from both Socrates and Seneca, can easily become a means not to self-knowledge but to self-regard.[27] In Shakespeare's Sonnet 3 it serves both ends:

> Look in thy glass, and tell the face thou viewest
> Now is the time that face should form another.

The mirror reflects a self-devouring beauty vowed to sterility:

> Or who is he so fond will be the tomb
> Of his self-love, to stop posterity?

The poet advises the young man to defy Time by refusing to keep his beauty to himself. By embracing the destructions of age he will renew himself in youth.

---

25 *The Enneads*, p. 63.
26 Vyvyan, *Shakespeare and Platonic Beauty*, p. 197.
27 In Nannus Mirabellius' *Polyanthea*, a schoolroom compilation of extracts from Latin and some Greek authors arranged in dictionary form, which T. W. Baldwin argues was used in grammar schools, Socrates' advice about gazing into the mirror of the self is placed under two headings: *Pulchritudo* (Beauty) and *Amor Sui* (Self-Love).

But in *Troilus and Cressida* the mirror offers no such advice. It betrays men and women into Narcissism. The self-loving man devours himself: 'He that is proud eats up himself. Pride is his own glass, his own trumpet, his own chronicle; and whatever praises itself but in the deed devours the deed in the praise' (2.3.149–53). Ulysses urges that men should cease to allow Achilles to see himself in the mirror of their deference:

> Pride hath no other glass
> To show itself but pride; for supple knees
> Feed arrogance and are the proud man's fees.
>
> (3.3.47–9)

Shakespeare no doubt recalled in this image of Pride gazing into its own glass Spenser's picture of Pride, 'a mayden Queene', in Book I of *The Faerie Queene*:

> And in her hand she held a mirrhour bright,
> Wherein her face she often vewed fayne
> And in her selfe-lou'd semblance took delight.[28]

The beauty, regality and vanity of Spenser's allegorical monarch audaciously laud and satirize the real Virgin Queen whose favour Spenser industriously and unsuccessfully courted. When Shakespeare came to show Richard II, a monarch whom Elizabeth I ruefully admitted to be her prototype, deposed by Bolingbroke, he has him call for a mirror in which to view his clouded majesty:

> Was this the face
> That every day under his household roof
> Did keep ten thousand men? Was this the face
> That like the sun did make beholders wink?
>
> (4.1.276–9)

The sun imagery looks back to Spenser's maiden 'that shone as *Titans* ray', forward to Helen, whose beauty 'Wrinkles Apollo's, and makes stale the morning' (2.2.79). But even more significant is the characteristic form in which Richard II's question is cast, with its obvious echo of Marlowe's Faustus:

> Was this the face that launched a thousand ships
> And burnt the topless towers of Ilium?[29]

When Shakespeare embarked on his own creation of Helen of Troy adulation of Elizabeth was over. The Queen who had seen herself mirrored in Richard II died the year that *Troilus and Cressida* was registered by the Stationers' Company. The Elizabethan myth she had cultivated was already dead. Shakespeare's Helen with her tarnished image, her vanity, her obsession, shared with Achilles and with Cressida,[30] with what other people see in her, bears witness to an emergent Jacobean consciousness of beauty corrupted by self-love and left succession-less. The maiden Queen fascinated by her own reflection had proved after all to be Time's subject, self-consumed in her own sterility.

When Achilles gazes into the mirror of the self, as Plotinus commands, he sees in his soul confusion rather than clarity:

> My mind is troubled, like a fountain stirr'd;
> And I myself see not the bottom of it.
>
> (3.3.303–4)

Shakespeare shows that eyes and ears fail to perceive a beauty at one with truth because the senses are deluded by self-regard. Unable to know themselves, the characters in *Troilus and Cressida* remain the slaves of beauty in its material forms, rather than the servants of its spirit.

IV

Troilus and Cressida dramatizes not the conjunction of the beautiful and the good but the inseparability of the fair and the foul in human experience. The consequence is the disintegration of language as the tool of rational discourse. This is evident early in the play when Paris argues for keeping Helen:

---

[28] Edmund Spenser, *The Faerie Queene*, ed. Thomas P. Roche, Jr. (Harmondsworth, 1978), i.iv.8, 10; p. 81.

[29] *Doctor Faustus*, 5.1.99, in *The Complete Plays of Christopher Marlowe*, ed. Irving Ribner (New York, 1963).

[30] Cressida's 'Tear my bright hair, and scratch my praised cheeks' (4.2.106) recalls Chapman's 'bright-cheekt Brysys' in *The Iliads of Homer*, I, reprinted in Bullough, *Narrative and Dramatic Sources of Shakespeare*, vol. 6, p. 118. The glass of other people's praise is equally vital to Achilles, as is apparent in the speech traditionally associated with Plato's *First Alcibiades*: 'The beauty that is borne here in the face / The bearer knows not, but commends itself / To others' eyes' (3.3.95).

I would have the soil of her fair rape
Wip'd off in honourable keeping her.

(2.2.148–9)

The antithetical responses evoked by the juxtaposition of 'fair' and 'rape' and of 'soil' and 'fair' rob language of stability. The word is no longer the signifier of the thing, but the evasion of its reality. The same coupling of beauty and falsehood in Cressida incites Troilus' outburst against discourse itself, which Ficino called 'the messenger of reason':[31]

O madness of discourse,
That cause sets up with and against itself.

(5.2.140–1)

The same inner divisions in language appear in the dialogue between Hector and Troilus about the conduct of battle:

Troilus.
When many times the captive Grecian falls,
Even in the fan and wind of your fair sword,
You bid them rise and live.
Hector.
O, 'tis fair play!
Troilus.
Fool's play, by heaven, Hector.   (5.3.40–3)

The now commonplace expression 'fair play' was first coined by Shakespeare some ten years earlier in *King John*, where it is twice used with its modern meaning of fair dealing.[32] But the fact that the compound was so new to the language allows Shakespeare to exploit in *Troilus and Cressida* its willingness to regress into its separate elements of 'fair' and 'play'. Hector uses the words in the new sense to mean 'just behaviour', Troilus in their separate senses of 'beautiful sport' or even, in the context of the play, 'sport for beauty'. The word 'fool', so nearly related in sound to 'foul', contains a linguistic augury of where Hector's sport will lead him, to his own foul slaughter at the hands of Achilles, which follows hard on the fool's play of hunting the warrior in fair armour. Just as beauty in the play is the carcass of itself, lacking inner life, so the language of the beautiful, the rich Elizabethan word 'fair', has disintegrated into empty compliment:

Pandarus. Fair be to you, my lord, and to all this fair company! Fair desires, in all fair measures, fairly guide them – especially to you, fair queen! Fair thoughts be your fair pillow.
Helen. Dear lord, you are full of fair words.
Pandarus. You speak your fair pleasure, sweet queen. Fair prince, here is good broken music.

(3.1.41–7)

The play records the breakdown of discourse as the badge of the rational being. At the end sweet notes fail. There is nowhere to go but silence.

v

The pursuit of beauty in *Troilus and Cressida* has thus brought its adherents to a vision of its worthlessness which trivializes even the burning of Troy. Shakespeare destroys the definition of beauty as the beautiful maiden more ruthlessly than Socrates himself without offering any alternative testimony to the reality of the spirit behind the physical form. Yet his other plays affirm that reality. He seems deliberately to have excluded from *Troilus and Cressida* some element vital to his drama as a whole.

In Plato's *Symposium* Diotima defines love as the desire to possess the beautiful and the good in perpetuity:

All men, Socrates, are in a state of pregnancy, both spiritual and physical, and when they come to maturity they feel a natural desire to bring forth, but they can do so only in beauty and never in ugliness.[33]

Physical procreation is the lower form, spiritual the higher. But in *Troilus and Cressida* there is no time for the creation of the beautiful in spirit, any more than there is any place for the creation of children. Andromache is not allowed the luxury of her Homeric lament for Astyanax, the child who will never carry his father's renown into the future. The legitimate are cut off, while gods stand up for bastards,

---

[31] *Five Questions Concerning the Mind*, in Cassirer (ed.), *The Renaissance Philosophy of Man*, p. 206.
[32] 5.1.67: 'Fair-play orders'; 5.2.118: 'According to the fair play of the world'; *OED*, entry for 'Fair', 10(c).
[33] Plato, *The Symposium*, trans. W. Hamilton (Harmondsworth, 1951), p. 86.

as Thersites boasts in his absurd encounter with Margarelon, bastard son of Priam: 'One bear will not bite another, and wherefore should one bastard? Take heed, the quarrel's ominous to us: if the son of a whore fight for a whore, he tempts judgment. Farewell, bastard' (5.7.19–24). Defence, the aim of war, is also the aim of love, as Cressida, loving a thousand-fold, knows, lying 'at a thousand watches': 'If I cannot ward what I would not have hit, I can watch you for telling how I took the blow; unless it swell past hiding, and then it's past watching' (1.2.256, 259–62). The whore is the physical emblem of the barrenness of beauty in the play. Helen has no posterity:

> He like a puling cuckold would drink up
> The lees and dregs of a flat tamed piece;
> You, like a lecher, out of whorish loins
> Are pleas'd to breed out your inheritors.
>
> (4.1.63–6)

From whores and wars men inherit only diseases. To such has the pursuit of beauty brought them.

The vital element missing from *Troilus and Cressida* is a commitment at the heart of the drama to the power of beauty to re-create itself. Dio Chrysostom recorded in his 'Twenty-First Discourse: On Beauty' his sense of decline in the Greek ideal of physical beauty: 'As if the beautiful have died out in the course of time just like some plant or animal – the fate which

they do say has overtaken the lions in Europe.'[34] Perhaps Shakespeare meant Troilus' comparison of Hector's generosity to that of the lion to forebode extinction. The play shows beauty unable to survive in a world pledged, with deep irony, to its defence. Without the power to propagate, either in body or spirit, its men and women remain trapped in time, obsessed with the past and the future, powerless to own the present. Their stake in the future lies in the slanders of Time itself.

Troilus' question about whether he will lie in publishing the truth of Cressida's faithlessness recalls Greek scepticism about the story of Helen. Yet despite Shakespeare's destruction of the myth, outside the play Helen retains symbolic stature.[35] Shakespeare defines beauty by giving it the power to generate life not in the time-bound past of the Trojan war but in the recreating present of the work of art, the play itself.

---

[34] *Discourses*, II.273. Hardy notes this decline in the face of Clym Yeobright, the sign 'that a long line of disillusive centuries has permanently displaced the Hellenic idea of life', *The Return of the Native*, Book 3, chap. 1.

[35] Douglas Cole, 'Myth and Anti-Myth: The Case of *Troilus and Cressida*', *Shakespeare Quarterly*, 31 (1980), 76–86, p. 84; R. A. Foakes, '*Troilus and Cressida* Reconsidered', *University of Toronto Quarterly*, 32 (1963), 142–54; p. 154.

THE PASTORAL RECKONING IN 'CYMBELINE'

MICHAEL TAYLOR

The most astonishing scene in *Cymbeline* unnerves us with the grotesque spectacle of its heroine waking up in a pastoral setting from a death-like sleep (induced by Dr Cornelius' box of drugs) to the sight of what appears to be her decapitated husband sprawled alongside her. *Et in Arcadia ego*, with a vengeance! Until this rude awakening, Imogen had imagined herself to be safe in her pastoral sanctuary, far from the corruption of Cymbeline's court, secure in the immediate and excessive affection displayed for her by Arviragus and Guiderius who, despite her male disguise, and despite the fact that they have never met her before, have instinctively and conventionally responded to the ties of blood between them. Horrified now by this change in her situation, Imogen at first concludes that she must be dreaming:

> I hope I dream,
> For so I thought I was a cave-keeper
> And cook to honest creatures. (4.2.297–9)[1]

The desired diminution of status from princess to pastoral skivvy has become mysteriously transformed into a nightmare degradation in which the honest creatures of her waking hours have vanished, leaving behind in their place a headless changeling whose reality can be only fleetingly doubted in those blurred moments 'twixt sleep and wake.

Imogen's enumeration of Posthumus' Herculean parts as she then inches her way up to the corpse's headlessness has shaken many critics; as Bernard Harris observes, the whole scene has a 'comic menace and near-demented ingenuity'.[2] 'Dramatically inexcusable' for Harley Granville-Barker,[3] Imogen's final confrontation with Cloten is a notoriously difficult one to bring off in the theatre without arousing a defensive risibility in an audience alarmed by the extent to which Shakespeare has already subjected his heroine to the unspeakable. In remorseless fashion, Imogen's lamentations over the body include *a fortiori* a prolonged outburst against the callous despoliation that makes the spectacle so remarkably uncomfortable for us:

> Damned Pisanio
> Hath with his forgèd letters – damned Pisanio –
> From this most bravest vessel of the world
> Struck the maintop. O Posthumus, alas,
> Where is thy head? Where's that? Ay me, where's
> that?
> Pisanio might have killed thee at the heart
> And left this head on. (4.2.317–23)

These last three lines in particular must be very troublesome for any actress to make properly affecting, even though the construction 'might have killed thee' need not entail the petulant delivery it so frequently calls for in modern usage. Shakespeare seems determined to invest Cloten's remains with a more remarkable potency than their owner ever managed when alive, while still maintaining his essential absurdity even when the cause of it has been so unceremoniously removed. Brainless while alive,

---

[1] References to Shakespeare are from *The Complete Pelican Shakespeare*, general editor Alfred Harbage (Baltimore, 1969).

[2] '"What's past is prologue": *Cymbeline* and *Henry VIII*', in *Later Shakespeare*, ed. John Russell Brown and Bernard Harris, Stratford-upon-Avon Studies, 8 (1966), p. 225.

[3] *Prefaces to Shakespeare*, second series (1930), p. 340.

Cloten's fate is grim poetic justice: his headless carcass a bizarre rebus for the conduct of his life. In death, his absurdity is infectious. In all the previous confrontations between Cloten and Imogen, Cloten has come halting off, his precarious intellect no match for Imogen's sarcastic tongue and unshakeable dignity; now, in mute triumph, his body, about which he had been so absurdly arrogant (that 'arrogant piece of flesh' (4.2.127) as Guiderius describes him), raises up a storm of emotion in Imogen's breast. The fact that she believes the body to belong to Posthumus makes the experience even more damaging to her dignity, especially when, in an excess of grief, she throws herself upon it in an action ironically – dementedly – almost farcically – precipitated by the name of the person (did she but know it) with whose blood she now daubs herself:

> This is Pisanio's deed, and Cloten. O,
> Give colour to my pale cheek with thy blood,
> That we the horrider may seem to those
> Which chance to find us. O my lord, my lord!
>
> (4.2.329–32)

In a superfluous piece of commentary, the play's Arden editor cannot conceal his distaste for the extravagance of Imogen's conduct: 'There seems no escape from the gruesome conclusion that she smears her face with his blood, or is about to do so.'[4]

There is no escape from this gruesome conclusion except at the text's expense. And however much as civilized readers we would like to spare Imogen and ourselves her necrophilic embrace, we can hardly fail to notice that it seems in some respects no more than fitting that she should suffer such an indignity, the like of which would be unimaginable for Marina and Perdita even during Marina's humiliation in the brothel at Mitylene. Although we may flinch from its painful accumulation of detail, in a powerful way the indignity to Imogen satisfies expectations aroused in us during the course of Shakespeare's treatment of the wager story in *Cymbeline*, bringing to a suitably grotesque climax an element of punitive behaviour in relationships and towards the self that is more fugitively intimated in *Pericles* and *The Winter's Tale*. While it may be true (as so many critics insist) that there has been something of an 'uneasy conflation'[5] of history

and romance in *Cymbeline*, or that the play as a whole fails to come together entirely satisfactorily, it is demonstrably true that in the story of Imogen, Iachimo, and Posthumus Shakespeare achieves a potent coherence in which the violation of Imogen's dream of pastoral innocence has an important role to play, as it also has in the play's action as a whole, making it one of those events of special significance in a work of art around which interpretation inevitably clusters.[6] After some forty lines or so of wild address over the decapitated body, Imogen falls into an exhausted sleep from which she wakens to another, more promising reality as attendant on her civilized Roman master, Caius Lucius. After Imogen's grotesque experience, malicious energy in the play as a whole flags – the scenes which follow act 4, scene 2 record a progressive amelioration: in act 4, scene 3, news of the Queen's fatal illness (we never see her again); in act 5, scene 1, Posthumus' repentance even before he knows Imogen to be guiltless; in act 5, scene 2, Iachimo's similar repentance following his defeat in battle by the disguised Posthumus; in the play's last three scenes, the military triumph of the Britons over the Romans, Posthumus' vision of Jupiter, Cymbeline's refreshed state of mind and his voluntary return to the *pax romana*.

In structural and emotional terms Imogen's degradation in act 4, scene 2 marks a watershed in the play's action; after it, with almost every wink of the eye some new grace will be born. Pivotally placed, Imogen's experience captures much of the play's accumulated significance, and the greater the interpretative burden the more daring Shakespeare's choice of the grotesque as an appropriate vehicle for this climax to the play's pastoral activity, in which an original dream of innocence – Imogen's – expressed in explicitly pastoral terms, undergoes such a savage assault. Earlier, in Cymbeline's court, with Posthumus banished, and pursued by the preposterous

---

4 James Nosworthy (ed.), *Cymbeline*, the new Arden Shakespeare (1955), p. 143.

5 See Howard Felperin, *Shakespearean Romance* (Princeton, 1972), p. 178.

6 See Frank Kermode's discussion of such events in his *Genesis: On the Interpretation of Narrative* (Cambridge, Mass., 1979), pp. 15 ff.

Cloten, Imogen had dreamt of a life exempt from courtly haunt and princely responsibility:

> Would I were
> A neatherd's daughter, and my Leonatus
> Our neighbor shepherd's son.   (1.1.148–50)

Instead of finding herself in a pastoral setting where she might play Flora to Posthumus' Florizel, Imogen finds herself in one where she must play a much more demandingly operatic role in a mad burlesque of sexual passion and shattered idyllic expectations. When Imogen clutches the decapitated body to her, daubs herself with its blood, and falls into an exhausted, dreamless sleep – the sleep of an emotional satiety – the coital sequence suggested by these responses supplies an equivocal, parodic answer to the earnest prayer of Guiderius and Arviragus: 'Quiet consummation have, / And renowned be thy grave' (4.2.280–1).[7]

Why at this important juncture does Shakespeare choose to subject his heroine (a heroine as militantly chaste, incidentally, as any in the late plays) to such a literal and symbolic besmirching? Any adequate answer has to take into account the extent to which *Cymbeline* has from the beginning played fast and loose with the narrative conventions normally governing the lives of young lovers in the romances, especially the one that insists on the narrative sequence that leads them through a troublesome unmarried state to a blissfully married one.[8] Not for Posthumus and Imogen (or so it seems) the traditional comedic role of their counterparts in the other romances and romantic comedies whose marriage prospects remain conventionally dim until the final scenes, their consummations impeded by a society that Northrop Frye characterizes as 'irrational or anti-comic':

The normal action [of Renaissance comedy] is the effort of a young man to get possession of a young woman who is kept from him by various social barriers: her low birth, his minority or shortage of funds, parental opposition, the prior claims of a rival. These are eventually circumvented, and the comedy ends at a point when a new society is crystallised, usually by the marriage or betrothal of hero and heroine.[9]

In the case of *Cymbeline*, Frye's various social barriers

seem already to have been hurdled by the lovers' impetuous marriage – consummated despite Posthumus' low birth, shortage of funds, the opposition of Imogen's father and step-mother and the rival claims, prior or otherwise, of Cloten, the Queen's son and Imogen's step-brother. Just as iconoclastically, however, Cymbeline and his supporters act in shocking defiance of both dramatic and social convention; they refuse to accept the validity of the lovers' contract, using all the arguments mentioned by Frye (with the exception of the hero's minority), as though the marriage itself – usually the holy grail in Shakespearian comedy – were nothing but a minor impediment to Cloten's more authentic courtship. In the enormity of its casualness, Cymbeline's advice to his step-son perfectly conveys this important aspect of his court's aristocratic perversity:

> The exile of her minion is too new;
> She hath not yet forgot him. Some more time
> Must wear the print of his remembrance on't,
> And then she's yours.   (2.3.41–4)

Not much spirit of *noblesse oblige* here: stripped of its fatuity (if that were possible) Cloten's version of what it is to be a nobleman (the obsession later of Belarius' moral reflections) – 'it is fit I should commit offense to my inferiors' (2.1.26–7) – epitomizes the values of Cymbeline's court.

Cymbeline begins then in the manner of *Pericles*; both plays open with the unsavoury spectacle of wayward kings disregarding moral or social norms, victimizing representatives of the younger generation, committing offences to their inferiors. (The general resemblance is made keener by the suggestion

---

7 Although 'consummation' meaning 'ending' has by far the longer history, the *OED* records the first use of 'consummation' as the 'completion of marriage by sexual intercourse' in 1530.

8 *The Comedy of Errors* and *Othello* are the only other plays by Shakespeare to begin in this way – one a tragedy of sexual jealousy, the other an untypical early comedy that presents the unromantic marriage between Adriana and Antipholus of Ephesus with cool and disdainful objectivity.

9 Northrop Frye, *A Natural Perspective* (New York, 1965), p. 72. The phrase 'an irrational or anti-comic society' occurs on p. 74.

of incest in Cloten's courtship of his step-sister.) In vivid contrast, the marriage of Imogen and Post-humus institutionalizes (or seems to do so) the larger virtues each possesses; yet even before we experience Posthumus' later weakness on his banishment to Italy – even (for that matter) before we meet either Imogen or Posthumus – the sense we have of the abnormality of the situation, of there being something posthumous about the action of a romance beginning where most end, infects even the play's opening conversation, a piece of explicatory dialogue between the two Gentle-men in which the First Gentleman – for the benefit of his conventionally ignorant colleague (and of our-selves) – extols the superior virtues of the newly married couple at the expense of the King's party. He does so in a verse typical of *Cymbeline* – one that has a 'hard corrugated texture ... [caused by] the persistent recreation of feelings of a particular kind of physical pain'.[10] The play's opening lines, 'tantalizingly ellip-tical' in Nosworthy's phrase,[11] make only tortuous sense, but are then followed by the crystal-clear exposition that the First Gentleman provides for the Second, as though he were at the same time mocking his own introductory style:

> She's wedded,
> Her husband banished, she imprisoned. All
> Is outward sorrow, though I think the King
> Be touched at very heart. (1.1.7–10)

To swing from one linguistic extreme to the other within the space of a few lines seems appropriate for a play throughout blown stylistically between the opposing winds of fairy-tale and case-history. If the semantic complexity of the First Gentleman's opening speech reflects the moral difficulty of living in a court so Janus-faced, then his later use of the hyperbole of punishment in his description of Posthumus reveals a more subtle difficulty; like the other courtiers, the First Gentleman cannot mould his language to the disposition of his subject without the use of punitive metaphor:

> I do extend him, sir, within himself,
> Crush him together rather than unfold
> His measure duly. (1.1.25–7)

This is the first of several instances in the play where the extreme worth of an object – something or someone beyond beyond, as Imogen says (3.2.56) – forces the eulogizer beyond (or rather beneath) conventional hyperbolic expression to draw extrava-gance from a darker area of the mind. If Cloten is 'a thing / Too bad for bad report' (1.2.16–17) then Posthumus and Imogen often seem to be things too good for good report, hence their superiority can only be conveyed in a strange hyperbolic exploitation of the vocabulary of bad report dominated by the imagery of forcible restraint – merit crushed in order to be unfolded duly. The lovers express their love for each other in terms equally punitive: Posthumus will drink down the words of Imogen's letters 'Though ink be made of gall' (1.1.101); rather than marry again were Imogen to die before him (itself a morbid notion) he would 'cere up my embracements from a next / With bonds of death' (1.1.116–17); in his eyes, the bracelet he gives Imogen on parting from her 'is a manacle of love; I'll place it / Upon this fairest prisoner' (1.1.122–3). Imogen is similarly afflicted. She can afford to ignore her father's anger, she says, because 'a touch more rare / Subdues all pangs, all fears' (1.1.135–6) – 'a touch more rare' is a fine phrase meaning (as Dowden tells us) 'a more exquisite pain', the pain, that is, of the enforced absence of her new husband whom she later describes as 'My supreme crown of grief' (1.6.4). Later still, she talks of the 'med'cinable' griefs that 'physic love' (3.2.34); and it is she who has to drink the gall of Posthumus' letter. 'The paper / Hath cut her throat already' (3.4.32–3) Pisanio observes in a typical metaphor. Love's afflic-tion becomes self-infliction for Imogen – or imagined self-infliction – when she responds to Pisanio's descrip-tion of Posthumus' embarking for Italy with

> I would have broke mine eyestrings, cracked them but
> To look upon him till the diminution
> Of space had pointed him sharp as my needle.
> (1.3.17–19)

Lovers in Shakespeare's plays do not usually talk of love's experience in this way except in problem comedies like *Troilus and Cressida* or tragedies of love

---

[10] F. C. Tinkler, '*Cymbeline*', *Scrutiny*, 7 (1938–9), 6.
[11] New Arden *Cymbeline*, p. 3.

like *Romeo and Juliet.* Do the lovers in *Cymbeline* linger in punitive terms over their love for each other simply because they have been forced to undergo the punishment of separation at that point in their lives when their counterparts in the other romances begin their hard-won freedom together? It hardly seems an adequate explanation. When Imogen describes Posthumus as 'My supreme crown of grief' (which follows the interesting ambiguity of her 'a wedded lady / That hath her husband banished' (1.6.2–3)), the phrase is a metonym not so much for Posthumus himself as for the punishment he cannot avoid inflicting on her by his banishment from Cymbeline's court – the 'pangs of barred affections' (1.1.82) in the Queen's hypocritical words. Yet Imogen's elliptical construction gives the phrase the force of an accusation (or even self-accusation), especially as it follows 'O, that husband', the traditional resigned or despairing cry of long-suffering wives of neglectful husbands (a class Imogen is about to join).

Neither the perilous situation in which Imogen and Posthumus find themselves at the beginning of the play, nor the irony of subsequent events, justifies the extravagant language each uses to and about the other, each the other's supreme crown of grief more mysteriously than can be explained by the circumstances of their separation. And as in *The Winter's Tale,* Shakespeare allows us the occasional fleeting insight into his characters' pasts to suggest more complicated psychic disturbances than at first seems to be the case. The impression we have of something hyperbolically and unnaturally over-ripe, where (as the First Gentleman says of Posthumus) spring has become autumn, and where value can be expressed only in punitive terms, suggests a deeper malaise, hinted at perhaps by Imogen when surprised by Iachimo's description of Posthumus' frivolous behaviour in Rome:

> When he was here
> He did incline to sadness, and ofttimes
> Not knowing why. (1.6.61–3)

Shakespeare begins *The Merchant of Venice* with a better-known and more elaborate confession of the same mysterious ailment. Antonio rejects the explanations for his melancholy suggested by his friends,

Salerio and Solanio; he suffers neither from unrequited love nor from a fear for his argosies at sea. As far as we can determine, like Jaques in *As You Like It,* he suffers obscurely from the melancholy of being human – it is Antonio he grieves for. It may well be Posthumus Posthumus grieves for (if 'sadness' here goes beyond the merely serious); as Imogen has indicated, his inclination to it pre-dates Cymbeline's harsh verdict on their marriage. What Imogen remembers about Posthumus has an ironically lurid light thrown on it by what Posthumus remembers about Imogen in parallel circumstances an act later (act 2, scene 5). Both memories surface under the pressure of Iachimo's accusations, both seem spontaneous and involuntary, each tells us something unexpected about the person concerned:

> Me of my lawful pleasure she restrained
> And prayed me oft forbearance – did it with
> A pudency so rosy, the sweet view on't
> Might well have warmed old Saturn – that I thought her
> As chaste as unsunned snow. (2.5.9–13)

These lines come in the middle of a soliloquy of great power and subtlety; one that George Steiner in *After Babel* chooses as his paradigm for the untranslatability of the 'complete semantic event'[12] in great poetry. To exhaust the significance (the meaning even) of such a complex speech, he argues, would involve us in ever-widening circles of legitimate application up to and including what he calls the 'informing sphere of sensibility' (p. 7) with the problem of 'infinite series' (p. 7) becoming an increasingly daunting one. We do not have to journey too far down the road to infinity, however, to notice how Posthumus' memory of Imogen exposes her innocence in an equivocal manner peculiar to *Cymbeline.* As opposed, say, to the sinless sensuality of the lovers in *The Winter's Tale,*[13] *Cymbeline* makes much of the treacherous eroticism of its lovers' innocence, with Imogen cast as the play's Isabella whose 'modesty may more betray our sense / Than woman's

---

[12] 1975, p. 7.
[13] The phrase is S. L. Bethell's in *The Winter's Tale: A Study* (1947), p. 31.

lightness' (*Measure for Measure*, 2.2.169–70). Post-humus couches his recollections of Imogen's modesty in words that convey how dangerous to itself it is: 'pudency so rosy' suggests the erotic image that warms old Saturn far more readily than, in this context, the more paradoxical one of a chastity as cold as unsunned snow. Posthumus remembers Imogen in terms that recall Iachimo aroused by her erotic vulnerability as she lies sleeping before him, whose encomium on her beauty comes to a climax with a de-scription of the intimate detail which for Posthumus will clinch the argument for her betrayal of him:

> On her left breast
> A mole cinque-spotted, like the crimson drops
> I' th' bottom of a cowslip. Here's a voucher
> Stronger than ever law could make. This secret
> Will force him think I have picked the lock and ta'en
> The treasure of her honor.   (2.2.37–42)

Nosworthy remarks: 'In the French versions of the wager-story the mole is likened to a rose and to a violet, but Shakespeare's flower analogy is almost certainly coincidental.'[14] Coincidental it may be, but Shakespeare's choice here of a flower more simple and demure than either the rose or the violet em-phasizes the corresponding delicacy and demureness of Imogen's sensuality, and hence her power to more betray men's sense than woman's lightness. Iachimo's fervid response to the charms of innocent abandon-ment is followed by its vulgar counterpart in the next scene (act 2, scene 3) where Cloten calls for an aubade from the musicians to awaken Imogen – in his greasy terminology, 'If you can penetrate her with your fingering, so; we'll try with tongue too' (2.3.13–14). He sees the performance of the song's words and music as a sexual invasion though, unlike Orsino, he would not want the appetite to sicken and so die as a result (except in the punning sense that Orsino probably did not have in mind). The song's lyrics, however, are as remote from Cloten's intentions as the cowslip from Iachimo's arousal:

> Hark, hark, the lark at heaven's gate sings,
>   And Phoebus gins arise,
> His steeds to water at those springs
>   On chaliced flowers that lies;

> And winking Mary-buds begin
>   To ope their golden eyes.
> With every thing that pretty is,
>   My lady sweet, arise,
>   Arise, arise !   (2.3.19–27)

The song's conventional pastoralism hardly squares with Cloten's lubricious expectations of its effect on Imogen; for that matter, it barely corresponds to Cloten's introduction of it as 'a wonderful sweet air with admirable rich words to it' (2.3.16–17). His fanciful transfiguration of its nature does square, however, though on a far more moronically brutal level, with similar transformations of innocence on the parts of Iachimo and Posthumus and is one of the ways in which Shakespeare builds up a network of associations between them in our minds.

'Pudency so rosy', 'crimson drops / I' th' bottom of a cowslip', 'chaliced flowers': images to warm the libidos of old Saturn, Iachimo, Posthumus, and Cloten. And Posthumus is not as much the odd man out on this list as he ought to be, considering that, until his banishment, he has had every reason to expect the provocative image to give way to the reality it advertises. Between wedding and banishment, how-ever, the image retains its provocation for him because of the frequency with which Imogen restrains him from his *lawful* pleasure – she 'prayed me *oft* for-bearance'. Appropriately enough, Iachimo squeezes the final equivocation out of Imogen's attitude in the last scene of the play: 'He spake of her as Dian had hot dreams, / And she alone were cold' (5.5.180–1). Exploiting yet another ironic parallel with Cloten, Britain's absurd, bungling Iachimo, Posthumus' ex-perience seems to confirm Cloten's vulgar opinion of love-making in which 'a woman's fitness comes by fits' (4.1.5–6). The inclination to sadness that Imogen remembers about Posthumus may therefore not be unconnected with what Posthumus remembers about Imogen's chaste behaviour, no matter how rosily managed (a management, by the way, that Pisanio de-scribes as 'More goddess-like than wife-like', 3.2.8). Such an inference need not go beyond the complete semantic event, even though it may go beyond the more usual interpretation of the lovers' recollections

---

[14] New Arden *Cymbeline*, p. 53.

which sees them as having only a limited application – Imogen's rosy pudency functioning simply as a kind of pathetic fallacy emphasizing Posthumus' savagery. Yet well within the informing sphere of sensibility lies the important connection that we make between Posthumus' prurient recollection of Imogen's sexual attractiveness and the relative ease with which he believes Iachimo's account of her fallen condition. As Geoffrey Hill says: 'there is a kind of naivete which asks to be devoured and a natural partly unconscious collusion between the deceived and the deceiver: between, for instance, Posthumus and Iachimo, Imogen and Iachimo, Cymbeline and the Queen.'[15]

Homer Swander has shown that Posthumus asks insistently (and deserves) to be devoured by Iachimo:[16] the collusion (if that is the right word) between Imogen and Iachimo is far more problematic. According to Angelo in *Measure for Measure*, no blame can possibly be attached to Isabella for the fact that her superior virtue has ensnared his lust. Angelo recognizes the injustice of calling someone a temptress who all unknowingly tempts; besides, a virtuous man, as he says (2.2.166–8), should be fortified in his virtue by Isabella's example, not carnally stimulated. But the play – Isabella herself – clouds the issue:

That is, were I under the terms of death,
Th' impression of keen whips I'ld wear as rubies,
And strip myself to death as to a bed
That longing have been sick for, ere I'ld yield
My body up to shame.   (2.4.100–4)

Isabella's militant defence of her purity does not escape the Viennese obsession with the carnal – no one in the play does (as the Duke himself discovers in his demeaning encounters with Lucio) – and in this quotation Isabella is obviously overwhelmed by what F. R. Leavis calls the 'sensuality of martyrdom'[17] which as much reveals the imperfect submergence of the woman in the ecclesiastic as encourages the concupiscence of Angelo's thoughts.

In *Cymbeline* imperfect submergences abound. However innocent the lovers, we cannot help but see them as sexual objects designed to provoke the conspiracy of suggestiveness that gives them their ambivalent and attractive power. How much more attractive (and no less ambivalent) must be Imogen's

appeal for us, when we hear not only from Iachimo how beautiful she is, but share with him in the actual vision of her loveliness, the naked extent of which will be determined only by the tact or bravado of the particular production in which she appears.[18] The moral precariousness of the moment is heightened when Iachimo bends to kiss her: 'But kiss, one kiss! Rubies unparagoned, / How dearly they do't!' (2.2.17–18).[19] Her lips in fact 'do' nothing, as she is asleep, but it is difficult to keep this in mind given the whispered fervour of Iachimo's remarks, all of which, incidentally, stress the magnetic power of Imogen's unconscious form – drawing the taper's flame to it – exuding a heady perfume. When Iachimo reports back to Posthumus, his description of Imogen's bedroom not only cruelly prolongs and as cruelly substantiates the claim made by his narrative, but recaptures the erotic cosmopolitanism of the trappings we have already seen with our own eyes: the tapestry of 'silk and silver' depicting Cleopatra's meeting with Antony where, in a mamillary image, 'Cydnus swelled above the banks' (2.4.71); the andirons shaped like 'winking Cupids' (turning thereby a blind eye on the proceedings); the cherubim sporting wantonly on the ceiling; and, in the near-oxymoron of the voyeur, the carving of 'Chaste Dian bathing' on the chimney over the fireplace. Typical of the

---

15 '"The True Conduct of Human Judgement": Some Observations on *Cymbeline*', in *The Morality of Art. Essays Presented to G. Wilson Knight by His Colleagues and Friends*, ed. D. W. Jefferson (1969), p. 25.

16 See his two important articles, '*Cymbeline* and the "Blameless Hero"', *ELH*, 31 (1964), 259–70, and '*Cymbeline*: Religious Idea and Dramatic Design', in *Pacific Coast Studies in Shakespeare*, eds. W. F. McNeir and Thelma N. Greenfield (Eugene, Oregon, 1966), pp. 248–62.

17 'The Greatness of *Measure for Measure*', in *The Common Pursuit* (1952), p. 169.

18 The first paperback edition of the new Arden *Cymbeline* featured Iachimo on its cover, notebook in hand, an insouciant feather in his cap, taking down Imogen's particulars as she lies in an abandoned manner, sleeping half naked, just behind him. The illustration is an engraving from Bell's 1774 edition of Shakespeare.

19 Some critics have argued that 'how dearly they do't' refers to how beautifully Imogen's lips kiss each other. This seems to me a strained interpretation.

'naïvety that asks to be devoured' (as well as, more obviously, of the irony of the event) is the detail that Iachimo does not bother to repeat to Posthumus (it does not help to prove his presence in the bedchamber), the fact that Imogen has fallen asleep while reading Ovid's account in the *Metamorphoses* of Tereus' rape of Philomela: fallen asleep over the very page 'Where Philomel gave up' (2.2.46). And, as we have seen, in the centre of all these seductive trappings, the cynosure, the goddess Imogen herself, whom Iachimo (like Milton's Satan) has already worshipped in his hushed recitation of her lovely parts, a devotional exercise we may well recall when listening to Imogen's catalogue of the headless corpse's Herculean ones.

In the light of this eventful history, it would be more accurate to view Imogen's grim experience with Cloten's body as a manifestation of a particular kind of symbolically appropriate pastoral reckoning than as the climax of a destructive counter-movement to the pastoral tradition as such. In recent years, Shakespeare's treatment of the pastoral convention has received much critical attention, most of it concentrating on the innovative and unconventional in his handling of traditional literary attitudes. But by Shakespeare's time, the pastoral experience itself in literature had lost much of its traditional sweetness; beneath its 'superficial loveliness ranked the wretchedness of man',[20] its nostalgia and idealization in the service of satire and moral allegory. In the opening chapter of *The Oaten Flute*, Renato Poggioli observes that Shakespeare and Cervantes are typically more complex in their response to the pastoral tradition than any of the other writers with whom he more centrally deals. In *As You Like It*, for instance, Poggioli notes that Corin's inability to provide the hospitality sought for in Arden by Rosalind and Celia 'is unique in the whole bucolic tradition', and that *As You Like It* as a whole and this episode in particular 'show that there are Arcadias where man may be as churlish as the wind'.[21] Although Poggioli confuses Corin with Corin's master (Corin actually says 'But what is, come see / And in my voice most welcome shall you be'; *As You Like It*, 2.4.81–2), he nonetheless places the emphasis correctly on Shakespeare's unsentimental version of a traditional idyllic setting. Even

though the pastoralism of the last plays is similar to that of the romantic comedies in its stress on the therapeutic function of a benign environment, it is clear that, to use Poggioli's terminology, the emphasis in the romances is on the pastoralism of innocence rather than on the pastoralism of happiness. The pastoral experience in *Cymbeline* and *The Tempest* is particularly harsh: innocence (rather than happiness) has to be renewed on a daily basis in a spirit of absorbed self-abnegation in a more formidable landscape than the traditional *locus amoenus* of Greek pastoral. Of this landscape in *Cymbeline*, Rosalie Colie writes: 'it is unmitigated hard pastoral, a rocky difficult terrain training its inhabitants to a spare and muscular strength sufficient to wrest their nutriment from its minimal, ungenerous, exiguous resources.'[22]

It is to this frugal landscape which makes 'tanlings' of her abducted brothers in the summer and 'shrinking slaves' (4.4.29–30) of them in the winter that Imogen comes in her traditional search for a pastoral sanctuary. She finds it – or thinks she does – in Belarius' 'pinching cave' (3.3.38), that 'cell of ignorance' (l. 33) in Guiderius' contemptuous words, whose symbolically low threshold 'bows' the brothers each morning 'To a morning's holy office' (l. 4). Despite the love that Imogen wins instinctively from her unknown brothers, she must share with them the life of 'hardness' that 'ever / Of hardiness is mother' (3.6.21–2). We might contrast, at this point, the different kinds of preparatory tutelage offered in similar circumstances in *As You Like It* and *Cymbeline*. In *As You Like It*, Rosalind encourages Celia at the beginning of their journey to Arden with jocular references to the necessity for her as the taller of the two to disguise herself as a man whereby her 'hidden woman's fear' (1.3.15) will be overlaid by a 'swashing and a martial outside' (1.3.115–16). In *Cymbeline*, Pisanio also urges Imogen to 'forget to be a woman' (3.4.155); but his lengthy exhortation on the importance of her transvestism for her survival sub-

---

[20] S. K. Heninger, Jr., 'The Renaissance Perversion of Pastoral', *Journal of the History of Ideas*, 22 (1961), 254.

[21] *The Oaten Flute: Essays on Pastoral Poetry and the Pastoral Tradition* (Cambridge, Mass., 1975), p. 38.

[22] *Shakespeare's Living Art* (Princeton, 1974), p. 295.

stitutes the doleful for the jocular. He seems overwhelmed by the inevitable degradation of her experience:

> Nay, you must
> Forget that rarest treasure of your cheek,
> Exposing it – but O, the harder heart!
> Alack, no remedy – to the greedy touch
> Of common-kissing Titan, and forget
> Your laborsome and dainty trims, wherein
> You made great Juno angry.   (3.4.160–6)

In a manner typical of *Cymbeline*, Pisanio views Imogen's exposure to the elements as yet another sexual violation in which the sun becomes some hulking commoner intent on defiling a refined aristocrat, one who, typically again, has in all innocence angered Juno with her 'laboursome and dainty trims'. (We may see at times, incidentally, some faint justification for Cloten's angry dismissal of Imogen as 'this imperceiverant thing', 4.1.13.) If Imogen follows Pisanio's grim prescription she should, he believes, 'tread a course / Pretty and full of view' (3.4.147–8). The naïve pastoralism of this metaphor, like Cloten's aubade and Iachimo's cowslip, contrasts vividly with Pisanio's extended description of the sexual degradation Imogen first has to suffer. And this too, as we have seen, is typical of *Cymbeline*. As soon as Imogen discovers Posthumus' murderous intentions towards her she leaps naïvely to be devoured. Convinced that Posthumus has been 'betrayed' by 'some jay of Italy' (3.4.49), 'some Roman courtesan' (l. 124), she offers herself up to Pisanio's sword in an ecstasy of sacrifice:

> Look,
> I draw the sword myself. Take it, and hit
> The innocent mansion of my love, my heart.
>
>   (ll. 66–8)

A little later she says: 'The lamb entreats the butcher' (l. 97).

In *Cymbeline* the lovers' renewal of innocence is completed only after a rigorous purging of their sexual frailty. Imogen's grotesque experience with Cloten's body is therefore part of a pattern of erotic punishment in which both lovers suffer for the naïvety of their expectations. In an ambiguous

manner peculiar to *Cymbeline*, Imogen, in Pisanio's words, is 'punished for her truth' (3.2.7); and part of that punishment – as Imogen herself half realizes – entails 'peril to my modesty, not death on't' (3.4.153). The lovers' punitive behaviour towards each other is brought to an appropriate climax in the play's last scene in a manner reminiscent of Pericles' initial rejection of his daughter, Marina. Imogen, still disguised as Fidele, attempts to interrupt another (this time the last) of Posthumus' outbursts of self-detestation and lamentation over Imogen's fate. Making the opposite of Imogen's mistake over Cloten, Posthumus spurns Imogen's intervention:

> Shall's have a play of this? Thou scornful page,
> There lie thy part.
>   [*Thrusts her away; she falls*]   (5.5.228–9)

The stage direction here is from the Pelican edition; Nosworthy in the new Arden edition has '[*Striking her: she falls*]' which seems to me closer to the savage spirit of the sequence. That blow brings to a climax and to an end the thwarted relationship between the lovers, the naïvety that asks to be devoured, the collusion between the deceived and the deceiver. When Posthumus next speaks some thirty or so lines later (apart from his Cymbeline-like bewilderment 'How come these staggers on me?', 5.5.233), he uses the play's most famous pastoral metaphor as the lovers embrace: 'Hang there like fruit, my soul / Till the tree die' (5.5.263–4). So this reconciliation is also part of the play's pastoral reckoning. Posthumus is now mature enough – and Imogen too – for him to be able properly to fulfil Jupiter's prediction: 'He shall be lord of Lady Imogen' (5.4.107).

Jupiter's way of putting it – courtly and zestful – anticipates a future for the lovers purged of all their sexual misconstructions and hesitancies. Posthumus' dense arboreal metaphor, however, goes beyond the assertion of mere swaggering lordship to provide us with a vision of married life as an entwining mutuality in which the spiritual (Imogen as Posthumus' soul) and the erotic and fructuous (Posthumus as the tree and Imogen as the fruit of it) merge in a complicated, slightly ambiguous union. The density of the metaphor matches the subtleties of the lovers' history. Some 150 lines later, when Posthumus next speaks, his last words in the play measure the extent to which he has achieved the authoritative maturity erroneously thrust upon him by the First Gentleman in the opening scene. All traces of that corrugated verbal texture have now vanished: like Leontes in the final scene of *The Winter's Tale* Posthumus has earned the right to speak with compelling clarity. Confronted with a penitent, kneeling Iachimo, Posthumus provides Cymbeline with his model for bringing the conflict between the Romans and the British and the play itself to an end:

> Kneel not to me.
> The pow'r that I have on you is to spare you;
> The malice towards you to forgive you. Live,
> And deal with others better. (5.5.417–20)

Cymbeline is suitably impressed:

> Nobly doomed!
> We'll learn our freeness of a son-in-law:
> Pardon's the word to all. (5.5.420–2)

Pardon to all and the new harmony between Britain and Rome mark the happy outcome envisioned in pastoral terms by the Soothsayer in which the 'majestic cedar' (5.5.456) of Britain is made whole. The play's pastoral reckoning, therefore, embraces not only the lovers' punishment and reward but also the British failure and recovery on the political and diplomatic fronts in which, as the appropriate last word for a pastoral vision, the play's last, lingering word – peace – is the word to all.

NEW CREATED CREATURES: RALPH CRANE AND THE STAGE DIRECTIONS IN 'THE TEMPEST'

JOHN JOWETT

The stage directions in *The Tempest* are amongst the best known and the least understood of those in Shakespeare's works. This paper suggests that, far from reflecting Shakespeare's genius, the very eloquence of some of their phrasing is part of the evidence for the intervention of a second hand. The obvious candidate for such part-authorship of the stage directions is Ralph Crane, the scrivener to the King's Men. He acted as scribe in the preparation of several play transcripts, including, it is believed, the copy from which the First Folio text of *The Tempest* (F) was set up.[1] The theory that Crane intervened suggests that Shakespeare's original directions were substantially different from those found in F. It therefore opens the way for a reappraisal of both the nature of the copy from which Crane himself worked and the way in which Shakespeare intended some of his most spectacular scenes to be staged in the theatre.

One explanation sometimes offered for the elaborate detail of these stage directions is that Shakespeare was working in semi-retirement at Stratford, and that the fullness of the directions remedies his inability to direct the players verbally.[2] Informative and detailed directions, however, are common in his later plays, and they reach their most extended and elaborate forms not in *The Tempest* but in the Shakespearian directions in *The Two Noble Kinsmen* and *Henry VIII*.[3] As we believe Shakespeare was collaborating with Fletcher in these plays, there is little likelihood that he was in Stratford while doing so. What is indicated is in part a change in his way of writing stage directions, as witnessed, for example, by those in *Coriolanus*, and in part the increasing prevalence of spectacular, ceremonial, and masque-like elements in the late plays.

The directions in *The Tempest*, however, are qualitatively different from those of any other Shakespeare play. Here the theory of the rural retreat does not help, and indeed the actual observed qualities argue against it: the elements which distinguish *The Tempest* are non-theatrical, and would be peculiarly ineffective in instructing the players.

As a point of departure, here is a typical detailed direction from part of *The Two Noble Kinsmen* attributed to Shakespeare:[4]

Still Musicke of Records.
Enter Emilia *in white, her haire about her shoulders, a wheaten wreath: One in white holding up her traine, her haire stucke with flowers: One before her carrying a silver Hynde, in which is conveyed Incense and sweet odours,*

---

[1] For Crane's responsibility for the transcripts, see T. H. Howard-Hill, *Ralph Crane and Some Shakespeare First Folio Comedies* (Charlottesville, 1972); on *The Tempest*, see Jeanne Addison Roberts, 'Ralph Crane and the Text of *The Tempest*', *Shakespeare Studies*, 13 (1980), 213–33.

[2] This is suggested by Dover Wilson in his and Quiller-Couch's New Cambridge edition (Cambridge, 1948), p. 80.

[3] By the conventional distribution of authorship in *The Two Noble Kinsmen*, the extensive and detailed directions are mostly Shakespeare's. The most widely-accepted statement on the joint authorship of *Henry VIII* is by Cyrus Hoy in 'The Shares of Fletcher and his Collaborators in the Beaumont and Fletcher Canon (VII)', *Studies in Bibliography*, 15 (1962), 71–90.

[4] Old spellings are quoted throughout. This should not be taken to imply that the quoted spelling form has any particular significance when the status of a word is discussed.

which being set upon the Altar her maides standing a loofe, she sets fire to it, then they curtsey and kneele.

(LIV; 5.1.136.2–6)[5]

Every single detail here is a precise indicator to theatrical effect. The only possible exception for the modern reader is '*a loofe*' ('aloof'), which suggests an adverb of manner; it actually means simply 'at a distance'. From 'Emilia' to '*odours*' the direction is descriptive; thereafter it prescribes action. In the descriptive section, the grammatical emphasis is on the substantive, indicating a theatrical concern with actual properties. The adjectives '*wheaten*' and '*silver*' indicate material appearances, and even '*sweet*' (like '*Still*') delimits a particular subclass and has a practical function that precedes its literary flavour. The direction is a model of exactness in the way it indicates the physical relation between people, properties, and sequence of action. Technically the syntax is irregular if not maverick, but the sequence of phrases is held together by the formal grammar of the ceremony.[6]

A similar flavour can be found in *The Tempest*:

Heere enters Ariel *before: Then* Alonso *with a franticke gesture, attended by* Gonzalo. Sebastian *and* Anthonio *in like manner attended by* Adrian *and* Francisco: *They all enter the circle . . . and there stand charm'd: which* Prospero *obseruing, speakes.*

(TLN 2009–13; 5.1.57.1)

Although less ambitious in its scope, this direction has marked similarities with that from *The Two Noble Kinsmen*. Both show an emphatic symmetry in the grouping of characters and in *The Tempest*'s strange re-enactment of the '*franticke gesture*'; this contributes to an audience's sense of the supernatural and ceremonious control which Prospero exerts. The comparison will convince most readers that the same hand is at work (note particularly the absolute '*before*' and the cavalier '*which*' in both directions). The phrase '*with a franticke gesture*' is characteristic of the Shakespeare stage direction in its latest, most explicit and most creative phase. It may be placed alongside '*The Cardinall in his passage, fixeth his eye on Buckingham and Buckingham on him, both full of disdaine*' (*Henry VIII*, TLN 176–9; 1.1.114.3–6).

But another element in the directions of *The*

Tempest does not conform to Shakespeare's practice in other late plays. Greg quoted the directions following 3.3.17 and 4.1.138, and commented,

This, except for the use of the present tense, is the language familiar to us in descriptions of many masques at court. I cannot imagine an author writing notes for the producer, still less a book-keeper, using the phrase 'with a quaint device': it is descriptive of the thing seen, a compliment to the machinist. I am inclined to believe that behind the folio text is a manuscript carefully prepared by Crane, in which the author's directions were preserved and elaborated and

---

5 This act and scene line-reference is to G. R. Proudfoot's Regents Renaissance Drama Series edition (1970). Act and scene line-references to other Shakespeare plays are to Alexander's edition (1951), and continuous text line-numbers (TLN) are from the *Norton Facsimile of the First Folio of Shakespeare* (New York and London, 1968).

6 Whatever the nature of the copy for Q, there are strong reasons to consider this direction as authorial. Such is the view of Paul Bertram in his *Shakespeare and 'The Two Noble Kinsmen'* (New Brunswick, 1965), p. 62, even though he believes that directions other than the handful of marginal directions may incorporate occasional earlier prompt annotations. Bertram proposes that the printer's copy was the prompt-book, consisting in an annotated fair copy in Shakespeare's hand. If the copy was indeed the prompt-book, the possibility at least arises that it is *The Two Noble Kinsmen*, not *The Tempest*, which demonstrates non-authorial characteristics in the stage directions. This would be a somewhat desperate line of argument. It is well established that Crane, a sophisticating scribe responsible to neither the dramatist nor the theatre, prepared the copy for *The Tempest*; there is no known agent other than Shakespeare himself who is likely to have introduced directions such as the one quoted into *The Two Noble Kinsmen*. One would expect that substantial non-authorial annotation, either in the printer's copy or in foul papers used as copy for a transcript, would be very obviously theatrical – in the manner of the marginal directions preserved in Q. The very oddity of many of the directions ('. . . with a short Thunder as the burst of a Battaile . . .') is in itself a reason for assuming their authorial origin. Whereas a playwright may well have wished to communicate their information to his players, some of the more expressive details are of a kind that are highly unlikely to have been added in preparing a prompt book. Indeed, they are the kind of detail that would often have been eliminated in a non-authorial transcript – despite their dramatic interest – as being superfluous to normal requirements.

the marks of stage use (supposing the original to have been used as a prompt-book) eliminated. [7]

Leaving aside for a while the question of whether Crane's copy was the prompt-book, Greg's key word is 'elaborated'. His comments are shrewd but impressionistic. Is it possible to investigate further how Crane may have elaborated, so as to put Greg's 'belief' on a firmer footing?

On the general character of Crane, though with specific reference to his orthography, Trevor Howard-Hill has written:

He was a sophisticating scribe, with strong opinions about what kind of orthography was desirable in texts of this period. He took pride in his manuscription and conceived it as his foremost task to deliver a legible, intelligible manuscript to his client or patron. His obligation was not to the author or to concepts of scholarly accuracy which are held at present. There is little hope, although his influence on orthography is clear enough, that all the points at which he altered the substantives of his copy texts have been detected by modern scholars and much of his influence will continue to elude detection . . . when editors come to a greater understanding of his habits, they can make suitable allowance for them. [8]

This conclusion is well attested by Howard-Hill's detailed observations. His opinion on the authority of the stage directions in *The Tempest*, however, is slightly curious. He holds that 'the fullness of the directions...undoubtedly derives from the copy, which, according to Greg, was foul papers', but that 'the language of the directions...probably owes much to [Crane]'.[9] The evidence for such 'fullness' lies in Crane's habits in treating directions elsewhere, though the evidence is open to a certain amount of interpretation, and Howard-Hill recognizes that Crane's treatment of his copy in other respects was variable. Yet the qualification about the 'language' is wide-sweeping in its potential application, and might include such evocations as are usually thought most Shakespearian. It also seems to imply a process of paraphrase without expansion which is not one of the most plausible. The emphasis of these assertions is designed to uphold the view that 'there is no evidence that Crane prepared copy for *Tmp.* in any special way'. In contrast, the starting-point adopted here is that there are *no* Shakespeare directions closely

comparable with some of these for *The Tempest*. This includes the other plays printed from Crane transcripts (*Two Gentlemen, Merry Wives, Measure for Measure, Comedy of Errors* and *Winter's Tale*), and in particular *Winter's Tale*, which is, like *The Tempest*, a late play. (Incidentally, I do not find, as does Howard-Hill, 'many points of similarity' between the directions of *Winter's Tale* and *The Tempest*, though some of the action in the former might invite more elaborate directions. But see pp. 113–14.) It must therefore be considered whether the features distinct to *The Tempest* are more likely to derive from the author's hand, perhaps indeed in a foul-paper manuscript, or from a Crane intervention. If the latter, it may be inferred that the transcript was prepared specifically in order to appear as the first play in F, this circumstance accounting for the exceptional attention which, by this view, he must have given it.

It is known that Crane did in fact interfere with stage directions. On occasion he omitted, reworded or added words and phrases. It is intervention of the latter two kinds that concerns us here. Several critics have examined Crane's habits in transcribing stage directions; the evidence they cite varies, but the conclusions are similar. After considering Crane's transcript of Fletcher and Massinger's *Sir John van Olden Barnavelt* which 'gives little information', F. P. Wilson noted:

In Crane's other transcripts the directions never smack of the theatre. Occasionally they are descriptive, and have a literary flavour. For example, in *Demetrius and Enanthe*, IV.iii: '*Enter a Magitian wth a Bowle in his hand. He seemes to Coniure: sweete Musique is heard, and an Antick of litle Fayeries enter, & dance about ye Bowle, and fling in things, & Ex^t.*' Again, in *A Game at Chess* (Lansdowne 690), IV.iii: '*Enter ye Black Q^r. Pawne (wth a Tapo^r in her hand) and Conducts the White Q^r. Pawne (in her Night Attire) into one Chamber: And then Conuaies the Black B^r. Pawne (in his Night habit) into an other Chamber: So putts out the Light, and followes him.*'[10]

---

[7] W. W. Greg, *The Editorial Problem in Shakespeare: A Survey of the Foundations of the Text*, second edition (Oxford, 1951), pp. 151-2.

[8] Howard-Hill, *Ralph Crane*, p. 138.

[9] Howard-Hill, *Ralph Crane*, p. 108.

[10] F. P. Wilson, 'Ralph Crane, Scrivener to the King's Players', in *The Library*, 7 (1926), 194-215, pp. 212-13. In the quotation from Wilson and the discussion which

Wilson does not establish how far Crane was responsible for these directions. The second can be compared with Middleton's holograph, the Trinity manuscript. This reads: 'Enter Bl. queenes pawne as conducting the White to a chamber, then fetching in the Bl. Bishops pawne the Jesuite conuayes him another puts out the light and shee followes'. The loss of 'another' character suggests a different staging; Crane tinkers with the wording throughout; and the material he brackets describing costume may be attributed to his own hand. The 1647 Beaumont and Fletcher Folio text of *Demetrius and Enanthe*, there entitled *The Humorous Lieutenant*, appears to be closer to Fletcher's directions than Crane's transcript. In his study of the Folio, R. C. Bald compared these directions. For the first direction Wilson quotes, the Folio text merely has '*Enter Mag. with a bowle*'. Elsewhere the Crane transcript adds '. . . (*in poore attire*)' to the Folio's '*Enter Celia*'; and '. . . *with a book*' becomes '. . . *with a Booke in her hand*'. Crane seems to have recast '*Great Shout within*' as '*A joyfull showt*' and introduced two directions reading '*She turnes over yᵉ Booke*'. Bald commented:

Those [directions] in the folio are more precise . . . Crane's directions in the manuscript, on the other hand, seem to have been 'written up' somewhat, with occasional touches of literary elaboration based perhaps on recollections of actual performances of the play; they are, one feels, less curt than the stage directions which a thoroughly experienced dramatist would insert during composition, and they are also written for the reader rather than the actor or producer.[11]

T. Howard-Hill comes to a similar conclusion after comparing the several Crane transcripts of *A Game at Chess* both with each other and with Middleton's holograph and another part-holograph manuscript: 'his tendency was to insert matter which might assist a reader'.[12] A particularly significant example is at 5.1.40, where the Trinity manuscript reads 'Musique an Altar discouerd and Statues, wth a Song'; Crane's Folger transcript has '*Musick An Altar discouerd, richely adorned, and diuers Statues standing on each-side*'. Jeanne Addison Roberts also cites this direction in her examination of the Archdall Crane transcript, and quotes another substantial addition in that manu-

script: '*– his vpper garment taken of, he appeeres Black-vnderneath*'. Other examples she gives are '*Enter both houses*' in Trinity, where Archdall names the specific characters, and '*Musique*' in Trinity, which is characterized as '*Lowd Musick*' in Archdall. Like Bald, she notes that the changes often indicate their instigator's familiarity with the play on stage.[13]

It is the literary quality of the directions in *The Tempest* which is their most distinctive trait. The term 'literary' as applied to directions has both a positive and a negative value. It makes the play more vivid, more attractive or more enjoyable for the reader, but in doing so gives a form of direction which at best will be neutral and at worst may be an impediment when the text is used in the theatre. Such directions will self-evidently give rise to suspicions that their author is not the dramatist – unless, of course, it can be shown that he was preparing his text for non-theatrical use. An example of the latter is Jonson's holograph of *The Masque of Queens*, which he prepared for Prince Henry after the unique performance. The directions, in the past tense, are elaborate, eulogistic and descriptive. This is an extreme and clear-cut case, however. In *The Tempest* the transcriber is the obvious agent for any such characteristics: there is no reason to suppose that Crane made a transcript of a transcript in Shakespeare's hand, nor is there evidence that Shakespeare would have written the kind of direction found in *The Tempest* even for non-theatrical use. Crane's supposed influence will give rise to a mixed stage direction. Some further enquiry is needed if we wish to understand the nature of his contribution.

follows below, 'literary' is used in a rather different, more 'literal' sense than is usual in discussions of stage directions, where it tends to have a limited specialist meaning. Partly for this reason, and partly because Shakespeare seems to have developed his style in stage directions to anticipate theatrical needs more accurately during his later career, this paper appears to reverse the common categorization whereby Shakespeare's directions (as opposed to playhouse annotations) are described as 'literary'.

[11] R. C. Bald, *Bibliographical Studies in the Beaumont and Fletcher Folio of 1647* (Oxford, 1938), Bibliographical Society Transactions, Supplement 13, pp. 76–7.

[12] Howard-Hill, *Ralph Crane*, p. 24.

[13] Roberts, 'Ralph Crane and the Text of *The Tempest*', pp. 216–18.

Here probabilities not certainties are involved. But if a problem of staging arises from the phrasing of a particular direction, and if that phrasing is striking or unusual irrespective of its significance for the stage, this coincidence of the 'negative' and 'positive' aspects of the literary direction will combine to suggest more strongly that its provenance lies with the sophisticator, not the dramatist. Another factor which might combine with either or both of these aspects is the vocabulary used in the direction. In dialogue, the occurrence of words not found elsewhere in the canon might actually argue for Shakespeare's authorship of the passage concerned. But stage directions are characteristically restricted in function and formulaic in expression. The word-range of the directions in *The Tempest* is remarkably great, and includes over fifty words which do not occur elsewhere in the stage directions of Shakespeare's plays.[14] This is surpassed only by the Shakespearian portion of *The Two Noble Kinsmen*, though *Cymbeline* compares quite favourably if one expresses the amount of innovation as a proportion of the available vocabulary.[15] However, it is clear that word-counts as such have limited value: one must allow for the creative scope of Shakespeare's late experiments with stage directions. Thus in the direction from *The Two Noble Kinsmen* quoted above, there is a considerable number of words unique to Shakespeare's stage direction vocabulary: '*shoulders*' (plural), '*wheaten*', '*wreath*', '*stucke*', '*Hynde*', '*conveyd*', '*Incense*', '*odours*', '*standing*' and '*curtsey*' (singular). Though the list is extensive in relation to the length of the direction, each word arises out of the exigencies of the action; most of the words are new to the stage-direction vocabulary because the action itself is unusually exotic and highly specific. What will make Shakespeare's authorship doubtful is new stage direction vocabulary which has no dramatic reference. Novelty without exactness, descriptive or non-dramatic novelty, will not be thought to characterize Shakespeare.

There follows a list of phrases from the directions in *The Tempest* which may, with varying degrees of probability, be attributed to Crane on the basis of these criteria. Material in square brackets is not in question, but provides context.

1. '*A tempestuous noise of* [*Thunder and Lightning*] *heard*' (TLN 2; 1.1.0.1). Thunder and lightning were standard effects, and in view of the limited resources of the theatres for sound effects, it is doubtful whether there would be an attempt to imitate the noise of wind and the sea. Lightning, of course, is not an aural but a visual effect; this is a possible indication of an original direction having been reworded. '*Tempestuous*' is new Shakespeare stage-direction vocabulary (henceforth shortened to 'new vocabulary'), and makes an obvious but literary allusion to the title of the play.

2. '[*A*] *confused* [*noyse within*]' (TLN 70; 1.1.56). There is a problem here, but it is one for the director rather than the readers. F sets the following speech, which gives the verbal substance of the '*noyse*', as verse. The lines do indeed scan – even to the first phrase 'Mercy on us', which runs on from the unfinished line of verse preceding the stage direction. It is therefore difficult to conceive that these lines should actually be prose.[16] However, spoken verse is defined by its metrical features; the verse-arrangement and the direction '*confused*' are therefore mutually inconsistent. It is quite possible that the individual phrases should come from different speakers and different directions offstage whilst retaining a semblance of sequence and rhythm. But Shakespeare is not likely to have described such an effect as '*confused*'. Moreover, it is new vocabulary.

3. '[*Burthen*] *dispersedly*' (TLN 525; 1.2.381). '*Dispersedly*' is similar in intent to '*confused*', and also new vocabulary. The exact musical meaning of '*Burthen*' in the present context has never been settled, nor has it been established how much of the

---

[14] Information on stage-direction vocabulary has been assembled from *A Complete and Systematic Concordance to the Works of Shakespeare* by Marvin Spevack, 9 vols. (1968–80), vol. 7, *Stage Directions and Speech-Prefixes*.

[15] By 'available vocabulary' is meant the words that remain after the elimination of character names, formulaic expressions such as '*Enter*', and common words such as prepositions and conjunctions.

[16] As E. K. Chambers demonstrated in *Shakespearian Gleanings* (1944), pp. 81–2, most of 1.1 can be set as approximate verse. Whereas the usual editorial procedure is probably correct in generally following F and setting most of the scene as prose, any director or actor should be aware of the verse rhythms that permeate this scene. A measure of stylization is perhaps suggested.

song constitutes the burden.[17] This direction and the ambiguous 'Burthen: ding dong' in the following song (TLN 546; 1.2.403) may be additions to the original manuscript. It will be suggested below that Crane's copy was probably not a theatrical manuscript, and this would leave Crane as the most likely originator of such annotations. But it is also possible that these directions have foul-paper origin.

4. '[*Enter Ariell with Musicke*] *and Song*' (TLN 999; 2.1.287.2–3). '*And Song*' is redundant in view of the direction '*Sings in Gonzaloes eare*' which follows within three lines, and misleading in its unlikely implication that Ariel enters singing. The intent of '*and Song*' is therefore far from clear. As an authorial direction it is conceivable only as a self-reminder at a point where Shakespeare left off working on the script for a time; as a theatrical annotation it seems to be nonsense ('to the accompaniment of music and prepared to sing a song'?). I would suggest that it is a non-theatrical addition made in formulaic imitation of '*playing & singing*' (TLN 519; 1.2.376.1).

5. '. . . *seuerall strange shapes* . . .' (TLN 1536; 3.3.18.2–3). This is highly unspecific. '*Shapes*' gives the vaguest of impressions, but does not give the basic information that it is the Spirits who enter;[18] it suggests the spectacle as seen through the eyes of the audience. The Spirits are described as '*shapes*' that vanish '*strangely*' in the dialogue that follows (ll. 37 and 40), but '*shapes*' is used to refer to their appearance, not to name them (Gonzalo thinks they are '*Island[er]s*'). '*Strange*' and '*shape(s)*' are both new vocabulary, and elsewhere Shakespeare's stage-direction use of '*seuerall*' is always to denote different '*doores*' or '*wayes*'. Moreover, two separate stage directions are run together: '*Solemne . . . inuisible*' and '*Enter . . . depart*'; the latter should be placed after l. 19. If '*shapes*' is a Crane alteration in this direction, it is also later in the scene at TLN 161; 3.3.82.1.

6. '. . . *with gentle actions of salutations* . . .' (TLN 1537; 3.3.18.4). The adjective and nouns are new vocabulary. In the case of '*actions*' this is probably for the very reason that it conveys minimal theatrical information. The phrase is imprecise, and once again the idea may be derived from the text: 'Their manners are more gentle, kinde . . .' (l. 32).

7. '. . . *they depart*' (TLN 1538; 3.3.18.5–6).

'*Depart*' for *exit/exeunt* is found elsewhere in the canon only in texts of disputed authorship. In conjunction with preceding phrases, this suggests that the entire direction was elaborately reconstructed by Crane.

8. '. . . *with a quient deuice* . . .' (TLN 1584; 3.3.52.3). Greg's essential comment is quoted on p. 108. '*Device*', like '*shapes*' and '*actions*', is of no practical value, and to someone involved in the theatre nothing is gained by the phrase that is not implicit in '*vanishes*'.

9. '. . . (*with mockes and mowes*) [*and carrying out the Table*]' (TLN 1617–18; 3.3.82.2–3). The '*with* . . .' qualifier seems to be favoured by Crane. For example, Folger *A Game at Chess* adds '*w*[th] *Lights*', which is not found in Middleton's holograph. The formula has a practical usefulness for additions in that it gives a neat parenthesis. Two '*with* . . .' phrases have already appeared in this list. '*Mockes and mowes*' as such occurs nowhere else in the Shakespeare canon, but it varies '*with mops, and mowe*', in the text seventy lines below and again referring to the Spirits ('*Mobing, & Mohing*' is found in the Quarto text of *King Lear*, H3, l. 17; 4.1.62).[19] The syntax is curious if not suspicious.

---

17 For editors' comments on the 'Burthen' see Peter J. Seng, *The Vocal Songs in the Plays of Shakespeare: A Critical History* (Cambridge, Mass., 1967), pp. 61–2.

18 '*Shapes*' undoubtedly suggests the supernatural, but as '*strange*' is implicitly contrasted with the commonplace and emphasizes physical appearance, as '*shapes*' also suggests 'disguise' (compare '*in shape of*'; TLN 1929; 4.1.254.1); and as *OED* nowhere mentions 'spirit' under shape, the word cannot be simply equivalent to 'spirit'.

19 The expression 'mock/mop and mow' seems to have entered Shakespeare's vocabulary through his reading of Harsnett (see Kenneth Muir, 'Samuel Harsnett and *King Lear*', *Review of English Studies*, 2 (1951), 11–21). Certainly *The Tempest* TLN 1048–50; 2.2.9–11 echoes Harsnett's 'mow, and mop like an Ape, tumble like a Hedgehogge'. The connection with an author Shakespeare is known to have read might suggest that he wrote the direction '*with mockes and mowes*', especially as it varies '*with mop, and mowe*'. But *mock/mop* were probably indifferent variants. The phrase was fairly common in the seventeenth century, and was not a distinctive expression as it now appears. Glosses suggesting grotesqueness of facial expression are perhaps exaggerated or misleading: it seems to indicate here a form of 'dumbe discourse' equivalent to the current northern expression 'me-mow'. As such it would be the obvious, if not the

As in the first example quoted from the Archdall transcript, Crane may have been so preoccupied with adding content to the direction that he dropped part of it – in this instance '*exeunt*'. '*Carrying out the Table*' could itself be an addition where Crane fell between writing '*exeunt carrying . . .*' and '*. . . Table, they depart*'.

10. '. . . (*properly habited:*) . . .' (TLN 1805; 4.1.138.1). This is an approbatory but otherwise unhelpfully vague expression. '*Properly*' could mean either 'as befits a reaper' or 'handsomely (as befits a masque)'. Both words are new vocabulary.

11. '. . . *towards the end whereof . . . after which . . .*' (TLN 1806–7; 4.1.138.3–4). Taken as a whole, this direction shows a tendency to draw events together into a sustained entry. This may be compared, tentatively at least, with the 'massed' entries Crane introduced in several transcripts including, it appears, the copy for F *The Two Gentlemen of Verona*.[20] Another instance of the habit of running events together which are separate in the text has already been observed above. The aspiration is towards continuous narrative. The unusual way in which actions are related is suggested by the fact that '*whereof*' is new vocabulary.

12. '. . . *to a strange hollow and confused noyse . . .*' (TLN 1807–8; 4.1.138.5). Despite the compounded epithets, we are not told what the noise actually is. Again, it is not the reader who is potentially inconvenienced. The epithets are all new vocabulary; '*confused*' recalls '*confusedly within*'. '*Strange*' is a key word in *The Tempest* but here could have been taken from its nearby occurrence in the text, just five lines below the direction. The phrase as a whole certainly has literary effectiveness, but in view of its dramatic defectiveness, this should not be taken as a sign of Shakespeare's authorship.

13. '. . . *in shape of Dogs and Hounds . . .*' (TLN 1929–30; 4.1.253.2). New vocabulary '*shape*' here deliberately but somewhat awkwardly recalls to the reader the '*shapes*' of previous directions. '*Dogs*' is also new vocabulary. It co-exists with the more usual term '*Hounds*', consequently duplicating the information.

14. '. . . (*in his Magicke robes*) . . .' (TLN 1946; 5.1.0.1). These have been tacitly assumed previously, even where it is necessary to understand that Prospero takes his robe off or puts it on. A singular '*robe*' would

accord with Shakespeare's practice elsewhere in stage directions. '*Magicke*' too is unique vocabulary; it is literary, though perhaps in a way compatible with foul papers.

15. '. . . *which* Prospero *had made . . .*' (TLN 2012; 5.1.57.5–6). This points very clearly to the consecutiveness of prose narrative. If a dramatist included a direction for an action, he would do so at the appropriate point (which is uncertain in F), not in retrospect. The mysterious back-reference found here is certainly conceived as an aid to the reader. Apart from one instance in the unauthoritative quartos of *2 Henry VI* – 'the man that had been blind' (C2; l. 36; 2.1.67.2) – 'had' occurs nowhere in Shakespeare's directions. This is, of course, significant in view of the commonness of the word. The reason is that the dramatist's directions do not relate temporally distant actions in this way; they are directed at the here-and-now.

Of the list put forward above, three examples are in round brackets. Crane favoured this form of punctuation. As I have found only one pair of brackets in directions in non-Crane transcript plays in F (*King John*, TLN 2250; 5.2.0.1), the eight examples in *The Tempest* and the two in *The Winter's Tale* can quite safely be attributed to his hand. A further three appear in one direction in *Cymbeline* (TLN 3065–71; 5.4.29.1–10); as two hands may have given rise to the curious over-explication there, it may at least be suggested that Crane annotated the manuscript at this juncture.[21] One phrase in particular, '(*as in an Apparation*)', is striking in that exactly the same words occur, again within brackets, in at least two of Crane's

---

only, way of describing the effect. However, it should be recognized that a more natural and accessible '*mockes and mowes*' not only opens up the possibility of its use by Crane but also adds to the theatrical value of the expression if Shakespeare introduced it.

20 The other plays in F are *The Merry Wives of Windsor* and *The Winter's Tale*. Massed entries are also found in the Malone transcript of *A Game At Chess* and the first quarto of *The Duchess of Malfi*, which is thought to be set from a Crane transcript.

21 The passage that follows has been suspected of being written by someone other than Shakespeare. This is probably not so; however the issue has little bearing on the present discussion.

transcripts of *A Game at Chess*.[22] (The distinctive spelling 'Apparation' is probably Compositor B's: it occurs twice in his stint in the stage directions of *Macbeth*.)

In *The Winter's Tale*, a Crane transcript play, the two occurrences both enclose vital descriptions of Hermione: '. . . (*as to her Triall*)' at TLN 1174–5; 3.2.10.0 and '. . . (*like a Statue:*)' at the opening of 5.3 (TLN 3185). This can scarcely be coincidence, though few qualifying phrases are available for styling in this way. Although there is no reason why Shakespeare should not have written these directions, there is a possibility that it was Crane who did so. In *The Tempest*, the same is true of '. . . (*bearing a Log*)' (TLN 1235; 3.1.0.1) and '. . . (*like a Harpey*)' (TLN 1583; 3.3.52.1–2). On the other hand, the evidence of *A Game at Chess* suggests that while about half of the parentheses introduced might contain entirely new material and others show minor rewordings, Crane sometimes introduced brackets where he made no other changes.[23] However, this evidence also suggests a greater likelihood of finding Crane additions within brackets than elsewhere. It should be noted that '(*to soft Musicke*)' (TLN 1616; 3.3.82.1) is one kind of addition that Crane seems to favour. Nowhere else in the canon does '*soft*' qualify music or any other substantive; '*still*' is the epithet Shakespeare prefers. Similarly '*solemn(e)*' is found only in *The Tempest* (three times), *Cymbeline* (twice, of which one instance is in the direction discussed above) and the Fletcherian part of *Henry VIII*; there are some reasons for supposing that it too is non-Shakespearian. Of the remaining directions in the brackets, the formulation of '(*a noyse of Thunder heard.*)' (TLN 1038–9; 2.2.02 recalls the suspect opening direction of the play, and '(*inuisible*: (TLN 1535; 3.3.18.2))' is found twice elsewhere in the text but nowhere else in the canon.[24]

These marginal examples show the proposed Crane additions cannot be definitively listed. However, it is possible to establish the general character of the non-Shakespearian stratum attributable to Crane. It is inevitable that at least some interpolations will not stand out as being distinctively different from Shakespeare's practice. The list necessarily tends towards conservatism. For example the phrase '. . . *with a franticke gesture*' contains two examples of new stage-direction vocabulary and follows the '*with* . . .' construction which Crane appears to favour; it is excluded from the list because it is a kind of direction which seems quite well exampled in Shakespeare's directions elsewhere. It may be thought that to present Shakespeare's stage direction vocabulary as a fixed and determined body is misleading in view of the playhouse annotations that may survive in some texts; if so, the effect will again be to increase the conservatism of the procedure by excluding certain words from the possible list of innovations in *The Tempest*. But any effect here will be marginal: theatrical annotation will tend towards the formulaic, and can only be imagined to introduce the occasional actor's name or unusual stage property that Shakespeare may not have specifically named in the particular context or elsewhere (and properties too are fairly standardized).

If the phrases discussed are inadequate for the theatre, they are mostly effective literary embellishments. Crane would have successfully translated from one medium to another. But it is almost certainly necessary to postulate that he was familiar with the play on the stage. We can therefore posit unrecorded performances, presumably at the Blackfriars theatre. This is consistent with Dryden's statement that the play 'had formerly been acted with success in the *Black-Fryers*',[25] which implies a reputation that would not have been established in a short run. Crane must have given some thought to his additions, and was probably in the habit of looking forward through his copy in search of apposite words. The additions are conspicuously ornamental, and contain a high proportion of adjectives and adverbs. It may be conjectured that as a rule Crane elaborated directions that were extant in

---

22 See Howard-Hill, *Ralph Crane*, p. 22. Middleton's wording was '*like an Apparition*'.

23 See Howard-Hill, *Ralph Crane*, pp. 18–24, for various examples of directions in Crane's hand.

24 Compositor B apparently regularized any Crane stage-direction brackets out of the text in F. No such brackets appear in his stints.

25 Preface to Davenant and Dryden's adaptation, *The Tempest; or, The Enchanted Island*, in *The Works of John Dryden*, edited by H. T. Swedenberg Jr., Earl Miner and Vinton A. Dearing, 19 vols. (Berkeley and Los Angeles, 1956–81), vol. 10, edited by Maximillian E. Novak and George R. Guffey, pp. 1–103; p. 3.

his copy; or, to put this another way, that he might not notice the need for directions when they were missing in his copy. The consistency of the directions is less than we would imagine Shakespeare producing in a fair copy at the end of his career.

On the basis of the evidence already given, there are some grounds for considering that the copy Crane used was foul papers. It has been suggested not only that he intervened in the stage directions, but that he intervened to a greater extent than was his usual practice. This may be connected with the occasion for his transcript. However the evidence of his changes to the stage directions reinforces the circumstance of his making a transcript in the first place in suggesting that his copy may have been in some ways deficient. To express this in a positive way, if Crane had found directions such as those in *The Two Noble Kinsmen*, his interventions would have been minimal. Shakespeare's late fair copies were well supplied with stage directions.[26]

Despite their detail, the stage directions in *The Tempest* are not always theatrically adequate. In the masque of 4.1 they vary from the highly descriptive to the non-existent to the point of becoming problematic. As Crane's transcript was itself non-theatrical, it is possible that a feature of foul papers has been preserved through the two subsequent stages of transmission.

Here it is necessary to question the idea that the spectacular nature of the masque is in itself evidence that it constitutes a revision of the play for one of the two known court performances. Where these would probably most specifically differ from the Blackfriars version is in the presentation of spectacles. In particular, it is very unlikely that the stage at the Banqueting House would have facilities for free flights. The proscenium arch of the court stage would not at this date have had sufficient depth to conceal flight machinery behind it.[27] Ariel and Juno would be discovered on an upper stage, from where they could be lowered by a 'cloud' type of machine or descend by way of steps. In the context of a stage play, the latter is more probable.[28] But it does seem that the suspended free flight of the Blackfriars or Globe would be an equally or more effective staging for the descents in *The Tempest*.

The evidence is not conclusive as to whether Shakespeare had court performance in mind when he wrote *The Tempest*. It was probably staged at the Blackfriars before the first court performance in either event, if only in order to present a polished performance at court. The occasion of the betrothal for the second court performance has encouraged some fanciful and self-indulgent writing from more than one critic.[29] The play demonstrably was not written for this occasion; the hypothesis of textual revision has probably been encouraged by those who wish that it had been. It has been shown elsewhere in some detail how the play could have been staged at court,[30] but the directions themselves are neutral and could be adapted to the Blackfriars or Whitehall equally well.

The crucial stage direction for the masque is '*Iuno descends*' (TLN 1730–1; 4.1.72.1). This is the only extraordinary direction before the end of the masque; moreover its position gives cause for disquiet. It is not placed by Juno's evident arrival on stage ('Great *Iuno* comes'; TLN 1763; 4.1.101), but appears almost thirty lines before. The new Arden editor, Frank

26 *Antony and Cleopatra* and *Coriolanus* are both considered to have been printed from 'a carefully prepared author's manuscript' (Greg, *Editorial Problem*, p. 187) and have directions which are 'unusually full' and show Shakespeare 'using the language of the theatre' (pp. 147–8).

27 We have no exact information on how plays were performed at the Banqueting House, but the stage would be fundamentally the same as that for masques. The permanent theatres' free flight descent was not only considered graceless and vulgar compared with masque machinery, but was beyond the resources of the proscenium-arched court stage until 1631 (John Harris, Stephen Orgel and Roy Strong, *The King's Arcadia: Inigo Jones and the Stuart Court* (1973), p. 90). For practical reasons the conventions of the masque-within-a-play were different from those of masques themselves.

28 John H. Long describes Juno appearing 'from behind the mountain-top on the upper scene'; she 'slowly descends by a ramp or stairway to the middle scene' – i.e. the main stage (*Shakespeare's Use of Music*, 3 vols. (Gainesville, Florida, 1961–7), vol. 2, *The Final Comedies* (1961), p. 124.

29 See, for example, Ernest Law, in his Shakespeare Association pamphlet 'Shakespeare's *Tempest* as Originally Produced at Court' (1920), and Quiller-Couch's Introduction to the New Cambridge edition.

30 Long, *The Final Comedies*, pp. 101–26.

Kermode, shows obvious unease at retaining its position in F, though clearly he cannot justify moving it. In his commentary he claims that 'unless those who suspect serious interference with the play at this point are right, Juno must be held to start or prepare her passage earthward here . . . The reference in l. 72 suggests an appearance'. This is indecisive enough, but in an additional note he puts forward a prompt-copy explanation that precludes an actual appearance: 'this S.D. looks like a survival in Crane's transcript of some prompter's note'.[31] This later explanation has several problems and improbabilities. It makes an extravagant exception to the generally accurate placing of directions in F (apart, that is, from Crane's rationalized groupings and the occasional anticipation by a line or two which is also characteristic of his work). A prompt-book anticipation would need a different formulation such as 'Iuno ready', for according to this interpretation the direction is some thirty lines before the actual descent. It must be supposed that Crane eliminated all other evident prompt-book annotations except this one; that (presumably against his experience of the play in production) he changed the wording of the direction in such a way as to change its meaning; that having thus mis-preserved the prompt note, he also reversed his normal practice in *The Tempest* when he came to the original Shakespearian direction, and suppressed it instead of expanding it.

Nor is Crane likely to have transposed the direction by mistake. If he added the directions after completing a sheet (or more) of manuscript, he would also add 'Enter Ceres', which appears in proximity a few lines after 'Iuno descends' in F. In other words, if he transposed 'Iuno descends', he must have altered the order of the directions and introduced the descent into an obviously wrong environment.

The difficulties surrounding the descent are such that Irwin Smith argues that 'Juno probably does not enter in flight'. He points out that a prolonged descent

. . . would leave Juno in full view for some thirty lines while Iris and Ceres remain unaware of her approach. It would keep her suspended aloft for all that time without uttering a word, and it would let her and her celestial car vie for attention with the masque on the stage below. Her car, having come to earth and discharged its passenger, must then either return to

heaven empty (which is unexampled in the stagecraft of the period) or remain on the ground, to the inconvenience of the reapers and nymphs in their dance. And finally, a descent from heaven conflicts with Ceres' announcement of Juno's approach at lines 101–102, which makes it clear that she is afoot:

> Highest queen of state,
> Great Juno, comes; I know her by her gait.[32]

If a continuous slow descent is imagined, the problem is real enough. 'Iuno descends' is not placed randomly in the text but, as Kermode observed, in the context of a reference to the goddess; this suggests that her descent actually begins here. It is not necessarily true that Ceres and Iris are unaware of her presence at this point: Iris's comment 'her peacocks fly amain' could be a reaction to seeing her. However, if Juno is visibly approaching them, it is curious that they continue their dialogue without further reference to her. The effect on stage would be peculiar, especially in view of the contrived extreme slowness of the descent. For the audience, the effect would be not only a division of its attention, but in all probability a bewilderment that would defeat the celebratory function of the masque.

However, the direction '*descend(s)*' does not necessarily, or even usually, indicate a descent to the stage. There was, on the contrary, what has been called 'the convention of the floating deity', whereby the deity would be expected, upon appearing from the heavens, to remain suspended in the air rather than to come down to the stage.[33] It is common enough to find such

---

[31] New Arden edition, edited by Frank Kermode (1954), pp. 98 and 170. Theobald and the old Cambridge and the Pelican editors moved the direction to around l. 101 (TLN 1761), the latter two rewording it 'Enter Juno'.

[32] Irwin Smith, *Shakespeare's Blackfriars Playhouse: Its History and Its Design* (New York, 1964), p. 416. An exception to Smith's assertion that a car returning to heaven empty is 'unexampled' may be found in Greene's *Alphonsus King of Aragon* (1578–8) where Venus is '*let downe from the top of the Stage*' when the play begins, but seems to walk offstage at the end of the scene. The reverse happens in the Epilogue: '*Exit* Venus. *Or if you can conueniently, let a chaire come downe from the top of the stage, and draw her vp*' (Malone Society Reprint (1926), ll. 2109–10). But Greene was writing at an early date and in an essentially naive way; the conventions of staging descents were not established until the seventeenth century.

an appearance signalled by the word '*descend(s)*', and it would not normally be taken as indicating a descent to the stage unless this was specified. Juno probably appears and descends to a stationary position in the air at the point where the direction is found in F, and Iris witnesses her do so. Iris' observation here is paralleled by 'Great *Iuno* comes' at l. 101, which marks the second stage of the descent to earth. The text, by this interpretation, simply lacks a second direction.[34]

The position in the text of Juno's final descent to the stage is at first sight rather arbitrary. It becomes less so if one considers, especially in view of the Virgilian echoes in the play, the traditional rivalry between Venus and Juno. The action of the masque, like Juno herself but not so literally, is suspended until it is established that Venus and Cupid can have no part in it. Ceres asks the question that establishes their absence, and misleadingly asks if they attend Juno – an unlikely event. By any interpretation of the masque this is awkwardly contrived, but in terms of its overall symbolism the banishment of Venus is a necessary prelude to Juno's meeting with Ceres. Ceres asks the questions, and Iris answers on Juno's behalf, but it is Juno herself who, silent and aloof (in several senses), visibly withholds assent until the questions are answered.

Some of Smith's objections remain. On the lines he finally quotes, it should be commented that 'gait' (F 'gate') does not make it clear that Juno is afoot. *OED* gives the meaning 'bearing or carriage while moving' and Milton describes Satan's flight in the guise of an angel as 'his airy gait' (*Paradise Lost*, IV.568). For Juno, queen of the heavens, of whom Jonson wrote 'With the *Greekes*, *Juno* was interpreted to the *ayre* it self',[35] flight would be the way of moving that would most befit her and by which she would be recognized. Ceres' line actually argues against Juno being on foot. But Juno immediately says 'goe with me . . .': has she in the space of a line arrived on the stage and disembarked? It is the circumstances of her leaving her descent chair or throne which causes Smith's other difficulty. Might not Juno invite Ceres to join her in her throne? If this was the case, the goddesses would then be raised to a halfway stance between the stage and the heavens for their song. This would not bring them closer to Ferdinand and Miranda, but would

suggest that blessings 'shower' or 'fall' on the couple. The spectacle of the suspended deities would justify Ferdinand's comment 'This is a most maiesticke vision' – far more so than three characters standing on the stage with a bathetically grounded throne. As the text might imply, Ceres would have joined Juno in her element, rather than the other way round. This arrangement would also enhance the significance of Iris's role as intermediary between the goddesses and the dancers. Apart from her presence, the masque area of the stage would be clear for the dancing. From their station aloft, Juno and Ceres would be rapidly pulled up to the heavens when the spirits '*vanish*'. The throne may require some careful balancing or extra wires to take first one, then two, characters (albeit boys). However, a later Blackfriars play, Cavendish's (and Shirley's?) *The Variety* (1639–42), provides a comparable and more demanding instance; in Smith's words, 'a throne descends to music with a boy in it, and Formall and a Wench are put in the throne and sent up to heaven'.[36] It may also be noted that in *Women Beware Women* (1625), Livia impersonates Juno and appears in flight, suspended in the air until she is poisoned and falls to the stage; Fabritio comments

> Look, Juno's down too!
> What makes she there? her pride should keep aloft.
> She was wont to scorn the earth in other shows.
>
> (5.2.135–7)

Juno in flight appears in Greene's *Orlando Furioso* (1591) and Heywood's *The Silver Age* (1611), but the early date of the former makes it unlikely that it was regularly revived on stage as *The Tempest* probably was. Although we can be less sure about *The Silver Age*, Middleton probably primarily recalls Shakespeare's play. This allusion therefore might confirm

[33] J. Nathan French, *The Staging of Magical Effects in Elizabethan and Jacobean Drama* (unpublished Ph.D. thesis, University of Birmingham, 1964), p. 141.

[34] To this point, Anne Righter conjectures similarly in her New Penguin edition (Harmondsworth, 1968), p. 168.

[35] Ben Jonson, *Hymenaei*, in *Complete Works*, edited by C. H. Herford, Percy and Evelyn Simpson, 11 vols. (Oxford, 1925–52), vol. 7, p. 216.

[36] Smith, *Shakespeare's Blackfriars*, p. 415.

that Juno stayed in her throne and spent most of the time suspended in the air.[37]

If this construction of the masque's staging can be allowed, the deficiencies of the text in F are primarily a shortage of stage directions. Nevertheless, there remain some infelicities perhaps too slight to be called textual problems. The model has its rough edges. Juno, through Iris, bids Ceres

> with her soueraigne grace,
> Here on this grasse-plot, in this very place
> To come, and sport. (TLN 1730–2; 4.1.72–4)

Though this seems to suggest that Juno does after all disembark, the further suggestion that Juno and Ceres 'sport' is itself misleading: the sport is the dancing, to which the goddesses are passive spectators. Iris' invitation can lead to confusion by any interpretation. The following expression 'her [F "here"] Peacocks flye amaine', suggests a slight difficulty if Juno is seen partially to descend then stop: 'amaine' can only mean 'at speed'. But a masque does not aim at realism in such matters. How Juno seems to share, by implication, Ceres' concern about Venus, and how 'attend' (TLN 1747; 4.1.88) works against this impression, have already been described. Not all these factors relate only to the particular staging that has been proposed here. They centre on peculiar or misleading words. But the entire diction of the masque is riddled with verbal oddities: 'Medes thetched with Stouer', 'pioned, and twilled', 'broome-groues', 'pole-clipt', 'boskie acres' for example. Precise meaning and coherence may be partially suspended in favour of verbal impressionism and visually spectacular effect. But such considerations cannot dispose of problems which must relate to the history of the text. The fact that the stage directions are sometimes defective in itself suggests this.

Irwin Smith describes the scene as 'mutilated'.[38] He does not develop this idea, though elsewhere he offers an ingenious account of how the masque could have been added after the original composition to adapt the play for the 1612–13 court performance in celebration of the wedding of Princess Elizabeth and the Elector Palatine.[39] This conjecture has little bearing on the internal problems of staging the masque because it supposes a finished text for the masque supplied for known staging conditions. Nor can the masque's oddities be explained in terms of its adaptation from a Blackfriars version to a court version, in that all the extant details of staging could be applied at either venue. The most satisfactory way of accounting for the history of the text is to postulate that Crane's copy was Shakespeare's rough draft.[40] It would seem that initially Shakespeare conceived of the masque in primarily verbal terms. The outline of an envisaged staging can be traced, but it has been imperfectly marked in the text. Fuller directions, hand in hand with textual revision, could be undertaken when the fair copy was made. In the extant text, the carefully phrased direction which ends the masque gives a spurious impression of finality to the state of the text; this direction shows every sign of having been heavily rewritten by Crane. In the masque, Shakespeare was attempting at least as sophisticated a spectacle as anywhere else in the canon, and was writing in a mode that was unfamiliar to him. One might expect his conception of this part of the play to be less clear and well-defined, and the consequent text less perfect, than elsewhere in the play.[41]

The implication of a foul-paper copy for Crane's work on the stage-directions is that he may have contributed considerably more than the phrases which seem distinctly non-Shakespearian. There is no reason why most of his changes should be detectable; indeed one would not expect them to be. Foul papers provides both a motive for a fairly drastic intervention (the inadequacy of the directions in a play with which he was familiar in the theatre) and an explanation as to

---

[37] Masques are not considered here because (a) at this time they did not stage free flights (see n. 27); (b) in view of the highly élite audience at a masque, the joke would miss its point for most of the wider audience at the theatre.

[38] Smith, *Shakespeare's Blackfriars*, p. 416.

[39] Irwin Smith, 'Ariel and the Masque in *The Tempest*', *Shakespeare Quarterly*, 21 (1970), 213–22.

[40] Most of the usual forms of evidence for foul papers cannot be expected to have survived into Crane's transcript. The nature of Crane's copy cannot be established through pure bibliographical argument, and discussion of it cannot therefore precede the more speculative issues of textual criticism.

[41] Nevertheless, it should be pointed out that the spectacles of 3.3 have no provisional air about them.

why the consistency of the directions is not such as Shakespeare would have provided in a finished text at this period of his work.[42]

A foul-paper explanation may also pertain to the direction 'Enter Ariell' (TLN 1583; 3.3.52.1), where Ariel almost certainly descends from the heavens. In a rough draft, Shakespeare may have made only a provisional note, even if he knew the staging he intended. Modern editions retain 'Enter Ariell' without comment, and Furness records no discussion of the subject.[43] Ariel represents himself as one of several 'ministers of Fate', who visit 'this lower world', and he is disguised as a harpy, a winged monster. This coincidence of the agent of the heavens and an explicitly airborne creature (not to mention the name of the character involved) very strongly suggests a descent. Ariel actually wears wings. The flight mechanism was available at the Blackfriars, and it is impossible to think of any reason why it should not be used here. It has been suggested that Ariel rises through a trap-door in the stage.[44] This would give the exact opposite of the symbolism required. Its only possible justification is to give a conventional interpretation for 'He vanishes...' (TLN 1616; 3.3.82.1), again making use of the trapdoor. But Ariel vanishes '... in Thunder', and as the sound of thunder in the Elizabethan and Jacobean theatre apparently came from the heavens, this can be taken to mean that he vanishes into the heavens.[45] The phrasing recalls Cymbeline, where 'Iupiter descends in Thunder and Lightning' from the heavens (TLN 3126; 5.4.92.1). The situation here in The Tempest appears to be the same as when Juno and Ceres vanish at the end of the masque: Ariel is rapidly raised from a station in the air. The occasion for him rising to the intermediate position would be when Alonso's party try to attack him with swords (TLN 1593; 3.3.60). In fact the similarities with the masque run further if the interpretations I have suggested are followed: there is a comparable brief engagement with the stage and then an ascent to an intermediate position. This visual parallel will suggest points of contrast both in the spectacles and in their significance. Ariel devours the banquet to deprive Alonso and his party of food, then rises into the air to give a sermon explaining this as a punishment for sin; Juno takes in her throne Ceres, the goddess of crops and hence food, and they ascend to sing a song which showers blessings on the betrothed couple as a reward for virtue. In each case the spectacle and the symbolism are determined by the controlling hand of Prospero.

The discussion offered here attempts to reach towards some conclusions, but is exploratory in spirit and cannot establish definite facts. What may be stated as a minimal conclusion is that many of the distinguishing stage directions of The Tempest have a style and function that is unprecedented in the work of Shakespeare, and that it is difficult to conceive of circumstances under which he would have prepared such directions. Although Crane is in many respects a suitable and likely candidate for the role of elaborator, once the possibility of such an elaboration is recognized, the idea that a scrivener rather than an author wrote such suggestive and eloquent phrases may be greeted with surprise and scepticism. There is another possibility which should be considered: that a third hand, the hand of an experienced author, is at work. One such author who might conceivably have had a hand in the preparation of the text for the Folio is Ben Jonson. Indeed the similarities of diction and phrasing between the directions in The Tempest and those in the Jonson masques invite such an association:

---

[42] Whereas Crane could lose an occasional word or phrase and has been suspected of cutting directions in The Two Gentlemen of Verona, it is unlikely that the inconsistency in The Tempest is his doing. In Two Gentlemen he was probably rationalizing the text and introducing a consistency not found in his copy, if he interfered at all. As an intelligent sophisticator, he would not embellish and cut the same text without good cause.

[43] On the other hand, Smith believes that a flight was probably intended (Shakespeare's Blackfriars, p. 416), John C. Adams supports the same interpretation in 'The Staging of The Tempest, III.iii' (Review of English Studies, 14 (1938), 404–19), and Ariel sometimes enters in flight in stage productions. For some pre-1905 stagings, see Arthur Colby Sprague, Shakespeare and the Actors: The Stage Business in His Plays (Cambridge, Mass., 1944, repr. New York, 1963), p. 43.

[44] This staging goes back at least to Bell's edition: 'Two Devils rise out of the Stage, with a Table decorated'. After nine lines, 'The Devils vanish with the Table. Thunder and Lightning. Enter Ariel' (9 vols. (1774), vol. 3, pp. 260–1).

[45] Smith, Shakespeare's Blackfriars, p. 144.

*The song ended: They fell sodain   into an antique dance,
full of gesture, and swift motion . . .*

*. . . there was heard a strange Musique of wilde Instruments.
To which a SPHYNX came forth dauncing, leading
LOVE bound.*

*Here they all stoope to the water, and dance forth their
Antimasque in severall gestures . . .*[46]

Yet there are differences too. Most important,
Jonson's directions, though elaborate and literary,
clearly indicate the dramatic effect required. Although
they are descriptive and convey a sense of wonder in
many cases, they also abound in specific and precise
details: they do not mystify, and unspecified shapes
and sounds are not typical. By nature of the genre they
connect complex actions ('*after which*' constantly
recurs), but they do not reach across sections of text. A
reconsidered verdict on the apparent Jonsonian influence is that it is most likely to reflect a conscious
imitation of his stage directions, an imitation successful
in literary terms, less so dramatically. The Jonson
directions quoted, and scores of others, were available
to a would-be imitator in the 1616 Jonson Folio. That
this pioneering venture should influence someone
connected with the Shakespeare Folio might well be
expected. More particularly, Crane is known to have
been influenced by Jonson, and probably by the 1616
Folio itself: '. . . whether or not Jonson initiated Crane
into the art of literary transcription, there are conspicuous similarities between the general features of
their manuscripts'.[47] The Jonsonian style of the

directions might be a further pointer towards Crane
himself.

A final question, and a crucial one, concerns the
implications for an editor of the probable Crane
intervention. There would appear to be four considerations.

(a) The case for a non-Shakespearian stratum
remains an unproved hypothesis.

(b) It is not possible definitively to separate out such
a stratum, or to establish the wording of original
directions they may (or may not) supplant.

(c) Most of the phrases which are likely to be non-
authorial are elaborations of necessary or helpful
directions.

(d) Despite the above, from the point of view of
anyone trying to interpret the play for performance or
imagine it performed, there are several instances
where directions are misleading or inadequate.

It therefore seems clear that an editor's policy
should be in general to retain the Folio directions, only
modifying or rejecting them in specific instances
where they are incorrect to the point of misleading or
confusing a reader. In practice there should not prove
to be many such occasions. However, where an editor
has doubts as to the dramatic intelligibility of a
direction, s/he may reflect that the direction concerned may well be non-authorial, and that in the
circumstances outlined above, the lack of such intelligibility may itself be evidence that this is the case.

---

[46] Jonson, *Complete Works*, vol. 7, pp. 351, 359 and 457.
[47] Howard-Hill, *Ralph Crane*, p. 10.

'ARDEN OF FAVERSHAM'

ALEXANDER LEGGATT

We do not know who wrote *Arden of Faversham*, but we know that it belongs to the late 1580s or early 1590s, a period when new and often ambitious talents were appearing and when dramatic genres were being self-consciously shaped and reshaped. It was a time when playwrights were staking out their territory, as Marlowe does in his Prologue to *Tamburlaine the Great*, a play roughly contemporary with *Arden*:

From jigging veins of rhyming mother-wits
And such conceits as clownage keeps in pay,
We'll lead you to the stately tent of War,
Where you shall hear the Scythian Tamburlaine
Threat'ning the world with high astounding terms
And scourging kingdoms with his conquering sword.
View but his picture in this tragic glass
And then applaud his fortunes as you please.[1]

The play is going to be exotic, heroic, exalted in language, tragic in dignity. The author of *Arden of Faversham* gives us a similar statement, staking out a very different territory:

Gentlemen, we hope you'll pardon this naked tragedy
Wherein no filèd points are foisted in
To make it gracious to the ear or eye;
For simple truth is gracious enough
And needs no other points of glozing stuff.
                                        (Epilogue, 14–18)[2]

He seems to turn away from the high-astounding terms of Marlowe as consciously as Marlowe had turned away from the jigs and rhymes of the contemporary clown. This is a straight recounting of the facts, with no literary heightening, plain truth, a slice of life.

Comparing the play with *Tamburlaine*, we may find the author's statement of his intentions fair enough.

This is certainly domestic tragedy, based on a real event – though an event, we might note, of some forty years earlier – and, bearing in mind Allardyce Nicoll's caution that realism is always a relative term,[3] its manner is by the standards of its time realistic. Yet the author did not achieve this simply by telling the story as he found it. Much of the play's reputation for realism is based, I think, on its acute and sometimes disconcerting psychological insight and M. L. Wine in his Revels edition has shown how carefully the playwright has gone to work to round the flat characters he found in his source material.[4] This is not the realism that comes from giving us just the facts; it is the deeper realism that a writer achieves by working on the facts. We should notice, too, that the playwright's statement of policy comes not, as in *Tamburlaine*, at the beginning of the play, but at the very end. We enter the world of *Tamburlaine* with a guide, as we do in, say, *The Jew of Malta* and *Romeo and Juliet*. We enter the world of *Arden of Faversham* without a guide, and we have to make of it what we can. When at the end a guide emerges to tell us where we have been, we can compare our assessment with his. We should note, too, that the guide is not an

A version of this paper was delivered to the Royal Shakespeare Theatre Summer School on Shakespeare and the Theatre in August 1982, in connection with Terry Hands's RSC production of *Arden of Faversham* at The Other Place.

[1] Revels edition, ed. J. S. Cunningham (Manchester, 1981), Prologue to Part One, 1–8.
[2] All references are to the Revels edition, *The Tragedy of Master Arden of Faversham*, ed. M. L. Wine (1973). Numbers refer to scene and line; there is no act division.
[3] *British Drama* (fifth edition, New York, 1963), p. 231.
[4] Introduction, pp. lxvi–lxxiv.

impersonal chorus but Franklin, one of the characters, whose judgements within the play are not always sound. We may not feel bound to take his final statement simply at face value, any more than we do the final statements of Horatio and Fortinbras summing up the tragedy of *Hamlet*. Fortinbras, the outsider, sees only a heap of princely bodies; Horatio, the relative insider, describes the action as one

> Of accidental judgments, casual slaughters,
> Of deaths put on by cunning and forc'd cause,
> And, in this upshot, purposes mistook
> Fall'n on th' inventors' heads.   (5.2.384–7)[5]

– which is part of the truth, but is really a better description of that fine Ealing comedy *The Ladykillers* than it is of *Hamlet*. I am not saying that Franklin at this point is *just* an imperfect character, and is simply wrong about the play; we know from other plays of the period that at a moment like this a character can be both himself and the author's spokesman; but I believe that by placing it at the end and in the mouth of one of his characters the author has invited us to think critically about this view of the play as 'simple truth' in relation to our own experience of the work. Like Marlowe, who tells us what sort of hero to expect but invites us to applaud his fortunes as we please, the author of *Arden* is guiding our judgements up to a point but leaving them ultimately free.

Indeed, much of the play's fascination stems from the way it keeps us guessing about the kind of play it is; is it a reporting of the facts, a slice of life – or are the facts consciously shaped to give a significant pattern? Connected with this question about the play's art are some of the favourite Elizabethan questions about life itself. Is it random or meaningful? Is man a free agent, or are his actions shaped by forces stronger than himself; if the latter, are those forces just and reasonable, or wanton and meaningless? These questions were turned by Shakespeare into familiar quotations: 'The fault, dear Brutus, is not in our stars, / But in ourselves, that we are underlings' (*Julius Caesar*, 1.2.140–1). Or is it? The same character later declares, 'Now I change my mind, / And partly credit things that do presage' (5.1.77–8). In *King Lear* there are two major assessments of the fate of Gloucester, one from his son –

> The gods are just, and of our pleasant vices
> Make instruments to plague us.
> The dark and vicious place where thee he got
> Cost him his eyes.   (5.3.173–7)

– and one from himself: 'As flies to wanton boys are we to th' gods, / They kill us for their sport' (4.1.36–7). Not so much by conscious statements from his characters as by the very manner of his play, the author of *Arden of Faversham* keeps us engaged with these questions. The metaphysical problems are also artistic ones: does the 'simple truth' the writer offers consist of a set of sordid facts presented for our inspection, without comment; or are those facts shaped and controlled for a critical, even a moral purpose?

At certain points we seem to be in an accidental world, whose violence lacks the meaning and dignity of violence in conventional tragedy. Whatever Horatio may say, the slaughters in *Hamlet* are never quite casual; even the crazy stabbing of Polonius is dignified by significance: 'Thou find'st to be too busy is some danger' (3.4.34). But Black Will's threat, 'I'll stab him as he stands pissing against a wall' (scene 2, 97–8), evokes a whole world of casual, meaningless violence in which death has no dignity at all. The first attempt by Alice and her lover Mosby to kill Arden is with a bowl of poisoned broth, and it fails not because of the intervention of the gods but because the broth tastes nasty: Mosby declares in some annoyance, 'But what a villain is this painter Clarke!' (who provided the poison) and Alice adds:

> Was it not a goodly poison that he gave!
> Why, he's as well now as he was before.
> It should have been some fine confection
> That might have given the broth some dainty taste.
> This powder was too gross and populous.
>
>   (scene 1, 420–5)

We are made to reflect not on the workings of destiny but on how hard it is to get good domestic help these days. After the murder Alice goes down on her knees in a vain attempt to scrape the blood off the floor with her nails. We think of Lady Macbeth; we note the moral significance of Alice reduced to an animal

---

[5] All references to Shakespeare are to the *Complete Works*, ed. David Bevington (Glenview, Illinois, 1980).

scratching the ground. But we also have to notice the servant-girl Susan, who has been ordered to fetch water, standing helplessly by; and we hear Mosby's exasperated comment, 'Why, strew rushes on it, can you not? / This wench doth nothing. . . . Fall unto the work' (scene 14, 263–4). It is like seeing a classic tragedy refracted through the medium of a realistic novel. At other times the effect goes in reverse. The aftermath of the murder is full of police-court details – footprints in the snow, a hand-towel, a knife, a bloodstain, rushes stuck to the victim's slipper. But the print of the body that lingers in the grass for over two years takes us to a different level altogether.

At times the playwright flirts with a high romantic style of the sort that other playwrights of the period were using quite seriously. In this writer's hands the romantic style has a deliberate instability. In the opening scene Alice, like Juliet, like Cressida, like lovers through the ages, chides her husband for leaving her bed too soon, and he replies:

Sweet love, thou know'st that we two, Ovid-like,
Have often chid the morning when it 'gan to peep,
And often wished that dark Night's purblind steeds
Would pull her by the purple mantle back
And cast her in the ocean to her love.
But this night, sweet Alice, thou hast killed my heart:
I heard thee call on Mosby in thy sleep.

(scene 1, 60–6)

The Ovidian decoration sits uneasily on the sordid reality, and the nasty twist at the end shows the irony is deliberate. It may be dangerous to make too much depend on the literary style of what may be a bad, reported text; but it appears that the various lovers of the play have read the right books and are trying to dignify their own grubby passions with a glamorous style they cannot quite handle. Clarke, thinking of his love for Susan Mosby, declares,

For, as sharp-witted poets, whose sweet verse
Make heavenly gods break off their nectar draughts
And lay their ears down to the lowly earth,
Use humble promise to their sacred Muse,
So we that are the poets' favourites
Must have a love.   (scene 1, 251–6)

Compare Shakespeare's 'And when Love speaks, the voice of all the gods / Make heaven drowsy with the harmony' (*Love's Labour's Lost*, 4.3.340–1) with

'Make heavenly gods break off their nectar draughts' and we see how the brusque, matter-of-fact tone threatens the romantic manner of the rest of the passage. Just before the murder Alice declares:

Mosby's arms
Shall compass me; and, were I made a star,
I would have none other spheres but those.
There is no nectar but in Mosby's lips!
Had chaste Diana kissed him, she like me
Would grow love-sick, and from her wat'ry bower
Fling down Endymion and snatch him up.

(scene 14, 145–51)

Here the writing, though offering no real competition to Shakespeare or Marlowe, does not seem at first to be consciously sinking – until we come to the brisk verbs, 'Fling' and 'snatch'. There is also an ironic incongruity with the dramatic situation: the sordid plotting of the murder and the all-too-realistic quarrels we have seen these lovers engage in.

As the lovers are given to attempting the golden style, Arden's friend Franklin is an exponent of the drab style, in this case the generalizing proverb. He advises Arden on his marital difficulties with comments like 'sweet words are fittest engines / To raze the flint walls of a woman's breast' (scene 1, 46–7) or, advising Arden not to act the jealous husband, 'For women when they may will not, / But, being kept back, straight grow outrageous' (scene 1, 52–3). This too is a familiar trick of style in contemporary writing, and again it sits uneasily on the facts of the play. Sweet words have no effect on Alice if they come from a man she does not love; and far from illustrating the principle that 'women when they may will not', Alice, when she may, does. Other standard formulae fare no better. As Northrop Frye puts it, tragic playwrights of this period are 'fond of putting up signs reading "Danger–God at work"'.[6] Here, when a chance meeting saves Arden's life, Greene declares, 'The Lord of Heaven hath preservèd him' and Black Will retorts, 'The Lord of Heaven a fig! The Lord Cheyne hath preservèd him' (scene 9, 142–3).[7]

---

[6] *Fools of Time* (Toronto, 1967), p. 80.
[7] Here Wine strengthens the effect by emending the original, which reads, 'Preserued, a figge'.

123

The play's resistance to reductive formulae, whether romantic, practical or religious, goes along with a full realization of a world the audience would have recognized as its own – a world concerned not with passions in the purified form they often take in tragedy, but with matters such as class and property. It is Juliet's nurse, not Juliet, who points out that 'he that can lay hold of her / Shall have the chinks' (1.5.117–18). Juliet never sees herself this way. The central characters in *Arden*, however, cannot separate their passions from the social world in which those passions arise. Arden is offended not just because Alice is dishonouring him but because she is doing so with a social climber:

> A botcher, and no better at the first,
> Who, by base brokerage getting some small stock,
> Crept into service of a nobleman,
> And by his servile flattery and fawning
> Is now become the steward of his house,
> And bravely jets it in his silken gown.
>
> (scene 1, 25–30)

When he takes away Mosby's sword it is not a gesture from the world of chivalry but a studied social insult:

> So, sirrah, you may not wear a sword!
> The statute makes against artificers.
> I warrant that I do. Now use your bodkin,
> Your Spanish needle, and your pressing iron,
> For this shall go with me.   (scene 1, 310–14)

Alice too, when she quarrels with Mosby, harps on her noble descent and his baseness.

The criminal classes are a little more stylized, perhaps; but even Black Will is not just a stage villain but a representative of a basic Elizabethan social problem, the discharged soldier. And there is snobbery in his world too: 'Why, Bradshaw, was not thou and I fellow soldiers at Boulogne, where I was a corporal, and thou but a base mercenary groom? "No fellows now" because you are a goldsmith and have a little plate in your shop?' (scene 2, 18–21). He has, in a comic way, his own social aspirations: 'Ah, that I might be set awork thus through the year and that murder would grow to an occupation, that a man might without danger of law – Zounds, I warrant I should be warden of the company!' (scene 2, 105–9).

But there is delicate shading here: in the first passage we recognize the bitterness of a man who thinks he has come down in the world; in the second, with its conscious audience-teasing paradox, we are closer to the voice of an Elizabethan clown. And this is a clue to one kind of shaping the playwright allows himself. He is interested in his characters as social beings, and like Middleton after him he is not at this level content with simple observation; he heightens and sharpens for critical effect – and often for effects that anticipate the work of Middleton.

One matter to which he returns almost obsessively is the striking of bargains. The play is full of oaths, obligations, words given and kept, given and broken. It is this kind of action that stamps man as a social being; society, as Rousseau discerned, is a contract. The playwright's interest in this matter is signalled quite early, when of all the ways he could have made Alice declare her adulterous passion he picks the following:

> Sweet Mosby is the man that hath my heart;
> And he [Arden] usurps it, having nought but this,
> That I am tied to him by marriage.
> Love is a god, and marriage is but words;
> And therefore Mosby's title is the best.
> Tush! Whether it be or no, he shall be mine
> In spite of him, of Hymen, and of rites.
>
> (scene 1, 98–104)

When she says 'marriage is but words', 'word' has a special meaning; at the centre of the marriage service is a set of promises, which she has violated. She sets her desires against her obligations; but before talking herself into this position she makes a brief attempt to give her choice a specious respectability: 'Mosby's title is the best.' In the next line she shrugs that idea off; but it may be she is more disturbed than she cares to admit by the fact that she has broken a promise.

She is not the only one. Mosby and Arden make up their quarrel and swear friendship just before Arden goes off to London; Alice professes that she cannot bear to be parted from her husband:

Alice....

> And, Master Franklin, seeing you take him hence,
> In hope you'll hasten him home I'll give you this.
> *And then she kisseth him.*

Franklin.

And, if he stay, the fault shall not be mine. –
Mosby, farewell, and see you keep your oath.

Mosby.

I hope he is not jealous of me now.

Arden.

No, Mosby, no. Hereafter think of me
As of your dearest friend, and so farewell.

(scene 1, 410–16)

Moments later Alice is telling Mosby to pay no attention to his vow of friendship: 'oaths are words, and words is wind, / And wind is mutable' (scene 1, 436–7). It is not long before Arden is voicing his old suspicions again, and Franklin, who has promised to speed his return home, is inviting him to stay in London (scene 4, 28). All this is no more than we would expect; but the way it is dramatized emphasizes how hard it is for these characters to keep their promises.

The same concern affects the low-life characters. There is a curious sort of honour among thieves. Black Will, after the first setback, grows restive, and complains to Greene, 'I have had ten pound to steal a dog, and we have no more here to kill a man. But that a bargain is a bargain and so forth, you should do it yourself' (scene 3, 73–6). He seems to feel that he has taken on this contract a bit hastily, but it is still a contract. Greene whips him back into line:

Remember how devoutly thou hast sworn
To kill the villain; think upon thine oath.

Will.

Tush, I have broken five hundred oaths!
But wouldst thou charm me to effect this deed,
Tell me of gold, my resolution's fee.

(scene 3, 87–91)

Will would hate to have Greene think of him as the sort of milksop who would keep an oath for the oath's sake; yet the fee, which he has just been grumbling about, seems enough to hold him to his word. And through a long series of frustrations he keeps on trying; we might even say that he takes his promises more seriously than Alice takes hers.

A professional, he despises amateurs, as we see when he confronts the unfortunate servant Michael:

'Tis known to us you love Mosby's sister;
We know besides that you have ta'en your oath
To further Mosby to your mistress' bed
And kill your master for his sister's sake.
Now, sir, a poorer coward than yourself
Was never fostered in the coast of Kent.
How comes it then that such a knave as you
Dare swear a matter of such consequence?

(scene 3, 144–51)

Professional snobbery comes into play here, related to the class-consciousness we have already seen in Black Will. Swearing is, it seems, only for high-class criminals like himself; it confers a certain dignity on the enterprise. At the same time – indeed, within three lines – he shows a child-like readiness to trust Michael, simply because Michael *has* sworn: 'Sith thou hast sworn, we dare discover all' (scene 3, 154). As he said earlier to Greene, a bargain is a bargain.

For Black Will the issue is ultimately simple: he is a professional, he has a contract, and he carries it out. Or he tries at least. His loyalty is to the job and (of course) the fee. For Michael, who is an amateur, it is not so simple; he is torn by conflicting loyalties:

My master's kindness pleads to me for life
With just demand, and I must grant it him;
My mistress she hath forced me with an oath
For Susan's sake, the which I may not break,
For that is nearer than a master's love;
That grim-faced fellow, pitiless Black Will,
And Shakebag, stern in bloody stratagem –
Two rougher ruffians never lived in Kent –
Have sworn my death if I infringe my vow,
A dreadful thing to be considered of.

(scene 4, 62–71)

There is something pathetic in watching the poor young man struggle with his conscience; but there may be an edge of wry, satiric comedy here as well. Alice could break her loyalty for the sake of her desire; and there is a certain integrity in that. Michael has his desires too, but what seems to weigh most heavily with him is that he has *promised* to help kill his master. He has obligations to Arden; but it is an awful thing to break a promise, and so he commits himself to murder. We may think of that other slave of duty, Mrs Solness in Ibsen's *The Master Builder*, who weighs her duty to stop her husband from killing himself against her duty to greet a party of ladies who have just arrived – and goes to greet the ladies, muttering, 'One has duties in so many directions.' Another factor that weighs with Michael, of course, is fear of what the ruffians will do; if he doesn't keep his oath, their oath is to kill him; and whatever Michael is he assumes Black Will and Shakebag are men of their word.

If there is satire here, it is muted by the pathos of the amateur criminal who has got out of his depth. The satire is not so muted elsewhere. A world held together by oaths and obligations needs only a slight turn of the screw to become a world held together by deals and bargains, in which human beings become commodities. This is what happens here, and it is in this respect that *Arden of Faversham* most clearly anticipates the work of Thomas Middleton (I should add that though Middleton may have been around twenty when this play first appeared I am not proposing him as the author). Michael is not quite so pathetic, perhaps, when he first swears the oath that will ultimately doom him. After Alice offers his fee, 'I say that Susan's thine', he replies:

Why, then I say that I will kill my master
Or anything that you will have me do.
Alice.
But, Michael, see you do it cunningly.
Michael.
Why, say I should be took, I'll ne'er confess
That you know anything; and Susan, being a maid,
May beg me from the gallows of the shrieve.
Alice.
Trust not to that, Michael.
Michael.
You cannot tell me; I have seen it, I. [8]
But, mistress, tell her whether I live or die
I'll make her more worth than twenty painters can;
For I will rid mine elder brother away,
And then the farm of Bolton is mine own.
Who would not venture upon house and land
When he might have it for a right-down blow?
(scene 1, 161–75)

Kill your master and get the girl; kill your brother and get the house: he lives in a world of easy satisfactions, which even Alice finds naïve. Servant though he may be, his descendant in Jacobean tragedy is Beatrice-Joanna in *The Changeling*.

In this world of bargains and deals human life is traded against money and land. Alice offers Greene an advance of ten pounds on Arden's murder, twenty more and the title to his land when the deed is done. Black Will tosses off a cheerful offer of parricide: 'and, if thou't have thy own father slain that thou may'st inherit his land, we'll kill him' (scene 2, 88–90). Arden seems to be a land-grabber himself, though he does not kill for it; that is a matter I want to return to later. Just before the murder Alice, sensing that Black Will may need a little extra incentive, promises,

You shall have twenty pound,
And, when he is dead, you shall have forty more;
And, lest you might be suspected staying here,
Michael shall saddle you two lusty geldings.
Ride whither you will, to Scotland or to Wales,
I'll see you shall not lack where'er you be.
Will.
Such words would make one kill a thousand men!
Give me the key. Which is the countinghouse?
(scene 14, 126–33)

In Will's reply there is a sudden drop from the Marlovian brag to the practical detail; and the counting-house seems altogether the appropriate place for Will to hide. In this world the promises that are kept are the promises that have an incentive attached to them; that is the difference between an oath and a deal. We see this even in a matter that is not literally material, the bargain that ends the lovers' quarrel between Mosby and Alice:

Mosby. . . .
I will forget this quarrel, gentle Alice,
Provided I'll be tempted so no more. . . .
Alice.
Then with thy lips seal up this new-made match.
(scene 8, 148–50)

Even between lovers forgiveness has a price tag, and Alice's words suggest the concluding of a business agreement.

As a social drama, then, *Arden of Faversham* shows not just observation but analysis. It is also a tragedy.

---

[8] Since, as Alice points out, such a means of rescue is unlikely, we may wonder if Michael has seen it in a popular play.

While the Elizabethans had no very elaborate theories of tragedy, they had certain expectations: disaster and death, and a sense of a world beyond. Their tragedies are full of omens, from the blood that congeals as Faustus tries to sign his pact with the devil to the night of storm and horror that precedes the murder of Julius Caesar. The signs of doom are not always external: when Romeo pauses before entering the Capulets' ball to express his fear of 'Some consequence yet hanging in the stars' (1.4.107) the moment looks artificial to us; to the first audience it may have looked like a striking variation on the expected device, internalizing the sense of disaster. Much later, in *The Changeling*, the external omen and the internal sense of doom are fused as Beatrice-Joanna says of her lover and destroyer De Flores, 'Beneath the stars, upon yon meteor / Ever hung my fate, 'mongst things corruptible'.[9] In *Arden of Faversham* there are no comets or thunderclaps; but there is a sense that the characters are doomed by their own compulsions, and there is a moment when Alice, like Romeo, seems to feel the touch of disaster. After a quarrel with Mosby, she has just allowed him to talk her around:

> So lists the sailor to the mermaid's song;
> So looks the traveller to the basilisk.
> I am content for to be reconciled,
> And that I know will be my overthrow.
>
> (scene 1, 213–16)

But it is typical of the play that this moment lacks the clarity of Romeo's sudden fear of the stars; it could be pouting, flirting, teasing or all three; it could be that Alice is not fully aware of the seriousness of her words. The speech both acts as a dramatic foreshadowing and reports, realistically, the movement of the character's mind.

The fusion between these two effects is even closer in Mosby's long soliloquy. He is doomed by his own compulsion, knows it, and is unable to stop himself. The way his mind works is disconcertingly recognizable; he is capable both of insight into his own feelings and of turning away from that insight because it is too uncomfortable:

My golden time was when I had no gold;
Though then I wanted, yet I slept secure;
My daily toil begat me night's repose;
My night's repose made daylight fresh to me.

But since I climbed the top bough of the tree
And sought to build my nest among the clouds,
Each gentle starry gale doth shake my bed
And makes me dread my downfall to the earth.
But whither doth contemplation carry me?
The way I seek to find where pleasure dwells
Is hedged behind me that I cannot back
But needs must on although to danger's gate.
Then, Arden, perish thou by that decree,
For Greene doth ear the land and weed thee up
To make my harvest nothing but pure corn.
And for his pains I'll heave him up awhile
And, after, smother him to have his wax;
Such bees as Greene must never live to sting.
Then there is Michael and the painter too,
Chief actors to Arden's overthrow,
Who, when they shall see me sit in Arden's seat,
They will insult upon me for my meed
Or fright me by detecting of his end.
I'll none of that, for I can cast a bone
To make these curs pluck out each other's throat;
And then am I sole ruler of mine own.
Yet Mistress Arden lives; but she's myself,
And holy church rites makes us two but one.
But what for that I may not trust you, Alice?
You have supplanted Arden for my sake
And will extirpen me to plant another.
'Tis fearful sleeping in a serpent's bed,
And I will cleanly rid my hands of her.

(scene 8, 11–43)

Like Macbeth he knows what is happening to him, but he can only go forward, not back, killing compulsively to protect himself. The difference is that so far Mosby has not killed anybody; we are watching not a man being trapped by the consequences of his deeds but a man trapping himself by accepting the consequences of deeds he has not even committed. He has, if you like, mortgaged himself on a property he does not yet own. The final twist of irony is that one of the key motives for doing so was his love for Alice – whom he now sees as a threat to be disposed of. He imagines himself marrying her and killing her; the vows of holy church hold him back a moment and are then brushed off. In that, ironically, he and Alice think alike.

Of the various motives for Arden's death the one to

---

[9] Revels edition, ed. N. W. Bawcutt (1958), 5.3.154–5.

which the playwright gives the greatest dramatic prominence is the adulterous love of Alice and Mosby; he also shows that love going sour right from the beginning. The two are bickering in their first scene together; they quarrel constantly about the murder. Mosby's soliloquy, and the serious altercation that follows it, cast doubt on all the protestations of constancy that come after. They go on to commit murder, and to suffer the consequences, for the sake of an affair that is deeply shaky, damaged, one suspects, by the very tension of working the scheme that is supposed to fulfil their desires. This is not to say that they have no love for each other at all, or that their reconciliations are always hollow. That irony would be too simple. We might even see this as the sort of passionate affair that is fuelled by regular quarrelling. But we are never quite sure how much they really mean to each other, and neither are they. All we – or they – can be sure of is the disaster their love will produce.

In shaping his work as a tragedy, then, the playwright relies not on the external machinery of Fortune, the gods, or the stars, but on the internal compulsions of the characters, the sense of fate they have created for themselves. And yet there is a section of the play in which we are made to wonder if some external power is taking a hand, where a series of chances accumulates in such a way as to suggest a design. The role of sheer bad luck in tragedy is always a controversial one; it is a standard complaint about *Romeo and Juliet* that it depends too much on the incompetence of the Italian postal service; and at the end of *Tess of the d'Urbervilles* Hardy feels called upon to dignify the novel's chain of accidents by declaring, 'the President of the Immortals, in Aeschylean phrase, had ended his sport with Tess'. In the extraordinary middle scenes of *Arden of Faversham* the President of the Immortals seems to be having some very strange sport indeed. The effect is not so much tragedy as anti-tragedy; by a series of accidents Arden's life is saved, over and over again. Whereas in conventional tragedy Fate seems to lead the hero to his doom, here Fate seems to be stubbornly holding him back. From the beginning of the play we have thought of Arden as a man marked for death; now he looks as indestructible as the hero of an animated cartoon. The effect is anti-

tragic in another way; in tragedy a chain of accidents has a cumulative effect, as each builds on the other to produce the inevitable end. Here by the very nature of things each accident is discrete and leads nowhere. The effect is not a cumulative movement but a series of stops and starts.

The author is aware, I am sure, that this material if not carefully handled will create the impression of incompetent playwriting, an attempt to pad out a thin action. He needs to assure us somehow that he is in control; and he does this by sharpening the comic irony of the sequence. Black Will is useful here; his habit of boasting sets him up for predictable, comic deflation. When Arden appears with Franklin and Michael he reacts automatically, 'Zounds, I'll kill them all three' (scene 3, 37), and Greene has to restrain him. But he kills nobody, for a moment later he is struck on the head by a shop window. The playwright emphasizes the element of sheer fluke in this episode by showing the apprentice who causes the accident simply going about his ordinary business: ''Tis very late; I were best shut up my stall, for here will be old filching when the press comes forth of Paul's' (scene 3, 50–1). Black Will is not just frustrated; he is humiliated and embarrassed. He and Shakebag go on boasting about what they are going to do to Arden, but their protestations begin to look futile:

> I tell thee, Greene, the forlorn traveller
> Whose lips are glued with summer's parching heat
> Ne'er longed so much to see a running brook
> As I to finish Arden's tragedy.
> Seest thou this gore that cleaveth to my face?
> From hence ne'er will I wash this bloody stain
> Till Arden's heart be panting in my hand.
>
> (scene 3, 100–6)

Later Will describes himself as

> the very man,
> Marked in my birth-hour by the Destinies,
> To give an end to Arden's life on earth . . .
>
> (scene 3, 159–61)

What Will is doing is trying to invest himself with the trappings of conventional tragedy; he himself uses the word 'tragedy' more than once. He is marked out, fated to be Arden's killer. But this attempt at tragic dignity looks increasingly futile as accident after accident intervenes, and Greene declares, 'I think we shall never do it; let us give it over' (scene 14, 2).

That cry of frustration is heard more than once towards the end of the play. Then, just as we ourselves have begun to wonder if Arden leads a charmed life, he is killed. There is, I think, a sense of fate in his tragedy, but it is an unconventional one. Fate is not so much inexorable as perverse. As it plays cat-and-mouse with Arden, so the dramatist plays cat-and-mouse with us. Once we are used to the idea of Arden as a murder victim he becomes unkillable; and as soon as we are used to the idea that he is unkillable, he is killed.[10] We feel that, as Clov in *Endgame* puts it, something is taking its course. And yet the nature of that something remains elusive. When Shakebag declares 'Arden, thou hast wondrous holy luck' (scene 9, 133), he summarizes our problem. The words 'holy' and 'luck' simply collide; they belong to two different metaphysical systems, a divinely ordered universe and a random one. There is, we are tempted to say, no such thing as holy luck. And yet the randomness of life seems to have been manipulated here in such a way as to produce a sense of design out of its sheer perversity.

The metaphysical problem is connected, as I have already suggested, with the artistic one: the playwright keeps us guessing about what sort of play he is writing. One scene that brings this into particularly sharp focus is that in which Will and Shakebag lose their chance by missing Arden in the fog, and Shakebag falls into a ditch. Here the playwright introduces an interesting minor figure, a ferryman. Given that this is a play about death, and given Michael's reference in the previous scene to Will and Shakebag as Arden's 'ferrymen to long home' (scene 10, 45), how symbolic in this ferryman? Is he meant to suggest what Clarence in *Richard III* calls 'that sour ferryman which poets write of' (1.4.46), Charon, who ferries souls across the Styx to Hades?[11] Is he, in other words, second cousin to the gloomy fellow with the scythe who accompanies the arrest of Edward II in Marlowe's play or the bony apothecary who sells Romeo the poison, creating an emblematic picture of the young man encountering death? The sequence opens with a dialogue between Arden and the ferryman:

Ferryman.
  Fie, what a mist is here!
Arden.
  This mist, my friend, is mystical,
  Like to a good companion's smoky brain,
  That was half-drowned with new ale overnight.
                                    (scene 11, 5–8)

When Arden says, 'This mist, my friend, is mystical', we prick up our ears. But he and the ferryman go on to jokes about drunkenness, curst wives, and later adultery – applicable to Arden, but not in quite the way we expected. Apart from a mild joke about opening a skull to let in a chimney (scene 11, 9–10) the ferryman's humour is not quite the gallows humour we would expect from a Charon figure. A few moments later Will and Shakebag seem to give us a mystical mist of the sort we were expecting, when Will declares he is 'almost in hell's mouth, where I cannot see my way for smoke' (scene 12, 2–3), but they too turn to sexual jokes, and when next they refer to the mist it suggests not death and hell but the workings of chance, as Shakebag says of their intended victims, 'they may haply lose their way as we have done, and then we may chance meet with them' (scene 12, 17–19) – and promptly falls into a ditch. We are just getting used to the idea that this is not the darkness of Hell but a normal English fog that produces a simply literal confusion, when the ferryman reappears and the following dialogue ensues between him and Shakebag:

Ferryman. . . . . What's his name, I pray you, sir?
Shakebag. His name is Black Will.
Ferryman. I hope to see him one day hanged upon a
  hill.
                                    (scene 12, 39–41)

Once again the playwright is toying with us. Our first temptation was to think of the ferryman as an omen of death for Arden; then he seemed to be no such thing; then he turns out to be ominous after all, not for the hero but for the killer.

---

[10] During an Actors' Forum at the Twentieth International Shakespeare Conference (August, 1982), the sequence was described in just these terms by John Bowe, the actor playing Black Will in Terry Hands's production.

[11] This suggestion is made by Wine, p. lxvii.

The real test of whether the world of the play is random or ordered is the final, successful attempt on Arden's life. The question is whether it is the fulfilment of a deeper pattern, or just one more attempt that this time happens to succeed as the earlier ones happened to fail. At one level the playwright does indeed seem to be drawing threads together: Arden's death is not just the last in an unconnected sequence of events but the culmination of a number of motifs introduced early in the play. There is a simple but compelling theatrical point: all his major adversaries are directly involved, as they were not in earlier attempts. The result is more satisfying dramatically than his death at the hands of a couple of hired assassins would be. Each of the three characters who stabs him gives a reason:

Mosby.
There's for the pressing iron you told me of. [*He stabs Arden.*]
Shakebag.
And there's for the ten pound in my sleeve. [*He stabs him.*]
Alice.
What, groans thou? – Nay, then give me the weapon! –
Take this for hind'ring Mosby's love and mine. [*She stabs him.*]
(scene 14, 235–8)

Mosby remembers a social insult, though our own memories may have to be fairly acute if we are to recall Arden's taunt about the pressing iron; Shakebag is thinking of his fee; and Alice announces the motive to which the play has given the greatest prominence, striking the last blow as she does so. Also, the circumstances of the murder have a certain resonance; Arden is not just killed while pissing against a wall. He is gaming; and gaming is one of the first ideas associated with the love of Mosby and Alice:

Bear him from me these pair of silver dice
With which we played for kisses many a time,
And when I lost I won, and so did he . . .
(scene 1, 122–5)

Also, we might say that throughout the play Arden has been winning a game of chance without even knowing he was playing it; and now at last his 'holy luck' runs out. The killers hide in the counting-house, and this too has significance, not just for their own mercenary natures but for his. Arden has been placed socially as a man of property and business, and a grasping one at that. If he has any guilt for which his death is a retribution it is in this area of his life. None of this makes his death as systematically emblematic as that of, say, the old Duke in *The Revenger's Tragedy*, who is forced to kiss the poisoned skull of the woman he lusted after and murdered. The resonance of Arden's murder is more a matter of suggestion than of emblem; but the resonance is there, and it is just enough to make the murder something more than the last event in an episodic story

It is also the final crisis for the other characters, and the way they behave under the stress of it shows the playwright's interest in surprise. This is not so much a matter of plot twists as of a lifelike unpredictability in the whole dramatic world. It is the same unpredictability that lends an eccentric rhythm to the series of murder attempts; here it shows itself in a number of surprising character developments. In the early scenes Mosby had seemed to be a somewhat ineffectual plotter, hankering after exotic devices like poisoned paintings and poisoned crucifixes, somewhat to the irritation of the more practical Alice. Perhaps his desire to do things in the grand Italian manner is part of his social climbing; in any case, the closest Arden comes to this sort of Websterian fate is the poisoned broth, and even that fails. Yet in the final sequence Mosby takes charge and it is his plot that succeeds. Alice has always seemed the more practical and resolute of the two; yet in the tense aftermath of the murder she is the one who cracks, unable to bear the word 'husband', and Mosby complains, 'She will undo us through her foolishness' (scene 14, 306). There is a similar reversal between the two hired thugs. Black Will appears throughout the play the more spectacular and bloodthirsty of the two; yet when he starts to particularize the crimes he has actually committed they sound more like undergraduate pranks:

For a cross word of a tapster I have pierced one barrel after another with my dagger and held him by the ears till all his beer hath run out. . . . I and my company have taken the constable from his watch and carried him about the fields on a coltstaff.
(scene 14, 13–21)

After the murder he flees to Flushing, confessing in soliloquy:

> I am so pursued with hues and cries
> For petty robberies that I have done
> That I can come unto no sanctuary.
>
> (scene 17, 2–4)

We had thought he had much more than petty robberies on his conscience. Meanwhile Shakebag, who is relatively speaking the quieter of the two[12] and has complained more than once of Black Will's boasting, turns out to be the real killer. He too, like Black Will, has a soliloquy concerning his flight, but the effect is very different:

> The widow Chambley in her husband's days kept;
> And, now he's dead, she is grown so stout
> She will not know her old companions.
> I came hither, thinking to have had
> Harbour as I was wont,
> And she was ready to thrust me out at doors.
> But, whether she would or no, I got me up;
> And, as she followed me, I spurned her down the stairs,
> And broke her neck, and cut her tapster's throat;
> And now I am going to fling them in the Thames.
> I have the gold; what care I though it be known?
> I'll cross the water and take sanctuary.
>
> (scene 15, 1–12)

At first the widow Chambley looks like a bit of picturesque local colour; nothing in the low-key, semi-comic tone of the speech's opening prepares us for its grim conclusion. Shakebag kills as a matter of course, casually and without flourish. Black Will brags like a backstreet Tamburlaine; but Shakebag, it turns out, is the real thing. Thinking back on the murder we realize that while Black Will pinned Arden down it was Shakebag who stabbed him; we may even wonder if Black Will has ever killed a man in his life.

In the end the two professionals, who have always worked as a team, scatter; and the amateurs, who have always been rather disconnected, come together for final sentencing. We are not surprised when Mosby and Alice turn on each other; but we may be a little surprised when Alice becomes a Christian penitent:

> Leave now to trouble me with worldly things,
> And let me meditate upon my Saviour Christ,
> Whose blood must save me for the blood I shed.

Mosby.
> How long shall I live in this hell of grief?
> Convey me from the presence of that strumpet.

Alice.
> Ah, but for thee I never had been strumpet.
> What cannot oaths and protestations do
> When men have opportunity to woo?
>
> (scene 18, 9–16)

She is as much given to cliché proverbs as Franklin was at the start of the play. And yet it may be that even here the playwright wants to keep us guessing. In her proverbs about female frailty, is she trying to shift the blame? And in 'Leave now to trouble me with worldly things' is she trying – absurdly and pointlessly, now that the game is up – to avoid further questioning? It looks like a conventional criminal's repentance, of the sort that ballad-makers were fond of. But is it? And can we take any final satisfaction in the workings of justice at the end of the play? The criminals are executed, but indiscriminately. We would recognize different degrees, even kinds of guilt in Alice, Mosby, Susan, and Michael, but the law evidently does not. And we do not recognize any guilt in Bradshaw, whose final words, 'My blood be on his head that gave the sentence' (scene 18, 38), turn the guilt upon the law itself. He is the last of the victims to speak before the epilogue, and if we are trying to see a clear pattern of retributive justice in the ending he strikes a jarring note. The others accept their sentences, but in a great variety of ways:

Alice.
> Let my death make amends for all my sins.

Mosby.
> Fie upon women! – this shall be my song.
> But bear me hence, for I have lived too long.

Susan.
> Seeing no hope on earth, in heaven is my hope.

Michael.
> Faith, I care not, seeing I die with Susan.
>
> (scene 18, 33–7)

---

[12] This relationship was well brought out in Terry Hands's production. Shakebag generally stood far upstage of Black Will, and his manner was still and guarded while Will's was expansive.

Susan and Alice, major and minor characters, are united in a conventional piety at the end. Mosby goes off with a snarl; for him, as we see in an earlier speech, *this* world is hell and he wants to be released from it. He has no thought of another one. While Mosby rejects his love, Michael remains true to his, and his acceptance of his fate has a simple, touching dignity that makes this weak young man, unexpectedly, the most impressive of the murderers at the end. Often in the drama of this period a character's last speech will be the touchstone of his nature, and will sum up his quality. Here the characters as they go to death seem to keep changing before our eyes, not because the playwright is inconsistent but because he has something like Shakespeare's awareness of the unpredictability of humanity under pressure.

In the end the pattern of the play seems to be drawing together, and yet the different components will not quite stay in place. The tension between an ordering vision and respect for intractable reality goes into Franklin's epilogue, to which we should now return:

> Thus have you seen the truth of Arden's death.
> As for the ruffians, Shakebag and Black Will,
> The one took sanctuary, and being sent for out,
> Was murdered in Southwark as he passed
> To Greenwich, where the Lord Protector lay.
> Black Will was burned in Flushing on a stage;
> Greene was hangèd at Osbridge in Kent;
> The painter fled, and how he died we know not.
>
> (Epilogue, 1–8)

Shakebag, who kills in passing, is killed in passing – literally. Black Will dies as the ferryman predicted, but he is burned, not hanged. The omen was only half effective. Greene is hanged; and with the rhythm thus established we expect to hear of the painter Clarke's execution in the next line; instead of which the playwright tells us that he doesn't know everything. It would have been so easy to slip in another execution; but the playwright does not want things to be that neat. Even in the final mopping-up, something eludes us.

That is the strongest touch of the random and accidental in the epilogue. It is followed at once by the most powerful indication that Arden's death fulfils a coherent pattern of retribution:

> But this above the rest is to be noted:
> Arden lay murdered in that plot of ground
> Which he by force and violence held from Reede,
> And in the grass his body's print was seen
> Two years and more after the deed was done.
>
> (Epilogue, 9–13)

In the confrontation between Arden and Reede it was not clear whether Arden held the land legally or not, because it was not clear which man was telling the truth. Now we know; and we recognize a final twist to the theme of oath and obligation we noted earlier; Arden holds this plot of land by force rather than agreement. And it is force that brings him to rest in it at the end. Earlier in the play the view of Arden as (in Greene's words) 'greedy-gaping still for gain' (scene 1, 475) was held in tension with the view of him as a kindly and innocent victim, best expressed by Michael: 'Ah, harmless Arden, how, how hast thou misdone / That thus thy gentle life is levelled at?' (scene 3, 195–6). Now that tension seems to be resolved; Arden is not an innocent victim; he is paying for his crimes. Beneath the actions of the characters Fate is working in its own way, and reveals its purpose at the end. But a number of factors make the final effect a little off-centre. One is that Reede's curse comes fairly late in the play. This makes it less powerful as a unifying device than, say, the curses of Margaret in *Richard III*, which are planted quite early and go off at regular intervals like time bombs. Another is that Reede provides so many options in his curse that the effect of inexorable fate is somewhat dissipated:

> That plot of ground which thou detains from me –
> I speak it in an agony of spirit –
> Be ruinous and fatal unto thee!
> Either there be butchered by thy dearest friends,
> Or else be brought for men to wonder at,
> Or thou or thine miscarry in that place,
> Or there run mad and end thy cursèd days.
>
> (scene 13, 32–8)

The curse that is fulfilled comes second in a list of four; it does not even have the force of a climactic position. A third factor is that Reede himself is not involved in the murder plot, which proceeds quite independently of his grievance, though admittedly Greene's motives are parallel to his. The retribution, if such it can be called, is indirect. This gives it, from one angle, greater power because it is more mysterious; but it also puts it closer to the realm of mere bizarre coincidence. Right to the end, the playwright keeps surprising us, and keeps us guessing.

And so to that final statement of artistic policy:

Gentlemen, we hope you'll pardon this naked tragedy
Wherein no filèd points are foisted in
To make it gracious to the ear or eye;
For simple truth is gracious enough
And needs no other points of glozing stuff.

(Epilogue, 14–18)

What the playwright disclaims, I think, is the intrusion of any artificial heightening to his story; but 'simple truth', when looked at closely, has its own sufficient order, is 'gracious enough'. In showing a world of oath-breaking and crude bargaining, a set of characters trapped by their own compulsions, and an action that combines the workings of perverse chance with a final sense of retribution, the playwright shows that he is not content simply to pile facts together. But he applies these ordering principles tentatively, with a due respect for the intractable and unpredictable world his characters live in, and for their own capacity to surprise and baffle. Appropriately, his ordering is most decisive on the social level, most tentative on the supernatural. He is concerned with what he can observe here and now, with things as they are, not with some hidden world. The hidden world is there, and we glimpse it occasionally. We might even say, paradoxically, that no fully developed realism can ignore it. But we can never be sure, and we are certainly not sure here, how it is operating and how much sense it makes in terms that we would understand.

What the *Arden* playwright has done, I think, is to open a vein of realism in Elizabethan drama to run beside and later enrich the heroics of tragedy and the romantic fantasy of comedy. It is a realism that consists of a hard, tough appraisal of things as they are, and a resistance to conventional formulae. He is not the only playwright to be doing so around 1590. Again, I say nothing about authorship but the other playwright I have in mind is Shakespeare and the play is *Henry VI, Part One*. It opens with a ceremony, the funeral of Henry V, during which the formal laments of the mourners are interrupted by news of English losses in France. Exeter demands, 'How were they lost? What treachery was us'd?' (He evidently assumes, like the Chaplain in Shaw's *St. Joan*, that no Englishman is ever fairly beaten.) He receives the chilling reply, 'No treachery, but want of men and money' (1.1.68–9). It is not a world of heroic action; it is a world of practical reality. Through the rest of the play the Agincourt generation dies off – one of them, Salisbury, killed by a sniper. Even Joan of Arc's spirits fail her. And Talbot, the flower of English chivalry, dies betrayed by York and Somerset, who engage in a bureaucratic wrangle about who should be sending him aid. To quote Shaw again, 'the British soldier can stand up to anything except the British War Office'. Shakespeare does for chivalric romance what the *Arden* playwright does for tragedy; he brings it down to earth. He allows the shaping patterns, of course – rise and fall, crime and retribution. But he shows us these patterns at work in a world of tough reality. The lead thus established as early as 1590 will be followed by Middleton and Webster and by Shakespeare himself in his later work.

In claiming to show us 'simple truth' the *Arden* playwright may be a little disingenuous. Realism is a sophisticated form, and realism as he practises it is often complex and mysterious. It also has great importance for the future of English drama. It is tempting to end by quoting, not Shaw this time but one of his contemporaries; and I do not intend to resist the temptation: 'The truth is rarely pure and never simple. Modern life would be very tedious if it were either, and modern literature a complete impossibility.'

'PICKLEHERRING' AND ENGLISH
ACTORS IN GERMANY

WILLEM SCHRICKX

Clown-names seem to have had a way of attaching themselves to individual English actors travelling on the Continent so that the companies to which they belonged between 1590 and 1620 apparently succeeded in popularizing certain clownish figures. Three of these, John Posset, Stockfish and Pickleherring, have come to be generally acknowledged as representative clownish types in the standard accounts of the Elizabethan and Jacobean stages.[1] Yet, having gone through the evidence on which this general consensus is based, I have come to the conclusion that, for the time being, there is only one clown-name for whose existence there is ample evidence, both in archival material and in printed texts, and that is the figure of John Bouset or Posset, a name that became associated with Thomas Sackville, an English actor at the court of Duke Henry Julius of Brunswick (1564–1613) in Wolfenbüttel. As to the fishnames for the clown, those of (Hans) Stockfish and Pickleherring have been all too carelessly attached to the actors John Spencer and Robert Reynolds, although there is very little that can be advanced in support of the identifications. It is the purpose of this paper to show that there is little justification for looking upon Reynolds as one of the chief actors to introduce the humorous character of Pickleherring on to the German stage; and that, on the contrary, archival evidence points to another English Pickleherring-player whose career has only quite recently begun to emerge from the records. Incidentally, one early student of the Elizabethan drama, Frederick Gard Fleay, a scholar whom it is as dangerous to trust as to ignore, had suggested a different equation. He thought that a member of Queen Anne's Men, Robert

Lee, was the progenitor of the Pickleherring type.[2] But before paying attention to the new evidence for the identity of Pickleherring, it is necessary to make available a will, recently discovered by Peter Brand, which enables us to define, with greater precision than has hitherto been thought possible, the identity of Robert Browne, the well-known actor of German fame who spent many years on the Continent visiting such places as Wolfenbüttel, Frankfurt, Lille and Brussels. The name of Browne is so common that confusion as to whom we are talking about seems almost inevitable. The Browne to be dealt with here should, for example, not be confused with another actor, the much-discussed 'Browne of the Boar's Head', whose death Joan Alleyn announced to her husband, the actor Edward Alleyn, in a letter of October 1603.[3]

Some time in 1623 a certain Robert Browne drew up his will in Shoreditch, Middlesex.

In the name of god Amen. I Robert Browne of the Parish of St Leonard, Shorditch in the countie of

---

[1] See E. K. Chambers, *The Elizabethan Stage*, 4 vols. (Oxford, 1923), vol. 2, pp. 285, 336, and G. E. Bentley, *The Jacobean and Caroline Stage*, 7 vols. (Oxford, 1941–68), vol. 2, p. 543.

[2] F. G. Fleay, *A Chronicle History of the London Stage 1559–1642* (1890), pp. 297, 329.

[3] For more information on the Brownes see my article 'English Actors at the Courts of Wolfenbüttel, Brussels and Graz during the Lifetime of Shakespeare', *Shakespeare Survey 33* (Cambridge, 1980), 153–68. I wish to thank Peter Brand for giving me permission to publish the will of Robert Brown Jr. See his study 'Der englische Komödiant Robert Browne, (1563–*ca.* 1621/39)', p. 95.

Middlesex yeoman beinge sicke of bodie but of perfect remembrance thanks be given to Almightie god And knowinge that nothinge is more certayne than death and nothing more uncertayne then the houre of death doe therefore make my last will and Testament in manner and forme followinge. Ffirst bequeath my soule to Allmightie god my maker hopinge for remission of my sinnes by the death and passion of Jesus Christ myne onely saviour and redeemer for his mercy onely and by [sic for my] bodye to the ground from whence it came to be buried in Christian buriall in the Church of St Leonards Shorditch if I die in Clarkenwell. And if I die ellswhere then in the discretion of my Executor hereafter named And touching the disposition of lands goods and chattels I give devise bequeath and dispose them in manner and forme followinge that is to say I give power and authoritie to my trusty and welbeloved mother Cissalie Robins my executor to give those legacies hereafter mentioned. Item I give unto my mother Cissalie Robins her heires executors and assignes all that one house messuage or tenement situate lying and being in the Parish of St Leonhards Shoreditch in the countie afore said. Item to my sister Jane Renaldes Tenn pounds to be paid a yeare after my decease. Item I give and bequeath unto my sister Elizabeth Browne Tenn pounds to be paid at the day of her marriage. Item to my Brother James Browne Judith Browne and my sister Awdrey Browne Tenn pounds to be devided equallie amongst them at the day of Theire marriages. Item to my ffather William Robins fforty shillings to buy him a ringe to weare for my sake after my decease all which legacies to be paid by my executor after my decease. In witness whereof I have hereunto put to [sic] my hand and seale in the yeare of our Lord god one thousand sixhundred and twenty three. The marke of Robert Browne, Miles Hill. The marke of Katherine Swainestone. The marke of Elizabeth Hill.

Probatum fuit testamentum suprascriptum apud London coram magistro Willimo Sames legum doctore Surrogato venerabilis viri domini henrici Marten militis legum etiam doctoris Curie Prerogatiue Cantuariensis magistri custodis sive Comissarii legitime constituti vicesimo die mensis Jannuarij Anno domini iuxta Cursum et Computationem ecclesiae Anglicanae millesimo sexcentisimo vicesimo quarto Juramento Cicilie Robins matrix dicti defunti ex [sic] executricis in huiusmodi testamento nominatae. Cui comissa fuit administratio omnium et singulorum bonorum Jurium

et Credetorum dicti defuncti de bene et fideliter administrando eadem ad sancta dei Evangelica indebita iuris forma Juratae.[4]

By pursuing the names of Browne's mother Cicely Robins and that of his sister Jane 'Renaldes' through the available records, we can establish with certainty that the Robert Browne of the will was a son of the Robert Browne of German fame. When Cicely Robins proved her son's will in London on 20 January 1625 she had been married for more than two years to the player William Robins.[5] The marriage was registered in Clerkenwell, which explains the appearance of the name of this parish in Browne's will. The will was apparently drawn up shortly after his mother's marriage. Yet another clue places Cicely Browne firmly within the theatrical orbit. When William Sly, an actor who had belonged both to the Admiral's men and to the Chamberlain's men (Shakespeare's company), made his nuncupative will on 4 August 1608, he left legacies to Cuthbert Burbage and James Sandes, and the rest of his property to Robert and Cicely Browne and their daughter Jane.[6] This Jane was somewhat more than eight years old at the time, as appears from an entry in a parish register of St Leonard's, Shoreditch, which shows that she was

---

[4] 'The above-written will was proved in London before Master William Sames, LL.D., surrogate to the Right Hon. Henry Marten, Knight, likewise LL.D., Master Warden or Commissary of the Prerogative Court of Canterbury, lawfully constituted on 20 January AD 1624 in accordance with the computation of the Anglican church, the oath being taken of Cicely Robins, mother of the deceased and appointed executrix of the will to this effect. To her was committed the administration of all and singular goods, rights and dues of the deceased and their good and trusty administering, after she had sworn to the Holy Gospel of God in the required legal form.' Public Record Office, London, PROB II 145, fol. 30. I thank the trustees of the PRO for sending me a photostat copy of the original.

[5] See Bentley, *Jacobean and Caroline Stage*, vol. 2 (1941, repr. 1949), p. 548: '1622, July 30 – "William Robins & Cisley Browne; lic" mar. St.J.C.'.

[6] See Chambers, *Elizabethan Stage*, vol. 2, p. 340. The maiden name of Cicely was Sands. She married Browne on 7 March 1594. See Guildhall Library MS 7493, marriages, fol. 17: 'Robert Browne and Cicely Sands were maryed the vij[th] day of March' (register for 1593/4).

baptized there on 13 January 1600.[7] By the time she was sixteen she had contracted a marriage with Robert Reynolds, for the Middlesex County Records name him and his wife for non-attendance at church on 1 January 1616, Jane being named subsequently on 1 March 1617, apparently at a time when Robert Reynolds was not himself in England.[8] The important family relationship that emerges from all this is that Reynolds was the son-in-law of Robert Browne, which accounts for their close association in June and July 1618 when they were playing in Strasburg, Robert Browne having apparently fallen ill during the latter part of their stay.[9] Since the last piece of information we possess about Robert Browne traces him to Frankfurt-on-Main in March 1620, the evidence of his son's will enables us to conclude that the man 'who did most to acclimatize the English actors in Germany' (Chambers) died between April 1620 and June 1622, probably in 1621. As for Jane Reynolds, J. G. Riewald has discovered her name in two licences to 'pass beyond Seas' preserved in the Public Record Office.[10] The first licence records, on 2 July 1629, that Jane intended to join her husband in Utrecht while the second, dated 17 October 1629, shows that Reynolds had in the meantime moved to The Hague, embarking upon a prosperous acting career in the Netherlands. But let us now turn to Reynolds's early fortunes and the problem of Pickleherring.

In England Robert Reynolds appears for the first time in June 1616 and 1617, as a Queen Anne's man in the documents known as the Baskerville papers (see Chambers, *Elizabethan Stage*, vol. 2, pp. 237–8). But his earliest introduction to the stage was apparently through his marriage with Jane Browne, the daughter of Robert Browne, the man who took relays of actors to the Continent and under whom another well-known actor, John Green, had started his theatrical career there around 1603. Green was to take over from Browne during the period the latter spent in England between 1608 and 1617, and as a result it was under his auspices that Reynolds left for the Continent, his name appearing as co-signatory with Green in a petition the actors submitted to the Danzig city council on 28 July 1616.[11] It is from this time that Reynolds, according to many authorities, began to acquire a reputation as a clown and thus Edwin Nungezer[12] writes that the

actor, though not otherwise known in England, 'evidently attained considerable popularity in Germany under the clown-name Pickleherring', a statement echoed by G. E. Bentley when he says that 'by 1616 Reynolds had begun an acting career in Germany, where he made no small reputation, often appearing under the clown-name of Pickleherring'. When we examine the evidence that can be adduced for the view that Reynolds often acted the part of this particular clown it appears to be extremely tenuous. The scholar ultimately responsible for spreading this view was the well-known German theatre historian Wilhelm Creizenach. In his influential book *Die Schauspiele der englischen Komödianten* (Berlin, 1889) he devoted a section, in the long introduction, to 'die lustige Person' in which he wrote (p. xviii) that 'Der Typus des Pickelhäring ist, wie ich im folgenden darzuthun hoffe, durch Robert Reynolds creirt worden'. But the paragraph on the adjoining page which contains the real gist of his argument is very condensed and constitutes a specious mixture of truth and misrepresentation.

Wir haben also den Namen Pickelhäring 1620 zuerst in Deutschland gefunden, wir haben gesehen, dass Robert Reynolds schon 1618 als Führer einer Truppe erscheint, dass er 1628 als einer der Hauptschauspieler der

---

[7] Guildhall Library MS 7493, fol. 42[r]: 'Jane Browne ye daughter of Robert Brown was baptised ye same day [13 January 1599/1600] Stebineth'. As was pointed out by C. Cooper, Keeper of MSS in Guildhall Library (letter of 25 May 1981), the wording of the entry suggests that Stepney is not the place of baptism but the place of residence of the child's parents. It was the expected birth of his daughter Jane which may have caused Robert Browne to leave Strasburg, where he had been acting 'sambt noch 12 personen', soon after 22 December 1599. See *Shakespeare Survey 33*, p. 159.

[8] J. C. Jeaffreson, *Middlesex County Records* (1886–92), vol. 2, pp. 120, 127; see Bentley, vol. 2, p. 543.

[9] See J. Crüger, 'Englische Komoedianten in Strassburg im Elsass', *Archiv für Litteraturgeschichte*, 15 (1887), 113–25, esp. p. 121.

[10] 'Some Later Elizabethan and Early Stuart Actors and Musicians', *English Studies*, 40 (1959), 35. See also *English Studies*, 41 (1960), 84.

[11] See J. Bolte, *Das Danziger Theater im 16. und 17. Jahrhundert* (Hamburg, 1895), p. 49.

[12] *A Dictionary of Actors* (New Haven, 1929), p. 295.

kursächsischen Truppe auftritt, dass der Darsteller der wichtigen Rolle der lustigen Person in dieser Truppe als Robert Pickelhäring bezeichnet wird und dass die Truppe zur Unterscheidung von anderen sich Bücklingshäringskompagnie nennt. Nach dem allen sind wir wohl zur Annahme berechtigt, dass Reynolds sich für seinen Gebrauch eine Abart des komischen Typus schuf und sich den burlesken Beinamen Pickelhäring zulegte, einem Gebrauche folgend, an den man durch Sackeville-Bouset und Spencer-Stockfisch in Deutschland schon gewöhnt war. Dieser Typus wurde dann von den einheimischen Schauspielern beibehalten, welche die Engländer ablösten.[13]

It is true that the name Pickleherring appeared for the first time in printed form both on the title-page and in some of the plays of the famous collection of the *Engelische Comedien und Tragedien*, which was published in Germany (presumably in Leipzig) in 1620, but Creizenach fails to bring to our notice that Reynolds's father-in-law Browne was still at the head of the company in both Nuremberg (28 May 1618) and Strasburg (22 June 1618). In July 1618, however, Browne had apparently fallen ill, which explains the wording of entries after 22 June in the archives, Reynolds acting for the leader only as spokesman ('*wegen* Engell. Comoedianten', 'on behalf of the English comedians').[14] Robert Reynolds does not, in fact, clearly emerge as the leader of the Elector of Saxony's players until May–June 1628, when his name appears, together with those of Thomas Robinson and 'Jacob Teodor', in the Cologne archives,[15] while in June 1628, when they were again in Strasburg, their leader was Edward Pudsey, so that, as we have seen, Reynolds must have decided to take the route to the Netherlands instead of going south. It is true, though, that the Elector of Saxony's players called themselves 'bieklingherings compagnia' when they submitted their petition in Nuremberg about 30 July 1627 – they were refused permission to play because of 'grosser Armut der Burgerschafft' ('the great poverty of the citizens') – but then the archival entry remained silent as to the identity of the company's leader. Who he was in 1627 must therefore remain unknown for the time being, though it should be emphasized that it has been generally assumed that John Green[16] was still at the head of the troupe, while it is also his name which has

usually been associated with the performances at the Dresden court in May 1626.

What, finally, is the source for Creizenach's statement that 'der Darsteller der lustigen Person als Robert Pickelhäring bezeichnet wird'? It is the housing-list which has survived from the actors' stay in Torgau in 1627. It was first printed by Albert Cohn and runs as follows:

Robertt: Pickelheringk mit zwei Jungen. Jacob der Hesse. Johann Eydwardt. Aaron der Danzer. Thomas die Jungfraw. Johann. Wilhelm der Kleiderverwahrer. Der Engelender. Der Rothkopf. Vier Jungen.[17]

On the strength of the Christian name Robert it is perhaps justified to argue that Reynolds was at the

---

[13] 'We have found the name Pickleherring in Germany for the first time in 1620 and seen that Robert Reynolds appears as an actors' leader from 1618 onwards and that in 1628 he was the chief actor of the Elector of Saxony's troupe whose clown was called Robert Pickleherring, the company itself being called "Bücklingshäringskompagnie". All this entitles us to assume that Reynolds created for himself a variant of the comic type and assumed the burlesque sobriquet of Pickleherring, thus following the practice of Sackville-Bouset and Spencer-Stockfish in Germany. This type was later adopted by the German players who took over from English strolling companies.'

[14] For the evidence see articles by K. Trautmann, 'Englische Komoedianten in Nürnberg bis zum Schlusse des Dreissigjährigen Krieges (1593–1648)', *Archiv für Litteraturgeschichte*, 14 (1886), p. 129 and J. Crüger, *Archiv für Litteraturgeschichte*, 15 (1887), p. 120.

[15] See Carl Niessen, *Dramatische Darstellungen in Köln von 1526–1700* (Cologne, 1917), p. 95. Chambers, *Elizabethan Stage*, vol. 2, p. 288, is in error in stating that the Electoral players of Saxony 'do not clearly emerge until April 1608' when a visit is recorded at Cologne. They then were, in fact, the Hessian comedians; see Niessen, p. 77.

[16] See J. Meissner, *Die englischen Comoedianten zur Zeit Shakespeares in Oesterreich* (Vienna, 1884), p. 86; E. Nungezer, *Dictionary*, p. 161; E. Mentzel, *Geschichte der Schauspielkunst in Frankfurt a. M.* (1882), p. 63, and W. Creizenach himself, see *Die Schauspiele*, pp. xi, xxviii.

[17] 'Pickelhering with two boys. James the Hessian. John Edward. Aaron the dancer. Thomas the maiden. John. William the keeper of the wardrobe. The Englishman. The red-haired. Four boys.' A. Cohn, *Shakespeare in Germany* (Berlin, 1865), pp. xcvi, xcvii. It was the similarity of the Christian name, as we have seen, which was enough for Fleay to claim that another actor, Robert Lee, was Pickleherring.

head of the company, but that he was also its clown is highly questionable. To begin with, in the printed text of the *Engelische Comedien* of 1620, Pickleherring, as is the case with all three clown-names with which we are here concerned, is also occasionally given the Christian name of Hans. Furthermore, it is this very collection which, in the period of Reynolds's rise to prominence, testifies to the newly-acquired popularity of the generic name Pickleherring, displayed as it is in prominent capitals in the middle of the title-page, while we should bear in mind that in the two years preceding 1620 Reynolds was still performing under the aegis of his father-in-law, and not with Green. The name soon came to be appropriated by the anonymous author of two jigs, or broadsides, as Cohn prefers to call them, which we find printed in J. Scheible's book *Die Fliegenden Blätter des XVI. und XVII. Jahrhunderts* (Stuttgart, 1850, pp. 81 ff.). They both belong to the year 1621 and are topical in nature in that they are clearly connected with the Bohemian troubles and the first years of the Thirty Years War. The first jig is entitled 'Engelländischer Pickelhäring' and the second 'Englischer Pickelhäring'. We will come back to these jigs at a later stage of this article and now turn to the explanation of 'Pickle-herring' given by the *Oxford English Dictionary* under that word, *sb.* 2.

A clown, a buffoon, a merry-andrew. This application of the term originated in German. It appears in 1620 in *Engelische Comedien vnd Tragedien . . . sampt dem Pickelhering*, where it is the name of a humorous character in one of the plays, and of the chief actor in a series of 'Pickelhärings-spiele' and 'Singspiele' (= Jig *sb.* 4). One of the latter is a version of R. Cox's *Singing Simpkin*, and a Dutch version of this, from the German, as *Singende klucht van Pekelharingh in de Kist*, 1648, is the first known evidence of the use in Dutch, to which Addison attributed it in 1711 – the first mention in English. (Grimm's Dictionary is in error in ascribing to it an English origin.)

This explanation is of course in general agreement with the foregoing account, but that the term originated in German must be revised in the light of an extremely interesting archival entry which has been overlooked by all the theatre historians of the period and in which we see it applied to an English actor (or,

perhaps better, musician or 'jig-maker'). It is an entry which pre-dates by at least a year the first appearance (in Danzig) of Robert Reynolds under the leadership of John Green. It comes from the very court where Thomas Sackville had successfully popularized the clownish figure of John Posset during the lifetime of Duke Henry Julius. In the account-books of the court of Henry Julius's successor at Wolfenbüttel we find the following entry (it can be dated about 20 May 1615).

Uff Ill*ustriss*imae befehlig ['On the orders of the very Illustrious Lady'] Georg Vincint alias Pickelhering 100 thlr.[18]

The 'very illustrious' lady who gave George Vincent a hundred Taler was no less a person than the recently-widowed Elizabeth, Duchess of Brunswick, whose husband had died in Prague in 1613. She was the daughter of King Frederick II of Denmark, her younger sister Anne having married James VI of Scotland in Oslo in 1589. On his way back to Scotland James had attended the wedding festivities of his wife's sister in Copenhagen, where the marriage of Henry Julius and Elizabeth was celebrated on Easter Day 19 April 1590. When Anne of Denmark later became Queen of England, she patronized her own players and among Queen Anne's Men there are quite a number who distinguished themselves as strolling actors on the Continent, among whom Robert Reynolds deserves to be singled out. The reigning duke in Wolfenbüttel in 1615 was Frederick Ulric (1591–1634), whose marriage on 4 September 1614 to Anna-Sophia, the daughter of John Sigismund, Elector of Brandenburg, had been celebrated with performances by the Brandenburg comedians. One

---

[18] The Kammerrechnungen are now preserved at the *Niedersächsisches Hauptstaatsarchiv* in Hanover. This entry comes from a special register indexed as *Cal.Br. 21* Nr 1756, where it is found on p. 49ʳ. The text reads 'Vincint'. Thanks are due to the staff of the archives for their permission to print material for which they provided photostat copies. H. Niedecken-Gebhart who, in his article 'Neues Aktenmaterial über die Englischen Komödianten in Deutschland' in *Euphorion*, vol. 21 (Leipzig and Vienna, 1914), pp. 72–85, made available extensive excerpts from the Wolfenbüttel archives, mistranscribed the name as 'Bieciet'.

detail of Frederick Ulric's life is worth recalling in this connection: in 1610 he had been on a visit to England at the invitation of Prince Henry at whose court another contemporary visitor, the German prince Lewis Frederick of Wirtemberg, was also staying. The two German princes met frequently and if it is recalled that Lewis Frederick saw a performance of *Othello* at the Globe on 30 April 1610, there is ample justification for claiming that in all probability the Brunswick heir to the dukedom also saw Shakespeare's play.[19] 'Pickelhering' George Vincent was apparently a player who, like so many others, had been welcomed at the court of Wolfenbüttel through the good offices of Queen Anne, for it was to him that the latter's sister extended her special liberality, which, perhaps, is one more reason for believing that the particular clown-name here discussed did not originate in Germany.

We are fortunately able to supply further information about George Vincent, for he has recently emerged[20] from the *Acts of the Privy Council* as an English musician in the service of the Prince of Poland. Under the date 12 June 1617 we find the following entry:

A letter to the Erle of Suffolke, Lord Highe Treasorer of England [22 June 1617].
Whereas George Vincent, servant to the Prince of Poland, hath made provision here of certeyne necessaries for the use of the Prince his master and for the King and Queene of Poland, vizt: 36 paire of silke stockinges, black and coloured, and 15 paire of gloves, and thereupon hath made humble suite unto us that hee might have leave to transport them custome free. Theese are therefore to pray your Lordship to give order to the searchers and other officers of the porte of London to license the sayd Geo[rge] Vincent to transporte those thinges above mentioned without paying any custome or impost for them. And this shall be unto your Lordship a sufficient warrant.
A passe for the sayd Geo[rge] Vincent to goe over the Prince of Poland, and to carry over with him to the sayd Prince his master these musitians. Richard Jones, Wm. Corkin, Donatus O'Chaine, Thomas White, Wm. Jackson, Tho. Sutton, Valentine Flood and John Wayd.

A further entry relating to Vincent and bringing confirmatory evidence of this musician's employment by the Prince of Poland, was overlooked by both J. G. Riewald and Jerzy Limon.[21] A pass was again granted by the Council on 24 August 1618.

A passe for George Vincent to retourne into Poland to the Prince, his master, and to take over with him such thinges as he hath bought for the Kinge, Queene and Prince of Poland vizt. a perfumed sweete bagge and two bever hattes, one wastcot and foure paire of ritch gloves, six wastcottes and six night capps, a dozen of ryding gloves and such instrumentes of musicke as he shall have use of for his maister's service, together with his wife and childrenn and also five musitians for the service of the Prince of Poland, and the wife of one Joanes residing in Poland [24 August 1618].

This passe was graunted upon significacion of his Majesty's pleasure by letter from Sir Robert Cary, knight.[22]

A comparison of the contents of the two passports makes clear that both George Vincent and Richard Jones (the leading musician) seem to have left England in 1617 without their wives, but in 1618 Jones must have decided to stay behind on the Continent leaving it to Vincent to make provisions for the return to Poland of their respective wives as well as Vincent's children ('the wife of one Joanes'). It is in the light of all this new information that two letters from Jones and one from his wife, all three addressed to Edward Alleyn, the celebrated Elizabethan actor, take on a new significance. The letters will be found published in W. W. Greg's edition of the *Henslowe Papers* (1907), p. 33 and pp. 94–5, and that which probably comes first chronologically is reproduced here for its great human interest.

19 See W. B. Rye, ed., *England as seen by Foreigners* (1865, repr. New York, 1967), p. 61: 'Lundi, 30 S.E. alla au Globe lieu ordinaire où l'on joue les Commedies, y fut representé l'histoire du More del Venise'.
20 See J. G. Riewald, 'New Light on the English Actors in the Netherlands, c. 1590–c. 1660', *English Studies*, 41 (1960), 65–92, esp. p. 89. Note, for what it is worth, that there was a London bookseller by the name of George Vincent, who was active between 1595 and 1620 (see *A Dictionary of Booksellers*, ed. R. B. McKerrow, 1910, p. 276).
21 Jerzy Limon, 'Komedianci Angielscy w Warszawie', *Pamietnik Teatralny*, 3–4 (Warsaw, 1980), 469–77.
22 *Acts of the Privy Council*, ed. J. V. Lyle, vol. 35 (1927), p. 267 and vol. 36 (1929), p. 247.

m^r allen J commend my love and humble duty to you geving you thankes for your great bounty bestoed vpon me in my sicknes, when J was in great want, god blese you for it, sir this it is, J am to go over beyond the seas with m^r browne and the company but not by his meanes for he is put to half a shaer, and to stay hear, for they ar all against his goinge now good sir as you have ever byne my worthie frend so healp me nowe J have asut of clothes and acloke at pane for three pound and if it shall pleas you to lend me so much to release them J shalbe bound to pray for you so longe as J leve, for if J go over and have no clothes J shall not be esteemed of and by godes help the first mony that J gett J will send it over vnto you, for hear J get nothinge, some tymes J have a shillinge aday, and some tymes nothinge, so that J leve in great poverty hear, and so J humbly take my leave prainge to God J and my wiffe for your health and mistris allenes which god continew,

Your poor frend to command
Richard Jones

Receved of master allen the   of february the somme of m^r Jones his Letter wher on J Lent Hym 3^1

'The reference to Browne as not going with the company has always been a puzzle', writes Chambers (*Elizabethan Stage*, vol. 2, p. 287), who suggests 'that the letter was written in or near 1615, and that Jones was one of the actors who started in advance of Browne under John Green'. That Jones did travel about this time is shown by another letter from him, also undated, where a mention of Henslowe indicates that it was written before the latter's death on 6 January 1616, the letter also showing that Jones and his wife were abroad. But Jones says in the letter just quoted that he is to go over beyond the seas but not by 'his [Browne's] meanes', for they were 'all against his [Browne] goinge'. We have seen Jones travelling in 1617 'by means' of George Vincent, while Chambers suggests that in 1615 the voyage was effected 'by means' of John Green. So far as we know Green never returned to England to take players back with him, but we can produce convincing proof that he was at the Wolfenbüttel court at the very time of George Vincent's presence there, so that it looks as though Vincent was an important intermediary in providing entertainers for the troupe headed by Green. I therefore suggest that the letter quoted above was written in February 1615, that Jones left soon after this to

join George Vincent ('Pickelhering', the musician-composer of jigs!) in Wolfenbüttel in May 1615 at a time when Green was also staying there. That Green himself did stay at the Brunswick court can be gathered both from the wording of the signed petition he submitted to the Danzig city council on 25 August 1615 and from an archival entry (in the Wolfenbüttel accounts) of expenses paid to English comedians. In the Danzig petition Green pointed out that he had come all the way from Wolfenbüttel ('so wier einen zimlichen wegk von Wolffenbüttel anhero, dieser Hochberümbten Stadt zu sondern ehren, schleünig gereiset'), and that 600 Taler had been paid to its visiting 'Englischen Comedianten'.[23] In other words, there can hardly be any doubt both that immediately after May 1615 Green and Vincent travelled in each other's company to Danzig and that Jones was also a member of the troupe.

The common characteristic of the Pickleherring of the two German 'jigs' (printed by Scheible) consists in his having changed his acting profession for the career of a prosperous iron-dealer. He is said to be peddling his wares while on his way to the marts of Frankfurt and Prague. This comic character thus followed the example of such well-known clowns as Thomas Sackville, who had also found trading more profitable. The Pickleherring who travelled to Prague ('jetzo vornehmer Eisenhändler, mit Aext, Beil, Barten gen Prag jubilirend') also found occasion to commemorate his theatrical career in the lines (my italics):

Vorm Jahr war ich nicht gering,
Ein aus der Massen gut Pickelhäring,
Mein Antlitz in tausend Manieren
Konnt ich holdselig figuriren,
Alles was ich hab vorgebracht,
Das hat man ja stattlich belacht.
Ich war der Niemand, kennt ihr mich?[24]

---

[23] A. Cohn, *Shakespeare in Germany*, p. xxxiv, prints this entry, dates it '1615. May 8', but fails to note that the reference is to Green and his men. See also *Euphorion*, vol. 21, p. 85, and J. Bolte, *Das Danziger Theater*, p. 47.

[24] J. Scheible, ed. *Die fliegenden Blätter des XVI. und XVII. Jahrhunderts* (Stuttgart, 1850), p. 87; translated by E. Nungezer (p. 295):

> Last year I was a mighty good Pickleherring,
> I could twist my face in a thousand ways,

This extract leads us to the repertoire of the wandering actors we are here dealing with. *Niemand und Jemand* was one of the plays acted at the court of Graz, before the Archduchess Maria and her family, in February 1608, though the character of Pickleherring does not appear as such in any of the three versions of the play *Nobody and Somebody* – one English and two German – which have come down to us. The actors who took part in the Graz performances can, however, be shown to have contributed to the creation of the comic type of Pickleherring, for they were led by John Green whose later proven association with George Vincent shows that it was his troupe which introduced the type on to the German stage.

We are informed of the Green repertoire of 1608 by an extremely important letter which the eighteen-year-old Archduchess Maria Magdalena wrote to her brother, later the Emperor Ferdinand II, who was the imperial representative at the Diet of Regensburg at the time the letter was written. This celebrated *Theaterbrief* has aroused considerable attention and has recently been edited by Irene Morris with an English translation, while Orlene Murad has studied the letter with particular reference to the repertoire mentioned.[25] What seems hitherto to have escaped the notice of all those who have studied the theatre letter is that Green's repertoire both before and after 1608 was chiefly indebted to that of the actors patronized by Queen Anne, and, at an earlier stage, by the players who enjoyed the patronage of the Earl of Worcester and the Lord Admiral during their tenancy of the Rose playhouse, the well-known theatre under the management of Philip Henslowe. One such Queen Anne's play, for example, was the anonymous and undated *Nobody and Somebody* just referred to. Its title-page informed the reader that 'it hath beene acted by the Queens Maiesties Seruants' and as it was printed for John Trundle to whom it was entered in the Stationers' Register on 8 January 1606, it is probable that the first performance of the play occurred between 1603 and 1605.[26] Of the other nine plays performed at Graz at least four can be attributed to dramatists working for Henslowe and later for the Queen's Men: *The Goldsmith's Wife*, *Doctor Faustus*, *The Jew of Malta*, and *Old Fortunatus*, that is to say one play by Thomas Heywood, *King Edward IV* (as *The Goldsmith's Wife* was also known), two Marlowe plays and *Old Fortunatus*, the author of which is Thomas Dekker. Thomas Heywood, who had started his theatrical career as an Admiral's man and then as a member of the Earl of Worcester's Company under the management of Philip Henslowe at the Rose playhouse, after 1603 wrote all his plays for Queen Anne's Men. These plays formed as it were the staple fare of the company, with Thomas Dekker, John Webster and John Ford functioning as less representative dramatists. The playhouse the actors regularly occupied was the Red Bull Theatre in Clerkenwell, outside the City of London's jurisdiction. The district, it is worth recalling, was the one with which Cicely Robins and her son Robert Browne, her daughter Jane and her son-in-law Robert Reynolds can all be associated. When a number of plays from the Red Bull repertoire were transferred to the Continent they of course underwent considerable modifications, adaptations and revisions, to the extent that the *Nobody and Somebody* given at Graz included references to suit the new audience, the more serious parts of the original English play being considerably altered so that the effect on a modern reader is one of extreme vulgarization. The Graz version was discovered and published in 1899 by Ferdinand Bischoff,[27] who wrote that the adapter of the German versions treated some scenes very coarsely, with the language becoming 'sehr nachlässig, unbeholfen und fehlerhaft'. The manuscript was presented by John Green to the Archduke Maximilian with a Latin dedication, signed 'Joannes Grün. Nob. Anglus', which established beyond doubt the identity of the troupe which played in Inner Austria. When *Eine schöne lustige Comoedia von Jemand*

Everything that I did gave great amusement,
I was Nobody: do you recognize me?

[25] See I. Morris, 'A Hapsburg Letter', *Modern Language Review*, 69 (1974), 12–22, and O. Murad, *The English Comedians at the Hapsburg Court in Graz 1607–1608*, Elizabethan and Renaissance Studies, 81 (Salzburg, 1978).

[26] See E. K. Chambers's *The Elizabethan Stage*, vol. 2, p. 37 and the *Stationers' Register*, ed. E. Arber, vol. 3, p. 308. There is a later entry on 12 March 1606.

[27] F. Bischoff, '"Niemund und Jemand" in Graz im Jahre 1608', *Mitteilungen des historischen Vereines für Steiermark*, 47 (1899), 127–92.

und Niemandt came to be published in the famous collection of *Engelische Comedien und Tragedien* of 1620, the *Nobody and Somebody* had again undergone extensive alteration, but the three versions bear an unmistakable relationship to one another. Neither in the English version of about 1605 nor in the German texts of 1608 or 1620 does Pickleherring appear, though this is the very play in which the jig singer 'Englischer Pickelhäring' claimed to have made his appearance. Yet there is one play in the Graz repertoire, Dekker's *Old Fortunatus*, to which the Pickelhering character will be found to have been added in the version preserved in the *Engelische Comedien und Tragedien*. The phrase 'Allhier agiret Pickelhering' appears five times in the printed text, at the close of the first and second acts respectively (thus providing a singing interlude), and three times in the course of the third act.[28] As was to be expected – it was of course a general feature of many contemporary plays – Dekker's drama itself includes quite a number of songs. Incontrovertible archival evidence and the two Pickleherring plays of the Green repertoire provide striking evidence that this troupe formed as it were the breeding-ground from which the special type of clown here discussed originated.

A second Heywood play which was also transferred to the Continent by Green's troupe was *The Rape of Lucrece*. The title-page of the 1608 edition stated that it was given by her Majesty's servants 'at the Red Bull neare Clarkenwell', dates between 1603 and 1607 having been suggested as the likeliest period for its composition and performance. Though the play did not appear in Maria Magdalena's *Theaterbrief*, its title was mentioned in one of the many petitions John Green addressed to the Danzig city council during the course of his wanderings. In August 1619 the English comedians were refused permission to play by decree of the council dated 28 August, but the petition they submitted was introduced by a reference to the fact that they had given a public performance of the 'Römischen Lucretia' for which they had been greatly applauded, the citizens having besought them to 'reiterate their action'.

Demenach ohnlängst von vnsz eine gantz neue Tragoedia von der Römischen Lucretia zuvor niemalsz

agirt, in theatrum publicé producirt worden, vndt wir aber damalsz nicht allein ein sonderlichen applausum Spectatorum vermercket, sondern werden auch von dem mehrern theil dieses orths Burgerschaft instendig ersucht, vorgemelte Action noch einest zu reiterien.[29]

Among the features of *The Rape of Lucrece* that have puzzled critics there is Heywood's use of the fantastic character of Valerius, a Roman nobleman who indulges in the singing of more than a score of lively songs. This feature accords well with the theatrical fare typically offered at the Red Bull where the noise and vulgarity of the audience required jigs and drolls to satisfy its taste for the spectacular. One early critic of the play, A. W. Ward, for example, thought it absurd that Heywood had introduced into a tragedy on such a subject as that of Tarquin's crime a novel sort of clown distinguished by his capacity for singing all the comic songs of the day.[30] Characteristically, the fusion of nobleman and singing clown was a notable feature of the *Nobody and Somebody* play at Graz in which the 'Nob. Anglus' John Green is believed to have acted the part of Nobody, a part later associated with

---

[28] For the text see *Spieltexte der Wanderbühne*, ed. Manfred Brauneck (Berlin, 1970), vol. 1, pp. 128–209. It is perhaps noteworthy that in Dekker's pamphlet *A Knight's Conjuring* (1607), there occurs the following passage in praise of Thomas Nashe: '. . . if they had given his Muse that cherishment which shee most worthily deserved, hee had fed to his dying day on fat Capons, burnt Sack and Sugar, and not so desperately have ventur'de his life and shortened his dayes by keeping company with pickle herrings' (sig. Lʳ). Shakespeare mentions 'pickleherring' only once, in *Twelfth Night*, 1.5.129, and it may not be entirely without significance that scene 5 marks the first appearance of the Clown Feste. Note also that at 3.1.30 ff. Feste says that 'fooles are as like husbands, as Pilchers are to Herrings' (F reading).

[29] 'As we have recently produced a new tragedy of the Roman Lucrece (never before acted) in a public theatre and as we have been singularly applauded, and because the majority of the citizens have earnestly entreated us to it, we make a request for a single further performance.' J. Bolte, *Das Danziger Theater*, p. 54. Though the petition does not bear Green's signature, it appears from the archive text made available by J. Limon, p. 473, that we have to do with Green.

[30] A. W. Ward, *A History of English Dramatic Literature* (1875), vol. 2, p. 581.

'Pickleharing'. Allan Holaday[31] has suggested that *The Rape of Lucrece* was taken to the Continent by the strolling actor Robert Browne after the Lucrece subject had been treated by Heywood around 1607, although Holaday had to concede that 'records of Browne's performances during his numerous Continental tours are discouragingly fragmentary and contain no mention of *Lucrece*'. We have just seen however that it was Green's repertoire which did include a *Lucrece* play and we know from his association in 1616 with Robert Reynolds, a notable Queen Anne's man and the son-in-law of Robert Browne, that it was perfectly possible for the play to have been made available to the Green troupe through Reynolds, or even more plausibly, through Thomas Greene, the leading actor of Queen Anne's Men, who was probably a brother of the John Green we have been concerned with here.

We must now turn our attention again to the fortunes of Richard Jones. We have discussed his (undated) letter to Edward Alleyn and have made the suggestion that it was written about February 1616 when he and his wife were abroad. In June 1617, it will be remembered, Richard Jones was back in England with George Vincent, while in August 1618 the latter returned 'into Poland to the Prince, his master' in order to take over with him 'five musicians for the service of the Prince of Poland and the wife of one Joanes residing in Poland'. In other words, Jones's wife must have been on her way to Poland in the latter half of 1618. Luckily, it so happens that one of her letters has overcome the vagaries of manuscript survival. In the letter Harris Jones addressed to him from Danzig on 1 April 1620, the celebrated actor Edward Alleyn was asked, as he had been in the past, to help the Jones family in its financial tribulations. From Danzig she expected 'Every daye' to join her husband who was 'with the prince'.

Ladvo[32] from dansicke The ffirste of Apriell 1620

my Aproved Good ffrinde m^r Allin your helleth wished in the lord witith your Good wife trvsting in God you Ar both in Good hellth As J was at the wryting her of thes few lines is to be in tre[a]te your worshype to stand owr Good frinde As you hath bin before J sente you A leeter of Atorny by m^r bapties

Abowte the lebickes hed J cnowe not whither you hath Reseafed it or no J wowlld intreate your worship to send me word how m^r Rowly hath delte with me for my Rente by this baer her of   my Husband Js with the prince And as yt J am here in dansicke lockinge Evry daye to Gooe to him thvs desierin God to bles you with your Good wife J Commyt you to the all myty God

> your pore frinde to
> Command haris
> Joones

(W. W. Greg, *Henslowe Papers*, pp. 94–5)

The identity of the prince has long puzzled commentators. W. W. Greg and George F. Warner believed that George William, Elector of Brandenburg (who succeeded his father in 1619 and died in 1640) was intended. George William's wife was Elizabeth Charlotte, the sister of the Elector Palatine and thus the sister-in-law of King James's daughter, Princess Elizabeth (the Elector's wife), who has become known in English literature as the 'Winter Queen' of Bohemia, celebrated in Sir Henry Wotton's remarkable poem. Jerzy Limon, however, thought that Philip Julius, Duke of Pommern-Wolgast was the person referred to, because it was at *his* court in Wolgast that Richard Jones can be shown to have resided in August 1623.[33] But then Limon has overlooked the fact that in the petition signed by Richard Jones, Johan Kostressen and Robert Dulandt, the musicians pointed out that they had been taken into the service of Philip Julius only the year before and that they expected to see their contract renewed for another year, for in case of non-renewal, they would have to decide to return to England. Incidentally, it has not usually been mentioned that Philip Julius's interest in London musicians was of very long standing, for in Chambers's account of the boy companies (*Elizabethan Stage*, vol. 2, p. 46) this enduring interest is left unmentioned. In his youth the

[31] A. Holaday, 'Robert Browne and the Date of Heywood's *Lucrece*', *Journal of English and Germanic Philology*, 44 (1945), 171–80.
[32] Unexplained, but 'ładvo' happens to be Polish for 'easy'.
[33] See C. F. Meyer, 'Englische Komödianten am Hofe des Herzogs Philipp Julius von Pommern-Wolgast', *Jahrbuch der deutschen Shakespeare-Gesellschaft*, 38 (1902), 196–211.

Duke of Stettin-Pomerania – this is how Chambers describes him – visited the Blackfriars Theatre. An account of this visit, which took place on 18 September 1602, has been preserved in the journal of Frederic Gerschow, a member of the Duke's retinue. But to return to the identity of the prince.

The solution to the enigma is of course to be had from all the archive material discussed in the preceding pages. John Green, George Vincent and Richard Jones must on several occasions have been the guests of the Warsaw court, Jones himself being on his way to Poland some time after June 1617 and being joined there by his wife after August 1618, each time under the safe conduct of George Vincent, who was specifically identified in his passport as a 'servant to the Prince of Poland'. At the beginning of July 1619 the Green troupe was again in Danzig. In the petition they submitted to the city council we find the following highly significant passage (my italics): 'Demenach Vnsere Compagnia Welche sich vf eine Zeit bey kön: Maijtt: in polen Verhalten, *auch gegen den Winter wiederumb dachinn begeben wirdt*, so Viel erlaubnusz gebten, diesie Undt andere angräntzendt Städte in etwasz zu frequentiren damenhero wir bedacht Zukünftige Dominici Mess auch allhier Vnter, E. Ehrnv. Vndt Weiszhh. löblichen Jurisdiction Vnsere wenige qualiteten zu exerciren.'[34] What is here revealed is that the company intended to spend the winter of 1619–20 at the Polish court in Warsaw, which they eventually did for when they emerged again in archival records in Cologne at the end of April 1620 – on 29 April to be precise – 'Johanssen Grein' can be seen displaying his freshly gained laurels when announcing proudly that his '*Polnische Comedianten*' desired to put on their plays and 'feats of activity'.[35] It ought to be abundantly clear now that when on 1 April 1620 Harris Jones was writing to Edward Alleyn that her husband was with 'the prince', this person was none other than Wladyslaw, the crown prince of Poland.

Wladyslaw IV Vasa (1595–1648) was born in Cracow on 9 June 1595, the son of Sigismund III and Anna, the first-born of the eight daughters of the Austrian Habsburg, Charles of Styria, and his wife Maria of Bavaria. But Anna (born 1573) died in 1598 and seven years later Sigismund, prompted by both the Pope and Rudolf II, decided to marry again, with a Styrian princess, Anna's younger sister Constantia (1588–1631). The marriage was celebrated in Cracow on 11 December 1605 and was followed by all sorts of festivities so that, as Jacques-Auguste de Thou, the well-known contemporary French historian and chronicler, reports, 'tout le reste de l'année se passa en carousels, en bals, en mascarades, en jeux, et en toutes sortes de divertissemens'.[36] Maria Magdalena (1589–1631), the writer of the famous *Theaterbrief*, was of course the younger sister of Constantia, the wife of Sigismund III, and so we begin to see that one of the important incentives for Green in establishing certain circuits in Europe was to enjoy the patronage and financial support of the illustrious house of the Habsburgs whose scions occupied the courts of Brussels, Graz, and Warsaw, at all of which places Green turned up regularly in the course of his itinerant theatrical career. Thus the Green troupe spent three consecutive winters at the Warsaw court between 1616–17 and 1619–20, also making its appearance in Prague on the occasion of Ferdinand of Styria's coronation as King of Bohemia on 19 June 1617.[37] Ferdinand was crowned by Franz von Dietrichstein, Cardinal of Olmütz, in the presence of the Emperor Rudolf. This Ferdinand was, as we have seen, the brother to whom the Archduchess Maria Magdalena addressed her *Theaterbrief*.

The last scion of the house of Styria was the posthumously born Archduke Charles (1590–1624), who from 1608 until his death was bishop of Breslau, with his residence in Neisse (in Polish, Nisa), a town about seventy kilometres south of Breslau. He, too, extended his patronage to the Green troupe and it was

---

34 'Our company having resided at the court of his Royal Majesty of Poland, we will return there for the winter and now request permission to visit this and other adjoining towns as we intend to exercise our profession under your jurisdiction during the coming Dominic Fair.' Petition (dated 7 July) made available for the first time by J. Limon, p. 473.

35 See Carl Niessen, *Dramatische Darstellungen*, p. 89.

36 J.-A. De Thou, *Histoire Universelle* (London, 1734), vol. 14, p. 467. It seems worth noting that on 2 August 1606 'Ettlichen *Polnischen* Comedianten' submitted a petition to act in Cologne. See Niessen, p. 76.

37 See J. Meissner, p. 58.

no doubt in anticipation of Green's contribution to the coronation ceremonies in Prague of his brother Ferdinand that he addressed a letter to Dietrichstein, dated from Neisse 18 March 1617, in recommendation of the players. One passage in it is extremely significant. It recalls the memorable visit to Graz in February 1608 where 'eben dieselbe Personen' he is now recommending delighted his late beloved mother, the Archduchess Maria, at the same time revealing that Green had just returned from Poland.

Wan wir vns dan zueruckh wol eryndern können, dass noch bei weilandt vnserer geliebsten Frawen Muetter hochehr- vnd Lobwürdigsten angedenckhens, lebens Zeiten, eben dieselbe Personen zue Gräcz, ihre Comedien, gancz Erbar vnd zichtig, mit der Vnserigen allerseits genedigistenn gefallen vndt begnügen verrichtet. An Yezo aber aus Pohln, darin Sy dergleichen bei Iher Königl. vndt Ldn. eczlich Monat Lang exhibiret mit Königlichen recommendationen vndt guetten Zeügnus, zue vns ankhommen, vndt sich gehorsambist angegeben habenn.[38]

The Archduchess Maria, whose death occurred in 1608, a few months after the visit of the English comedians, had exercised an undisputed authority in her family since the death of her husband, the Archduke Charles (1540–90), who, it deserves to be recalled, had once been considered as a suitor for the hand of Queen Elizabeth. Maria was a remarkable woman in her own right and she played a significant role in the matrimonial negotiations preceding the marriages of her daughters, by whom she continued to be greatly honoured, as is evident from the family correspondence after 1608. Her personal family relationships can no doubt explain why Cologne was such a favourite stopping-place for Green and his men. Maria's brother was Duke Ernest of Bavaria (1554–1612), who had been archbishop of Cologne since 1583, evidently an office of weight in such a Catholic city as Cologne undoubtedly was in the early years of the seventeenth century. One of Ernest's cousins was Duke Maximilian I of Bavaria (1573–1651), whose political power and influence were considerable. A younger brother of Maximilian, Ferdinand (1577–1650), held an appointment as coadjutor to his uncle the archbishop so that on the latter's death in 1612 Ferdinand became the Elector of Cologne. Naturally, these two ecclesiastical authorities were bound to exercise a certain control over theatrical performances in their city. Their adviser was the Count of Hohenzollern, 'Choirbischoff des Hohendoimstifts', who on two occasions can be shown to have intervened on behalf of the English comedians, though unfortunately the identity of the actors is not disclosed in the archive material.[39] Indeed, it seems significant that Green did not visit Frankfurt-on-Main in early April 1620, whereas Robert Browne did.

In the present account of the wanderings of Green's troupe we have as yet made no reference to the simmering revolt of Bohemia which began to break into the open on 23 May 1618 with the 'defenestration of Prague' during which members of the board of Regency, which met in the castle of Prague and had been set up by the Emperor Matthias, were flung from a window eighty feet above ground level. This new situation was of course bound to affect the position of the Habsburg rulers all over Europe, though it is a measure of Green's continued Polish allegiance that he visited the Warsaw court on two occasions in the period of the Bohemian troubles following the defenestration. After the death of Matthias on 20 March 1619 Wladyslaw made his first journey to the West for a visit to his uncle Charles, the bishop of Breslau, staying in Neisse from the middle of May to 27 September, arriving back in Warsaw on

---

[38] 'When we remember that, during the lifetime of our late most beloved lady mother of high and praiseworthy memory, just these same persons have performed their comedies at Gratz, quite honorably and decently, always with our most gracious pleasure and satisfaction, but that now they have come to us with royal recommendations and good testimonials from Poland, where they have some months long exhibited such comedies at their Royal Highnesses, and have respectfully announced themselves.' A. Cohn, *Shakespeare in Germany*, pp. xciii–xciv. The original letter is in Brno in the Boček collection 12.265. I wish to thank the Director of the State Archives of Brno for sending me a photostat copy of this letter. See also J. Polišenský, 'England and Bohemia in Shakespeare's day', in *Charles University on Shakespeare*, ed. Z. Stříbrný (Prague, 1966), pp. 65–81.

[39] See C. Niessen, *Dramatische Darstellungen*, pp. 75–85.

7 October 1619. In November we have reports that the Prince would travel to Grodno but on 6 April 1620 his letter of that date to the Elector of Brandenburg shows that he was then in Warsaw;[40] Harris Jones's letter, it will be remembered, bore the date 1 April 1620 and was addressed to Edward Alleyn, who had won his theatrical laurels in the early nineties but who in later years must have performed some sort of banking function for a number of actors, while Harris's husband, for his part, had earlier been involved with the Queen's Revels company, when he had been named on 4 January 1610, together with Robert Browne and others, as one of its patentees. But the earliest association of Browne and Jones dated from the late 1580s, which is also the period with which we can perhaps connect George Vincent.

It is tempting indeed to suppose that the 'servant of the Prince of Poland' is one and the same as the Vincent who appeared in the episode illustrating Sloth in the 'Plot' of 2 Seven Deadly Sins, a play which must have been acted in the years 1589 to 1591 and of which the cast mentioned is exceptionally complete. W. W. Greg[41] notes that a Vincent appeared as one of three musicians in a single scene of Sloth, the others being Cowley and Sincler, and goes on to say that the Thomas Vincent who is known as a book-keeper or prompter at the Globe could hardly have already held that post in about 1590. It is therefore indeed highly likely that the 'musician' who performed in 2 Seven Deadly Sins is none other than the musician who later travelled to the Polish court. By a strange coincidence Richard Jones, 'Engelender und Musikant', addressing a petition to the Duke of Stettin on 24 April 1624, mentioned that he had received an invitation from 'Jürgen mein Landtman' to travel to England with the purpose of entering the service of Prince Charles, but added that, seeing his hopes of employment dashed, he had been forced to return to Wolgast a disappointed man. Could this George by any chance be the subject of our enquiries, George Vincent, with whom we know Jones had thrown in his lot ever since 1617?[42]

There is no question that the present account of certain aspects of the theatrical situation both in England and abroad has shown that the theatrical patronage of Queen Anne is a connecting factor in the development of certain forms of drama. Not only were there the London players who acted as the Queen's Men at the Red Bull, but also and more significantly there were continental actors who under the leadership of John Green brought the more successful plays of the Red Bull repertoire to the courtly stages of Brussels, Wolfenbüttel, Graz, and Warsaw, where music, singing and 'jigs' formed an important added attraction through the talents of such noted musicians as 'Pickleherring' George Vincent and Richard Jones.

---

40 I wish to thank Professor W. Czapliński for kindly supplying this information, shortly before his sad death on 17 August 1981. His book *Władysław IV i jego czasy* (1972) established him as an authority on the period. See also A. Przybos, *Podróz Królewicza Wazy do Krajów Europy Zachodniej w Latach 1624–1625. Wydawnictwo Literackie* (Cracow, 1977), pp. 12–13.

41 W. W. Greg, *Dramatic Documents from the Elizabethan Playhouses. Commentary* (Oxford, 1931), p. 50.

42 See Meyer, 'Englische Komödianten', p. 210. Furthermore, an entry in Alleyn's Diary under the date of 7 August 1619 with its reference to 'm^r Vincent' and Mr. Geratt (Alleyn's counsel) implies that (George?) Vincent was then in London for financial negotiations with Alleyn. See W. Young, *The History of Dulwich College* (1889), vol. 2, p. 146. Note also that George Vincent's second passport carried the date 24 *August* 1618. On the other hand, Robert Dowland (who was at Wolgast with Jones in August 1623), was apparently more successful than his friend in finding employment with Prince Charles, who soon after becoming King engaged him. See Diana Poulton, *John Dowland* (1982), p. 88. It is also noteworthy that Edward Alleyn was acquainted with many court musicians about 1620.

SHAKESPEARE PERFORMANCES IN STRATFORD-UPON-AVON AND LONDON, 1981—2

NICHOLAS SHRIMPTON

These have been two years of transition for the Royal Shakespeare Company, and awkward ones at that. Three circumstances combined to make things difficult. The company's London home moved, in June 1982, from the Aldwych and The Warehouse to the Barbican Theatre and The Pit. Several young directors were learning to use the main stage at Stratford. And all the work lay under the long shadow of a hit production which had nothing to do with Shakespeare. After the extraordinary success of *Nicholas Nickleby*, Ken Campbell renamed its creators the Royal Dickens Company. At times it looked as if the joke had been taken to heart.

The ensemble manner, the musical punctuation and, on occasion, the Victorian décor of *Nicholas Nickleby* all reappeared. *Henry IV* was played on a larger version of its set and, appropriately enough, echoed its crowd effects to evoke the low life of medieval London. *King Lear* borrowed its striking Fool and many of its spectacular tricks from the nineteenth-century popular theatre. Even *Macbeth*, otherwise studiously ahistorical in setting, brought on a Victorian doctor for the sleep-walking scene.

All's Well That Ends Well, the masterly production which closed the 1980–1 season, was explicitly and persuasively Edwardian; Proust rather than Dickens was its tutelary novelist. Rossillion was here very much provincial France, hot, dusty and contentedly remote. The Countess interviewed her clown (a rustic Toulouse-Lautrec) against a background of grey shutters and potted orange trees, while a distant bell and a twitter of bird song sketched in the landscape of Provence. Marcellus was Marseilles Station in the era

of the steam train, and the King of France in the final scene looked like nothing so much as Napoleon III on a private visit to the Riviera. Throughout, the vivid sense of life in a late nineteenth-century French country-house was reinforced with touches of *Upstairs, Downstairs*. In the gaps between scenes a covey of maids romped or tidied, and when Helena returned from Paris in 3.2 her late arrival got them excitedly out of bed to let her in (a piece of atmospheric timing which led to some discreet re-writing – this Helena proposed to 'steal away' not with the 'dark' but with the 'dawn').

Trevor Nunn and his designer, John Gunter, carried off this chronological transposition with immense assurance. But the distinction of the production was that the striking décor was not merely picturesque. Helena's uncomfortable self-assertion was given an intellectual context by dressing her as a nineteenth-century New Woman. And, more subtly still, the sleepy sense of eternal afternoon which hung about this rural Rossillion made it possible to feel a degree of sympathy for Bertram.

At Stratford everybody's least favourite Shakespearian hero appeared as an overgrown adolescent desperate to escape from home and mother, and to live in a world of men. The manifest charm and comfort of Peggy Ashcroft's Rossillion *ménage* merely made this need more imperative. A teenage crush on a flashy cad like Parolles was natural enough when life as a mother's boy loomed and the only other models of male behaviour were an elderly steward and a crippled clown. Mike Gwilym's Bertram, consequently, treated Helena less as a social inferior than as one of the apron strings which he needed so urgently to sever, and played the first scene in a breathless rush to get out of the front door before he was stopped.

The nineteenth-century setting brought faint memories of Julien Sorel or Lucien Chardon to this eagerness to shake the dust of the *terroir* from his feet and make a career in Paris. The cluster of solicitous maids underlined his hunger for the company of men. Suffocating in a provincial boudoir, he clearly could not wait to breathe the sour air of the locker-room.

By one of this production's most brilliant touches, a locker-room was precisely where he next found himself. The King of France, though confined to a wheelchair, was in the gymnasium with his officers when the young Count Rossillion arrived at court. Their fencing and vaulting were so exciting that Bertram could scarcely keep his eyes on his monarch; the delivery of urgent dispatches by a pair of pioneer aviators brought an intoxicating whiff of the great world outside. An exquisite transition from this electrifying activity to the remoteness and tedium of the country, at the beginning of 1.3, brought the point unforgettably home.

Back in the country, meanwhile, a very remarkable performance was being given by Peggy Ashcroft, returning to the Stratford stage after an absence of thirteen years. Her hands flickering with the nervous precision of pointers on a dial, she handled Harriet Walter's raw and uneasy Helena with surgical delicacy. This, one felt, was a woman who had suffered and remembered the sensation, and who could combine worldly wisdom with profound personal engagement. 'Yes, Helen, you might be my daughter-in-law' was delivered with extraordinary warmth and weight while a distraught Helena, unable to face such frankness, stared desperately into the audience.

A mother of this emotional power and intellectual skill might indeed drive a Bertram, however incoherently, to flight. And when, the gymnasium having given way first to an officers' mess and then to a *belle époque* ballroom, he was picked out by his bride in an elegant version of musical chairs, a sense of being dragged home to mother lay behind his dismay. In this production 'the dark house and the detested wife' seemed, simultaneously, an absurd description of domestic life with Helena on the Countess's sunny and gracious domain, and an entirely reasonable account of how a young man in Bertram's position might see it. Helena did not seem wrong to want Bertram. But she did seem wrong to want him so soon.

This remarkable transformation of an unsympathetic play about worth rewarded into a sympathetic play about growing-up involved, of course, a certain amount of playing against the text. When the production transferred to the Barbican in July 1982, and Philip Franks replaced Mike Gwilym, the interpretation became more coherent but less exciting. Franks offered adolescent weakness rather than adolescent self-assertion. The benefit of this was that it came as less of a shock when, in the final scene, Bertram's horror at the prospect of marrying Diana reveals him to be a snob after all. The cost was a distinct lowering of the erotic temperature. Gwilym's rude and reckless Bertram might be immature, but he was clearly worth waiting for, even suffering for, as a sexual partner. This, importantly, meant that the customary contradiction between Helena's public intelligence and private stupidity was for once abolished. The New Woman seemed no more a fool when picking a husband than she had done when curing fistulas.

Trevor Nunn gave Helena's final entry an appropriate air of the Late Plays – an orange evening glow and a hush as absolute as that which greets the waking of Hermione's statue. But the sanctified atmosphere, magical though it was, rapidly modulated into something else. At the end of the play (the Epilogue was cut) Bertram and Helena were left nervously together, just touching hands. Shame and shyness were the predominant emotions. But under them was a distinct sub-text of aroused curiosity, and turbulent memories of a night spent together in Florence some months before. A prologue had shown two shadowy figures waltzing together. It combined excitingly with the final tableau to suggest a couple both together and apart.

Two other aspects of this important production demand to be mentioned. The Florentine wars were played as an exuberant version of the First World War on the Italian Front (Caporetto, after all, was very much Parolles's sort of battle). Cheryl Campbell's Diana, at some peril to her 'most chaste renown', appeared as a popular *chanteuse* in a crowded soldiers'*estaminet*, stray shells interrupted Bertram's promotion, and Helena's pilgrimage was to serve as a VAD in a casualty clearing station. The other matter of note was Stephen Moore's astonishing performance as Parolles. Arriving silently on Florence Station, at the end of 3.1, equipped for the war with his golf clubs, he survived a genuinely disturbing interrogation (spoons scraped against the *estaminet*'s tin trays cruelly suggesting instruments of torture) to give a riveting account of 'Simply the thing I am'. Standing motionless in a cold, blue light, Moore seemed on the verge of tears, yet judged and aimed the moral language of his self-analysis with cold precision. This was Trevor Nunn's last production at Stratford before the opening of the Barbican absorbed his energies. It combined sympathetic intelligence and emotional daring in a way which will make it a landmark in the company's history.

For the 1982 season, which opened in March with Howard Davies's production of *Macbeth*, the Stratford stage was rebuilt. A raked thrust-stage projected deep into the stalls, and two wooden gangways were constructed to exits in the side walls of the auditorium. For *Macbeth*, part of the audience was put on tiers of seats at the side of the forestage, and the gallery and dress circle were plastered with RSC posters. The effect was the nearest the main stage at Stratford is ever likely to come to looking like The Warehouse, where Howard Davies had done much of his previous work for the company. On the bare stage an austere scaffolding platform carried two well-equipped percussionists. Fierce white light beat down almost throughout.

The anthology of critical fragments with which Stratford fills its programmes ended on this occasion with an attack by D. J. Enright on the idea of Macbeth as a victim of external evil. A humanized *Macbeth* of this kind was a natural enough reaction, after the image of black magic and malign destiny which Trevor Nunn had presented so memorably in 1976. The directness of the staging clearly served this end. But Howard Davies's purposes seemed also to go beyond this simple and immediate shift in emphasis. The programme's penultimate fragment was Mary McCarthy's comparison of Macbeth with Babbitt, and her description of him as 'a bourgeois type'.

At least one reviewer found the resulting production explicitly and coherently Marxist. 'Here,' wrote Victoria Radin in *The Observer*, 'Mr Davies would have us believe, is Capitalism: for is not the Elizabethan age reckoned to be the dawning of it?'[1] On stage, and without the help of the programme, the point was not, in my judgement, quite so clear. Bob Peck's Macbeth was certainly not much affected by supernatural solicitings. This was a plain and practical man who rolled his sleeves up before the murder of Duncan and delivered 'Is this a dagger' in the down-to-earth tones of a sceptic's first encounter with extrasensory perception. His rise to power (a rise from the ranks according to his Lancashire-lad accent) was conducted with corresponding efficiency and detachment. Whether the play can thereby be made to talk about capitalism, however, is a rather different matter.

The style could broadly have been described as Brechtian and some of the characterization had a deliberately contemporary air. Jonathan Hyde, for example, played the Porter (and third murderer) as a grumpy, trades-unionized caretaker with the comic aggression of what has come to be called an alternative comedian. But the production's main effect was simply to make us believe in Macbeth the successful general. For once we understood how the Thane of Glamis could have turned the tide of battle single-handed and saw him running a competent administrative machine. Peck was at his best when interviewing his team of murderers. Seated at a desk, doing a spot of work on the accounts, his tone was chillingly brisk, practical and untroubled. Only on 'Malice domestic, foreign levy, nothing / Can touch him further', in 3.2, did he finally push the ledgers away, with the weary sigh of an over-worked executive.

Touches like this, or like Lady Macbeth's acquisition of an expensive fur coat (worn over costumes which could otherwise have done duty in anything from a medieval mystery play to *Star Wars*) were perhaps meant to suggest their specifically bourgeois status. Actually they merely spoke of the Macbeths' practicality and worldliness. The trouble was that practicality and worldliness, though pertinent, are not in themselves enough. Bradley explained the difficulty

[1] *The Observer*, 4 April 1982.

perfectly well in 1904. 'Here is the outward conflict,' he wrote of *Macbeth*, 'here is the inner. And neither by itself could make the tragedy'.[2] Howard Davies placed such stress upon the outward that he left himself with only half a play. The tone of the great soliloquies was not appalled, not deranged, not even self-questioning, but merely frustrated – Macbeth's native efficiency was being denied its outlet. Stephen Wall made the point very cogently in the *Times Literary Supplement*: 'The horror of the act so powerfully insisted on in the poetry is not communicated because this Macbeth does not have the sensibility to understand the language he uses.'[3] To put it more crudely, you couldn't understand why this strong, silent man bothered to talk so much.

Much Ado About Nothing, which opened in April, was very different. This was a pretty and playful production by Terry Hands, featuring a bravura display of comic charm from Derek Jacobi. Ralph Koltai supplied an exquisite set, consisting of a mirror floor and upright perspex panels, variously bronze or transparent according to the light that was shone on them. Elegantly costumed Caroline courtiers moved, as a consequence, in a golden Claude Lorrain glow and a flicker of multiple reflections.

Audiences were delighted by this visual feast. Critics, such as Emrys Jones, pointed to its thematic significances: 'That the senses can't be trusted, not even the eyes, is one of the play's leading assumptions; and the eye-teasing, kaleidoscopically dissolving images which the mirror-set projects at us reinforce the point with dazzling but almost exhausting profusion.'[4] The human drama was rather less satisfactory. Jacobi gave a star performance, constantly entertaining but also full of subtle interior detail (his strangled 'I do love – nothing in the world – so well as you' came as the appropriate climax to a long process of introspective struggle). But even his interpretation was marred by some oddly camp touches, and his sparring partner wasn't up to his weight. Sinead Cusack is a fine actress but not, I think, a natural comedienne. Her Beatrice was a gloomy girl, only really at home in her tender moments. In many ways the most arresting performance came from John Carlisle as a gaunt, sinister, and utterly disillusioned Don John. With a real sense of inner fire burning beneath his stock malice, he seemed half malcontent, half sketch for Milton's Satan.

June brought *King Lear*, directed by Adrian Noble and played in repertory with Edward Bond's *Lear* at The Other Place. The Shakespeare play was the second of the season from a director new to the main Stratford auditorium and, like *Macbeth*, it strained every nerve to establish a distinct identity. The Fool and his relationship with his master were the core of the production, and most of its imaginative energy had clearly been poured into their scenes together. This had certain notable disadvantages. After the Fool's death, accidentally stabbed by Lear as he cowered in the hovel's dustbin, the sense of coherence was much reduced. *King Lear* the history play (that is, the plots and battles of the later acts) was not performed with much conviction. At the same time the stylistic detail – everything from Russian soldiers with sandbags to Japanese Kendo fighters – began to be whimsically diverse. Equally notable was the diminished status allowed to Edmund. Properly the play's only intellectual, Clive Wood gave him in this interpretation plenty of brio but not many brains. Appropriately enough, in the circumstances, his repentance was cut.

Such ruthless transference of interest did, however, also produce some memorable benefits. From the moment when the first spotlight went up on a tableau of Cordelia and the Fool apparently hanged (though actually playing, on the throne, with a length of rope) we knew that it was Antony Sher whom we should be watching. He richly merited our attention. His Fool was a clown – a Charlie from the late Victorian circus with Dan Leno boots, a Grock violin and a red button nose on a length of elastic. When his lines were not funny he amused his audience by miming, or fooling, or – in extremity – strumming his violin like a tuneless George Formby. The immediate consequence of this was that we understood, for once, why he was tolerated. However bitter his comments became, his act remained ludicrous. He was, simply, the political artist who uses his skills as an entertainer to win himself a platform.

[2] A. C. Bradley, *Shakespearean Tragedy* (1904), p. 19.
[3] *Times Literary Supplement*, 16 April 1982.
[4] *Times Literary Supplement*, 7 May 1982.

But there were also some deeper advantages to this vaudevillian Fool. Lear and he were, we realized, an old-established cross-talk act, long accustomed to claiming the spotlight for their banter. This explained something about Lear's irascible public manner. It also made possible a marvellous effect at the onset of the madness. Act 1, scene 5 was played over a set of music hall footlights. The Fool struggled like a comic whose straight man has suddenly forgotten his lines, authentically petrified by the advent of mental decay.

Michael Gambon's shaggy terrier of a Lear made splendid use of such opportunities. His most touching moment in the later scenes, indeed, came when he and Gloucester, reunited as a pair of aged and garrulous tramps, were able to revert to a kind of vaudeville manner. In the storm he and his Fool together generated an extraordinary excitement. First seen perched in a crow's nest against a cloudy cyclorama, they launched their lines against great blasts of music and matched the elements for energy. The Fool's prophecy was an elaborate climax from the circus ring, with a funny dance in a rose-pink spotlight. Yet what followed it was an agonized Beckettian moment – a scuttling exit and a snarl of hate.

Such absurdist touches set the interpretative tone of the production. The dustbin and the naked lightbulb in the hovel put us firmly into the world of *Endgame*, and the play's conclusion was raggedly subdued. But for all the austerity of its reading, this was an oddly spectacular *Lear*, full of tricks from the nineteenth-century theatre. Poor Tom, for example, emerged from a sprung trap like a Victorian demon king.

Lear was chiefly the Fool's property. *Henry IV*, which opened the Barbican Theatre in June 1982, was entirely Falstaff's. Joss Ackland gave a rich and provoking performance as an oddly melancholy King of Misrule. He was not, in fact, particularly funny. But his manic-depressive Falstaff, by turns insufferable and subdued, had an insistent sense of life. His domination of the stage, unfortunately, was not entirely the consequence of his own success. On the opening night the critics greeted this historic production with distinctly subdued enthusiasm. Seen, as I saw it, two months into its run, it prompted very mixed feelings indeed.

The detail was ragged (Sir Walter Blunt, to take a trivial but characteristic example, was brought in with a blindfold for the parley in *Part 1*, 4.3, took it off to embrace Hotspur, and was then allowed to leave without putting it back on again). The set was frequently cumbrous. And, above all, Gerard Murphy's interpretation of Prince Hal was mystifyingly weak.

This was a hippy Prince, with long blonde hair and a petulant manner, who had dropped out without much liking the alternative society. His evident lack of relish for Falstaff's company might, of course, have had something to do with his menial status. At the opening of *Part 1*, 1.3, he was busy making breakfast for the fat knight, and 'I know you all' was delivered while doing the washing-up. Less hell-raiser than housemaid, he found it hard to establish the right emotional register and the speeches veered abruptly from one tone to another. His costumes were almost as much of a nuisance as his inappropriate business. His armour, for instance, a complete suit of shiny plate, gave him the easy mobility of a beached lobster and obliged Hotspur more or less to kill himself.

The upshot of this incoherence was that the play's serious interests fell more and more on to the broad shoulders of Falstaff. The 'honour' speech was given, not humorously, but with savage indignation, emerging as a political catechism which Hal and his soldiers stayed on stage to hear. Patrick Stewart successfully sketched in King Henry as an austere civil servant with religious qualms, helped by an elaborate chorus of cowled monks. Falstaff's troubled humanism remained, indomitably, the focus of the plays.

Three brilliant cameos stood out from the rest of the acting. Miriam Karlin's Mistress Quickly was an aboriginal Cockney. Gemma Jones played Doll Tearsheet with raw and raucous vulgarity. And Mike Gwilym provided, at last, a convincing modern interpretation of Pistol. Instead of the customary, and irredeemably archaic, braggart, he gave us what the criminal classes call a nutter – a psychopathic hit-man whose violent impulses are as much suicidal as murderous. 'Obsque hoc nihil est', in the final scene of *Part 2*, he chanted as an aggressive football slogan, and his trigger-happy habits provoked some remarkable comic chases. This was original interpretation of a kind which was not much evident elsewhere, and may in the end prove the most influential aspect of this uncertain production.

The Tempest, which opened at Stratford in August, was better designed, more intelligently interpreted, and altogether more coherent. Maria Bjornson, the designer, gave us, firstly, a vast ship's prow and mainsail. These collapsed in the storm to reveal a beached wreck, amidst whose spectacular timbers the rest of the action was played. Stephen Oliver wrote elaborate (sometimes over-elaborate) music to accompany the masque and the magic. Ron Daniels, the director, supplied magical action to match.

The most conspicuous of these effects was the multiplication of Ariels. Prospero's brave spirit, played by Mark Rylance, was a slim youth in a silver body-stocking covered with multi-coloured veins. Wherever he went five look-alikes accompanied him, and joined him in his songs. Robert Cushman, in *The Observer*, wittily christened them 'Ariel and his Full Fathom Five'.[5] 'Ariel and the Clones' might more precisely catch their New Wave appearance. Caliban, meanwhile, was a Rastafarian, played by Bob Peck in blackface, dreadlocks and a copious beard.

The master of these picturesque servants was an admirably youthful, energetic and angry Prospero. Derek Jacobi replaced the serene stage-manager, conventional in recent productions, with a man who was not afraid to shout, weep or show weakness. Ariel's 'Do you love me, master?' prompted a deeply felt 'Dearly', and Prospero's final words before the Epilogue were a distressed appeal to a spirit who had already deserted him. Even more strikingly, 'Our revels now are ended' was a murmured reverie by a man who seemed pleased to shed the burden of his magic. 'Unassertive humanity' was David Nokes's description of this characterization.[6] Prospero's ethical struggles were observed with the scrupulous care which such an interpretation would suggest.

All these things are thoroughly welcome developments in the theatrical interpretation of *The Tempest*. The fact remains, however, that for all the intelligence of its intentions the production lacked a certain edge. The clowns (perhaps unsettled by their rather dignified monster) were not very funny. Both Antonio (Robert O'Mahoney) and Alonso (Paul Webster) were distinctly weak. And even Jacobi failed at times to give his moral language quite sufficient point. The attempt to balance visual brilliance and intellectual weight was an admirable one. But in the end it was hard not to feel that the scales remained tilted towards the former.

August also saw the first Shakespeare production in The Warehouse (now The Donmar Warehouse) since the departure of the Royal Shakespeare Company, and it was one of which that company might itself have been proud. Jonathan Miller returned to *Hamlet*, which he first directed for the Oxford and Cambridge Shakespeare Company in 1970, in his characteristically thoughtful and observant manner. Certain features of the earlier production, such as Ophelia's clinically accurate symptoms of insanity, were revived. Elsewhere he moved his interpretation in new directions, while keeping the family and its emotional tensions very much at the centre of his thoughts.

The intimacy and austerity of the Warehouse stage were reflected in the set (which survived a subsequent transfer to the Piccadilly Theatre). Two bleached benches stood on a bare planked floor. Black drapes and a grey wall formed a simple box, with a catwalk across the back. Against this minimal background the actors played in Jacobean costumes of uniform grey and white. Darkness and mystery were rigorously eliminated (when lights were called for at the end of the play-scene, they were neither needed nor brought). The ghost was solemn rather than sinister.

Studio-production, in other words, encouraged a steady concentration on the political dynamics of the Danish court and the interior life of the principal characters. John Shrapnel gave an extraordinary performance as an astute and courageous Claudius, in the grip of an unmasterable sensual fascination with Gertrude. Susan Engel's Gertrude returned his feelings with equal subtlety, and they died hand clasped in hand. Alan MacNaughtan's Polonius was a dignified and diligent senator whose laughs came because he refused to play for them. Most strikingly of all, in a production full of illuminating detail, Ian McNeice's Osric was not a fop but the King's

---

[5] *The Observer*, 15 August 1982.
[6] *Times Literary Supplement*, 3 September 1982.

menacing bodyguard – a bullet-headed minder who shadowed his monarch in every scene.

For some critics this marvellously complete articulation of the life of the court produced merely a *Hamlet* without Hamlet. Amidst the urgency and intricacy of his setting Anton Lesser did indeed seem slight and inconsiderable. Occasionally this was the consequence of a careless rapidity with the lines. But fundamentally, of course, it was the product of a deliberate interpretative decision. This was the most extreme version we are ever likely to see of Hamlet the disturbed adolescent. John Grillo's grizzled Horatio was clearly the eternal graduate student who'd been supervising him. Rosencrantz and Guildenstern were callow contemporaries from the JCR. 'If this Hamlet has any plan,' wrote James Fenton in *The Sunday Times*, 'it is that by persisting in a certain kind of bad behaviour he will precipitate events in a way which will take matters out of his hands.'[7]

Such playing produced certain notable benefits. Lesser's Hamlet was, for example, extraordinarily good at insulting and annoying the old. Teenaged audiences responded to him, as a consequence, with thrilled attention. Others may perhaps have felt that something of Hamlet's intellectualism had been sacrificed to the stress upon his immaturity. What nobody could deny was the sustained intellectual pressure which lay behind this production even when it chose, quite consciously, to make that sacrifice. In an uneven year on the English Shakespearian stage it shone as brightly, and as reassuringly, as *All's Well That Ends Well*. And like *All's Well* it showed, once again, that fine Shakespearian productions are achieved by thinking outwards from the text.

---

[7] *The Sunday Times*, 22 August 1982.

IIIA *All's Well That Ends Well*, Royal Shakespeare Theatre, 1981.
The Countess (Peggy Ashcroft) and Lavache (Geoffrey Hutchings)

B *All's Well That Ends Well*, Royal Shakespeare Theatre, 1981.
Parolles (Stephen Moore) and Bertram (Mike Gwilym)

IVA *All's Well That Ends Well*, Royal Shakespeare Theatre, 1981.
The King of France (John Franklyn-Robbins) gives Bertram to Helena (Harriet Walter)

B *All's Well That Ends Well*, Royal Shakespeare Theatre, 1981. Bertram and Diana (Cheryl Campbell)

VA *Macbeth*, Royal Shakespeare Theatre, 1982.
Macbeth (Bob Peck) and his wife (Sara Kestelman) at the end of the banquet scene

B *Much Ado About Nothing*, Royal Shakespeare Theatre, 1982.
Act 1, scene 1: left, Beatrice (Sinead Cusack) questions the Messenger; centre, Edward Jewesbury as Leonato

VIA *Much Ado About Nothing*, Royal Shakespeare Theatre, 1982. 'Lady Beatrice, have you wept all this while?';
Derek Jacobi as Benedick

B *Much Ado About Nothing*, Royal Shakespeare Theatre, 1982.
John Carlisle as Don John (left) with Borachio (Ken Bones)

VIIA *King Lear*, Royal Shakespeare Theatre, 1982.
Lear (Michael Gambon), the Fool (Antony Sher), and Edgar disguised as Poor Tom (Jonathan Hyde)

B *King Lear*, Royal Shakespeare Theatre, 1982.
Act 4, scene 6: Edgar watches the reunion of Gloucester (David Waller) and Lear

VIIIA *1 Henry IV*, Barbican Theatre, 1982. Left, Joss Ackland as Falstaff

B *2 Henry IV*, Barbican Theatre, 1982.
Miriam Karlin as Mistress Quickly, Gemma Jones as Doll Tearsheet, and Joss Ackland as Falstaff (act 2, scene 4)

IXA *The Tempest*, Royal Shakespeare Theatre, 1982.
Act 1, scene 2: Prospero (Derek Jacobi) and Miranda (Alice Krige), with Ariel (Mark Rylance)
on the ship behind them, and Ferdinand (Michael Maloney) in foreground

B *The Tempest*, Royal Shakespeare Theatre, 1982.
One of the goddesses in the masque, act 4, scene 1

XA *Hamlet*, Donmar Warehouse Theatre, 1982.
Anton Lesser as Hamlet

B *Hamlet*, Donmar Warehouse Theatre, 1982.
Hamlet with Gertrude (Susan Engel), act 3, scene 4

THE YEAR'S CONTRIBUTIONS TO SHAKESPEARIAN STUDY

I   CRITICAL STUDIES
reviewed by BRIAN GIBBONS

In several ways the most penetrating piece of book-length Shakespeare criticism in 1981 is John Russell Brown's *Discovering Shakespeare*,[1] a short, essentially modest invitation to explore the plays as texts for performance. A valuable companion to his earlier book *Shakespeare's Dramatic Style*,[2] *Discovering Shakespeare* is addressed to the solitary reader, who must find inadequate, for Shakespeare's plays, those methods of literary study proper for non-dramatic texts. Brown also focuses attention on the limitations of present-day staging of Shakespeare, a no less topical issue:

The very substance of drama is changeable, and a reader must recognise this fact as much as a dramatist, even though it is more difficult to do so. It is very likely that the reader has never seen actors testing one interpretation against another in rehearsal. Most modern theatres show only productions that are carefully controlled so that they give a clear – and therefore strong – enactment of a single interpretative idea. At school or university the reader may have been trained to read a text so that he can be sure that he understands precisely what is on the page: whereas he should have been encouraged to play with conjecture and to enter imaginatively within a forever-changing image, or mirage, of another life.   (p. 9)

Another problem facing everyone is the number of highly specialized, difficult branches of Shakespeare studies, constantly developing, hard to keep up with, harder still to keep coherently related and integrated in an approach to the plays. There are few critics so widely qualified at such an authoritative level of scholarship as Russell Brown who also have his practical experience of theatre; fewer still are able to speak as lucidly, scrupulously and excitingly as he

habitually does. In *Discovering Shakespeare* he encourages the reader to believe that he can learn to explore many outwardly daunting aspects of Shakespeare, from textual variants to verse speaking, once their relation to performance is recognized; and the goal is the reader's own possession of a play in imagined performance, always remembering that 'As time passes our view of each play will change, because we ourselves alter and our knowledge of the text becomes more complete . . . Whenever the life that we imagine in a play becomes fixed and familiar, it is time to question our engagement' (p. 7).

On the text itself, for instance, the reader is shown, through brief and unfussy but revealing examples, how to take possession of specialist investigation and exercise his critical faculties so that the artistic questions are more sharply defined. Brown takes the reader through some lines from act 5, scene 2 of *Hamlet*, considers the Q and F variants, and then offers sensitive critical commentary on the implications of a choice between readings. Here, as persistently throughout the book, Brown invites the reader to share in the activity of questioning and exploration, resists any prompt 'solution' and prefers to leave questions open (even when one feels sure he has himself a clear conviction as to the right answer). Evidently Brown suspects that many intelligent, responsive students are put off by the exclusive tone, the dense specialist terminology, and alienating presentation of much Shakespeare scholarship.

His chapter on the text in *Discovering Shakespeare* is

---

[1] Macmillan, 1981.

[2] Heinemann, 1970.

certainly an admirable corrective, and perhaps the best short introduction to this subject available anywhere. It is, of course, no more than a stimulus to further enquiry, but without such an initial impulse many students and readers, we must fear, will avoid the subject and consequently remain blind to a fascinating and critically important issue. If the text is often unstable, if an actor's interpretation must be based on choices from moment to moment (as we are shown in close analysis of several episodes from different plays) Brown is able to show how, nevertheless, in a complete performance, Shakespeare's design ensures that continuity and rhythm draw both actor and spectator to seek the inner truth of role and action, how Shakespeare's art at the deepest level has not a watery vagueness but a structural integrity, which declares itself palpably and which exposes false and distorted or incoherent interpretation:

As horses are tested in battle, so the principal persons in a tragedy reveal their true mettle in the last Acts. In comedy, pretences and masks drop quite suddenly, as the plot brings everyone together at the close, but in the history plays and tragedies it is conflict and suffering that draw the truth out of the protagonists inch by inch; a 'bloody spur' strikes again and again, and so makes 'trial' of manhood. The climax of Macbeth's role is the wordless fight with Macduff. King Lear 'knows not what he says' during most of his last moments, and his final words are capable of many interpretations:

> Do you see this? Look on her. Look, her lips.
> Look there, look there!

Does he think Cordelia is alive or is he once more asserting his will? Are these words strong or weak? The text does not tell us and each actor must find what his performance as a whole directs him to do. Lear then 'faints' (line 311), but it is four lines later that Edgar says 'He is gone indeed'. How much does Lear suffer or resist at the end? Is he at peace? Has he slipped back into madness? The theatrical excitement at the end of a play cannot be evaluated by studying the matter of the text or the manner of its utterance, or the actions, gestures and movement that the words imply. The drama is expressed now in the total being of the actor, operating with heightened sensibility and power, and totally involved. Paradoxically, where Shakespeare seems to have given most freedom of choice, a performer may find he has least ability to choose (p. 63).

Brown is exceptionally good in discussing the strangeness of the plays – set in foreign places, ancient periods, exploring uncharted experience and reaching fantastic endings, but he insists that the plays offer no escape from life, no rest, are the work of a responsible mind, and quotes Edward Bond's view that Shakespeare spent his creative life struggling with such questions as: 'The nature of right and wrong, in what way an individual should be part of his society, why some men are tyrants and others nearly saints . . .' (p. 22). The key to Brown's argument in the book as a whole is contained in the difficult and exacting demand that we 'remain open to whatever the plays offer, however strange that may seem', like good actors in an inspired rehearsal, and that we should then try to imagine complete performances. The solitary reader must imagine the audience and its responses too, presumably; but Brown gives less attention to the question of audiences, rather surprisingly and disappointingly.

The book is full of excellent practical ideas to bring a play's many codes and signs to life: we should type out the text afresh with only minimal punctuation; we should ask not simply 'what can the words mean' but 'why does this person in the drama say this word at this moment'; we should label matchboxes with the names of the persons and make them meet one another as the text requires during a reading, so keeping ourselves aware at all times of how the stage looks, of the physical relationship of the persons to one another; however shy, we should read the text out aloud in private, noting any striking or surprising features such as the effect of its weight and length, its demand upon the wits of the actors, the moments when a speaker must stop and unravel a long sentence before he can make any kind of sense, or other moments when speech seems to glide over great and complicated happenings: 'these elementary first-hand perceptions are worth far more than the pleasures of responding to a sound recording made by practised actors, and can be just as enjoyable' – so Brown argues, and so it may be (one responds), if one is given the kind of enthusiastic guidance offered here.

The book takes seriously the needs of those who *read*

Shakespeare, and it is very practical, but its concern is with critical appreciation and critical method. It is designed to encourage the student, and is free of self-importance, it is hospitable to a wide variety of approaches to the plays; but it assumes that the reader seeks a personal imaginative experience, and that the more fully he takes into account the essential elements of instability, changeableness, surprise and challenge, integral to the plays in performance, the closer he will come to recognizing these works of art in themselves as they really are, and himself as changing and changeable. The book is short, in places impressionistic, it communicates excitement; it is impatient with static conceptions; but it offers a demanding critical approach to Shakespeare which has rigour and dignity.

Anyone involved in the teaching of Shakespeare who believes it important that the plays are better discussed in their full dimensions rather than as moral or political homilies, peculiar novels, elaborate long poems or galleries of characters, will see at once how welcome and valuable *Discovering Shakespeare* is. Anyone who regularly visits professional or amateur productions of the plays will wonder how often director and actors begin their rehearsals in the spirit Russell Brown recommends, trying to read the text as if it were entirely new, closely scrutinizing words, phrases, speeches, asking searching questions, openmindedly trying out this interpretation against that, above all trusting Shakespeare's design and persevering in it, not changing the order of scenes, not cutting – or deliberately upstaging – episodes which may seem unpalatable for one reason or another. (Adrian Noble's 1982 Royal Shakespeare Company production of *King Lear*, dominated by three superb performances by the actors playing Lear, the Fool and Gloucester, was marred unnecessarily in these ways.)

To ask for such trust in Shakespeare's design is not to refuse interpretations animated with the spirit of the times, of course; and in his short and interesting book *Changing Styles in Shakespeare*[3] Ralph Berry considers the fortunes of *Coriolanus*, *Measure for Measure*, *Troilus and Cressida*, *Henry V*, *Hamlet*, and *Twelfth Night* on the professional stage in the three phases of contemporary theatre life, 1945–56 (postwar), 1956–68 (the sixties), and 1968 onwards (the present). Berry believes that 'in the last half-generation the revalua-

tion of Shakespeare has been led by the stage' (p. 5), and he locates the centre of this dynamic in the RSC (though he notes that since Trevor Nunn took over, the RSC 'has adopted a more relaxed attitude to textual integrity . . . Textual fundamentalism was a stronger movement in the early 1960s than it is today'). He considers that the institution of three-year contracts to RSC actors, and hence the creation of a strong sense of company community and ensemble playing, permitted the RSC under Peter Hall to mount interesting and unusual reappraisals of certain plays by performance, at the same time as academic critics of Shakespeare increasingly came to regard awareness of performance values as essential to first-rate criticism.

Berry does not shrink from adducing large-scale social and political changes as well as swings in fashion to help account for the major changes in interpretation of his chosen plays, but his central argument goes as follows: 'Scholarship, which is well aware of the schizoid nature of *Measure for Measure* (the metaphor is Tillyard's) has not changed its readings substantially over the past generation. What has changed is the general audience. It is not, as I take it, receptive to the proposition that Authority Knows Best; and half of it consists of women, who tend now to a certain scepticism at the idea that Isabella will *of course* accept the Duke's hand. We are talking of a shift in the general perception. The changes in the staging of *Measure for Measure* relate, at bottom, to a changed directorial sense of what the audience can perceive, and tolerate in its action. What is true for *Measure for Measure* is equally, though less spectacularly, true for other plays in the canon' (pp. 11–12). Berry finds the change in interpretation of *Coriolanus* to be away from either right-wing or left-wing political bias to emphasis on human relationships, beginning with Peter Hall's production starring Olivier of 1959. *Henry V* was set on its modern course by Gerald Gould's view in 1919 that 'the play is ironic', but the theatre was slow to take up this critical reappraisal, and it is only with Olivier's film of 1944, dedicated to the Allied airborne forces at the time of D-Day, that Berry identifies the end of the nationalistic tradition of

---

[3] George Allen and Unwin, 1981.

interpreting the play. The anti-war feeling and in-sights in Shakespeare's *Henry V*, the reservations in that text, had been cut out by Olivier with 'a surgical intelligence and precision. And it is the "other" play that has exercised its fascination over a later genera-tion' (p. 70). *Troilus and Cressida*'s dissonances and ironies, its acrid view of the great, its openly anti-war stance, its stress on the imperative pressures of time and occasion on the lovers, have meant that modern audiences recognize and respond to it, and directors have exploited its hostility to military and political leadership; but Berry notes interestingly that the complexities of Troilus himself have eluded modern actors, and the usual interpretation of Cressida similarly diminishes her importance in modern inter-pretations on stage. Furthermore, 'just as academics are now ready to read "degree" in context as a stratagem, not a credo, so directors decline to regard it as the moral centre of the drama'. The darkness seems to be strong in modern productions of *Twelfth Night*: 'we know too much about the sadistic undercurrent of much practical joking to be at ease with it . . . Its passing means that the entire network of assumptions sustaining the old *Twelfth Night* has collapsed' (p. 118). Berry concludes that today's *Twelfth Night* appears as a machine for inducing laughter, only to disclose itself in the end as a machine for suppressing it. His account of *Hamlet* isolates the de-romanticizing of the Prince, and the interest in Claudius, as significant modern emphases, and records the Stratford Ontario produc-tion of 1976 as emblematic in its alternation of two different actors in the part of Hamlet with an otherwise unchanged cast; one actor performed the part oriented towards Gertrude, the other towards his absent father.

These plays for Berry constitute the new 'inner repertory of the Shakespearean canon', to which *King Lear* would have been added had the dominant single production by Peter Brook (and the later films by Brook and by Kozintsev) not been already so well documented. Berry's judgement in selection and emphasis seems sound and well-reasoned; his selective use of reviews and prompt-books illuminating; and he has a wide and alert grip on modern academic criticism of the plays. He offers suggestions about what constitutes the modern 'inner repertory' and

about which plays are still seen in the terms a mid-Victorian playgoer would assent to – here Berry suggests *Macbeth*, *Richard III*, *Julius Caesar* or *Love's Labour's Lost*. Berry does not discuss the reinterpreta-tion of the late Romances in modern criticism and performance, which might be thought a major area of critical and theatrical advance, but any reader will find his guide-lines valuable when applied elsewhere in the canon – say to *The Comedy of Errors*, *All's Well*, or *Timon*, which some may feel have their place in a discussion of recent revaluation in criticism and performance. Among incidental points of interest in the book is the plausible suggestion that what caused both Tillyard and Empson to declare mistakenly, and in print, that at the end of *Measure for Measure* Isabella consents to marry the Duke, was not merely the critics' human fallibility, but that they were 'faith-fully reporting their recollection of the play as seen'. Not until John Barton's production of 1970, ap-parently, was this stage tradition broken, when Isabella's silent resistance to the Duke's overtures was felt as a shocking and brilliantly inspired new departure.

James E. Hirsh undertakes a modest, painstaking investigation of *The Structure of Shakespearean Scenes*,[4] designed to follow up Empson's proposition that Shakespeare used a system of dramatic construction by scenes which 'clearly makes the scenes, the in-cidents, stand out as objects in themselves, to be compared even when they are not connected', so establishing ironic relationships and other kinds of pattern that serve to unify the play and complicate its significance.

Hirsh proposes that act divisions were not re-cognized in the Elizabethan theatre as legitimate dramatic units, so he suggests that future editors of the plays should erase all act divisions from the text, simply numbering the scenes sequentially – and only marking off scene divisions where the scene is cleared of all living characters (unconscious or sleeping characters preserve continuity). Hirsh argues that a clearing of the stage marks a significant break in the action, and he stresses that episodes without dialogue but preceded and followed by a cleared stage are

---

[4] Yale University Press, New Haven and London, 1981.

important dramatically and deserve to be marked and recognized as scenes. Richard III meets his death in a scene without dialogue, yet even in the new Arden edition of 1981 this is recorded only in stage directions which *open* the *following* scene. This is one tradition which Hirsh would like to see brought to a speedy end, and at least some modest moves have been made, in more recent series, to suppress intrusive act divisions.

Hirsh has lively things to say in his opening chapter about Shakespeare's variation of scene endings to control audience response (and mislead, as when the corpse of Falstaff revives after Hal's exit seemed to have marked the end of the scene), and there is a good discussion of montage effects (when an action on stage may be associated with a character asleep on another part of the stage). Yet the main part of the book is an oddly mechanical tabulation and catalogue of scenes as 'solo', 'duet', 'unitary group', 'two-part' and 'multi-partite'. Some better moments come in discussing larger patterns of symmetrical arrangement of scenes and mirror-effects, but Hirsh has not added to the subject which Emrys Jones explored in his *Scenic Form in Shakespeare* (Clarendon Press, Oxford, 1971), which is certainly a major work of modern Shakespeare criticism.

In his book *Shakespeare and the Dance*[5] Alan Brissenden shows how exact and particular are the references to and uses of dance in the plays, gives too brief an account of the origins, structures and appropriate social occasions of the types of Elizabethan dance referred to or required in the plays, and in a series of surveys considers the dance in terms of the dramatic action, imagery and theme. His analysis is illuminating when discussing the witty play on dance terminology, and repeated frustration of actual dancing, by the ladies in *Love's Labour's Lost*; he shows how actual dancing reflects major themes in *A Midsummer Night's Dream* and suggests that the different kinds of dance contribute an important (and today perhaps much underestimated) distinct source of meaning: Oberon and Titania dance at their reconciliation:

> Come, my Queen, take hands with me,
> And rock the ground whereon these sleepers be.
> Now thou and I are new in amity,

> And will to-morrow midnight solemnly
> Dance in Duke Theseus' house triumphantly
>
> (4.1.82–7)

Brissenden suggests that they begin this solemn dance at line 83, completing it before the line 'Now thou and I are new in amity', and so confirm their domestic harmony as Sir Thomas Elyot would approve. The 'earth feet, loam feet' of the Bergomask dancers, soon to follow, would be (in Brissenden's words) rustic, perhaps acrobatic, earthbound certainly, with the dance's stamping feet and tong-and-bone accompaniment (Brissenden's approach persistently reminds one of Benjamin Britten's operatic version of the play). The singing and dancing of the fairies which follows at Titania's command is in a carole: Brissenden links this ancient form of dance with the play's wider scope: 'The "glimmering light" Oberon tells the fairies to give through the house hints at starlight, and the stars are a reminder of the heavenly harmony existing in the greater universe, so that in this way their dance widens out in its implications' (p. 45).

By contrast with the restricted functions of dance in plays by his contemporaries, Shakespeare relates all the dances in his plays to the dramatic structure 'both of the particular scenes in which they occur and of the complete plays'. Brissenden's main concern is to develop this argument, showing how Shakespeare's use of dance contributed to the articulation of his ideas, especially ideas concerned with order. There are particular close commentaries on dances in *Much Ado*, *All's Well*, *Twelfth Night*, and *Romeo and Juliet* which indicate the precise significance of the various dances, how they are integrated into the dramatic action and what they contribute to the plays. As with music and song, a dance can present a miniature image revealing the whole inner design of a play; Brissenden's contribution is to alert us to the many *exact* meanings of dance terminology and dance performance in the plays he discusses.

Another feature of Shakespeare's art only fully appreciated in performance is his frequent use of aesthetic metaphors to remind an audience of what it is at that moment experiencing: as when an actor self-

---

[5] Macmillan Press, London and Basingstoke, 1981.

consciously alludes to his part, or when – at a larger scale – an episode is presented in such a way as to call attention to its artifice. The self-consciousness of actors and the self-consciousness of audiences are the subject of Sidney Homan's agreeable and modest book *When The Theater Turns To Itself*,[6] in which he seeks to explore the wide and diverse significance of Shakespeare's metadrama, beginning with the Induction to *The Taming of the Shrew* and ending with the Epilogue to *The Tempest*. The first part of the book considers three early comedies and the theatrical self-consciousness which, by means of word-play, high artifice in style and manner (whether of courtiers or rustics), and the presentation of on-stage audiences watching plays-within-a-play, presents the Renaissance paradox that the stage is a little world as the world is itself a stage. So Shakespeare, by appealing directly to the immediate moment as the audience is experiencing it, achieves a deconstruction within a perfectly serene frame. The central section of the book considers certain 'controlling figures' who manage the action, manipulate other characters by the use of a role, and serve as ironic reflectors of the general art of the playwright in their plays: Homan's contrast between Iago, a tragic controller, and two comic controllers, Rosalind in *As You Like It* and the Duke in *Measure for Measure*, is productive and interesting. The book concludes with discussions of *Hamlet*, *Antony and Cleopatra*, and *The Tempest* which persuasively exhibit the importance of the idea of acting and of theatre in these plays.

Certainly it is fascinating to reflect on those moments in which a character, in a moment of crisis wrought to the uttermost, suddenly looks up and out beyond the present time and place: as when Hamlet ironically speaks of the 'mutes or audience' to the events in act 5, scene 2, or when Cassius cries

> How many ages hence
> Shall this our lofty scene be acted over
> In states unborn and accents yet unknown!
> (*Julius Caesar*, 3.1.112–14)

or when Cleopatra stage-manages her own death and Charmian adjusts the crown: 'I'll mend it and then play' (5.2.317). Homan stresses the divided attitude to the theatre and to playing, as metaphor for human existence, both in *Hamlet* and *Antony and Cleopatra*; the 'baseless fabric' is certainly an ambivalent phrase, and the pressure is transferred to the audience who must interpret the play according to their own sense of truth and capacity for faith.

Important criticism of Shakespeare is to be found in part of a new book which is also concerned with Donne, Herbert, and Milton. Camille Wells Slights, in *The Casuistical Tradition in Shakespeare, Donne, Herbert, and Milton*,[7] provides two chapters on the tradition of casuistry and its method and then discusses certain cases of conscience in Shakespeare's tragedies. It is not possible in a brief review to reduce this discussion to a few sentences without damaging loss, but the interest of this topic is strong both in itself and in its relation to drama. The first chapter clarifies the conceptual framework common to Anglican and Puritan English casuists from Perkins in the 1590s to Baxter in 1673; the second chapter looks at specific cases to identify features of the casuistical habit of mind, something simultaneously structural and thematic: the casuists' insistence on 'the inviolability of the individual conscience, the relevance of particular circumstances to moral absolutes, and the role of reason in resolving problems of moral doubt' led them to see 'the operation of the conscience as essentially the process of discovering proper relationships among various kinds of knowledge' (p. 16); furthermore modern pejorative connotations of the word casuistry are misleading; casuistical analysis was designed precisely to prevent laxity and hypocrisy. Jeremy Taylor observed that Reason 'is such a box of quicksilver that it abides nowhere; . . . it is like a dove's neck, or a changeable taffata; it looks to me otherwise than to you, who do not stand in the same light that I do' (p. 31). Here we feel palpably a scepticism which alerts us to its own rhetorical procedures even as it seeks to persuade; it is almost as if Taylor's words were designed to teach the higher truth of the casuistical method – approaching moral problems without a single authority to follow unquestioningly, requiring 'skillful balancing' (in Slights's words) 'of the claims of reason, scripture and tradition in the context of

---

6 Bucknell University Press, Lewisburg, 1981.
7 Princeton University Press, 1981.

particular circumstances'. In turning to Shakespeare, Slights considers 'Sinning Against Conscience' in *Richard III*, 'Evasions of Doubt' in *Julius Caesar*, 'Struggles With Doubt' in *Hamlet*, 'Equivocation and Conscience' in *Macbeth*; she traces increasing emphasis on the ambiguity of circumstances, the difficulty of choice, and the inadequacy of simple good intentions. It is characteristic of the fastidious and discriminating particularity of Slights's discussion that she insists that 'The plays are informed by, but not confined within, the casuistical paradigm, so that the same assumptions about the moral decision-making process yield strikingly different dramatic forms.' The result of this approach is to illuminate more precisely how sheer intelligence, sheer vitality of mind, is a central quality of Shakespeare's art.

In discussing Brutus and Hamlet Slights gives a first-hand demonstration of how to follow the plays by employing rigorous casuistical skills in exploring the complex dialectic between general theory and particular circumstance while resisting oversimplification and exploring subtleties of temperament, personality and doctrine, so as to judge – and Slights certainly does make judgements: thus Brutus makes a tragic error in his crucial decision 'not because he chooses public duty over private affection or because he opts for republicanism in a world providentially destined for monarchy but because he decides to act on insufficient evidence and then banishes doubt'; Hamlet will kill Claudius 'not because he has received, from an inexplicable apparition, a dread command that confirms his intuitive revulsion, but because he has ample proof that Claudius killed his king and father, corrupted his mother, seized the throne, and tried to kill him, and because allowing this moral poison to continue to spread is damnable' (p. 104). These judgements are reached by close analysis of the plays, adducing with illuminating frequency apposite premises and arguments of contemporary casuists, and convincingly demonstrating an affinity between casuistical and Shakespearian treatments of the operation of conscience and approaches to problems of moral doubt, with sharp focus on individual and particular circumstances.

For Colin N. Manlove, in *The Gap In Shakespeare*,[8]

Shakespeare is preoccupied with dichotomy and division, but where other critics argue that Shakespeare's use of opposites in his plays is 'more or less conscious and deliberate' Manlove claims originality for his concern with opposites and divisions 'often far less intentional' which point to an essential dividedness in Shakespeare's own character. This is not an entirely novel idea, yet the procedure Manlove adopts is an all-too-conventional one of commentary on theme and character, play by play, with large-scale assertive generalizations providing regular interruption. His overall thesis proposes that 'dividedness increasingly dominated Shakespeare's vision to the point where it began to lose coherence'. The late plays are seriously flawed: 'the comic element consistently emasculates rather than subsumes the tragic, confining the insights of these plays to those of the middle comedies' (p. 182); 'the late romances ... do not convince' (p. 196).

This intemperate assertive tone is characteristic of many passages in the book; there is apparently no awareness of how Shakespeare's sheer intelligence is thus grossly underestimated, no consideration of how clearly demonstrable is Shakespeare's deep preoccupation with mode, genre and design – to go no further. Since hostile reaction to the mode of tragicomedy is scarcely new, and since Manlove cannot command the eloquence of Dr Johnson in expressing it, the reader might instead have been offered a rather more scrupulous account, in more detail, of the plays; instead we are told for instance that in *Measure for Measure* 'The Duke schemes to frustrate the evil that Angelo lets loose by purely mechanical means; Isabella's character is submerged until she suddenly appears as a marriageable woman at the end of the play... And all this can be seen as deriving from the basic severance of mind from body in the play' (p. 59). This cannot stand as a satisfactory account, nor does this bald statement engage in any way with the power, range, and subtlety of mind at work in the play. Tired old critical stereotypes are produced by Manlove with an air of discovery; but although we learn nothing new about Shakespeare's own character as it relates to his works, the subject remains an interesting one.

---

[8] Vision Press, 1981.

What depresses the reader of *The Gap In Shakespeare* is the crass interpretation of individual plays, as when for instance *The Winter's Tale* is described thus:

The remaining 'evil' in the play, following on from the character of that of Leontes, is similarly comic while supposedly real. Antigonus is killed and eaten by a bear, and the ship that bore Perdita to Bohemia is wrecked and the sailors drowned, but most of this is reported in the comic idiom of a gibbering clown. And all this, it should be added, emerges not from the fact that the play is a comedy, but from its being a failed tragi-comedy... (p. 186)

The only serious response to such comment must be embarrassed silence.

The contributors to a volume of essays on *Shakespeare as a Political Thinker*[9] include specialists in philosophy and politics, as well as literature, who all took part in a conference on the subject in Dallas in 1978. The plays discussed include *Troilus and Cressida*, *Timon of Athens*, *Measure for Measure*, *The Merchant of Venice* and *The Tempest* as well as, more predictably, *Richard II* and the Lancastrian cycle. The term 'political' has as a consequence some elasticity, but the essays share a concern to relate the plays to the major currents of thought in Shakespeare's time. This aim is welcome, and it is only a pity that many of the essays cover familiar ground in familiar ways rather than giving concerted attention to the stimulating view offered in the first essay, by John Alvis, that we may see in the diversity of the plays' settings, in ancient Greece and Rome, past and modern Britain and Denmark, and Renaissance Italy, 'an indication of Shakespeare's attempt to explore the alternative conceptions of the best civil life offered respectively by classical antiquity, Christianity, and modernity'. Several contributors make instructive use of ancient, and contemporary Renaissance, political theory in discussing the plays as, in a sense, discursive explorations of political ideas as they inform a particular society; Alvis rightly points out that 'England and Venice appear to serve as locales for inquiries into the problems specific to Christian societies and, at the same time, to offer public situations appropriate for confronting some of the issues posed by modern politics' (p. 12). There are good essays on some plays

with British settings – by Allan Bloom on *Richard II* and Dain Trafton on *Henry IV*. There is less attention to *Cymbeline*, *Henry VIII* or *Henry VI* than might have been expected, and *Titus* among the Roman plays is neglected. If this suggests a certain lack of adventurous spirit, nevertheless some ample propositions are made: John Alvis observes how Shakespeare's Grecian dramas 'appear to rehearse the range of forms one encounters in the Platonic-Aristotelian classifications of constitutions', and certainly in the Roman plays Republican and Imperial regimes are inspected not without fidelity to Roman history. Shakespeare's attention to constitutional ideas, and the specific problems they produce, begins to seem almost more than accidental.

Writing on 'Falstaff's Encore' Harry Levin[10] considers the relation of the second to the first part of *Henry IV*. He is prepared to entertain the possibility that a certain emphasis on comic material in Part 2 might suggest that the audience's delight with the character of the fat knight in Part 1 virtually required Shakespeare to produce a sequel. This essay has a late-summer quality itself in the mature ease, fullness and firmness of its substance and movement; it has a light touch, is not so green as to insist on some mere thesis for the sake of novelty, and it treats its readers hospitably as adults who have some idea of how to read Shakespeare, and who have already given the questions some thought. For Levin the comic scenes of Part 2 of *Henry IV* are particularly important, turning the play into a tragicomedy of human frailty, concerned with mutability, age, discontent and decay; we may see this play pointing from the histories and comedies of the 1590s towards the world of *Measure for Measure* and the mature tragedies. However generously speculative Levin's writing here may be, it is always underpinned by intellectual nimbleness. It is profitable to read his essay alongside J. McLaverty's discussion of 'The Prince and Falstaff in the Tavern Scenes of *Henry IV*',[11] for McLaverty

---

[9] Ed. John Alvis and Thomas G. West, *Shakespeare as a Political Thinker* (Carolina Academic Press, Durham, North Carolina, 1981).
[10] *Shakespeare Quarterly*, 32 (1981), 1–17.
[11] *Shakespeare Survey 34* (Cambridge University Press, 1981), pp. 105–10.

also is more instructive in renewing our sense of how the play works upon us than in proposing any new thesis. He shows how closely Hal and Falstaff share companionship in Part 1, not only appearing together in eight scenes (alone together on stage in four of them) but paradoxically 'when they are exchanging abuse . . . we are most aware of how close they are and how much they share. In their efforts to cap insults they reveal their familiarity with, and dependence on, one another' (pp. 106–7). Their shared command of language in 2.4 presents them as sharing fellowship. McLaverty compares the tavern scene in Part 2, the one scene in the play in which they properly meet, and finds many large and small parallels with the scene in Part 1; the differences, he argues, are designed to prepare for the coming rejection scene. In the tavern scene of Part 2 Hal is not necessary to the comic world as he was in the Part 1 scene; comedy arises partly from parallels and echoes of the earlier scene, which an audience has already experienced, reinforcing the later scene's concern with the past, with age, regret, diminishing powers. McLaverty notes how Falstaff's abuse of the Prince in the Part 2 tavern scene makes us aware of his exclusion from Hal's new society of youth and energy; and Falstaff finally will not confront Hal, but backs away: their changed relationship means that Falstaff can no longer generate comedy from antagonism with Hal, from such half-faced fellowship.

An excellent discussion of Falstaff is also offered by Samuel Crowl, in 'The Long Goodbye: Welles and Falstaff'.[12] Writing about the movie *Chimes at Midnight*, Crowl argues that it is the 'richest' of Welles's adaptations of Shakespeare. The essay is full of valuable detail, offering a memorable aide-memoire to those who have, like me, seen the film no more than a few times. Crowl sees *Chimes at Midnight* as Welles's farewell to Falstaff rather than any celebration of Hal's homecoming. Falstaff's winter dominates the texture of the film, beautifully shot in black and white, its opening reminiscent of Bergman, its battle scenes Kottian in their chilling and brutal immediacy. Crowl sees here a mid-European reading of the histories as depicting rule in terms of armed aggression not the sanctity of hierarchy, and Welles presents the battles in deliberate antithesis to the Technicolor battles of Olivier's film of *Henry V*. In the last image, of the great genius Falstaff being carted off to the grave, Welles obliquely hints at personal reasons for the powerful reshaping he has imposed on Shakespeare's *Henry IV* plays and claims the right to share some credit for the new work of art which is the result. No doubt Welles sees in Falstaff a continued allegory or dark conceit of the life of the director of genius who stars in his own films; but his personal version of the Falstaff story is a deeply felt interpretation of character and play – and who can forget the deathly chill of Gielgud's King Henry IV in *Chimes at Midnight*, an image of the appalling consequences for Henry himself, no less than for his subjects, of his power and his rule.

Irreducible ambiguities, the conflict of mighty opposites, are terms more often satisfactory when applied to history than to a particular play. Frank V. Cespedes in discussing 'The Sense of History in *Henry VIII*'[13] describes the historical person Henry VIII as 'a restless and amoral historical force', but shows that in the play Shakespeare exploits the discrepant awareness of the Jacobean audience who, unlike the persons in the play, are aware of the ironies of history since the end of Henry's actual reign. The golden age is only a dream in the future to the persons on stage as the play ends; it is not available to the audience in 1613 because the Elizabethan age is past: Elizabeth's birthday is a 'holiday in the midst of history's grim and implacable business'. This is a worthwhile essay, and leaves further room for speculation on how a Court audience, including Elizabeth's successor, and trained by the new masques, might have read the possible applications of the play, in 1613. To celebrate the providential protection of English protestantism, to expose these particular failings in an earlier English king, to dwell on the disappointed hopes earlier generations had focused on the nation's future, and to do all this before King James! This is a serious matter, surely.

In 'Lying Like Truth: Riddle, Representation and Treason in Renaissance England' Stephen Mullaney[14]

---

[12] *Shakespeare Quarterly*, 31 (1980), 369–80.
[13] *English Literary Renaissance*, 10 (1980), 413–38.
[14] *ELH*, 47 (1980), 32–47. There is an article on 'The Gowrie Conspiracy Against James VI: A New Source

writes on the language of treason and applies his ideas to *Macbeth* as a 'staging of treason'. There is some connection with Camille Slights's work on the Casuistical Tradition here. Mullaney quotes Sir John Cheke, who in *The Hurt of Sedition* of 1569 observed that traitors abuse words and are in turn betrayed by them, and Puttenham, who calls amphibology the worst vice in rhetoric and warns of the social and political threat the figure poses. Mullaney gives an interesting account of the Gowrie plot in relation to *Macbeth*: at the point of execution the traitor recovers the decorum of self. On a related topic Joseph M. Lenz writes on 'The Politics of Honour: The Oath in *Henry V*'[15] and points out that Henry V honours his oaths and teaches subjects and enemies to do likewise. Lenz has a brief survey of oath-taking in Shakespeare's plays and places its importance in Tudor society, though this approach to *Henry V* results, predictably perhaps, in a somewhat simplistic view of the play. Paul Dean considers the play's structure in terms of a contrast of modes, meanwhile, in his essay 'Chronicle and Romance Modes in *Henry V*'.[16]

Two essays approach a Shakespearian male hero in terms of sexual stereotyping. Thus Carolyn Asp[17] finds sexual stereotyping highly developed in the play *Macbeth* and central to the tragic action: Lady Macbeth perceives that her society equates feminine qualities with weakness and therefore adopts a male mentality; her husband associates the male stereotype with violence. Only a fully human warrior such as Macduff, who in feeling his grief 'like a man' is seen to integrate male and female responses, is able to confront the fiend Macbeth has become. The mechanical operation of Carolyn Asp's own set of stereotypes is all too apparent, though there is a lighter moment (of a kind) when we are invited to see in Lady Macbeth's line 'You lack the season of all natures, sleep' a 'subtle hint expressing her need for the intimacy of the boudoir'. For Edward A. Snow on the other hand, considering 'Sexual Anxiety and the Male Order of Things in *Othello*',[18] what erupts in the hero is not primitive barbaric man but the voice of the Father. We must see Othello as acting for men in general in a society where patriarchal restraints and Oedipal prohibitions domesticate women to the male order of things. Part of Othello is convinced of the sinfulness of

Desdemona's sexual appetite and his own relationship to it. It is a pity that the essay is marred by overstated assertion, and that it does not explore the ideas about male-dominated society in relation to Othello's origins as a Moor. Snow's chosen frame of analysis proves too predictable too soon.

Sexual ambiguity and disguise are the subject of two rather more intelligent essays. William W. E. Slights in his essay 'Maid and Man in *Twelfth Night*'[19] relates the play's concern with sexual ambiguity to several myths treated in non-dramatic Elizabethan poetry: self-love and self-consumption in Narcissus and in Actaeon, the unwilling boy in Venus and Adonis and the ambiguous union in Salmacis and Hermaphroditus. It is notable in connection with *Twelfth Night*, too, that the androgyne in classical art could be represented by twins. Slights appropriately refers to the illustrations of Barthélemy Aneau's *Picta Poesis ut Pictura Poesis Erit*. Several relevant woodcuts by Aneau, I would add, are reproduced by William Keach in his *Elizabethan Erotic Narratives* (Rutgers University Press, 1977), a study which admirably discusses the tonal and thematic complexities of this topic as it is treated in Elizabethan writing. As a symbol of ideal union and, in its opposite aspect, of fear and anxiety, the treatment of the hermaphrodite absorbs powerful and deep Renaissance currents which flow just beneath the surface of Shakespeare's *Twelfth Night*. This essay by William Slights helps to remind us of that tradition.

For Nancy K. Hayles[20] Shakespeare's progression from the early plays to *Twelfth Night* shows an increasing willingness to regard the disguised heroine as androgynous, so that there is a corresponding increase in the psychological complexities of her

for *Macbeth*' by Stanley J. Kozikowski in *Shakespeare Studies*, 13 (1980), 197–212.

[15] *Journal of English and Germanic Philology*, 80 (1981), 1–12.

[16] *Shakespeare Quarterly*, 32 (1981), 18–27.

[17] 'Be bloody, bold, and resolute': 'Tragic Action in Sexual Stereotyping in *Macbeth*', *Studies in Philology*, 78 (1981), 153–69.

[18] *English Literary Renaissance*, 10 (1980), 384–412.

[19] *Journal of English and Germanic Philology*, 80 (1981), 327–48.

[20] 'Sexual Disguise in *Cymbeline*', *Modern Language Quarterly*, 41 (1980), 231–47.

disguise. When disguise assumes a more fundamental relation to the heroine's identity, it will, evidently, be discarded less easily. The moral implications of disguise become a centre of dramatic interest when we come to *Cymbeline*, where Imogen/Fidele evokes the doubleness of psychic life. In the fourth act, when the heroine enters into a state combining male/female, waking/dream, conscious/unconscious life, her androgynous condition aids in the reordering and restoring of integrity in the self and in the family. Nancy Hales proposes that in *Cymbeline* this positive aspect of the androgyne is conclusively affirmed; perhaps her argument underestimates the degree of horror and the acuteness of risk involved for Imogen, and it may be truer to say that the truth represented by the androgyne is irreducibly and ultimately double. The strain of the conclusion to *Cymbeline* might then be seen as arising from a need to accommodate dramatic form to its paradoxical meaning.

Leonard Barkan in a valuable essay[21] also approaches Shakespearian romance by way of Ovid, who has a pattern of stories in which life hardens into stone or stones soften. Michelangelo well knew *The Metamorphoses*, and Barkan compares the sculptor to Shakespeare in his use of the tradition of stone statues being the signs of essential life within. Michelangelo's *Night* is a long-sleeping, perhaps dreaming mother. 'Night is frozen life, as is sleep, as is the statue of *Night*, as is all sculpture', and Barkan quotes Vasari: 'the stillness of one who is sleeping but also the grief and melancholy of one who has lost something great and noble'. Shakespeare, it is speculated, may have got Giulio Romano's name from Vasari; and Romano, the *trompe l'œil* master of the Palazzo del Te, is trumped by Shakespeare, who in *The Winter's Tale* translates Michelangelo's term for the creations of nature, 'living sculpture', into the medium of drama where art triumphs over nature as the sculpture comes to life, only to awaken us to a deeper sense of their mutuality.

The language produced by Leontes in reaction to the revival of Hermione is described in an article by Garrett Stewart[22] as 'dazed, reeling, elliptical', its shifting and ambiguous quality comparable in kind, though not in key, to that of Bottom reacting to Titania in *A Midsummer Night's Dream*. The two episodes from widely separated plays have in common, Stewart argues, a concern with an extraordinary kind of experience involving submission and detachment simultaneously, in dream-ordered actuality.

The ambiguities of the verb 'do' in *Antony and Cleopatra* serve to focus the value of action in the play, according to Peter Berek.[23] 'Do' can mean to make love or to make war; the nobleness of life is to 'do thus', embracing in love and ease; 'to do thus' is also – later on in the play – for Antony to fall upon his sword; evading the world's great snare is, in a sense, 'doing', while in another sense it is 'undoing'. A military action can turn into political defeat, success can lose one the love of those who helped make that success, while failure can win popular affection. For Peter Berek the intricate and paradoxical structure of thought and dramatic action in the play is destined to focus on the differing senses, substantial and illusory, of ruling and self-rule, and on how it may make sense to say that Antony and Cleopatra themselves 'what they undid, did'.

Barbara Mowat[24] approaches the transcendent element in *The Tempest* by discussing Prospero as a wizard, a pagan enchanter, brought like his dramatic antecedents Friar Bacon and Dr Faustus into a Christian world. Prospero is a human being with moral concerns who also has magic powers, yet his language seems foreign to the world of hermeneutic magic and daemons. The essay offers interesting examples from earlier drama of the several traditions ·which we are invited to see as informing Shakespeare's depiction of the magician in Prospero. Much more emphatically

---

[21] 'Living Sculptures: Ovid, Michelangelo, and *The Winter's Tale*', *ELH*, 48 (1981), 639–67.

[22] 'Shakespearean Dreamplay', *English Literary Renaissance*, 11 (1981), 44–69.

[23] 'Doing and Undoing: The Value of Action in *Antony and Cleopatra*', *Shakespeare Quarterly*, 32 (1981), 295–304. Other articles in this volume include Louis Adrian Montrose, '"The Place of a Brother" in *As You Like It*: Social Process and Comic Form' (pp. 28–54); Heather Dubrow, 'Shakespeare's Undramatic Monologues: Toward a Reading of the *Sonnets*' (pp. 55–68); René E. Fortin, 'Desolation and the Better Life: The Two Voices of Shakespearean Tragedy' (pp. 80–94).

[24] 'Prospero, Agrippa, and Hocus Pocus', *English Literary Renaissance*, 11 (1981), 281–303.

learned, and courtly, is the perspective in which Ernest Gilman invites us to see *The Tempest*, in his article '"All Eyes": Prospero's Inverted Masque'.[25] Gilman suggests that the interrupted masque in *The Tempest* hints at Prospero's own 'bedazzled, insulated self-regard' and is an instance of the play's broader strain of satire against Court theatre. We are to see the 're-surgent anti-masque' of Caliban's 'foul conspiracy' as inverting the norm of the Court masque convention. Gilman sees the resurgent conspiracy as a 'mis-placed anti-masque' which prompts the audience to replot what it has just seen, to return to the shattered masque and wonder again at this fragile and unstable creation. Surely it is stretching terminology and blurring proper distinctions to describe the Caliban–Trinculo–Stephano group as the anti-masque? Nevertheless the general case Gilman makes out is interesting: Prospero's masque, thus dislocated, makes us aware of other kinds of dislocation in the play, which open the flow of future action but only as a part of a process of re-enactment ebbing back through the channels of memory. Prospero's mind enacts a future by recalling the past, his masque is of 'baseless fabric' (both free of what is base yet tottering and uncertain) displaying vanity and grandeur, like Prospero himself, and needing inner tempering to order an inner tempest and purge mystification and self-indulgent display. The essay's claim to associate Shakespeare with anti-Court theatre satire is not substantiated.

Discussion of the character of Prospero would have brought a welcome complication to Russ McDonald's comparison[26] of visionary characters in Shakespeare's tragedies and Jonson's comedies, in an essay in *Shakespeare Survey 34*, devoted to characterization in Shakespeare. McDonald argues that while Jonson conceives of the collision between a harmonious vision and a corrupt world as comic, Shakespeare conceives of it as tragic. For Kenneth Muir, in the first article in the same volume, 'Shakespeare's Open Secret', it is precisely ambiguities and ambivalences which are essential to Shakespeare's art of characterization. Muir's use of the term 'stereoscopic' aptly defines the impression of three-dimensional reality in Shakespeare's characters, given by conflicting impressions from different directions – from 'the disparity between source and play, the disparity between

what different characters say about each other, the contrast between metaphysical and psychological motives, the shattering of stereotypes, the complicating effect of the poetry, the poet's presumed identification with some of his characters more than others, the difference between one production and another, one actor and another'. Muir does not hesitate to declare that these effects were calculated, that some are peculiar to Shakespeare, and that 'these methods run counter to all orthodox prescriptions of dramaturgy'.

Brian Vickers gives an admirably lucid and thoughtful account of 'The Emergence of Character Criticism, 1774–1800', the period when critics abandon discussion of plot or language and write simply about individual characters in the plays. Vickers provides ample illustration to support his argument, which is convincing: where previous generations had attacked Shakespeare for creating inconsistent characters, this generation, who shared the same belief in the need for consistency and morality, set out to defend him: the more highly developed their conception of Shakespeare's wider dramatic design, the greater the real advance in understanding that was achieved.

In a weighty essay Robert Weimann[27] is concerned with social relationships as a means of identifying character in the plays; these are more important in the early comedies and 'must obviously be differentiated from a more highly specified definition of identity through, say, a nexus of several layers of role-playing or through a more highly complex combination between typifying and individualizing features each, in its turn, linked with a certain set of circumstances with which, in the tragedies, the images of individuality are made to interact. It is by the degree of such interaction between self and circumstance that the merely functional definition of dramatic identity may be said to give way to some character "more dearly parted".'

Next, A. D. Nuttall[28] offers a trenchant argument

[25] *Renaissance Quarterly*, 33 (1980), 214–31.
[26] 'Sceptical Visions: Shakespeare's Tragedies and Jonson's Comedies', *Shakespeare Survey 34* (Cambridge University Press, 1981), pp. 131–47.
[27] 'Society and the Individual in Shakespeare's Conception of Character', *ibid.*, pp. 23–31.
[28] 'Realistic Convention and Conventional Realism in Shakespeare', *ibid.*, pp. 33–7.

that Shakespeare reached in the *Henry IV* plays a freedom from 'that early restless impulse to register his own consciousness of what is formally involved ... with this fracturing of the more obtrusive symmetries comes an intuition of reality'. Many will share Nuttall's contempt for those teachers of literature who, confronted with a literary opposition of convention and nature, react in a reflexive manner that the so-called 'nature' half of the antithesis is itself a conventional trope. Nuttall observes 'This, indeed, seems to mark the point of maximum strenuousness in much modern criticism. In Shakespeare it represents an early and (for him) undeveloped phase of his art which he effortlessly outgrew.'

Three well-written essays, which it would be improper to summarize but which are worth consulting, follow: Herbert Weil 'On Expectation and Surprise', with analysis of episodes from *Richard III*, *Much Ado*, and *King Lear*; Leo Salingar's 'Shakespeare and the Ventriloquists', concerned with our belief in the spontaneity of the characters as separate centres of consciousness, as illustrated by the case of Hamlet; and Giorgio Melchiori on 'The Rhetoric of Character Construction: *Othello*', a close analysis of the precision with which each character has been endowed with a personal linguistic code and rhetorical habits of constructing speeches, and of the play's overall pattern of keywords and rhetorical structures.

Other essays include Michael Goldman, 'Characterizing Coriolanus', Richard Levin disparaging 'The Ironic Reading of *The Rape of Lucrece*', T. J. Cribb on 'The Unity of *Romeo and Juliet*', and two essays on *Twelfth Night*, by Ralph Berry and Karen Greif. In the first[29] Berry concludes that the play's ending offers 'theatre as blood sport' with the effect of making the audience ashamed of itself, in the second[30] Greif finds the play plays with the idea of playing without coming to any very firm conclusion. Finally worthy of note are the conclusions of Harriett Hawkins, reviewing current critical studies of Shakespeare in this volume.[31] She stresses the need for scholarly journals to give fresh thought to their readership, whose appetite and judgement are often disappointed by being underestimated in various ways, and warns of the blight of selective citation, whereby previous

discussions which make the same points or demolish the theories propounded are simply ignored.

Since some eccentricity of the library caused two volumes of the annual *Shakespeare Studies* to arrive simultaneously on the shelf, it is possible to review them now together. Volume 13 begins with one of Richard Levin's zealous assaults on the modern critical thematizers and allegorizers.[32] Levin packs his mine with quotations from early eyewitnesses of the plays, who stress the lifelikeness of the literal representation of event and character and minimize abstractions, and this enables Levin to question the validity of such abstracting tendencies in modern criticism, and to point out that allegorical plays such as *A Game at Chess* were recognized as such at the time of first performance. Readers will enjoy the examples Levin gives of recent allegorical interpretations of *The Winter's Tale*. In the next article Lennet J. Daigle is entirely concerned with thematic and allegorical interpretation of a work by Shakespeare, but allowably so, and she offers some long perspectives terminating in a conclusion; her '*Venus and Adonis*: Some Traditional Contexts' argues that in the poem a 'value-system directed towards insuring the continuous order of nature' vindicates the demands of Venus. Three essays on individual characters come next: Gerry Brenner on 'Shakespeare's Politically Ambitious Friar' in *Romeo and Juliet* (pp. 47–58), Jacqueline Trace on 'Shakespeare's Bastard Faulconbridge: An Early Tudor Hero' (pp. 59–69), and Philip Goldstein on 'Hamlet: Not a World of His Own' (pp. 71–83), in which we are asked to recognize allusion to the history of sixteenth-century England, with a corrupt aristocracy opposed by a Platonic humanism enforced by 'the idealist concept of action of the Puritan movement' – in the shape of the Prince of Denmark.

There follow three essays on plays seen as a whole: one important, scrupulous and refreshing account, by Charles R. Forker and Joseph Candido, on 'Wit,

---

[29] '*Twelfth Night*: The Experience of the Audience', *ibid.*, pp. 111–19.
[30] 'Plays and Playing in *Twelfth Night*', *ibid.*, pp. 121–30.
[31] *Ibid.*, pp. 161–77, especially the first and last pages.
[32] 'The Relation of External Evidence to the Allegorical and Thematic Interpretation of Shakespeare', *Shakespeare Studies*, 13 (1980), 1–29.

Wisdom and Theatricality in *The Book of Sir Thomas More*' (pp. 85–104), then a straightforward account of '*Troilus and Cressida*: The Worst of Both Worlds' by M. M. Burns (pp. 105–30), and an essay by Richard A. Levin on '*All's Well That Ends Well* and "All Seems Well"' (pp. 131–44) that begins by noticing that opposing interpretations of Helena, like the play as a whole, 'almost like a Rorschach test' reveal our predispositions, but then baldly asserts that he will adopt a simply hostile attitude, 'show that Helen's success depends on guile'. A tone of brisk philistinism accompanies the reductive and assertive exercise.

Three articles consider *Othello*; in 'Othello's Threnos: "Arabian Trees" and "Indian" Versus "Iudean"' (pp. 145–67), Joan Ozark Holmer concentrates on the hero's death speech and the lines

> . . . whose subdu'd eyes,
> Albeit unused to the melting mood,
> Drops tears as fast as the Arabian trees
> Their med'cinable gum.   (5.2.351–4)

She would identify the Arabian trees as myrrh, and the 'base Iudean' as Judas: 'Unlike Myrrha's tearful and prayerful repentance that proves "medicinal" in her metamorphosis, Othello's "melting mood" bears the consequences of Judas' woe and transforms him utterly.' W. D. Adamson, in 'Unpinned or Undone?: Desdemona's Critics and the Problem of Sexual Innocence' (pp. 169–86), vindicates Desdemona as innocent, an absolutely positive moral person, who knows sexual passion but not shame. Ann Jennalie Cook, in 'The Design of Desdemona: Doubts Raised and Resolved' (pp. 187–96), observes that contradictory critical views of the heroine, as either embodiment of grace or something of a slut, seem to be prompted by contradictions which Shakespeare has 'quite deliberately structured into the play itself'. This is a good essay which notices the successive impressions an audience receives of Desdemona, and stresses the scandal of her elopement, and the absence of advance assurances as to her virtue. Furthermore at the very point in the middle of the play where the audience's doubts begin to be resolved, Othello's begin to be aroused; and this sequence begins with her appearance before the garrison on her bridal night and ends with the mock brothel scene where Othello calls her whore. The essay makes a persuasive case for symmetry in Shakespeare's design of the process of spawning and settling doubt in the play.

Volume 14 of *Shakespeare Studies*, for 1981, has a broadly similar coverage of Shakespeare's work, beginning with *Lucrece*, then six essays on early plays, two on *Julius Caesar*, one apiece on *As You Like It*, *The Merry Wives of Windsor*, and *Measure for Measure*, and concluding with three on *The Tempest*.[33] Of these perhaps Barbara Freedman's essay 'Falstaff's Punishment: Buffoonery as Defensive Posture in *The Merry Wives of Windsor*' may be singled out for its choice of a work still suffering relative critical neglect, and as a welcome match for the previous year's article on *The Book of Sir Thomas More*. Attention to the early plays, so long as it is not condescending, is also very welcome, and the editor of *Shakespeare Studies* includes a variety of critical approaches in the volume.

A. Robin Bowers in 'Iconography and Rhetoric in Shakespeare's *Lucrece*' reflects on traditional Renaissance treatments of the Lucrece story and provides some illustrations of paintings on the theme by Titian and a follower of Cranach. Bowers notes a coincidence of literary and painterly treatments of the subject in stressing the heroine's virtues. Bowers then considers the internal debates of Shakespeare's villain and heroine in the poem: they 'pit will against reason, illogic against logic, despair against hope'; although the essay rather keeps the verbal and musical texture of the poem at a distance, it does usefully explore its rhetorical structure.

Terry Comito[34] works through the whole corpus of Shakespeare's plays in pursuit of garden scenes, garden images: 'the root from which the garden image most compellingly flourishes is the imagination's need to convert time to place, to make itself at home in time

---

[33] These are Margreta de Grazia's '*The Tempest*: Gratuitous Movement or Action Without Kibes and Pinches' (pp. 249–65), Sister Corona Sharp, 'Caliban: The Primitive Man's Evolution' (pp. 267–83), and David G. Brailow, 'Prospero's "Old Brain": The Old Man as Metaphor in *The Tempest*' (pp. 285–303). Other articles are Marilyn L. Williamson, 'Romeo and Death' (pp. 129–37) and David Evett, 'Types of King David in Shakespeare's Lancastrian Tetralogy' (pp. 139–61).

[34] 'Caliban's Dream. The topography of Some Shakespearean Gardens', pp. 23–54.

by giving it a spatial contour' (p. 42). It is not often that one feels a piece of critical writing about Shakespeare is too compressed, but this essay provokes such a thought. Comito pursues an old-fashioned Theme through the whole corpus of Shakespeare's works, but subjects his theme, the garden, to so many changes of sense in such a short space that paths become rapidly overgrown and critical pronouncement, feeding on whole groups of plays to nurture ever more grandiose assertions, chokes. I do not want the particularity of critical discourse about Shakespeare drowned in such strained metaphors as 'the fallen gardens that constitute the landscape of tragedy', or abused by referring to Perdita's speech as 'sweet prattle' or blunted by the locution 'a figure like Iago' – which figure except Iago is like Iago? – nor do I find it impressive that Comito finds himself 'tempted to propose, only half playfully, that if the comedies and tragedies give us speech for gardens (*parole*), the tragicomedies give us the garden's very language (*langue*), restore us to the whole system of its possibilities' (p. 42).

Dolores M. Burton is by contrast modest and specific in her discussion of 'Discourse and Decorum in the First Act of *Richard III*'; she approaches the wooing of Lady Anne from a different but complementary direct to that of Herbert Weil in his article in *Shakespeare Survey 34*, 'On Expectation and Surprise'. Two essays follow on *Titus*: Robert S. Miola considers the play in the context of 'The Mythos of Shakespeare's Rome', and argues for a recognition of ironic recollection of the *Aeneid* behind the explicit use of Ovid's *Metamorphoses*. Miola seems to doubt the artistic unity and dramatic effectiveness of *Titus*; G. Harold Metz, writing on 'The Early Staging of *Titus Andronicus*', takes a sustained careful look at the 'varied, theatrically expert and resourceful' exploitation of the resources of the Elizabethan stage, as revealed by dialogue and stage-directions, with 'no signs of apprenticeship' on Shakespeare's part. The discussion is admirably accurate, restrained, reasoned, and should help a reader who has not seen the play performed, to respond and comprehend more fully.

King John is approached from another Elizabethan viewpoint by Douglas C. Wixson[35] who cites some contemporary pamphlets to support his argument that the play 'echoes the language and rhetoric' of pamphleteering and, in playing against a background of popular attitudes and opinions as well as traditional sources of information about King John in Bale, Foxe, Grafton and Holinshed, presents a dialectical staging of polemic: 'The episodes of *John* are composed of semi-autonomous scenes that find their unity in the minds of the audience, who are encouraged rather to see the complexity of politics than be taught a moral lesson' (p. 121). There are sixty footnotes to this article: among them is a solitary reference to the New Penguin edition of the play, but there is no apparent acknowledgement of the degree to which the Introduction to that edition, by R. L. Smallwood,[36] anticipates much of Wixson's drift.

Another variety of critical approach is exemplified in the intelligently grounded and lively essay by Barbara Freedman, 'Falstaff's Punishment' (pp. 163–74). She is concerned to show how 'The play expresses an obvious pleasure in being caught, in being humiliated, in being punished for sexual transgressions' (p. 165). Although no reader will feel obliged to follow Freedman's invitation to compare *The Merry Wives of Windsor* with *Othello* and *King Lear* (which she says Shakespeare wrote 'around the same time') on the grounds that Shakespeare's plays 'in this period' focus on 'an aging male protagonist' declining in powers and facing 'fantasies of emasculation and humiliation by women', and although her citation of a case study from *The Psychoanalytic Review* takes up too much space, nevertheless her argument that Falstaff, in a sense, asks for ridicule and humiliation, serves to focus the serious critical difficulty of trying to understand the place and meaning of the playful, parodic element in the scapegoat ritual at the play's centre – unless that centre is hollow.

Naomi Conn Liebler[37] considers *Julius Caesar*'s 'Ritual Ground', focusing on the play's beginning with the Feast of Lupercal, Rome's 'most ancient

---

35 '"Calm Words Folded Up in Smoke". Propaganda and Spectator Response in Shakespeare's *King John*', pp. 111–27.

36 Harmondsworth, 1974.

37 '"Thou Bleeding Piece of Earth": The Ritual Ground of *Julius Caesar*', pp. 175–96.

festival of purgation and fertility', which we are to see overshadowed and swallowed up by the more modern and pragmatic, secular concerns of politics, to emerge in the ritualistic images in which Brutus describes the assassination. Antony, not Brutus, is the official Lupercus, however, and it is he not Brutus who addresses the body of Caesar as 'thou bleeding piece of earth'. The 'ceremony of purgation and fertility is replaced by one of holocaust'. Liebler suggests possible analogies between the Feast of Lupercal and Elizabethan popular festivals. In David Kaula's essay '"Let Us Be Sacrificers": Religious Motifs in *Julius Caesar*' (pp. 197–214), Christian overtones in the language and stage-action of the play are suggested as offering 'oblique or parodic versions of familiar scriptural events'; intimations of Christian ritual in other Shakespearian plays with classical settings, Kaula argues, are an expression of that typological mode of thought which is important though not highly conspicuous in Shakespeare's art.

Two essays argue the importance of a particular perspective for understanding a play; Alice-Lyle Scoufos considers the symbolic setting of the *paradiso terrestre*, and the tradition of the testing of various levels of love, descending from the Florentine

Academy to Castiglione, Lyly and Sidney, in relation to *As You Like It* (pp. 215–27); and Mathew Winston considers 'Morality Play Elements in *Measure for Measure*' (pp. 229–48).

The year's critical studies are of a mingled yarn, but some final pieces serve to point to virtues: S. Nagarajan writes with dignity, and welcome gravity, on 'Shakespeare and the Nature of Politics: The Example of *Coriolanus*', in *The Journal of Literary Studies*; R. A. Foakes devotes his excellent British Academy Shakespeare Lecture to 'Forms to his Conceit: Shakespeare and the Uses of Stage-Illusion';[38] Jonathan Miller is lucid, engaging and honest in discussing a number of plays in an interview with Tim Hallinan,[39] and J. L. Styan, discussing 'Teaching through Performance' with Derek Peat,[40] observes 'the true learning process does not involve being given facts, especially in the arts and the humanities where facts are of no final account at all ... the closest you will come to understanding the nature of a play is to put it on ... a play is a changing, growing creature'.

[38] *Proceedings of the British Academy*, 66 (1980).
[39] *Shakespeare Quarterly*, 32 (1981), 134–45.
[40] *Shakespeare Quarterly*, 31 (1980), 142–52.

2 SHAKESPEARE'S LIFE, TIMES AND STAGE
reviewed by LOIS POTTER

The three categories specified in the title of this review are difficult to distinguish and still more difficult to delimit: how does one trace the circumference of a circle in the water? As I write, for instance, the *Times Literary Supplement* is the scene of a mild scholarly debate, caused by Eric Sams's contention that Shakespeare might have written *Edmund Ironside* during the so-called 'missing years' before the first mention of him in Greene's *Groatsworth of Wit*.[1] Whether this news item belongs to Shakespeare's Life or only to his Times depends on how one feels about the argument. Like many others, I rushed out and read the play at once: it doesn't *sound* much like Shakespeare, but then the argument is that early Shakespeare wouldn't have

sounded like Shakespeare anyway. Less subjective rebuttals (based on the Common Source argument) have since appeared; Sams has replied to these;[2] and I suspect that the excitement will have died down by the time this is read.

One feature of this year's work has been its interest in those early years of Shakespeare. I think it is connected with the current critical movement towards demystification of the creative process. A Shakespeare who appears out of nowhere at the relatively late age

[1] '*Edmund Ironside*: a Reappraisal', 13 August 1982.
[2] See the *Times Literary Supplement* for 3 September, 10 September, and 17 September, and Sams's reply, 24 September.

of twenty-eight bears an uncomfortable resemblance to Jesus Christ, whose life and works are equally hard to subject to derogatory criticism. Getting rid of that Shakespeare is the chief design of E. A. J. Honigmann's stimulating book, *Shakespeare's Impact on His Contemporaries*.[3] It attempts to replace the 'sweet' and 'gentle' image of Shakespeare the man with something more human and complex, to push the dates of his early works back into the empty spaces of the 1580s, and to establish the existence of a contemporary literary and critical debate in which he was a participant as well as a theme of controversy.

Professor Honigmann has not unearthed any new material on any of these topics; rather, he is concerned to restore familiar allusions to their contexts and to point out the possibility that other works already known may also constitute allusions to Shakespeare. The most dubious part of the enterprise, inevitably, is that which relates to the man's personality. It is not really a debunking: he suggests that 'sweet' and 'gentle' meant something more like 'civilized' and draws attention to familiar evidence of Shakespeare's financial hard-headedness. But he also relies on negative evidence, such as Shakespeare's failure to make a bequest to Ben Jonson. I hate to think what a biographer would make of my life if he concentrated on all the nice things which I might have done but didn't.

A good deal of the book is given over to a discussion of the relation between *King John* and *The Troublesome Reign*, concluding that the latter is an imitation rather than a source, and that Shakespeare's play dates from 1590–1, as does his *Richard III*. It is an attractive theory, since, as Professor Honigmann points out, it makes Shakespeare an exact contemporary rather than a follower of Marlowe; it also turns *King John* and *Richard III* into companion pieces. Still more interesting is the discussion of Shakespeare's relation to Jonson. Though he treats Fuller's and Dryden's accounts of the contrast between the two as mythical, Professor Honigmann seems finally to endorse their view; he claims that Shakespeare was felt, even in his own time, to be a writer hovering dangerously on the edge of bombast and improbability, and that *The Winter's Tale* both embraces and answers such criticism.

Some support for Honigmann's backdating can be found in Ann Thompson's compilation of parallels between *A Knack to Know a Knave* (1592) and the two *Shrew* plays; she convincingly argues that *The Shrew*, as the source play for *A Shrew*, can be no later than 1591–2.[4] Another writer concerned with Shakespeare's early years, David George, draws the opposite conclusion to Honigmann from his reading of Chettle's reference to Shakespeare in 1592; he thinks it implies that the actor was still 'fairly new to dramatic composition'.[5] He goes on to offer a closely argued case against Shakespeare's having been a member of Pembroke's Men between 1592 and 1594. Proving a negative is not very exciting, but the article also gives a good picture of the miserable state of theatrical companies during the plague years and (with acknowledgement to two articles by Paul E. Bennett in *Notes and Queries*, 200) offers a contribution to the sorting out of the confusion as to who acted *Titus Andronicus*.

Robert Giroux's decision to refer to the 1609 Quarto of the Sonnets and *A Lover's Complaint* as Q gives *The Book Known as Q* (first chapter: 'The Story of Q') an appearance of sensationalism which it does not deserve.[6] Mr Giroux treats the sonnets as autobiographical, but his interpretation of the available evidence is sensible, well-written, and unstartling. He thinks that the sonnets were written to the Earl of Southampton over a three-year period (1592–5), apart from Sonnet 107, which celebrates Southampton's release from prison in 1603; he takes Marlowe to be the rival poet, reserves judgement about the Dark Lady, and thinks that the absence of contemporary references to Q means that someone (probably Southampton) managed to get it suppressed. (In fact, the edition did not go totally unnoticed: Leo Daugherty has noted 'A 1614 Borrowing from Shakespeare's Sonnets'.[7]) The book, which also surveys the critical history of the sonnets, and contains a complete

---

[3] Macmillan Press, London and Basingstoke, 1982.
[4] 'Dating evidence for *The Taming of the Shrew*', *Notes and Queries*, NS 29 (1982), 108–9.
[5] 'Shakespeare and Pembroke's Men', *Shakespeare Quarterly*, 32 (1981), 305–23.
[6] Weidenfeld and Nicolson, 1982.
[7] *Notes and Queries*, NS 29 (1982), 126–7.

photographic facsimile of the Quarto, would make a good introduction to the subject for anyone who is not opposed to the biographical approach in principle. I hope that it will not be lumped in the same category as Charles Connell's *They Gave Us Shakespeare: John Heminge and Henry Condell*,[8] where a groatsworth of information about the two men is padded out to £6.95 worth of unscholarly and misleading speculation.

Though not about 'early' Shakespeare, Arthur Melville Clark's *Murder Under Trust* also attempts a bit of backdating.[9] Its theory is that Shakespeare wrote *Macbeth* in 1601, drawing on a manuscript history of Scotland in the Royal Library in Edinburgh and on the recent Gowrie conspiracy; he may have been in Edinburgh at the invitation of James VI, and he may have been glad to go there in any case in order to live down the embarrassment caused by the involuntary linking of *Richard II* with the Essex uprising. I should like to read a novel based on this idea. As evidence, Mr Clark provides a good deal of information on Scots law, Scots feuds in the sixteenth century, and James VI's relationship with the theatre. It is interesting to know that traitors in Scotland were 'put to the horn' – that is, proclaimed at market crosses to the sound of trumpets – but it seems unnecessary to look so far afield for a source of the trumpet-tongued angels who will blow Macbeth's horrid deed in every eye, when the Bible was probably the source for the custom, as for the image. It does, however, seem likely that Shakespeare had the Gowrie conspiracy as well as the Gunpowder plot in mind when he wrote *Macbeth*. This possibility has already been the starting-point for a stimulating essay by Steven Mullaney, reviewed by Brian Gibbons on pp. 165–6, which links the play's equivocation and prophecies with those associated with Gowrie and Garnet.[10]

Two reference works will serve as an introduction to Shakespeare's 'Times'. *Who's Who in Shakespeare's England*, by Alan and Veronica Palmer, is attractively presented and makes enjoyable browsing.[11] I noticed one minor error, the assumption that Old Adam is Rosalind's servant rather than Orlando's (this occurs in the account of a figure new to me, the Warwickshire shepherd Thomas Whittington, who has been proposed as the original of Shakespeare's

character). Entries are alphabetical (the decision whether to list aristocrats by titles or family names is not consistent), but a useful table in the front further classifies them by profession, status, links with Shakespeare, and so on. The choice of items for the glossary, on the other hand, seems arbitrary; one can see the point of Copyholder and Separatist, but why Civil War and Trial of Mary Queen of Scots?

L. C. Stagg's *The Figurative Language of the Tragedies of Shakespeare's Chief 17th-Century Contemporaries* (first published in 1977) is much less fun, but this is its third edition, so someone must find it useful.[12] The dramatists included are Chapman, Heywood, Jonson, Marston, Webster, Tourneur and Middleton. Each author is indexed separately, with the images in alphabetical order, but there is also – a new feature in this edition – a subject-index based on Caroline Spurgeon's image-categories, which allows for cross-referencing. My heart sinks to contemplate all the simple-minded imagery studies that can be based on this book. Properly used, however, and with the aid of more sophisticated linguistic techniques than it offers, it could be a valuable means of distinguishing between images which are genuinely personal and those which belong to a shared world of archetypes, clichés, and proverbs. And someone is no doubt using it even now to settle the authorship of *The Revenger's Tragedy*.

Even without the aid of the Index, most of the contributors to *Webster: the Critical Heritage* seem to have noticed that, as Professor Stagg says, his tragedies are dominated by images of 'devils, wild animals, sickness, and death'.[13] This collection naturally overlaps with G. K. Hunter's excellent Penguin Critical Anthology, but the editor, Don D. Moore, has included some interesting new material: extracts from

---

[8] Oriel Press (Routledge and Kegan Paul), Stocksfield, 1982.
[9] *Murder Under Trust, The Topical Macbeth, and Other Jacobean Matters* (Scottish Academic Press, Edinburgh, 1981).
[10] 'Lying Like Truth: Riddle, Representation and Treason in Renaissance England', *ELH*, 47 (1980), 32–47.
[11] Harvester Press, Brighton, 1981.
[12] Garland Publishing, New York and London, 1982.
[13] Ed. Don D. Moore (Routledge and Kegan Paul, London, Boston and Henley, 1981).

the adaptations by Tate, Theobald and Horne, and reviews of nineteenth-century revivals. There is not much variety in the assessments offered here, most of which suggest only vague or second-hand knowledge of the plays. (The historian Hallam is one of the few to notice either humour or theatrical skill in Webster.) Presumably it was his suspicion that the whole heritage should be traded for a mess of pottage that led the editor to provide a table of 'Comments' instead of 'Contents'. If you want to know what is actually in the book, you will have to turn to the index, since the Comments are a series of crossword puzzle clues. Thus, Charles Kingsley's attack on Webster appears (because Kingsley happened to be Canon of Westminster) under the heading 'The Canon Fires'.

The *literary* heritage of Shakespeare's contemporaries and successors is a more interesting topic: their relation to him has been seen, at least since T. S. Eliot, as in many ways analogous to our own relation to literary tradition. R. L. Smallwood's comparison of ''Tis Pity She's a Whore and Romeo and Juliet' attempts to go beyond the obvious plot similarities of the two plays to larger structural ones, like the killing-off of the principal comic character half-way through and the self-conscious allusion to the title in the closing line.[14] It is a comparison which could be extended still further; the play's echoes of *Othello* are equally strong. What Dr Smallwood leaves unexplained, however, is *why* Ford should have engaged in such obvious variations on a famous model: Homage? Satire? Parody?

From the problem of Shakespeare-as-source, I shall turn to the numerous speculations about Shakespeare's sources. Roland M. Frye's note on 'The "Shakespearean" Portrait of Richard III in Edward Alleyn's Picture Collection' looks at first as if it might belong to both categories.[15] Professor Frye speculates as to whether Alleyn's picture, which depicts a more obviously villainous Richard than the one in the National Portrait Gallery on which it is based, might have been inspired by, or have inspired, the Shakespeare play. But he himself recognizes that 'there was enough already present in Tudor iconography to influence Shakespeare's conception' – in which case, it might also have influenced the artist. (All scholarly

articles in this field ought to include a guarantee whose small print disclaims liability for any damage done by the discovery of a Common Source.)

Studies of the classical sources, not surprisingly, are dominated by Ovid. Barry Nass offers a modest and plausible note, '"Of one that loved not wisely but too well": Othello and the *Heroides*', and Roger Warren notes a parallel between 'Trembling Aspen Leaves in *Titus Andronicus* and Golding's Ovid'.[16] Two articles on *Titus Andronicus* complement each other interestingly. Robert S. Miola finds the play positively over-determined by classical references: Saturninus as Saturn devouring his own children, the fall of Troy, the four ages of the world, and the double role of Lavinia (whose name is linked with the beginning of Roman history in Virgil, with the end of its greatness in Shakespeare).[17] For Grace Starry West, the very obviousness of the Ovidian references, together with the fact that Ovid actually *inspires* the crime against Lavinia, is Shakespeare's way of depicting a decadent society whose members are unable to act without reference to literary models.[18]

Brief notes include J. J. M. Tobin's suggestion that the *Apologia* of Apuleius, who was charged with gaining his wife's love through witchcraft, might be a source for Othello's speech to the Senate.[19] Joseph Rosenblum thinks that the relation of Bottom and Titania might derive from a personification, illustrated in Ripa's *Iconologia*, of Obstinacy as a woman holding an ass's head.[20] (This view obliges one to see Titania as a symbol of Obstinacy; I don't, but in the circumstances am reluctant to argue about it.)

Leonard Barkan draws on both Ovid and Michelangelo for his stimulating interpretation of the statue

---

[14] *Cahiers Élisabéthains*, 20 (1981), 49–70.

[15] *Shakespeare Quarterly*, 32 (1981), 351–4.

[16] *English Language Notes*, 19 (1981), 102–4; *Notes and Queries*, NS 29 (1982), 112.

[17] '*Titus Andronicus* and the Myth of Shakespeare's Rome', *Shakespeare Studies*, 14 (1981), 85–98.

[18] 'Going by the Book: Classical Allusions in Shakespeare's *Titus Andronicus*', *Studies in Philology*, 79 (1982), 62–77.

[19] '*Othello* and the *Apologia* of Apuleius', *Cahiers Élisabéthains*, 21 (1982), 27–33.

[20] 'Why an Ass? Cesare Ripa's *Iconologia* as a Source for Bottom's Transformation', *Shakespeare Quarterly*, 32 (1981), 357–9.

scene in *The Winter's Tale*,[21] which Brian Gibbons has already summarized (p. 167). Professor Barkan scrupulously points out that there is no evidence that Shakespeare had ever heard of Michelangelo, so it may be worth drawing his attention to Webster's line, 'That cardinal hath made more bad faces with his oppression than ever Michael Angelo made good ones' (*Duchess of Malfi*, 3.3.51–2), which implies at least a general name-dropping familiarity with the artist.

The April 1982 edition of *Notes and Queries* included the usual collection of notes on possible sources. Apart from those already mentioned, the most convincing, I thought, were Jacqueline Pearson's 'The Influence of *King Leir* on Shakespeare's *Richard II*' (pp. 113–15), which draws attention to parallels of staging as well as language, and M. R. Woodhead's discovery of another parallel between Montaigne and *The Tempest* (p. 126). J. J. M. Tobin tries to link Nashe's *Summer's Last Will and Testament* with the references to summer and winter in Richard III's opening soliloquy (pp. 112–13). Other scholars offer parallels from Chaucer, Wilson's *Three Ladies of London*, the Geneva Bible, and Biblical commentaries,[22] and Margaret Hotine moves into the area of study pioneered by R. Chris Hassel, pointing out that *Measure for Measure* and *King Lear* were both 'Plays for St. Stephen's Day', on which the Old Testament readings deal with such topics as the nature of the bad ruler and the threat of madness (pp. 119–21).

Hugh Richmond's *Puritans and Libertines, Anglo-French Literary Relations in the Reformation*,[23] is an ambitious if uneven study of a fascinating topic, and a reminder that the Protestant movement in France counted for much more than, with hindsight, one tends to think. Professor Richmond's least convincing claim is for the influence of the *Heptameron* on Shakespeare's Sonnets; and he is generally inclined to turn general influences into specific sources. But his study of *Love's Labour's Lost* (some of which has already appeared in the *Huntington Library Quarterly* of 1979) provides interesting information both on the Elizabethan idealization of Henry of Navarre and on the Mata Hari role of the maids of honour of his Catholic antagonist, Catherine de Medici. His larger argument, that Shakespeare's witty ladies and their witty courtships derive from a French model (already visible in the fascination exerted by the French-educated Anne Boleyn), seems to me unprovable. A curious aspect of the book is that its highly speculative content is presented with a lot of unnecessary quotation from secondary sources, where a paraphrase would usually be neater and shorter. It is as if his pursuit of other people's sources and influences had made Professor Richmond determined to allow absolutely no doubt about his own.

The value of source study is normally taken for granted rather than discussed, yet it is likely that only one person ever benefits from it: the scholar who actually sees a spark leap from one work to another. It is an experience whose excitement is incapable of communication, and what survives is only the bare footnote. Howard C. Cole's *The All's Well Story from Boccaccio to Shakespeare* does at any rate consider the implications of the assumption that it *must* be useful to read all available versions of a story used by Shakespeare.[24] Arguing that one should look at what each writer did to his material rather than simply at what Shakespeare happened to take from it, he pays sympathetic attention to writers representing a wide variety of approaches to the Helena–Bertram situation, and thus is able to show that there is more behind *All's Well That Ends Well* than simply a 'fairy tale convention'. His own interpretation, which is developed only sketchily, takes the title to be ironic. Bertram's marriage is seen as a highly topical example of the abuse of the Court of Wards, and Helena's apparent gentleness as destructive and self-seeking: he notes the double-edged quality of 'Ah, what sharp stings are in her mildest words!' There is some suggestion here of a

---

21 'Living Sculpture: Ovid, Michelangelo, and *The Winter's Tale*', *ELH*, 48 (1981), 639–67.

22 R. A. L. Burnet, 'Some Chaucerian Echoes in *The Merchant of Venice*?' (pp. 115–16); J. A. B. Somerset. '*As You Like It*, III.iii.10–13, and *King Lear*, II.iv.125: Analogues from Robert Wilson's *Three Ladies of London*' (pp. 116–18); R. A. L. Burnet, 'Shakespeare and the First Seven Chapters of the Genevan Job' (pp. 127–8); R. A. L. Burnet, 'A Further Echo of Gilby's 'Commentary on Micah'' in *Macbeth*' (pp. 123–4).

23 University of California Press, Berkeley, Los Angeles, and London, 1981.

24 University of Illinois Press, Urbana and London, 1981.

resemblance between Helena and the Shakespeare that Professor Honigmann thinks he can detect in the Sonnets and elsewhere – both gentle and grasping. But the ambiguity seems to me inherent in the whole concept of self-sacrificing devotion, especially when it turns out to be rewarded after all. Ironically, Professor Cole's source study ends up becoming an argument against source study. His view of All's Well will stand or fall for most readers, not because of anything he shows about earlier treatments of the story, but according to whether it corresponds with their own sense of the play.

Matters of principle also arise in connection with two articles on The Rape of Lucrece, both in answer to Roy Battenhouse and Don Cameron Allen, who use Augustine's condemnation of Lucretia's suicide as evidence for an ironic reading of Shakespeare's poem. A. Robin Bowers attempts to counter this argument by putting Augustine's remarks into context and then by looking at other Renaissance depictions of the heroine in art and literature.[25] Richard Levin refuses to fight on this ground.[26] Listing and quoting all available contemporary references to Lucretia, some of which seem to be specifically about Shakespeare's poem, he shows clearly enough that, whatever they thought about Augustine's argument, Renaissance readers *were* sympathetic to Shakespeare's Lucrece. What his quotations also show is that the context in which most readers saw the poem was that which Shakespeare had already provided by the writing of its companion-piece, Venus and Adonis.

Since few of Shakespeare's works inspired so many contemporary references as his narrative poems, it is rarely possible to turn one's back on other contexts so completely as Professor Levin does. But it is difficult to balance response to the individual text with awareness of its infinite links with other things. An example of one type of over-emphasis is Alice-Lyle Scoufos, 'The Paradiso Terrestre and the Testing of Love in As You Like It',[27] in which Jaques's final exit is seen as a return to Plato's cave because he cannot face the light of love; the Platonic and Neoplatonic analogues do not so much illuminate the play as replace it altogether. On the other hand, Sister Corona Sharp's 'Caliban: the Primitive Man's Evolution', though it starts from the current debate as to whether American Indians were

human or subhuman, soon develops into a rewriting of the play from Caliban's point of view, something which she could have done equally well without this scholarly preface.[28]

A context which has attracted a number of writers is that of the dramatic tradition before 1576. James A. Reynolds's *Repentance and Retribution in Early English Drama*[29] starts from a premise which he never properly justifies: that the post-Reformation church preached mercy but the stage preached retribution instead. The plays discussed here are an odd assortment: Faustus, Richard II, The Massacre at Paris, and Webster's two best-known tragedies. Professor Reynolds is at his most useful when he points out echoes of the Justice vs. Mercy debate in isolated episodes like the scenes with the Old Man in Faustus and the pardoning of Aumerle in Richard II, but the approach is essentially reductive and, when it tries to encompass the whole of Webster's plays, totally inadequate. John W. Velz relates the dramaturgy of medieval conversion plays – a journey between two settings, with a neutral space between them in which the change of heart happens – to what might be called Shakespeare's conversion plays.[30] The neutral space is the forest in As You Like It, and the island in The Tempest, half-way between Carthage and Italy, recalls both Aeneas's journey and St Paul's. Mathew Winston looks at the implications of treating Lucio in Measure for Measure as a Vice.[31] These turn out to be extremely awkward, since the Duke ends up playing the roles of both Equity and Everyman, and the analogy becomes too general to be useful. Marjorie Garber's wide-ranging discussion of Memento Mori

[25] 'Iconography and Rhetoric in Shakespeare's *Lucrece*', *Shakespeare Studies*, 14 (1981), 1–21.

[26] 'The Ironic Reading of "The Rape of Lucrece" and the Problem of External Evidence', *Shakespeare Survey 34* (Cambridge University Press, 1981), pp. 84–192.

[27] *Shakespeare Studies*, 14 (1981), 215–27.

[28] *Ibid.*, pp. 267–83.

[29] Salzburg Studies in English 96, Salzburg, 1982.

[30] 'From Jerusalem to Damascus: Biblical Dramaturgy in Medieval and Shakespearian Conversion Plays', *Comparative Drama*, 15 (1981–2), 311–26.

[31] '"Craft Against Vice": Morality Play Elements in *Measure for Measure*', *Shakespeare Studies*, 14 (1981), 229–48.

elements in Shakespeare takes in stage effects (like the presence of a dead body on stage), the use of death figures like Mercade, and the ways in which the plays remind us that in the midst of life we are in death – and vice versa.[32]

As Gāmini Salgādo pointed out last year, Anne Barton's article on 'The King in Disguise' seems to have inaugurated a new and attractive approach to the history plays in the light of romance. Joanne Altieri's 'Romance in *Henry V*' suggests that the darker, Machiavellian side of the play, so often emphasized recently, coexists somewhat uneasily with a structure which is basically romantic: war, like the green world of the comedies, sorts out the problems of the court; Henry not only plays the role of the tongue-tied suitor but also, in his discovery of the traitors, anticipates Vincentio and Prospero.[33]

On the other hand, David Evett's 'Types of King David in Shakespeare's Lancastrian Tetralogy' leads him to such unlikely figures as Shallow's servant Davy and Davy Gam, Esquire, while Absalom is identified first with Richard II and then with Hotspur.[34] Shakespeare does indeed play around with Biblical allusions, and his characters frequently pun on one another's names; the trouble is not that this sort of evidence can't be found, but that there is too much of it. A researcher would get equally good results if he decided to look for types of John the Beloved Disciple (Falstaff and Prince John, for a start) or of Peter (who, significantly, is asked to 'stay at the gate' in *Romeo and Juliet*).

A final sign of Shakespeare's (and our) 'Times' can be seen in a number of studies of the androgyne. In addition to those already mentioned by Brian Gibbons, there is one by Robert Kimbrough, who distinguishes androgyny, which he defines as psychic wholeness, from the bisexuality of the hermaphrodite.[35] Apparently, Shakespeare wanted to 'bring home to the audience that androgyny has no necessary connection with any particular sexual orientation'. It's wonderful how many helpful messages Shakespeare left for posterity; one only wishes that he had expressed this one a bit more clearly, so that we could have had it earlier.

Some of this year's most exciting work is being done on Shakespeare's stage. The work is manual as

well as verbal: you can almost hear the hammering when you read *The Third Globe*,[36] a collection of the papers given at a 1979 symposium where scholars and practical theatre people pooled their resources as they prepared to build a replica of the second Globe in, of all places, Detroit. Unlike most such collections, this one actually conveys something of the excitement of the occasion. Extracts from the discussion, included in an appendix, are especially enjoyable ('Can we say how wide the stage pillars would have to be?'; 'I like the idea of the background being painted to represent stone'; 'The engineering department would tell you...').

The papers themselves include both specialized studies of Renaissance theatre (Herbert Berry on the legal documents relating to the Globe's owners and shareholders, Richard Hosley and John Orrell on the evidence provided by Hollar and contemporary surveyors' methods, Stuart Rigold on the carpenter's viewpoint, John Ronayne on 'Decorative and Mechanical Effects' for which his model is the Teatro Olympico) and more general discussions of the project from a theatrical point of view (John Russell Brown speaking from his experience at the National Theatre, Glynne Wickham warning against allowing speculation to harden into bricks-and-mortar certainty, Bernard Beckerman on Elizabethan staging, and C. Walter Hodges, whose enthusiasm seems to permeate the whole book, on the intellectual defensibility of reconstruction). W. M. H. Hummelen's paper on the Dutch Rhetoricians' Theatre is somewhat tangential to the discussion, except in so far as it constitutes an argument for an inner stage, but it is valuable in its own right, supplementing Kernodle s *From Art to Theatre* and reminding one how little work has been done on this topic.

[32] '"Remember Me"': *Memento Mori* Figures in Shakespeare's Plays', *Renaissance Drama*, NS 12 (1981), 3–25.

[33] *Studies in English Literature*, 21 (1981), 223–40.

[34] *Shakespeare Studies*, 14 (1981), 139–61.

[35] 'Androgyny Seen Through Shakespeare's Disguise', *Shakespeare Quarterly*, 33 (1982), 17–33.

[36] *Symposium for the Reconstruction of the Globe Playhouse*, Wayne State University, 1979, ed. C. Walter Hodges, S. Schoenbaum, and Leonard Leone (Wayne State University Press, Detroit, 1981).

Things have moved on since the 1979 symposium: Berry has published more work on the legal documents connected with the Globe;[37] Orrell's work on the methods of Elizabethan surveyors has been challenged by John Cranford Adams;[38] Hodges no longer proposes building a stage without supporting pillars.[39] Moreover, a similar, English project is now underway. Whereas the American Globe will have central heating, air-conditioning, a concealed sprinkler system, and a glass roof on which the rain can beat down, the English one, characteristically, is going to make a virtue of its absolutely authentic discomfort. It will thus re-create the conditions which prevented John Chamberlain from getting to *A Game at Chess* in 1624 because he wasn't well enough to arrive several hours early and squeeze in with the rest of the crowd. At least, the eminent scholars involved in both projects recognize the potential absurdity of their aim: re-creating Merrie England is no longer something we can take seriously. And the scheme has already justified itself by the publication of *The Third Globe*, a beautifully produced volume which every library should have.

Two new pieces of work on the Elizabethan-Jacobean stage will be of interest to the Third Globe planners. John B. Gleason puts the De Witt sketch into context.[40] In view of the debate over its reliability, it is useful to know that both De Witt and his friend Van Buchel, who copied the drawing, had some artistic talent. Gleason thinks that the two men thought of the Swan in classical terms because of the influence of Lipsius's *De Amphiteatro*, and that some puzzling features of the drawing result from De Witt's desire to represent several things simultaneously while taking others (such as the presence of an audience) for granted. Maria Jansson Cole has found 'A New Account of the Burning of the Globe', in a letter which corroborates the date of the fire (29 June 1613) and describes *All is True* as having been acted 'not passing 2 or 3 times before'.[41] I am not sure about one of her inferences; the fact that a child was rescued from the fire could mean, as she suggests, that the audience included children, but the child might also have been a member of the company.

The composition of audiences at the Globe and other public playhouses is the subject of Ann Jennalie

Cook's *The Privileged Playgoers of Shakespeare's London, 1576–1642*, whose references in fact include performances both before and after London became 'Shakespeare's'.[42] Her argument is that his audience did not represent a cross-section of the London population, still less of the country as a whole, but only that relatively small proportion of it who had enough money and leisure to go to the playhouses. The book is heavily documented and provides a lot of information about Londoners' wages, hours of work, leisure pursuits, and behaviour in the playhouses – much of which seems to have justified the complaints of the anti-theatre faction. Even if the public theatre audience was not after all like the mob in *Savonarola Brown* ('a vast seething crowd that is drawn entirely from the lower orders . . . Cobblers predominate'), there must have been greater differences between it and that of the private theatres than Professor Cook allows for. After all, the private theatres held fewer people and cost more.

Perhaps W. Reavley Gair's forthcoming book on the Children of Paul's will throw more light on this question. Meanwhile, Michael Shapiro has attacked Professor Gair's earlier publications about them, arguing that there is no real evidence about their playhouse's location, appearance or clientele.[43] He thinks that it was 'a small banqueting hall fitted out as a theatre, in which a chorister troupe led and directed chiefly by its choirmaster performed plays on a commercial basis'. In another article, Professor Shapiro offers an approach to *Antony and Cleopatra* in the light of the 'pathetic heroine' plays of the children's companies.[44] Though I can't see much

[37] 'The Globe, Its Shareholders, and Sir Matthew Brand', *Shakespeare Quarterly*, 32 (1981), 339–51.
[38] 'How Large Was the Globe Playhouse?', *Shakespeare Quarterly*, 33 (1982), 93–4.
[39] Paper given at the International Shakespeare Conference, Stratford-upon-Avon, 23 August 1982.
[40] 'The Dutch Humanist Origins of the De Witt Drawing of the Swan Theatre', *Shakespeare Quarterly*, 32 (1981), 324–38.   [41] *Ibid.*, p. 352.
[42] Princeton University Press, 1981.
[43] 'The Children of Paul's and Their Playhouse', *Theatre Notebook*, 36 (1982), 3–13.
[44] 'Boying Her Greatness: Shakespeare's Use of Coterie Drama in *Antony and Cleopatra*', *Modern Language Review*, 77 (1982), 1–15.

resemblance between Shakespeare's Cleopatra and any of the heroines discussed here, there may be something in the suggestion that the play uses Cleopatra's self-dramatization to invite our admiration for the boy actor's artistry.

A promising field of study is the use of rhetoric and other specifically oral techniques in Shakespearian drama. In 'Shakespeare's Oral Text', Marion Trousdale compares the dramatic use of pattern and repetition with the formulaic devices of oral epic.[45] Her examples are strikingly different from the image patterns so often pointed out, which might well be perceptible only to the critical reader. Coburn Freer's *The Poetics of Jacobean Drama* is a more ambitious attempt at coming to terms with the concept of oral poetry.[46] Drawing his evidence from lines like 'Nay, then, God buy you, and you talk in blank verse', and from the fact that schoolboys were trained in Latin verse composition, Professor Freer maintains that 'It must not have been uncommon to see poets and scholars in the audience, listening critically to the meter of every line.' When he goes on to look at the poetic language of various plays, especially *Cymbeline*, however, he seems frequently to be tone-deaf himself. Take, for instance, his comment on Imogen's reading of Ovid: 'A master's stroke, that: the Elizabethan best-seller has put the heroine to sleep at the very height of the narrative. It is a fine satiric touch that leads nowhere.' Still, the book is entertaining; it is better on Webster than on Shakespeare; and it explores some interesting territory, if with a somewhat unreliable compass.

Articles on staging include a good one by Robert R. Hellenga on 'Elizabethan Dramatic Conventions and Elizabethan Reality',[47] which supplements G. K. Hunter's 'Flatcaps and Bluecoats' in *Essays and Studies*, 33 (1980). Its point is that what we call conventions of character in Elizabethan drama are no more conventional than our own assumption that there is such a thing as an inner core of personal identity. Ralph Berry discusses the way in which an audience could be asked to imagine the stage itself as the set of a play: a ship in *Pericles* and *The Tempest*, a promontory, the cliff at Dover.[48] His most interesting suggestion is that, at the end of *The Tempest*, the audience's 'breath' and 'hands' are meant to transform it, imaginatively, from an island back into a ship.

Two articles on stage lighting by R. B. Graves provided a useful correction to my too-simple assumptions about the contrast between the daylight at the public theatres and the candlelit stage of the private theatres.[49] Pointing out that both types of theatre gave afternoon performances, and that the age's preference was for indirect, even lighting, he maintains that most performances apart from 'Nocturnals' and those given at night relied chiefly on daylight, supplemented with candles. Paradoxically, the night scenes for which extra lights were brought on stage would have been better lit than those that were supposed to take place by day – unless the candles and lanterns were merely symbolic and left unlit. Annette Drew-Bear writes on 'Face Painting in Renaissance Tragedy', with particular attention to its symbolic implications like the appearance of spots indicating sin or poison.[50] It seems possible that face painting and masks were more widely used than is usually assumed. A vast amount of evidence about their use in medieval and Renaissance drama has been compiled by Meg Twycross and Sarah Carpenter in *Medieval English Theatre*, 3 (1981) and 4 (1982).

On post-1642 stagings of Shakespeare, there is little to report. H. W. Pedicord, with the aid of a newly-discovered Garrick prompt-book of 1756, is able to show that Garrick's replacements of Tate's lines in *Lear* by Shakespeare's were much less extensive than those of Spranger Barry or George Colman.[51] Jan Macdonald gives an account of Poel's production of *The Taming of the Shrew* in 1913.[52] It managed to

---

45 *Renaissance Drama*, 12 (1981), 95–115.
46 Johns Hopkins Press, Baltimore and London, 1981.
47 *Renaissance Drama*, 12 (1981), 27–49.
48 'Metamorphoses of the Stage', *Shakespeare Quarterly*, 33 (1982), 5–16.
49 'Elizabethan Lighting Effects', *Renaissance Drama*, 12 (1981), 51–69; 'Daylight in the Elizabethan Private Theatres', *Shakespeare Quarterly* 33 (1982), pp. 80–92.
50 *Renaissance Drama*, 12 (1981), 71–93.
51 'Shakespeare, Tate, and Garrick: New Light on Alterations of *King Lear*', *Theatre Notebook*, 36 (1982), 14–21.
52 '"An Unholy Alliance": William Poel, Martin Harvey and *The Taming of the Shrew*', ibid., 64–72.

offend no one, probably because Petruchio was played by Martin Harvey, who regarded him as 'the greatest gentleman Shakespeare ever drew'. Volume 9 of *Nineteenth-Century Theatre Research* (1981) consists of two articles on Shakespearian productions. Edith Holding describes the *Love's Labour's Lost* of Madame Vestris, whose final pageant seems to have been its only successful feature'[53] and Ralph Berry defends the

pageantry of Herbert Beerbohm Tree's productions: he points out, for instance, that those notorious rabbits in *A Midsummer Night's Dream* were *meant* to be funny.[54] What a relief!

---

[53] 'Revels, Dances, Masques, and Merry Hours: Madame Vestris's Revival of *Love's Labour's Lost*, 1839', pp. 1–22.
[54] 'The Aesthetics of Beerbohm Tree's Shakespeare Festivals', pp. 23–51.

3 TEXTUAL STUDIES
reviewed by GEORGE WALTON WILLIAMS

Of the eight editions and the many studies to come before this review this year, the crowning achievement is Professor Harold Jenkins's monumental and magisterial edition of *Hamlet* for the new Arden Shakespeare.[1] There is every likelihood also that this edition will prove to be the crown of the entire series. The edition is 592 pages in length – by far the largest of the series. The single element that occasions this substance is the section of 'Longer Notes'. We must be grateful to the publishers for having accepted the proposition that *Hamlet* could not fully be edited without these Notes – 150 pages of detailed and thoughtful analysis of the specific problems in the play. On most of them Jenkins finds ways to surprise with the unexpected simplicity and cogency of his argument. At the other end of the volume the Introduction offers another 159 pages, treasure troves of fresh ideas.

Among many valuable insights one may notice in the Longer Notes Jenkins's treatment of Ophelia and of her two 'fathers' – the fishmonger (2.2.171–2) and Jephthah (2.2.398–9). Jenkins explains for the benefit of directors that Polonius's precepts are not funny (1.3); he argues that Horatio and Marcellus swear three times on Hamlet's sword (1.5) – pointing out that three different oaths are proposed to them by Hamlet; he declares that the 'nunnery' (3.1) 'for Ophelia is a sanctuary from...the world's contamination' (p. 496), yet he admits that Hamlet's iteration of the word does not rule out the possibility of

ambiguity; he justifies Hamlet's 'more horrid hent' in postponing the death of Claudius (3.3): 'the convention enables revenge to be shown in its most repulsive aspect' (p. 515); and he sees Hamlet's apology to Laertes (5.2) as representing the fact that Hamlet 'wrongs Laertes not by "a purpos'd evil" but "when he's not himself"' (p. 567).

He is very clear that the play presents Gertrude as having been unfaithful to her first husband while he lived, basing his conviction on the ghost's description of her as 'seeming virtuous' and of Claudius as 'adulterate'. 'To suppose otherwise is to ... lose the force of the implied contrast with love that was faithful to marriage-vows (ll. 48–50), and leave ll. 55–7 without point. Moreover, l. 105 suggests that Hamlet ... had received from the Ghost some new revelation of his mother's wickedness' (p. 456). If – to borrow a phrase from Philip Edwards – Gertrude's 'hospitable loins' had indeed entertained Claudius, we may ask why Old Hamlet had taken no action to correct his wife. We are not to think that he, too, was content to prey on garbage? Or are we to suppose that he discovered her infidelity only after his death?

In matters of staging, the Notes are equally interesting; Jenkins discusses the two pictures that

---

[1] The new Arden editions here reviewed are published by Methuen (London and New York, 1981, 1982); the New Penguin volumes by Penguin Books (Harmondsworth, 1981, 1982).

Hamlet shows Gertrude (3.4), Ophelia's distribution of flowers (4.5), and the exchange of rapiers (5.2); he emphasizes the fact that the action is continuous between act 3 and act 4 (yet he nevertheless retains the traditional act division at that point).

The edition is not marked by any extraordinary new readings, but five relocations of commas catch us up with surprise, requiring fresh analysis:

Hamlet, of the appearance of the Ghost (1.2.230):

What look'd he, frowningly?

Hamlet, to Ophelia (3.1.121–2):

Why, wouldst thou be a breeder of sinners?

Hamlet, contemplating the skulls (5.1.95–6, 198–9):

Why, may that not be the skull of a lawyer?

Why, may not imagination trace the noble dust of Alexander...?

For the first of these Jenkins identifies the initial monosyllable as 'not an exclamation.... Hamlet is ... introducing a new question' (p. 195); he interprets 'what' as meaning 'how'. For the next three, Jenkins identifies the initial monosyllable as 'not part of the question, ... but an interjection' (p. 387), a justification brief but suggestive for these three. Perhaps we may call the form a trick of Hamlet's speech. The fifth of this series seems less convincing:

Hamlet, in response to Claudius (3.2.232–3):

The Mousetrap – marry, how tropically!

Jenkins sees this punctuation as 'Hamlet's delighted exclamation at his own conceit.... There is no point in ... making *how* a question and *tropically* the answer to it' (p. 302).

In the stage direction concluding act 3, the Folio and all editors read: '*Exit Hamlet tugging in Polonius*'. Jenkins reads '*lugging in*', basing his emendation on Hamlet's statement 'I'll lug the guts' (3.4.212). He sees the Folio text as 'an editorial addition deriving, via a misprint, from the dialogue' (p. 333). This argument may not persuade all critics.

The Introduction is a beautiful piece of work with excellent sections on 'Delay', 'Ophelia', 'Revenge', and 'The final act'. In 'The central act' – that is 3.1 to 4.4 – Jenkins argues that 'at the centre of all, with the

nutshell truths inside it, is the play-within-the-play which re-enacts the murder' (pp. 140–1); one might quibble with the definition of what is the centre of the centre, for though the *Murder of Gonzago* is probably the symbolic centre of the play, to some critics 'The Murder of Polonius' – that other play-within-the-play which also re-enacts the killing of a king – is the critical point. That scene is, as Jenkins recognizes, the event that initiates the 'second revenge action'; it thus becomes the central action in the narrative. In discussing 'The second revenge', Jenkins aptly contrasts the violence of Laertes and Fortinbras; these foils to Hamlet stand at the extremes of action: Laertes fails because he is militant, Fortinbras succeeds because he is military.

Harold Jenkins's *Hamlet* is a noble achievement. It sets standards for the Arden series and for all editors. One cannot praise too highly the attention to detail, the largeness of scope, or the elegance of style. The volume is both a challenge and a guide to the profession.[2]

Of even greater length is the three-volume edition of *Henry VI* by Norman Sanders in the New Penguin edition – some 850 pages for the three volumes. The editing of these three long plays – though the 'Account of the Text' offers roughly the same material for both Part 2 and Part 3 – is, like the editing of *Hamlet*, massive. It may be remembered that J. Dover Wilson (and the Pelican Shakespeare) combined Parts 2 and 3 for discussion in a single Introduction; Sanders has provided a separate Introduction for each part. Each Introduction builds on the reader's knowledge of the preceding Parts, but only the last demands significantly an awareness of its successor play. It is commendable that Sanders has managed to keep these Introductions separate and, at the same time, contributory to the whole.

2 Another *Hamlet* item: Glen D. Hunter's 'Shakespeare's *Hamlet*: A Comprehensive Bibliography of Editions and Paraphrases in English 1876–1981', *Bulletin of Bibliography*, 38 (1981), 157–72. Hunter lists some 350 separate-volume editions published since the Furness Variorum of 1877, providing comments on some of them. His list will be most useful to those attempting to locate paraphrases, condensed versions, or versions in simplified modern English which are often omitted from 'scholarly' bibliographies.

In the Introduction to Part 2 we have the statement of the necessity of order in the kingdom and the fulfilling of that need in the figure of Duke Humphrey, the standard by which the other characters are judged. That the figure of that symbol is toppled is hardly surprising when we consider the way the warring nobles harvest the 'bitter fruits' (p. 35) in the garden of Part 1. In Part 3, as Sanders points out, the absence of a 'clearly articulated shaping of the action' bespeaks the 'erosion of all values that people have traditionally shored up against the encroachment of chaos in public life' (p. 9). Again in Part 2, Sanders cites the exposure of 'Saunder, ... the lying'st knave in Christendom' (2.1.126–7), as an indication of Duke Humphrey's 'shrewdness in the application of the law and the pursuit of truth' (p. 11), yet he observes that even the good Duke, failing to apply his own instruction to himself, cannot frustrate 'the awful energy of unscrupulous self-interest' (p. 24) intent on destroying him, the same urgency of destruction that moves the Duke of York in Ireland and Jack Cade on Blackheath who meets 'a suitably symbolic end' (p. 37) in Iden's Kentish garden. Cade's threats, York's threats, Clifford's threats are frightening because they constitute 'that human capacity to translate the political into terms of the individual which the play [Part 2] has shown to be the source of chaos and self-perpetuating strife' (p. 39).

The Introduction to Part 1 begins with a statement that, to the Elizabethan, history was 'neither an academic exercise nor an indulgence of antiquarian tastes: it had an awesome relevance' (p. 7), and it concludes with an analysis of the playwright's approach to a history play – 'a piece of shaped incompleteness ... dramatized in the full knowledge of prior event and sequent outcome', as Sir Walter Raleigh said, 'a pleasing analysis' (p. 38). In the Introduction to Part 3 Sanders explains the techniques the poet uses to shape that analysis: patterned imagery and character development. Part 3 is clearly an early expression of Shakespeare's particular skill in joining these two techniques so that a 'dense poetic texture ... works with ... the actions of the characters' (p. 33). As it emerges in Part 3, the character of Richard is supported by the imagery of 'acted savagery' (p. 33) and cannibalism. Richard becomes in his own play the personification of Ulysses' progress – power, will, appetite, the universal wolf – and last eats up himself and his England. Richmond gives him his quietus, praying that those who are treasonous to England's peace may 'not live to taste this land's increase' (5.5.38). Sanders has brought his reader through the ravages of the Wars of the Roses with unusual clarity and sureness.

It appears that in Parts 2 and 3, Sanders has advanced no new readings; in Part 1 he has proposed two. The more interesting of these involves the reassignment of a speech prefix at 5.2.16–18. All editors follow Folio in giving lines 16 and 17 to Burgundy:

Bur. I trust the Ghost of *Talbot* is not there: 16
Now he is gone my Lord, you neede not feare. 17
Pucel. Of all base passions, Feare is most accurst. 18

Sanders is admirably correct in recognizing that, as line 17 answers line 16, it requires another speaker. Two solutions occur that involve a single change only: either the prefix '*Bur.*' should be one line lower so that line 16 (continued to Charles) is answered by Burgundy with line 17; or the prefix '*Pucel.*' should be one line higher so that line 16 (spoken by Burgundy) is answered by Pucelle with line 17. Sanders has 'preferred the first of these because (a) both Burgundy and Pucelle seem intent on bolstering the Dauphin's confidence; (b) Pucelle's *Charles* in line 19 is more typical of her manner of blunt speech than the *my lord* in line 17' (p. 225). This reviewer prefers the second because (a) Burgundy says nothing in this scene beside this single line 17 to bolster the Dauphin's confidence, and it is therefore not inappropriate for him to express his own uneasiness at the presence 'of the ghost of the man he has betrayed' (p. 225), which Pucelle rebukes as a means of bolstering the Dauphin's confidence as she continues to do in lines 18–20; (b) the nobles do not address Charles as 'my lord' (with the single exception of Reignier, himself a king – 1.2.124, 2.1.66, 5.4.155), but Pucelle does indeed bluntly address Burgundy as 'thou wandering lord' (3.3.76).

The second emendation is less significant. Folio reads '*la pouure gens*' (3.2.14). Most editors correct and modernize 'pouure' to 'pauvre' and delete the article, recognizing that 'gens' (in modern French) is plural. Sanders has discovered that 'gens' 'was originally ...

the plural of "la gent"', and he has therefore emended to 'la pauvre gent' (p. 199). Cairncross (new Arden edition, p. 69) tells us that 'gens' as singular was 'a contemporary French form'. It seems unprofitable to spend much time in discussing the singular or plural of this French word when Shakespeare reveals a similar inexactness in the use of its English parallel in the next line, 'Poor market folks'.

This reviewer, however, cannot let pass without comment a refusal to emend in Part 1. The Folio consistently spells the name of the cowardly knight 'Falstaffe' and Sanders follows. Since the Chronicles consistently spell the name 'Fastolfe', it is almost certain that Shakespeare followed that spelling in his manuscript and highly probable that the name in the Folio is a later addition, deriving from the popularity of Prince Hal's fat friend. Surely it is evidence of some tinkering that the Folio spellings of this name are absolutely uniform while for other names 'there is a more than normal variation' (p. 239).[3]

Another refusal to emend is adroitly justified. In Part 3, the Folio stage direction 'on the Walles' (5.6.0.2) is usually rejected in favour of the bad Octavo reading 'in the Tower'. Sanders retains the Folio but lets it apply to the Lieutenant only; the result, faithful to the copy-text, produces a rather curious staging: Richard and Henry enter below (as they should, of course), the Lieutenant enters above 'on the walls', from which lofty position he is soon dismissed. The significance of the two levels in the staging, not evident in the dialogue, is not discussed by Sanders in the Commentary.

Sanders concludes the Introduction to Part 3 by leading directly to the concluding play of the tetralogy. The edition of *Richard III* by Antony Hammond for the Arden series carries on where Sanders in the New Penguin leaves off. Hammond effectively analyses the 'many thematic and historical connections between the *Henry* trilogy and *Richard III*': 'That Shakespeare wrote the plays in a single creative phase seems likely. . . . That they were performed as a cycle at the time cannot now be shown, though it seems likely enough' (pp. 116–17).

There are many virtues in Hammond's critical Introduction, but one may praise particularly the paragraphs on the theology, on the ritualism, and on the role-playing in the play. Of especial note is Hammond's long study of the text. Hammond concludes:

The evidence that Q originates in a memorial reconstruction has survived the challenges made against it. When allowance is made for compositorial corruption, the reconstruction appears extraordinarily good.[4] . . . Shakespeare could well have been among the people involved in this collective reconstruction. . ,. . Behind the actor's memories lies the prompt-book of the play, prepared from a fair copy probably written by Shakespeare himself, and preserving changes made by Shakespeare and the book-keeper to fit the play to the stage. . . . The F text is based on the collation of a manuscript which was probably the author's foul papers with a mixture of Q3 and Q6. Probably two collators were at work, one on the earlier quarto, and the other [on the later]. . . . The evidence that has been brought into play in an attempt to determine which quarto was used [as copy for the F] is so far inconclusive. . . . Nor is it certain that annotated Q was the form of copy supplied: against the probability of printed copy must be set some slight evidence that a manuscript transcript may have been made. . . . The F, being based as it seems on foul papers, misses a good deal [of the 'practical material' of Q], but because no memorial link is involved, it is generally a much more reliable guide to Shakespeare's text. (pp. 49, 48)

This complex conclusion is reached only after intense study, and it is surely one of the most sensitive to have been advanced; yet on two occasions Hammond speaks of the need for a complete investigation possible only through a computer (pp. 38, 39). It may be that for the final conclusion to this problem we must still await that exercise. Of a minor textual problem Hammond writes: 'It is all rather puzzling' (p. 15); the same observation may be applied to the whole.

Brian Morris's edition of *The Taming of the Shrew*

---

3 Editors who follow Folio in this spelling must explain to their readers that this Falstaff is not that Falstaff, who died before Henry VI came to the throne. Sanders's explanation is not wholly satisfactory, if it is not, indeed, somewhat misleading.

4 Hammond's analysis of the compositors of Q1 follows that of MacD. P. Jackson, reviewed below (p. 192).

for the new Arden treats a play as unlike *Richard III* in its early printing as can well be imagined. Though both plays appeared first in bad Quartos, the bad Quarto of *Richard III* is an unusually good bad Quarto; the bad Quarto associated with *The Taming of the Shrew* is so bad that some have thought it a different play. Both bad Quartos, however, bespeak the literary interest in Shakespeare's works at the beginning of his career as well as their theatrical popularity.

And just how early that beginning was, we are now coming to learn. Antony Hammond in *Richard* and Brian Morris in *Shrew* give extensive space to the problem of the dating of their plays. They both argue, surprisingly, for dates earlier than those we have been accustomed to assign to the plays: *Richard III* late in 1591 and *The Taming of the Shrew* in 1589. Since the editors have come to these dates only after the closest arguments, their conclusions carry weight; but the mysteries of the theatrical world in the early 1590s are great, and these dates will require careful evaluation. (In an article noticed on p. 173, Ann Thompson dates *The Shrew* 1591–2.)

Critics approach a new edition of *The Taming of the Shrew* to discover how the editor handles the problem of the bad Quarto of the play. For this reviewer, Morris has handled it perfectly. Following Richard Hosley, he makes it clear that *A Shrew* is a text derived with much confusion and innovation from *The Shrew* and that there is no *Ur-Shrew* to be considered. Hosley's challenge to 'find another dramatist, around 1593, capable of writing such a play' (p. 26) must remain unaccepted. Morris's early dating for *The Shrew* would push the date of a supposed *Ur-Shrew* back to 1590 at least and so render Hosley's argument even more telling.

The second major textual problem of *The Shrew* is the absence of an epilogue to conclude the business of Sly. In this matter, Morris follows Karl P. Wentersdorf's analysis of the ending of the play, agreeing that the exit and immediate re-entry required of Katherina and Petruchio in the Folio text can best be explained as the result of the omission of a Sly scene (which is, as it chances, preserved in the bad Quarto). Though Morris may not, of course, write the scene for Shakespeare or print the bad Quarto lines

in his edition, he includes them in the appendix. Here, at least, directors may find them. Wentersdorf had argued that demands on personnel were too great to permit the casting of the final Sly episodes, and Morris supports him vigorously.

A not unimportant consequence of the assumption of a Sly Epilogue is that it allows Sly to be a parallel figure to Katherina; both of them put on disguises in the play and take them off at the end. Morris sees this parallel in terms of bewilderment. Sly 'is perpetually bewildered, and in this he is the prefiguration of Katherina, who . . . is never allowed to be sure of her own nature until she surrenders to the character [that Petruchio] has created for her' (p. 135), i.e. her genuine self, just as Sly the 'supposed' Lord surrenders to become again Sly the real tinker.

We may note also Morris's observation in his section on sources of the shrew tradition that 'no one has discovered a version in which the tamer goes to work [as] . . . Petruchio does. Some beat their wives, and some trick them. Petruchio deliberately treats Katherina as if she were an untamed bird of prey, "mans" her, tames her, and makes her obedient by "killing her in her own humour". This would appear to be Shakespeare's original contribution to the shrew tradition. It is the treatment, and that alone, which has "no identifiable source"' (pp. 75–6). To have said so much is to have given us a valuable insight into the uniqueness and the peculiar Shakespearian quality of this play.

The proof of that taming lies in Kate's great speech at the end of the play, and another test of the quality of an edition is how the editor has faced the problem of the delivery of that speech. Kate's speech on order is one of the set speeches that Shakespeare gives on this topic, a topic he treats most significantly in the contemporary *Henry VI* plays, as we have noted, on the political level. Kate talks on order in the home, as does the Abbess in *The Comedy of Errors* (5.1.68–86). Lorenzo talks on order in music (*The Merchant of Venice*, 5.1.54–65), the Archbishop of Canterbury on order in the state (*Henry V*, 1.2.183–213), and Ulysses on order in the cosmos (*Troilus and Cressida*, 1.3.78–136); they all speak to the same point. And no matter what we may think of the character of the speaker or the context of his speech, the content is serious, earnest, and unexceptionable. That is clearly the view of Morris: 'the great final speech of *The Shrew* is a solemn affirmation of the great commonplace. . . . Shakespeare cannot possibly have intended it to be spoken ironically' (p. 146). He goes on, however, most shrewdly to speak positively and movingly of the last scene not as a test of love but as a statement of love. 'We . . . know from the last lines of V.i. that Katherina and Petruchio have made their peace' (p. 147) – 'it is *possible* to play [these] . . . lines as yet another example of Petruchio imposing his will on his unwilling wife, but to do so is to fly in the face of Shakespeare's obvious intention' (p. 286).[5] 'Act V, scene ii opens with a wit-bout in which Petruchio attacks the Widow and Katherina surreptitiously comes to his aid. The alliance between them is . . . another example of their developing trust. . . . When Grumio comes for her she obeys her husband's command, but it is no cowed, broken-spirited compliance, but a duty which she does and a gift which she offers freely. . . . With the stage-direction [5.2.98.1] "Enter Katherina" the test is over, . . . and the love relationship triumphs' (p. 147). The great speech itself is another such gift of love; 'I believe that any actor striving to represent Petruchio's feelings [at the end of that speech] should show him as perilously close to tears, tears of pride, and gratitude, and love' (p. 149).

To move from the textual tangles of the plays just noticed to the clean lines of *Much Ado About Nothing* is to breathe free breath.[6] A. R. Humphreys observes in his edition for the new Arden that, 'actually, Q's text is too good to require much emendation' (p. 81). For the most serious crux of the play – 'And sorrow, wagge,' (5.1.16) – Humphreys follows the received text (Capell's 'Bid sorrow wag'), but he lists some ten conjectures other editors have offered for this problem (another is mentioned below in this review). The critical sense of the Introduction is, however, at a high level. Caught up in the play's 'spirit of affluent gaiety' (p. 61), Humphreys notes that 'all is so fresh as to seem spontaneous and inevitable, yet nothing is casual or automatic' (p. 59). He demonstrates how the two lovers' plots interweave harmoniously and the watchmen's plot is deployed 'with an impeccable sense of timing' (p. 63). All this is true enough, but readers and viewers know there is more. 'Not every

strand is tightly tied up; some strands are not tied up at all' (p. 65). In dealing with the serious problem of Hero's chamber-window, Humphreys contributes several speeches of Lewis Carroll's verse that Hero or Beatrice[7] might have said. The speeches are charming, but they may not be admitted. Humphreys recognizes finally that Margaret's behaviour is inexplicable: 'Margaret was to be forgiven whatever folly she had committed, and with that we must rest content' (p. 67).

Much Ado is a play so eager to embrace gravity in its gaiety that it is very nearly thrown irretrievably off its balance. Humphreys's Introduction in effect follows that model; while dealing firmly and clearly with the dark side of the play, it lets the brightness shine through regularly and steadily. Humphreys points to the structural parallel between *Much Ado* and *The Merchant of Venice* in both of which the anguish of act 4, scene 1, deepens the tone of the comedy. The music of Belmont clears the air of the stratagems of Shylock in the one; in the other the music of Messina's pipers leads the dance that symbolizes matrimony and social communion (p. 218).

Not in life, no more in Shakespeare, does it always work so pleasingly. John Kerrigan's edition of *Love's*

---

[5] The key to Shakespeare's 'intention' must be the speech, 'Nay, I will give thee a kiss; now pray thee, love, stay' (5.1.133). In it, Kate makes precisely the request she had made earlier, 'Now, if you love me, stay' (3.2.200), but what a world of difference between the tones of the two requests! The word is 'love', used in act 3 of his love to her and in act 5 of her love to him. The second use is the first time that she has called him 'love', though he has called her 'love' several times. The actress who misses the significance of this word and of Kate's kiss has missed the play. Love has wrought this miracle (see 5.1.110).

[6] Another clarity in this play is the dating. Humphreys locates *Much Ado* comfortably 'in the latter part of 1598' (p. 4) before *As You Like It* (thereby correcting the sequence in the Pelican Shakespeare), *Julius Caesar*, and *Henry V* (in that order) in 1599. Harold Jenkins proposes to place *Hamlet* perhaps in the same year, certainly in 1600 (p. 13). If these plays are correctly dated, the year 1599 becomes a year of extraordinary productivity, probably Shakespeare's most productive year.

[7] Humphreys suggests that the name was 'in Elizabethan pronunciation *Bettris* or *Betteris*. Pronounced this latter way . . ., it pairs better with *Benedick* than *Be-a-trice* does' (p. 88).

Labour's Lost for the New Penguin series speaks movingly of the separation of the lovers. Kerrigan points out that the contest between Ver and Hiems, Spring and Winter, ends out of logical sequence with the foul ways of winter, parallel to the foul ending of the play. He encourages us that 'the owl and the cuckoo assure us that the labour of love will not be very long lost' (p. 36). But the time scheme is a twelvemonth and a day, and even though that is 'too long for a play' (5.2.866), it is not too long for life.

The most interesting aspect of Kerrigan's edition is his treatment of the Katharine–Rosaline textual tangle of 2.1.113–92.[8] Aside from the minor errors of misnaming of the Ladies, easily corrected, there is also in the Quarto the major confusion of Berowne's two flirtations. Kerrigan very rightly invokes the principle of first and second versions here, since, as none of the other Lords has any flirtation with his Lady, it does not seem appropriate that Berowne should have two flirtations with two Ladies, Katharine and Rosaline. Berowne's Lady is Rosaline; he may flirt with her only. (Such a restriction is based, of course, not on prudishness, but on the necessary balance of the play.) There needs to be dialogue while the King reads the letter (lines 113–27). Kerrigan has then, with some justice, excised the first flirtation (with Katharine) and transferred the second flirtation (with Rosaline) to its place. The procedure is not improper in this play which has several clear instances of just this sort of error requiring just this sort of correction. What are the consequences?[9] Kerrigan's version discards what is probably the more engaging encounter (who will prefer the humdrum 'Lady, I will commend you to mine own heart' to the joyous 'Did not I dance with you in Brabant once?'?), and adds a most awkward problem in staging which requires Dumaine to leave and re-enter simultaneously. (The staging problem can be solved by direction, but it is not Shakespeare's way to present us with such a problem. Though Berowne's situation at line 178 in the Quarto is similar, Berowne is a special character; Dumaine is not.)

The matter being serious, we must be grateful to Kerrigan for having honestly and boldly made the attempt to grapple seriously with it. We may draw two conclusions about the problem, neither of which

is attractive: Kerrigan has not solved the tangle by merely cutting the knot as the Worthy did; the text does not provide enough material for a solution. A correct text will require (1) one flirtation to cover the King's reading (lines 113–27); (2) an *exeunt* for the King and all his Lords (line 178) so that the Lords may make their surreptitious re-entries one by one (lines 193–213); (3) dialogue – presumably Boyet and the Princess – to take the place of lines 179–92 and to provide a space between the *exeunt* and the re-entries. The textual editor will find there can be no satisfactory solution; the director, forced to find a satisfactory solution, should (1) retain the text of the first flirtation and assign it to Rosaline and Berowne; (2) withdraw all the Lords; and (3) devise dialogue between Boyet and the Princess. Confronted with a difficult problem in *Much Ado*, as we noted above, Humphreys offered some of Carroll's blank verse to solve it. A clever director could engage Kerrigan to offer some of his.

Kerrigan's Introduction is imaginative and energetic; it is also startling. It tells us that the play is 'today celebrated as the first work of Shakespeare's genius' (p. 8). If this ambiguous phrase means that the play is the earliest work in which Shakespeare showed his full artistic power, it will gain incomplete assent; if it means other things, it will gain even less. Kerrigan's enthusiasm has betrayed him. Similarly, it carries him confidently through his dismissal of the theory of the 'school of night'. Though he may be correct in arguing that there is no reference to any specific coterie, he does his argument no kindness by explaining the passage 'Black is . . . the school of night' (4.3.250–1) with the gloss 'black is the school where

---

8 Kerrigan argues this matter at greater length in 'Shakespeare at Work: The Katharine–Rosaline Tangle in *Love's Labour's Lost*', *Review of English Studies*, 33 (1982), 129–36.

9 Kerrigan's article, '*Love's Labour's Lost* and Shakespearian Revision', *Shakespeare Quarterly*, appeared too late for consideration here; Paul Werstine has an essay forthcoming that argues convincingly that the 1598 Quarto is a reprint (in *Play-Texts in Old Spelling*, AMS Press, New York, 1982). Not available to Kerrigan was Andrew Sabol's publication of 'The french Kinges Maske' for lute in *Four Hundred Songs and Dances: Supplement I* (University Press of New England, Hanover and London, 1982), pp. 663, 679. Sabol believes it 'very likely' that this tune was used for the masque of Muscovites in act 5.

night learns to be black' – 'a strange circularity' (pp. 10, 9). His remarks on the inevitability of death are excellent; describing the entrance of Marcade (5.2.702.1), he recalls two memorable productions, one of which gave the impression at Marcade's entry that 'Death himself were taking shape among the vulnerable mortals' (p. 21). That good directors can produce this effect with clever lighting does not support the statement that 'Shakespeare has crafted V.2 in such a way that... Marcade's actual entry is not noticed' (p. 21). Kerrigan's remarks on the name of 'Marcade' point out its intense suggestiveness: the name is Marcadé (it requires three syllables in 5.2.703, the only time it is mentioned), it suggests 'mar Arcady', and 'Mercury', 'the god responsible for conducting souls to the underworld' (p. 232). Though the arrival of Marcade is not to many viewers 'the greatest shock in Shakespeare' (p. 20), that figure from the outside world darkly interrupting the joy of love's labours prepares us for the wintry song of that curiously merry owl.

Fredson Bowers takes the occasion of a response to Paul Werstine, whose uneasy concern for the validity of including modern editions in historical collations for old-spelling editions was published in *Analytical and Enumerative Bibliography* (1980), to provide a full *defensio* for the system of apparatus as used in the series of Beaumont and Fletcher volumes now being published by the Cambridge University Press. His article is notable in its clarifying of the differences that exist between the two views, but its significance lies in its careful explication of the philosophy behind the historical collation. The article goes far beyond the specific occasion; it is a new introduction – much amplified in its particulars – to the Beaumont and Fletcher series. It proposes one major variation in the traditional concept of an historical collation, suggesting a collation 'that would provide complete records of editions up to 1700 but would confine its records of modern editions to those in the major twentieth-century tradition ... [starting] with the Globe' (pp. 253–4). It may well be that this technique offers the solution to those practical problems in a 'complete' collation that produced Werstine's uneasiness.[10]

Paul Bertram's monograph *White Spaces In Shakespeare*, after tracing the editorial history of the printing of the text, addresses the phenomenon of 'white spaces' that appear when successive part-lines are successively indented.[11] Bertram's primary example is *Antony and Cleopatra*, 2.2.28–32, where ten words are divided among five speeches (p. 28). Since the time of Steevens, most editors (not Alexander) have considered this series of speeches as one line and have indented accordingly; the result is 'white space' with a diagonal of text dropping through it.[12] (Though there is as much white space when the part-lines are set flush left, Bertram takes offence only when the line of text slopes across the page.)

In dealing with this situation there are three choices before editors: they may print all such part lines flush left (as usual in the Folio); they may indent successively (as usual in editing); they may print all on the same line (as Ben Jonson did). It is clear that Jonson regarded part-lines as constituting a single line of verse. Though Jonson's style is not Shakespeare's, we would do well to follow the example of Jonson's Folio of 1616 in thinking of the verse line as one line.[13] That printing short speeches on successively indented lines does affect the 'continuous stream of subtle relationships between sound and sense that... impinge on the mind of any reader' (p. 71) may well be allowed, but it is not evident that printing short speeches on successively un-indented lines does not also produce a stream of subtle relationships. Indenting part-lines shows a reader that the short speeches make one line;

[10] 'The Historical Collation in an Old-spelling Shakespeare Edition: Another View', *Studies in Bibliography*, 35 (1982), 234–58; Werstine's article is reviewed in *Shakespeare Survey 35* (Cambridge University Press, 1982), p. 185.

[11] Paul Bertram, *White Spaces in Shakespeare* (Bellflower Press, Case Western Reserve University, Cleveland, Ohio, 1981).

[12] It is perhaps worthy of comment that Maynard Mack (whose Foreword to Bertram's volume supports Bertram's thesis) follows Steevens in printing this series of speeches on successive indentations (Pelican edition).

[13] This system is carefully followed with prefixes inserted in the verse line in Herford and Simpson's edition (Clarendon Press, Oxford, 1925–52); Steevens's system of indentation, however, is the method of the new edition revised by G. A. Wilkes (Clarendon Press, Oxford, 1979–81).

demonstrating that fact visibly on the page is an editorial task not negligible.

But the real test lies in the hearing, not in the seeing. In spite of a fairly long discussion of a comic passage, mostly in prose (*Tempest*, 2.2.54–154), Bertram fails to prove that actors' responses to indentation or non-indentation can be communicated to auditors. If his speech is indented in his script, an actor will know, at least, that he is sharing a line of verse; if it is not so indented, he will very likely not know, and his response may frustrate Shakespeare's intentions.

All will agree that it is essential to restore 'much of the original lineation and punctuation that was "improved" by the eighteenth-century editors in the interest of correctness' (p. 58), but not all will agree that it is then desirable to reprint the typography of the Folio without any editorial attention to metrics.[14]

The Textual Seminar at the annual session of the Shakespeare Association of America under the direction of Gary Taylor discussed Textual Evidence and Methodology; among many interesting papers one may be mentioned: Scott McMillin's 'revolutionary' argument that though Q1 is shorter than Q2 of *Hamlet* it requires more actors for performance than does Q2. The notion that Q1 is reduced to accommodate a travelling company of limited number is thus brought into question.

Michael Warren's pioneering statement on the two texts of *King Lear* was delivered in 1976. Since then larger and confirming studies by Steven Urkowitz, P. W. K. Stone, and Gary Taylor have been published. E. A. J. Honigmann reviews the validity of these studies and accepts their basic premise that there are two texts and that the reviser was Shakespeare.[15] He cites the reviser's 'awareness of the minutiae of characterization', 'a quite exceptional sensitivity to "background" plotting', 'the cleverness' with which additions are 'stitched into existing material', and 'the variety of the reviser's styles, all of them "Shakespearian" styles'. 'Who, other than Shakespeare, was capable of dramatic thinking at this level?' (p. 155). With this conclusion safely in hand, Honigmann turns in the second part of his article to 'the wider implications' – *Othello*. Here, by a pleasing parallel, Honigmann reviews the validity of three studies – Coghill's essay in *Shakespeare's Professional Skills*

(1964), Greg's comments in *The Shakespeare First Folio* (1955), and Honigmann's own observations in *The Stability of Shakespeare's Text* (1965) – and accepts their basic premise that there are two texts and that the reviser was Shakespeare. The parallelism continues, for the kinds of revision in *King Lear* are found also in *Othello*. In both plays 'metre, grammar or textual dislocations' indicate that Folio passages are later additions (not merely material omitted in the printing of the Quarto); in both plays 'strategies of revision . . . strengthen the play' in characterization (in Edgar, in Emilia) and in plotting (act 4 in *Lear*, act 1 in *Othello*); in both plays, the reviser sharpens the morality (in the Fool's speeches in *Lear*, in sexually specific references in *Othello*); in both plays the additions consist of short passages scattered through the plays (instead of long passages or complete scenes usually offered by non-authorial revisers). Honigmann has provided more than a shrewd analysis of *Othello*; he has offered a technique and a standard by which to judge the arguments for the two-text theory in *Henry VI* and in *Hamlet* and in many others that will no doubt be coming along. 'The fact that Shakespeare is thought to have re-touched not one but two of his greatest tragedies [perhaps it is significant that they are near-contemporary works], and to have strengthened both in similar (and unusual) ways, makes the "revision-theory" more compelling – and more exciting' (p. 171). Though he recommends caution, Honigmann's arguments provide sure ground for proceeding with confidence.

The two-text theory of *Lear* is to many critics not comforting. Keith Brown speaks his discomfort as he watches the editorial *Lear*, a perfectly constructed ship, doomed and sinking.[16] Still keeping his head

---

[14] Bertram here quotes James G. McManaway's annual review of 'Textual Studies' in *Shakespeare Survey 2* (Cambridge University Press, 1949), p. 150, but he is not sufficiently sensitive to McManaway's caution in making this observation: 'there will be disagreement about some of the details'.

[15] 'Shakespeare's Revised Plays: *King Lear* and *Othello*', *The Library*, 4 (1982), 142–73.

[16] 'Chimeras Dire? An Analysis of the "Conflated" *Lear* Text', *Cahiers Élisabéthains*, 20 (1981), pp. 71–83. Though the perceptions of this paper are literary rather than

above water, Brown provides a very careful analysis of the structure of the received text; it indicates, act by act, a system of almost exact contrasts and reflections centring precisely on Edgar, historically, as his name suggests, the 'heroic' figure of the play. Though he can sympathize with the despair of the traditionalist critic, this reviewer would offer a challenge – would throw out a life-preserver or two – suggesting that what is needed now is literary criticism clearly based on one text or another (and that means, of course, edited texts of each version). Let us find out what Brown's statistical analysis can tell us about the centrality of Edgar in the Q-*Lear* and in the F-*Lear*. Swimming in that direction brings us to dry ground.

A few technicalities may be mentioned here. After examining earlier counts of the number of exemplars of the third Quarto (1611) of *Titus Andronicus*, G. Harold Metz concludes that there are seventeen.[17] One of the copies that has been most difficult to trace is Metz's 1206a, now at Haverford College. This copy, sold at Sotheby's to Maggs in March 1906, was bought from Maggs by Dodd, Mead & Co. and later bought in October 1906 from Dodd by H. C. Folger. Perhaps Mr Folger sold it from his collection after he bought the Kemble–Devonshire copy (1199) in 1918. It becomes, thus, one of the very few quartos that Folger released from the collection that he was assembling as the Folger Shakespeare Library.

In a highly speculative paper, Robert F. Fleissner calls attention to the spacing of the Dedication of the Sonnets – 'M[r]. W. H. ALL. – as Thorpe's way of privately calling attention to the name 'Hall', which he was publicly attempting to conceal.[18] The Textual Reviewer is obliged to concede that the lineation of the dedication and the idiosyncratic use of periods are both very careful and that the em space (it is not technically a lacuna) between 'H.' and 'ALL.', unique on the page, calls attention to itself. Fortunately it is someone else's task to determine whether the embarrassing em is a clue to W. Hall's name or merely a device to signify the rhetorical pause after the introductory nomination and before the pre-posited direct object.

On surer typographical ground is Richard Levin's observation, made *en passant* in the article cited below (footnote 34), that the term 'turned letter' when applied as it commonly is to the *u/n* error is a misnomer. He makes the point that if letters were regularly turned, we should expect as many examples of the turning of other letters as we find of *u* and *n*. In fact, few letters are turned; the nick in the body of the type is designed to guard against just this specific error. It is more likely than not that the *u/n* error is an example of foul case (p. 61, n.3).

Important studies address the identification of the copy used in printing the Folio texts of *King Lear*, *Love's Labour's Lost*, and *Romeo and Juliet*. For *King Lear*, T. H. Howard-Hill examines the orthographical patterns of Compositors B and E and demonstrates that (a) the 'unusual' spellings in the Folio do not derive from the Quartos and that (b) the 'unusual' spellings in the Quartos do not reappear in the Folio.[19] He concludes, therefore, that neither of the Quartos was used as printer's copy for the Folio. Then 'in general fashion' (p. 22), he reconstructs the process by which Q1 press variants, Q2 orthography and accidentals, and manuscript substantives all find their way into the Folio text. 'The collator decided to make a current transcript of the prompt book, aided by Q2. . . . It is not inconceivable that he could . . . attempt a *concurrent collation and transcription*. [By such a process,] the scribe would produce the melange of forms which characterizes the Folio text' (p. 23). This argument, ingenious as it is persuasive, takes a giant step in solving the *Lear* mystery.

For *Love's Labour's Lost*, Stanley Wells concludes firmly that 'the Quarto from which the Folio was printed had been compared with a manuscript, and that this manuscript was one which presented the play in a form closer to that in which it was performed than the foul papers from which the Quarto was

---

textual, they are specific responses to a textual problem of first consequence.

[17] 'How Many Copies of *Titus Andronicus* Q3 are Extant?', *The Library*, 3 (1981), 336–40. ('Sotheby's' is misprinted 'Southeby's' (p. 337).) I am obliged to Miss Elizabeth Niemyer of the Folger Library for the provenance of the 'Folger' copy, 1206a.

[18] 'The Case of the Embarrassing Lacuna: A Textual Approach to the W. H. Mystery', *Res Publica Litterarum* (University of Kansas), 3 (1980), 17–27.

[19] 'The Problem of Manuscript Copy for Folio *King Lear*', *The Library*, 4 (1982), 1–24.

printed' (p. 146).[20] Wells is forced to argue that the agent preparing the Quarto was reprehensibly lazy, working thoroughly at the beginning and then giving the appearance of thoroughness at the end. He recognizes that it is not an attractive hypothesis, but it makes the pattern comprehensible. The thesis of consultation, of course, requires that 'all the Folio variants have to be considered potentially authoritative' (p. 147).

Accepting the view that the Folio *Romeo and Juliet* derives with a minimum of alteration from its Quarto copy, S. W. Reid examines closely that minimum.[21] He confirms the traditional view that the Folio was set from the third Quarto (1609) and not from the fourth,[22] and, with newly discovered information on Compositor E's methods and on his stints in this play, Reid demonstrates that there are many divergences from the Q3 text in Folio stage directions, prefixes, and dialogue that cannot be attributed to the compositor. He posits therefore a play-house editor – perhaps Knight or Heminge and Condell – who exhibits 'a general familiarity with the play and an understanding of both the on-stage and off-stage action that . . . [are] rather remarkable' (p. 65). The editor worked with 'considerable care, annotating the printer's copy where it struck him as deficient and relying mainly on the context to do so, though perhaps occasionally . . . consulting a playhouse manuscript' (p. 66). One small difficulty suggests itself in the hypothesis. Reid notes that E set the last page of the play and that this page, having been cancelled, was reset by B. He points to additional editorial alterations made prior to the resetting. Such an argument depends on the unlikely assumption that the playhouse editor was attending the press when the cancellation – a phenomenon exclusive to the printing-house – occurred. This is a minor objection to an argument that is a model of clarity and logic.

Studies of compositorial patterns continue in the Folio and the Quartos. In an attempt to conclude the identification of cases and compositors in the Folio comedies that Hinman left to others, Paul Werstine has analysed in detail the printing of the first section of the volume.[23] He finds Jaggard began with three compositors and three cases – B at y, C at x, and F at z. Though Compositor D and Compositor F alternated

stints (at case z) in quires F–H, a clear pattern of three-compositor work (one or two of the compositors setting at any time) is maintained from quire A through quire Q. Though 'type-recurrence patterns indicate that complex distributional practices persisted . . . , there is nothing to indicate that the availability of three compositors and cases sowed confusion in the production of the Folio' (p. 233). At quire R begins the two-compositor, two-case pattern of composition that is standard for the rest of the Folio.

Richard Knowles provides in his exhaustive study of the Pavier Quarto of *King Lear* (1619) data which bear notably on the printing of others of the series.[24] He argues that two compositors set sheets A–H and a third compositor set sheets I–L of *King Lear*. He finds – regardless of the specific pages set by the compositors – that the 'somewhat unusual pattern' (p. 193) of two-skeleton work, alternating by sheets rather than by formes, obtains throughout the Quarto and, indeed, through the first nine of the ten Pavier Quartos. He supposes that this system may reflect a decision of Pavier and Jaggard to prepare a collected works of Shakespeare; 'they might well have organized such a regular pattern of work to be adhered to from the beginning of the series to the end' (p. 206). Knowles's study is extremely careful and exact.

If we assume, as we may reasonably do, that Knowles is correct about this pattern in Pavier's shop and that Werstine is correct about another complex pattern in Jaggard's shop, we may infer a grand design established by Jaggard in the printing and press work of the plays.

On the salutary assumption that new techniques of compositor analysis may yield new information,

[20] 'The Copy for the Folio Text of *Love's Labour's Lost*', *Review of English Studies*, 33 (1982), 137–47.
[21] 'The Editing of Folio *Romeo and Juliet*', *Studies in Bibliography*, 35 (1982), 43–66.
[22] Though the undated Q4 was assigned by bibliographical means to 1622 in an article published in 1965, it is of interest to record that the *British Museum General Catalogue of Printed Books* (1964) had already assigned it (for reasons not given) to '[1620?]'.
[23] 'Cases and Compositors in the Shakespeare First Folio Comedies', *Studies in Bibliography*, 35 (1982), 206–34.
[24] 'The Printing of the Second Quarto (1619) of *King Lear*', *ibid.*, pp. 191–206.

MacD. P. Jackson has re-examined Quartos already studied by other scholars.[25] He argues that *Richard III* Q1 (1597) was set in two shops: sheets A–G by a single compositor in Valentine Simmes's shop; sheets H–M by two compositors in Peter Short's shop. He bases his distinction between these two (called N and O) on the spacing/non-spacing after commas and before question marks and colons. The division between the two occurs regularly half-way through each sheet. He notices also the pattern of two-skeleton printing, each skeleton printing and perfecting alternate sheets.[26] *1 Henry IV* Q1 (1598) also was printed in Short's shop, also by two compositors (called X and Y), alternating on the same basis (but not so exactly as in the earlier Quarto), and also with the same pattern of two-skeleton printing. Jackson thinks it likely that Compositors N and X are the same person.

An extra benefit of this survey is the examination of *1 Henry IV* Q0 (?1598). Jackson concludes that Compositors X and Y probably also set the single surviving sheet of this Quarto. He concludes further on the basis of demonstrated fidelity to copy between Q0 and Q1 that Q0 (hence Q1) is an accurate representation of the manuscript. As Q0 exhibits an 'absence of elisions' and a presence of non-Shakespearian connectives (i.e. between/betwixt, etc.), Jackson infers that the manuscript was not authorial, and that therefore 'an editor should have no compunction about introducing colloquial and metrical elisions into his text' (p. 190).

Proposals for emending seem particularly interesting this year. Suggestions include corrections for single words and descriptions of new techniques or approaches. Of the latter type are the articles by Alan E. Craven and Gary Taylor. Craven builds on his earlier work with Compositor A in Valentine Simmes's shop to argue imaginatively for emendation in twenty passages of *Richard II* and *Much Ado about Nothing*.[27] In these passages, never emended or variously emended, he demonstrates how the knowledge of A's practices in mis-setting reprints and so creating errors of substitution, omission, interpolation, and transposition can guide an editor. Some of the emendations he offers are simple substitutions – 'the' for 'thy', for example – but others are ingenious proposals – 'sorrow raze' from 'sorrow, wagge'

(*Much Ado*, 5.1.16). Critics of this technique will say that there is no 'evidence' for Craven's emendation, but the evidence, though it may seem shaky and unpersuasive to many, is deduced from the behaviour of the compositor. This technique is the logical conclusion of a generation of compositorial studies. It should be welcomed.

Gary Taylor isolates a particular class of error for analysis, the press variant.[28] He would out-guess the guesses of proof-correctors, who, it is acknowledged, did not consult copy before correcting a compositor's errors. So in *King Lear*, he finds four proof 'corrections' that deserve correcting. At 4.2.45 uncorrected Quarto reads 'beneflicted'; corrected reads 'benefited'. Taylor is right in objecting to the notion that the compositor would set a non-word with an easy one before him, and he reads 'benefacted'. Similarly at 2.4.129, uncorrected Quarto reads 'fruit'; corrected, 'tombe'. Taylor's attractive guess is 'scrine' (= shrine). At 2.2.162, uncorrected Quarto reads 'not'; corrected, 'most'. Taylor's 'now' is not impossible. At 1.4.341, uncorrected Quarto reads 'after your returne'; corrected, 'hasten your returne'. Taylor shrewdly suggests that the error is not in 'after' – that the corrector corrected the wrong word. He retains 'after' and corrects 'returne' to 'retinue'. Ready to commend the idea that one may seek to find the correctible word elsewhere than did the corrector, one is reluctant to accept this particular correction. 'Retinue' is a word used only twice by Shakespeare. It suggests more of a supporting company than Oswald might be thought to have (see *2 Henry IV*, 4.3.103–6), and as it is used by Goneril in line 200 of this scene to describe the King's attendants it is unlikely that it

---

[25] 'Two Shakespeare Quartos: *Richard III* (1597) and *1 Henry IV* (1598)', *ibid.*, pp. 173–90.

[26] It is difficult to see why this system should have been followed, but as it is the technique used also in the Pavier quartos, it must have had its economies. Jackson finds it 'very common' (p. 189), but to the present reviewer and to Knowles, it is 'somewhat unusual' (p. 193).

[27] 'Compositor Analysis to Edited Text: Some Suggested Readings in *Richard II* and *Much Ado about Nothing*', *PBSA*, 76 (1982), 43–62. See also *Shakespeare Survey 33* (Cambridge University Press, 1980), p. 206.

[28] 'Four New Readings in *King Lear*', *Notes and Queries*, 29 (1982), 121–3.

would be used by Goneril again in line 341 to describe Oswald's. Furthermore, Goneril's supposed command to Oswald, 'after your retinue', can scarcely mean either 'get your retinue' or 'have your retinue follow'; it must mean 'follow your retinue'. (But surely 'retinue' are 'followers' themselves? Compare 'after your master', Goneril to the Fool, line 315.) But to return to the main: Taylor is to be commended for directing critical attention to the proof-correctors' guesses; they have no sanctity. Either 'after' or 'returne' may be erroneous. Since both 'hasten' and 'retinue' seem unlikely guesses, critics have a double opportunity to exercise their 'inspired or uninspired guesses, without reference to the manuscript'.

Taylor elsewhere suggests a single emendation on the basis of misreading:[29] to explain the strange 'Humfrey Hower' of *Richard III* (4.4.175), he proposes a misreading of *e* for *o* (not so easy an error in italic as in secretary) and suggests 'Humfrey Hewer', 'the name of a [posited] table-servant who called the Duchess of York to breakfast once' (p. 96). The invention of such a table-servant and the supposition that his domestic action would be common knowledge one hundred and fifty years after the event seem strained, but the emendation provides a meaning to the passage better than any yet advanced.

R. L. Horn treats the interesting metathesis at *Hamlet*, 3.2.381: F1 (and modern editors) – 'such bitter business as the day'; Q2 (and Steevens) – 'such business as the bitter day'.[30] He argues that 'since the word "bitter" is part of an alliterative phrase in the F1 reading, there is little likelihood that it would have been shifted by a compositor to the position it occupies in Q2. We can assume with far greater justification that the shift occurred in the direction of the alliterative phrase' (p. 179). This assumption has immediate appeal, but Horn gives no indication that it has ever been tested as a working proposition. Steevens retained 'the bitter day' on the basis of his assumption that though the phrase was 'vulgar', it might not have been so in Shakespeare's time, and Maurice Charney in 1969 has glossed the bitter day as Doomsday. Horn supports Charney's acceptance of the Quarto reading with many instances from medieval sermons and poetry of 'bitter' used to describe the taste of Doomsday. In none of these,

however, do we find the precise phrase 'the bitter day', and none of these texts is later than the early fifteenth century. With the conceivable exception of one phrase (2 Samuel 2:26), there is no example in Scripture of 'bitter' as a modifier for the Last Day, nor does the association exist in proverbial lore, in the regular use of the word (see *OED*), or elsewhere in Shakespeare. It is abundantly clear that 'The Bitter Day' provides an intriguing reading, more bitter than the 'bitter business', but it is not clear that an Elizabethan would have understood it so.

James P. Hammersmith argues that in spite of editorial tradition two speech assignments in the Folio *Winter's Tale* are correct and should be retained.[31] At 5.1.12 the single word 'true' should be restored to Leontes, and at 5.1.75 the phrase 'I have done' should be restored to Cleomenes. He demonstrates that the Folio setting depicts the proper dramatic situation intended and is consistent with the characterizations of the play. There is certainly no bibliographical support for the editorial position. And Giorgio Melchiori recommends the Quarto 'thou blacke weede, why art so lovely faire?' over the Folio 'thou weed:/Who art so lovely faire' (*Othello*, 4.2.67–8), seeing the earlier version as representing the rhetorical principle of paradox; he finds support in Sonnet 94: 'Lilies that fester smell far worse than weeds.'[32]

A greater problem in *Othello*, one which has received much attention in recent months, is Othello's likening himself to an Indian (Q) or a Judean (F) (5.3.350). This review noted last year Joan Ozark Holmer's substantial support for the reading 'Judean'.[33] But one of the impediments in accepting

---

29 'Humfrey Hower', *Shakespeare Quarterly*, 33 (1982), 95–6. In the new Arden edition, Hammond suggests: 'a satirical reference to some unidentified contemporary' (p. 284).

30 '*Hamlet*, III.ii.376: A Defence of Q2's "The Bitter Day"', *Shakespeare Quarterly*, 33 (1982), 179–81. The new Arden rejects Q2 and Charney's gloss: 'the antithesis is between *day* and *night*' (p. 311).

31 'Two Speech-Assignments in *The Winter's Tale*, F1 (1623)', *PBSA*, 75 (1981), 171–4.

32 '"O thou blacke weede"', *Shakespeare Quarterly*, 32 (1981), 355–7.

33 See *Shakespeare Survey 35* (Cambridge University Press, 1982), p. 187 and nn. 20, 21.

'Judean' has always been that the *OED* did not recognize the word in English before 1832. Robert F. Fleissner reported last year also that the new Supplement had found it in 1652. This year Richard Levin has continued the argument against 'Judean' by stressing the fact that a single use in 1652 is not evidence for currency fifty years earlier.[34] The word, however, did exist in 1602, for it appears in the Lady Elizabeth Cary's *Mariam*,[35] written 1602–5 (published 1613), probably known to Shakespeare in manuscript.[36] Constibarus is here addressed: 'well met[,] *Iudean* Lord' (2.4.1; p. D2). The word is scanned as a trisyllable, the accent on the second syllable.

But 'Judean' certainly was not standard, and Levin notices that the compositor of F2 changed the word (presumably on his own initiative) to 'Indian' and that Q2, set from a copy of Q1 collated against F1, also reads 'Indian'. The evidence from F2 is more significant than that from Q2,[37] though the concurrence is interesting. (It is scarcely arguable that F2 consulted Q2.) Levin, furthermore, objects to Naseeb Shaheen's attempt to draw a parallel between Geoffrey Fenton's version of the fable where Judas Iscariot is twice mentioned and Shakespeare's treatment which, as Levin correctly points out, is 'so different . . . that no connection between Othello and Judas can be discerned' (p. 65).[38] Levin is again correct in addressing the question of the appropriateness of the simile to Othello himself, the speaker. Levin points out that the action of the Indian is based on ignorance; that of the Judean (i.e. Judas) on 'deliberate deception . . . [and] cold-blooded treachery' (p. 67). Othello sees himself as ignorant and perplexed, not as deceiving – that is the part of Iago. In taking this position, Levin is not indeed advancing a new thesis, for it is clearly Alice Walker's view: 'Judas . . . was the archetype of treachery, of which Othello . . . never accuses himself, . . . through ignorance [like the Indian's], Othello has thrown away his perfect chrysolite';[39] but Levin's arguments support this position with such vigour and clarity that it will be impossible to discount them.[40]

Several new glosses or interpretations have been offered during the year – some more persuasive than others. Douglas H. Parker suggests that 'Limander' and 'Helen' in *A Midsummer Night's Dream*,

5.1.195, 196, are mispronounced references not only to Leander and Hero but to Lysander and Helena as well.[41] Such a thesis supposes that Bottom (or Peter Quince) is aware of the existence of these two citizens of Athens and of their respective infidelity and fidelity; that is to suppose too much. More effective is the argument of David-Everett Blythe that when she speaks of Phebe's 'bugle eye-balls' (*As You Like It*, 3.5.47), Rosalind is using a dialect variant of 'bucolic' to describe the beauty of those eyes.[42] Phebe's eyes are thus compared to the beautiful ox-like eyes of many classical goddesses or (in modern times) to the 'large, dreamy, . . . mellow, kindly [and] soft' eyes of the Channel Island cattle, most conspicuously the Jersey. This extraordinary gloss supports the Folio reading 'mo beauty' (3.5.37) as against the editorial 'no beauty'.

Two items for *Love's Labour's Lost* are noteworthy. Manfred Draudt thinks that when Longaville replies to Berowne – 'A high hope for a low heaven'

---

[34] 'The Indian/Judean Crux In *Othello*', *Shakespeare Quarterly*, 33 (1982), 60–7. Mr Levin advises me, privately, that he has discovered another instance of the word in the early seventeenth century.

[35] See T. L. Berger and W. C. Bradford, Jr., *An Index of Characters in English Printed Drama to the Restoration* (Microcard Editions Books, Englewood, 1975).

[36] Lucy Brashear, 'A Case for the Influence of Lady Cary's Tragedy of *Mariam* on Shakespeare's *Othello*', *Shakespeare Newsletter*, 26 (1976), 31.

[37] Fleissner has already noted the fact that F2 'corrected' F1 in 'Othello as the Indigent Indian', *Shakespeare Jahrbuch* (Weimar), 114 (1978), 98.

[38] See *Shakespeare Survey 34* (Cambridge University Press, 1981), p. 196. Mr Fleissner has, privately, communicated to me his disagreement with Shaheen's interpretation.

[39] Edition of *Othello* (New Cambridge Shakespeare, 1957), pp. 218–19.

[40] This reviewer has gone to and back on this crux, lackeying the varying tide, but it now appears that it is no longer possible to consider (with Lucy Brashear) the base Judean to be Herod (see footnote 36), who is described in the prose Argument to *Mariam* as the son of Antipater, an Idumean (A2), and as an 'Idumean' (A4) and a 'Base [!] *Edomite*' (A4), or (with Shaheen and Joan Holmer) Judas (see footnotes 33 and 38). We must read 'Indian', the word that scans smoothly in the line.

[41] '"Limander" and "Helen" in *A Midsummer Night's Dream*', *Shakespeare Quarterly*, 33 (1982), 99–101.

[42] 'Ox-eyed Phebe', *ibid.*, pp. 101–2.

(1.1.191) – he refers to the 'heavens' of the Elizabethan theatre.[43] Draudt does not, however, explain what is to be gained by terming the ceiling over the stage 'low'. And M. C. Bradbrook glosses the song of the Owl (5.2.906, 915), 'Tu-whit, Tu-who', as 'To it! to woo!' – a call which perfectly speaks the merriment that comes in the winter.[44] Though it is rare that we encounter a merry owl in Shakespeare, perhaps this owl's ambiguity speaks also the muted joy of the close: love's labour is indeed lost.

One of the most celebrated cruxes, still being variously glossed, is the 'runnawayes eyes' of *Romeo and Juliet*, 3.2.6. Joan Ozark Holmer supports Johnson's and Delius' gloss that the term is plural possessive and that it refers to 'such fugitives and vagabonds as tramp about at night' (p. 97).[45] Though one is ready to accept the irony that Romeo is just such a runaway, one may well hesitate to accept the notion that Juliet should concern herself with such unspecified agents of whom she knows nothing. Indeed,

that there should be runaways wandering about the streets of Verona is most unlikely, for the watch, whom the Friar specifically fears, would surely have picked them up. Perhaps the solution lies in the verb 'wink'. The verb here signifies to sleep or to die, not to close the eyes for the express purpose of not seeing someone. (Why should the vagabonds wink when Romeo runs by them?) But there is no confidence that we may yet close our eyes on this crux.

---

[43] *Love's Labour's Lost*, I.i.196. "Low Heauen"', *Notes and Queries*, 29 (1982), 109–10. Kerrigan suggests in the New Penguin edition '*high words* are a *low* sort of *heaven* to *hope* highly for' (p. 156).

[44] '"To-whit, To-who, a Merry Note"', *Shakespeare Quarterly*, 33 (1982), 94–5.

[45] '"Runnawayes Eyes". A Fugitive Meaning', *ibid.*, pp. 97–9. Holmer is not quite correct in asserting that 'no notice has been taken of . . . "runnagate"' (p. 98); the Variorum records the notice of, at least, Hunter (1853) and Keightley (1867) in the word (pp. 376, 393).

James G. McManaway, editor, bibliographer, educator, scholar, and friend, left Shakespearians deeply indebted to him. Believing that many of those who knew and loved Mac would welcome an opportunity to create a tribute to his memory, we have formed a committee to establish a James G. McManaway Memorial Fund at the Folger Shakespeare Library. We plan to use contributions to purchase books and manuscripts for the Library in fields in which Mac did research over his long career. Committee members are John F. Fleming, Elizabeth Niemyer, Jeanne A. Roberts, S. Schoenbaum, Robert K. Turner, Jr, John Velz, and Susan Zimmerman. Contributions in any amount (tax deductible) may be made payable to the Folger Shakespeare Library: McManaway Fund, and mailed to Elizabeth Niemyer, Folger Shakespeare Library, Washington DC, 20003, USA.

Jeanne Roberts and John Velz
for the committee

INDEX

Abbott, Charles D., 30n
Ackland, Joss, 153
Adams, John Cranford, 119n, 179
Adamson, W. D., 170
Addison, Joseph, 139
Admiral's Men, the, 136
Aeschylus, 11–19
Agate, James, 81
Alexander, Nigel, 44
Alexander, Peter, 53n, 188
al-Hakim, Tawfik, 1
Allen, Don Cameron, 177
Allen, Michael J. B., 91n
Alleyn, Edward, 135, 140–1, 144, 145, 147, 175
Alleyn, Joan, 135
al-Subair, Shayk, 2, 3, 8, 10
Altieri, Joanne, 178
Alvis, John, 164
Amory, Mark, 28n
Aneau, Barthélemy, 166
Anna, wife of Sigismund III of Poland, 145
Anna-Sophia, wife of Frederick Ulric of Wolfenbüttel, 139
Anne of Denmark, later Queen of England, 139, 140, 142, 147
Anscombe, G. E. M., 22n
Apuleius, 175
Arber, E., 142n
Archdall Manuscript, 110, 113
Aristotle, 17, 28
Ashcroft, Dame Peggy, 149, 150
Asp, Carolyn, 166
Auden, W. H., 29–37
Ayrton, Randle, 73, 74, 78–9

Bach, J. S., 74
Badawi, M. M., 2
Ba-Kathir, Ali Ahmad, 1, 10

Bald, R. C., 110
Baldwin, T. W., 85n, 92n
Bale, John, 171
Barkan, Leonard, 167, 175–6
Barry, Spranger, 180
Barton, Anne, 178: see also Righter, Anne
Barton, John, 160
Battenhouse, Roy, 177
Bawcutt, N. W., 127n
Baxter, Richard, 162
Bayley, John, 48, 49
Beauman, Sally, 73, 74n
Beaumont, Francis, and Fletcher, John, 107n, 110, 188
Beckerman, Bernard, 57n, 63, 178
Beckett, Samuel, 21, 22, 23n, 24, 25, 28
Bedford, Brian, 60
Bell, John, 103n, 119n
Bellori, Giovanni Petro, 85
Bellow, Saul, 49
Bennett, Jonathan, 23n, 24, 25n
Bennett, Paul, E., 173
Bennett, Vivienne, 82
Benson, Frank, 74
Bentley, G. E., 135n, 136n, 137
Berek, Peter, 167
Berger, T. L., 194n
Bergman, Ingmar, 65–72, 165
Bergom-Larsson, Maria, 69n
Bergson, Henri, 27
Berlin, Normand, 21n
Berman, Ed, 26
Bernard, Anthony, 82
Berry, Herbert, 178, 179
Berry, Ralph, 159–60, 169, 180, 181
Bertram, Paul, 108n, 188–9
Bethell, S. L., 101n

Bevington, David, 31n, 122n
Bigsby, C. W. E., 21n, 23n
Bischoff, Ferdinand, 142
Björkman, Stig, 68n
Bjornson, Maria, 154
Blake, William, 78
Bloom, Allan, 164
Blythe, David-Everett, 194
Boleyn, Anne, 176
Bolte, J., 137n, 141n, 143n
Bond, Edward, 2, 28, 152, 158
Bowe, John, 129n
Bowers, A. Robin, 170, 177
Bowers, Fredson, 188
Bradbrook, M. C., 195
Bradford, W. C., Jr, 194n
Bradley, A. C., 43, 53, 56n, 78, 151–2
Bradshaw, Jon, 27n, 28n
Brailow, David G., 170n
Brand, Peter, 135
Brand, Sir Matthew, 179n
Brandenburg, Elector of, 147
Brashear, Lucy, 194n
Brauneck, Manfred, 143n
Brecht, Bertolt, 2
Brenner, Gerry, 169
Bridges-Adams, W., 75
Brissenden, Alan, 161
Britten, Benjamin, 161
Brook, Peter, 60, 74, 79, 80, 83, 160
Brown, Ivor, 74n, 82
Brown, John Russell, 50n, 97n, 157–9, 178
Brown, Keith, 189–90
Browne, Jane, 137
'Browne of Boar's Head', 135
Browne, Robert, 135, 137, 138, 141, 142, 144, 146, 147

Browne, Robert, Jr, 135–6
Bruno, Giordano, 41n
Brustein, Robert, 21n
Bullough, Geoffrey, 86n, 87n, 93n
Bunyan, John, 45
Burbage, Cuthbert, 136
Burnet, R. A. L., 176n
Burns, M. M., 170
Burroughs, Josephine L., 91n
Burton, Dolores M., 171
Byford, Roy, 77
Byron, Lord, 49

Cairncross, A. S., 184
Cairns, Huntington, 85n
Campbell, Cheryl, 150–1
Campbell, Ken, 149
Candido, Joseph, 169–70
Capell, Edward, 186
Carlisle, John, 152
Carpenter, Humphrey, 29n, 37n
Carpenter, Sarah, 180
Cary, Lady Elizabeth, 194
Cary, Sir Robert, 140
Cassirer, Ernst, 91n, 94n
Castiglione, Baldassare, 172
Cavendish, William, 117
Caxton, William, 87n
Cervantes, Miguel de, 104
Cespedes, Frank V., 165
Chamberlain, John, 179
Chamberlain's Men, the, 136: see
    also King's Men
Chambers, E. K., 111n, 135n,
    136n, 137, 138n, 141, 142n
Chapman, George, 93n, 174
Charity, A. C., 16n
Charles, Archduke, Bishop of
    Breslau, 145–6
Charles of Styria, 145
Charles, Prince, later Charles I, 147
Charney, Maurice, 193
Charques, R. D., 74n
Chaucer, Geoffrey, 87, 89n, 176
Cheke, Sir John, 166
Chekhov, Anton, 73
Chesterton, G. K., 49, 50n
Chettle, Henry, 173
Chramostova, Vlasta, 26
Christ, Jesus, 18, 67, 173
Clark, Arthur Melville, 174
Clowes, Richard, 82
Clunes, Alec, 82
Coghill, Nevill, 189

Cohn, Albert, 138, 139, 141n,
    146n
Cohn, Ruby, 23n
Cohoon, J. W., 85n
Cole, Douglas, 95n
Cole, Howard C., 176–7
Cole, Maria Jansson, 179
Coleridge, S. T., 53
Colie, Rosalie, 48n, 104
Collingwood, R. G., 33
Colman, George, 180
Colothus, 85n
Comito, Terry, 170–1
Conacher, D. J., 14n
Condell, Henry, 174, 191
Connell, Charles, 174
Constantia of Styria, 145
Cook, Ann Jennalie, 170, 179
Cooper, C., 137n
Corballis, Richard, 21n
Corkin, William, 140
Cowley, Richard, 147
Cox, R., 139
Cranach, Lucas, 170
Crane, Ralph, 107–20
Craven, Alan E., 192
Creizenach, Wilhelm, 137–8
Cribb, T. J., 169
Crosse, Gordon, 79, 81n, 82, 84
Crowl, Samuel, 165
Crüger, J., 137n, 138n
Cunningham, J. S., 121n
Cusack, Sinead, 152
Cushman, Robert, 154
Czapliński, W., 147n

Daigle, Lennet J., 169
Daniels, Ron, 154
Dares Phrygius, 87n
Darlington, W. A., 76
Daugherty, Leo, 173
Davenant, Sir William, 114n
Davies, Howard, 151–2
Dean, Paul, 166
Dearing, Vinton A., 114n
De Grazia, Margreta, 170n
Dekker, Thomas, 142, 143
De la Primaudaye, Pierre, 85n
Delius, Nikolaus, 195
Delle Colonne, Guido, 87n
De Madariaga, Salvador, 53n
De Medici, Catherine, 176
De Sainte-Maure, Benoît, 87n
De Thou, Jacques-Auguste, 145
De Witt, J., 179

Dexter, John, 61n
Dickens, Charles, 149
Dietrichstein, Franz von, 145, 146
Dio Chrysostom, 85, 87, 95
Donne, John, 39, 40, 41, 162
Donner, Jörn, 69n, 71n
Dowden, Edward, 100
Dowland, Robert, 147n
Drake, Fabia, 75
Draudt, Manfred, 194–5
Drew-Bear, Annette, 180
Dryden, John, 114, 173
Dubrow, Heather, 167n
Dulandt, Robert, 144

Edwards, Philip, 88n, 181
Ek, Anders, 65n, 70–1, 72
Ek, Ingrid, 65n
Eliot, T. S., 6, 18, 21, 175
Elizabeth, Duchess of Brunswick,
    139
Elizabeth, Princess, later Queen of
    Bohemia, 118, 144
Elizabeth I, Queen, 93, 146, 165
Elizabeth Charlotte of Branden-
    burg, 144
Elyot, Sir Thomas, 161
Empson, William, 160
Engel, Susan, 154
Enright, D. J., 151
Ericson, Sture, 67
Eriksen, Roy T., 41, 42
Ernest, Duke of Bavaria, 146
Euripides, 13, 14, 16, 17, 18, 85
Evans, G. Blakemore, 32n
Evett, David, 170n, 178
Ewing, Kenneth, 21

Felperin, Howard, 98n
Fenton, Geoffrey, 194
Fenton, James, 155
Ferdinand, Elector of Cologne,
    146
Ferdinand of Styria, 145
Ferdinand II, Emperor, 142, 146
Ficino, Marsilio, 86n, 90, 91, 94
Fielding, Henry, 3
Fleay, Frederick Gard, 135, 138n
Fleissner, Robert F., 190, 194
Fletcher, John, 107, 109, 110, 114
Flood, Valentine, 140
Flower, Sir Archibald, 73
Foakes, R. A., 95n, 172
Folger, H. C., 190
Ford, John, 142, 175

Forker, Charles R., 169–70
Formby, George, 152
Forster, E. M., 33
Fortin, René E., 167n
Foxe, John, 171
Franks, Philip, 150
Franz Josef, Emperor, 77
Frederick II, King of Denmark, 139
Frederick Ulric, Duke of Wolfen-büttel, 139, 140
Freedman, Barbara, 170, 171
Freer, Coburn, 180
French, J. Nathan, 117n
Freud, Sigmund, 19, 53
Frye, Northrop, 99, 123
Frye, Roland M., 175
Fuller, Thomas, 173
Furness, Horace Howard, 61n, 119

Gair, W. Reavley, 179
Gambon, Michael, 153
Garber, Marjorie, 177–8
Gardner, Dame Helen, 31
Garnet, Henry, 174
Garrick, David, 180
George, David, 173
George William, Elector of Brandenburg, 144
Gerschow, Frederic, 145
Gibbons, Brian, 174, 176, 178
Gibran, 1, 10
Gielgud, Sir John, 73n, 81, 84, 165
Gilman, Herbert, 168
Girard, René, 48, 49n
Giroux, Robert, 173
Giulio Romano, 167
Gleason, John B., 179
Goddard, Harold, 44
Golding, Arthur, 86, 175
Goldman, Michael, 169
Goldmann, Lucien, 45, 46
Goldstein, Philip, 169
Gordon, Giles, 22n, 25
Gould, Gerald, 159
Gowrie, Earl of, 166, 174
Grafton, Richard, 171
Granville-Barker, Harley, 79, 80, 97
Graves, R. B., 180
Graves, Robert, 39–42
Green, John, 137, 138, 139, 141–7 *passim*
Greenblatt, Stephen, 51
Greene, Robert, 116n, 117

Greene, Thomas, 144, 172
Greenfield, Thelma N., 103n
Greg, W. W., 108, 109, 112, 115n, 140, 144, 147, 189
Greif, Karen, 169
Grigson, Geoffrey, 30n
Grillo, John, 155
Grimm, Wilhelm and Jakob, 139
Grock, 152
Guffey, George R., 114n
Gunter, John, 149
Gwilym, Mike, 149, 153

Hackforth, R., 85n
Hagberg, Carl August, 70
Halio, Jay L., 31n
Hall, Sir Peter, 159
'Hall, W.', 190
Hallam, Henry, 175
Halliday, F. E., 55n
Hallinan, Tim, 172
Hallström, Per, 70
Halstead, William P., 74n
Hamilton, Edith, 85n
Hamilton, W., 94n
Hammersmith, James P., 193
Hammond, Antony, 184, 185, 193n
Hands, Terry, 59, 63, 120n, 129n, 152
Hankins, J. E., 85, 91n
Harbage, Alfred, 58n, 97n
Hardy, Thomas, 95n, 128
Harris, Bernard, 50n, 97
Harris, John, 115n
Harsnett, Samuel, 112n
Harvey, Martin, 180n, 181
Hassel, R. Chris, 176
'Hathawa, Hanna', 10
Hathaway, Anne, 10
Hawkins, Harriett, 169
Haydn, Franz Joseph, 82
Haydn, Hiram, 45n
Hayes, George, 75, 78
Hayles, Nancy K., 166–7
Hayman, Ronald, 22n, 26n
Hellenga, Robert R., 180
Heminge, John, 174, 191
Heninger, S. K., Jr, 104n
Henry Julius of Wolfenbüttel, 135, 139
Henry, Martha, 60
Henry IV (of Navarre), King of France, 176
Henry, Prince, 110, 140

Henryson, Robert, 87
Henslowe, Philip, 141, 142
Herbert, George, 11, 19, 45, 162
Herford, C. H., 117n, 188n
Heywood, Thomas, 117, 142, 143, 174
Hill, Geoffrey, 103
Hillebrand, Harold N., 85n
Hinman, Charlton, 191
Hirsh, James E., 160–1
Hodges, C. Walter, 178, 179
Hohenzollern, Count of, 146
Holaday, Allan, 144
Holding, Edith, 181
Holinshed, Raphael, 171
Hollar, W., 178
Hollingdale, R. J., 46n
Holmer, Joan Ozark, 170, 193, 194n, 195
Homan, Sidney, 162
Homer, 85
Honigmann, E. A. J., 173, 177, 189
Höök, Marianne, 69n
Horn, R. L., 193
Horne, Richard H., 175
Hosley, Richard, 178, 185
Hotine, Margaret, 176
Howard-Hill, T. H., 107n, 109, 110, 114n, 120n, 190
Hoy, Cyrus, 107n
Hummelen, W. M. H., 178
Humphreys, A. R., 186, 187
Hunter, Joseph, 195n
Hunter, G. K., 50n, 174, 180
Hunter, Glen D., 182n
Husak, Gustav, 27
Hyde, Jonathan, 151
Hyland, Frances, 58

Ibsen, Henrik, 65, 125
Irving, Sir Henry, 74
Isaiah, 15
Isherwood, Christopher, 30

Jackson, MacD. P., 184n, 192
Jackson, William, 140
Jacobi, Derek, 152, 154
Jaggard, William, 191
James, Clive, 23n
James I, King (James VI), 139, 165, 174
James, Henry, 32, 33n, 36
Jayne, Sears Reynolds, 90n
Jeaffreson, J. C., 137n
Jefferson, D. W., 103n

Jenkins, Harold, 23n, 55, 181–2, 186n
John Sigismund, Elector of Brandenburg, 139
Johnson, Samuel, 28, 163, 195
Jones, Emrys, 152, 161
Jones, Gemma, 153
Jones, Harris, 144, 145, 147
Jones, Inigo, 115n
Jones, Richard, 140–1, 144, 145, 147
Jonson, Ben, 53, 110, 117, 119, 120, 168, 173, 174, 188
Jowett, Benjamin, 86n
Joyce, James, 44, 49
Judas Iscariot, 194
Jump, J., 44n

Kafka, Franz, 21, 22, 28, 71
Karlin, Miriam, 153
Kaula, David, 172
Kavli, Karin, 71
Keach, William, 166
Keats, John, 44
Keightley, Thomas, 195n
Kemp, T. C., 79
Kermode, Frank, 98n, 115–16, 119n
Kernodle, G. R., 178
Kerrigan, John, 186–8, 195n
Khayyam, Omar, 7
Kierkegaard, Søren, 30, 31, 32, 33, 50, 51
Kilroy, Thomas, 1n
Kimbrough, Robert, 178
King's Men, the, 62, 83, 107: see also Chamberlain's Men
Kingsley, Charles, 175
Kitchin, Laurence, 72n
Klein, Joan Larsen, 24
Knight, Edward, 191
Knight, G. Wilson, 43, 44, 48, 49, 52
Knights, L. C. 44, 48
Knowles, Richard, 63, 191, 192n
Kohout, Pavel, 26
Koltai, Ralph, 152
Komisarjevsky, Theodore, 73–84
Kostressen, Johan, 144
Kott, Jan, 165
Kozikowski, Stanley J., 166n
Kozintsev, Grigori, 160
Kristeller, Paul Oskar, 91n

Lamb, Charles, 53, 78
Lamb, Margaret, 81

Lamb, Mary, 53
Landovsky, Pavel, 26, 27
Laurier, Jay, 82, 83
Law, Ernest, 115n
Leavis, F. R., 103
Lee, Robert, 135, 138n
Leech, Clifford, 57n
Lefevre, Raoul, 87n
Leighton, Margaret, 81
Leno, Dan, 152
Lenz, Joseph M., 166
Leone, Leonard, 178n
Leontovich, Eugenie, 81
Lesser, Anton, 155
Levin, Harry, 164
Levin, Richard, 169, 170, 177, 190, 194
Lewis, C. S., 44, 45
Lewis Frederick of Wirtemberg, 140
Liebler, Naomi Conn, 171–2
Limon, Jerzy, 140, 143n, 144
Lin Shu, 53
Lipsius, 179
Livesey, Peggy, 81
Londré, Felicia Hardison, 21n
Long, John H., 115n
Long, Michael, 48, 49
Lowrie, W., 50n
Lukács, Georg, 45
Luterkort, Ingrid, 67
Luther, Martin, 50
Lydgate, John, 87n
Lyle, J. V., 140n
Lyly, John, 172

McCarthy, Mary, 151
McCrindle, Joseph F., 22n
Macdonald, Jan, 180
McDonald, Russ, 168
Mack, Maynard, 44, 80, 188n
MacKenna, Stephen, 91n
McKerrow, R. B., 57, 140n
McLaverty, J., 164–5
McManaway, James G., 189n
McMillin, Scott, 189
MacNaughtan, Alan, 154
McNeice, Ian, 154
McNeir, W. F., 103n
Macrobius, 91n
Magnani, Anna, 3
Mallarmé, Stephane, 44
Malmström, Ulla, 65n, 70
Manlove, Colin N., 163–4
Manus, Torsten, 68n

Margesson, J. M. R., 57n
Maria Magdalena, Archduchess, 142, 143, 145, 146
Maria of Bavaria, 145
Marker, Frederick J., 65n
Marker, Lisa-Lone, 65n
Markus, Tom, 58
Marlowe, Christopher, 10, 40, 93, 121, 122, 123, 129, 142, 173
Marshall, Norman, 84n
Marston, John, 174
Marten, Henry, 136n
Marvell, Andrew, 7
Mary, Queen of Scots, 174
Masefield, John, 50n
Massinger, Philip, 109
Matchett, W. H., 40, 41–2
Matthias, Emperor, 146
Maximilian, Archduke, 142
Maximilian I, Duke of Bavaria, 146
Meissner, J., 138n, 145n
Melchiori, Giorgio, 169, 193
Mendelson, Edward, 29n, 31n
Mentzel, E., 138n
Metz, G. Harold, 171, 190
Meyer, C. F., 144n, 147n
Michelangelo, 167, 175, 176
Middleton, Thomas, 110, 112, 114n, 117, 124, 126, 133, 174
Miller, Jonathan, 61, 154, 172
Milton, John, 104, 117, 152, 162
Miner, Earl, 114n
Miola, Robert S., 171, 175
Mitchell, Lee, 62
Molière, 65
Monette, Richard, 59
Montaigne, Michel de, 176
Montrose, Louis Adrian, 167n
Moore, Don D., 174n
Moore, Stephen, 151
Morgan, Charles, 81
Morris, Brian, 184–6
Morris, Irene, 142
Morris, J., 142n
Moss, Peter, 59
Mowat, Barbara, 167
Mozart, Wolfgang Amadeus, 82
Muir, Kenneth, 55n, 112n, 168
Mullaney, Stephen, 165–6, 174
Mullin, Michael, 76
Munk, Kaj, 66
Murad, Orlene, 142
Murphy, Gerard, 153

Murry, John Middleton, 45
Mutran, Khali, 10

Nagarajan, S., 172
Nannus Mirabellius, 92n
Nashe, Thomas, 143n, 176
Nass, Barry, 175
Nelson, Gerald, 32n
Nicoll, Allardyce, 121
Niebuhr, Reinhold, 30
Niedecken-Gebhart, H., 139n
Niemyer, Elizabeth, 190n
Niessen, Carl, 138n, 145n, 146n
Nietzsche, F. W., 19
Nims, John Frederick, 86n
Noble, Adrian, 152, 159
Nokes, David, 154
Norak, Maximillian E., 114n
Nosworthy, James, 98n, 100, 102, 105
Nungezer, Edwin, 137, 138n, 141n
Nunn, Trevor, 149–51, 159
Nuttall, A. D., 168–9
Nyerere, Julius, 2

O'Casey, Sean, 1, 3, 10
O'Chaine, Donatus, 140
Oliver, Stephen, 154
Olivier, Lord, 61, 159–60, 165
O'Mahoney, Robert, 154
Omotoso, Kole, 2
Orgel, Stephen, 115n
Orrell, John, 178, 179
Ovid, 86, 104, 167, 171, 175, 180

Palmer, Alan and Veronica, 174
Panofsky, Erwin, 86n, 91n
Parker, Douglas H., 194
Pascal, Blaise, 45
Pavier, Thomas, 191, 192n
Payne, Ben Iden, 73
Peake, Joseph J. S., 86n
Pearson, Jacqueline, 176
Peat, Derek, 172
Peck, Bob, 151, 154
Pedicord, H. W., 180
Pembroke's Men, 173
Perkins, William, 162
Philip Julius of Pommern-Wolgast, 144–5
Phillips, Robin, 60, 63
Pinter, Harold, 21
Pirandello, Luigi, 21, 22, 28

Plato, 85, 86, 90, 91, 92, 93n, 94, 177
Plotinus, 86n, 91, 92, 93
Plummer, Christopher, 84
Plutarch, 18
Poel, William, 180
Poggioli, Renato, 104
Polišensky, J., 146n
Poulton, Diana, 147n
Prince, F. T., 40n
Prosser, Eleanor, 44
Proudfoot, G. R., 108n
Proust, Marcel, 149
Przybos, A., 147n
Pudsey, Edward, 138
Puttenham, Richard, 166

Queen Anne's Men, 135, 137, 139, 142, 144, 147
Quiller-Couch, Sir Arthur, 107n, 115n

Racine, Jean, 45
Rackoff, Louis, 59
Radin, Victoria, 151
Raleigh, Sir Walter, 40, 183
Reid, S. W., 191
Reynolds, James A., 177
Reynolds (Renaldes), Jane, 136–7, 142
Reynolds, Robert, 135, 137–8, 139, 142, 144
Ribner, Irving, 93n
Richards, I. A., 85n
Richmond, Hugh, 176
Riewald, J. G., 137, 140
Righter, Anne, 117n: see also Barton, Anne
Rigold, Stuart, 178
Ripa, Cesare, 175
Roberts, Jeanne Addison, 107n, 110
Robins, Cicely (Cissalie), 136, 142
Robins, William, 136
Robinson, F. N., 89n
Robinson, Thomas, 138
Roche, Thomas P., Jr, 93n
Ronayne, John, 178
Rosenblum, Joseph, 175
Rousseau, J.-J., 124
Rudolf II, Emperor, 145
Rey, W. B., 140n
Rylance, Mark, 154

Sabol, Andrew, 187n
Sackville, Thomas, 135, 138n, 139, 141
Salgādo, Gāmini, 81n, 178
Salingar, Leo, 169
Salvini, Tommaso, 61
Sames, William, 136n
Sammelles, Neil, 21n
Sams, Eric, 172
Sanders, Norman, 182–4
Sandes, James, 136
Sands, Cicely, (later Browne), 136n
Saunders, James, 21n
Saxony, Elector of, 138
Scheible, J., 139, 141
Schmitz, L. D., 44n
Schoenbaum, S., 178n
Scofield, Martin, 44n
Scoufos, Alice-Lyle, 172, 177
Seneca, 92
Seng, Peter J., 112n
Shabbakah, Elias Abu, 7
Shaheen, Naseeb, 194
Shakespeare, William
  editions
    Alexander, Peter, 86n, 108n
    Bevington, David, 122n
    Cambridge, 116n
    Complete Pelican, 58n, 97n, 105, 116n, 182, 186n
    Folios, 47, 63, 79, 80, 83, 107, 108n, 109, 111n, 113, 114n, 116, 117, 118, 120, 143, 157; textual studies of, 182–94 passim
    New Arden, 23n, 40n, 63, 98, 100n, 102n, 103n, 105, 116n, 119n, 161, 181, 184, 185, 186, 193n
    New Cambridge, 107n
    New Penguin, 117n, 171, 181, 182, 184, 186, 195n
    New Variorum, 61n, 63, 85n, 182n, 195n
    Quartos, 63, 79, 80, 108n, 112, 113, 157, 173, 174, 184, 185, 186; textual studies of, 184–94 passim
    Regents Renaissance Drama Series, 108n
    Riverside, 79
  plays
    All's Well that Ends Well, 60,

Shakespeare William, (cont.)
149, 155, 160, 161, 170,
176–7
Antony and Cleopatra,, 2, 3, 4,
5–10, 14–15, 18, 58, 73, 81,
83, 115n, 162, 167 179–80,
188
As You Like It, 9, 60, 63, 101,
104, 162, 167n, 170, 172,
177, 186n, 194
Comedy of Errors, The 81–2,
99n, 109, 160, 185
Coriolanus, 2, 5, 61, 107, 115n,
159, 169, 172
Cymbeline, 84, 88, 97–106,
111, 113, 114, 164, 167, 180
Hamlet, 2, 21–8, 32, 43–52,
53–6, 57, 122, 154–5, 159,
160, 163, 169, 181, 186n,
189, 193
Henry IV, 17, 25, 34, 58, 59,
149, 153–4, 164–5, 169, 192
2 Henry IV, 164
Henry V, 62, 65, 159–60, 165,
166, 178, 185
Henry VI, 59, 113, 133, 164,
182, 186, 189
1 Henry VI, 183
2 Henry VI, 182, 183
3 Henry VI, 182, 183
Henry VIII, 107, 108, 114,
157, 164, 165
Julius Caesar, 2, 5, 8, 14, 17,
57, 122, 127, 160, 162, 163,
170, 186n, 171–2
King John, 94, 113, 171, 173
King Lear, 2, 14–16, 32, 37,
45, 53n, 57, 58, 60, 63, 73,
78–9, 81, 82, 83, 88, 112,
122, 149, 152–3, 158, 159,
160, 169, 171, 176, 180, 189
190, 191, 192
Love's Labour's Lost, 74n, 89n,
123, 160, 161, 176, 181,
186–8, 190–1, 194
Macbeth, 2, 5, 10, 26, 28, 31,
62, 63, 65–72, 75–6, 83, 84,
114, 127, 149, 151–2, 158,
160, 163, 166, 174
Measure for Measure, 4, 14,
102, 103, 109, 159, 160, 162,
163, 164, 170, 172, 176, 177
Merchant of Venice, The, 2, 3,
10, 53n, 61, 73, 74–5, 83,
101, 164, 185, 186

Merry Wives of Windsor, The,
76–8, 83, 109, 113n, 170,
171
Midsummer Night's Dream, A,
2, 10, 60, 65, 161, 167, 175,
181, 194
Much Ado About Nothing, 152,
161, 169, 186, 187, 192
Othello, 3, 8, 14, 53n, 58, 61,
62, 92, 99n, 140, 162, 166,
169, 170, 171, 175, 189,
193, 194n
Pericles, 2, 98, 99, 180
Richard II, 9, 164, 174, 176,
177, 192
Richard III, 2, 58, 129, 132,
160, 161, 163, 169, 171, 173,
176, 184, 185, 192, 193
Romeo and Juliet, 1, 10, 14, 21,
25, 31n, 53n, 55, 61, 101,
121, 127, 128, 161, 169, 178,
190, 191, 195
Taming of the Shrew, The, 2,
82, 162, 173, 180, 184–6
Tempest, The, 10, 31–7, 84,
104, 107–20, 154, 162, 164,
167–8, 170, 176, 177, 180,
189
Timon of Athens, 87n, 160, 164
Titus Andronicus, 4, 14, 74,
164, 171, 173, 175, 190
Troilus and Cressida, 4, 8,
85–95, 100, 159, 160, 164,
169, 185
Twelfth Night, 65, 83, 92,
143n, 159, 160, 161, 166,
169
Two Gentlemen of Verona, The,
109, 113, 119n
Two Noble Kinsmen, The, 107,
108, 111, 115
Winter's Tale, The, 60, 88, 98,
101, 106, 109, 113, 114, 164,
167, 169, 173, 176, 193
poems
Lover's Complaint, A, 173
Phoenix and the Turtle, The,
40–2
Rape of Lucrece, The, 169, 170,
177
Sonnets, 7, 173, 176, 177, 190
Venus and Adonis, 169, 177
Shapiro, Michael, 179
Shaqui, Ahmad, 4, 5, 10
Sharp, Corona, 170n, 177

Shattuck, Charles, 75n, 76, 79, 82,
83
Shaw, George Bernard, 2, 133
Sher, Antony, 152
Shirley, James, 117
Short, Peter, 192
Shrapnel, John, 154
Sidney, Sir Philip, 172
Sigismund III, King of Poland, 145
Sima, Jonas, 68n
Simmes, Valentine, 192
Simpson, Percy and Evelyn, 117n,
188n
Sincler (Sincklo), John, 147
Sjöberg, Alf, 65
Sjögren, Henrik, 65n, 71n
Slights, Camille Wells, 162–3, 166
Slights, William W. E., 166
Sly, William, 136
Smallwood, R. L., 171, 175
Smith, Irwin, 116, 117, 118
Smith, Maggie, 60, 81
Smyth, H. W., 13n
Snow, Edward A., 166
Socrates, 86, 88, 91, 92
Somerset, J. A. B., 176n
Southampton, Henry Wriothesley,
3rd Earl of, 173
Soyinka, Wole, 11–19
Spears, Monroe K., 30n
Spencer, John, 135, 138n
Spender, Stephen, 29, 30
Spenser, Edmund, 93
Spevack, Marvin, 111n
Sprague, A. C., 119n
Spurgeon, Caroline, 174
Stagg, L. C., 174
Steevens, George, 188, 193
Stein, Arnold, 88n
Steiner, George, 101
Stesichorus, 85
Stettin, Duke of, 147
Stewart, Garrett, 167
Stewart, Patrick, 153
Stone, P. W. K., 189
Stoppard, Tom, 21–8
Stříbrný, Z., 146n
Strindberg, August, 65
Ström, Carl-Johan, 65n, 68–9
Strong, Sir Roy, 115n
Styan, J. L., 81n, 172
Suffolk, Thomas Howard, 1st Earl
of, 140
Sutton, Thomas, 140

Suzman, Janet, 81
Swander, Homer D., 59n, 103
Swendenberg, H. T., Jr, 114n

Tang Xianzu, 54
Tate, Nahum, 175, 180
Taylor, Gary, 189, 192–3
Taylor, Jeremy, 162
Teodor, Jacob, 138
Theobald, Lewis, 175
Thompson, Ann, 173, 185
Tian Han, 53
Tillyard, E. M. W., 159, 160
Tinkler, F. C., 100n
Titian, 170
Tobin, J. J. M., 175, 176
Toucatt, Ralph, 25n
Toulouse-Lautrec, Henri de, 149
Tourneur, Cyril, 174
Trace, Jacqueline, 169
Trafton, Dain, 164
Trautmann, K., 138n
Tree, Sir Herbert Beerbohm, 74, 181
Trewin, J. C., 79n, 81n
Trousdale, Marion, 180
Trundle, John, 142
Twycross, Meg, 180
Tynan, Kenneth, 21n, 61n
Tyndale, William, 50, 41

Ulrici, Hermann, 44–5, 49
Urkowitz, Steven, 189

Van Buchel, Arend, 179
Van Doren, Mark, 34n

Vasari, Giorgio, 167
Velz, John W., 177
Vestris, Madame, 181
Vickers, Brian, 168
Vincent, George, 139, 140, 141, 142, 144, 145, 147
Vincent, Thomas, 147
Virgil, 41
Vyvyan, John, 85, 91n, 92n

Waldock, A. J. A., 46n
Walker, Alice, 194
Wall, Stephen, 152
Walter, Harriet, 150
Ward, A. W., 143
Warner, George F., 144
Warren, Michael, 189
Warren, Roger, 175
Watson, Thomas, 85n
Way, A. S., 14n
Wayd, John, 140
Webster, John, 133, 142, 174, 175, 176, 177, 180
Webster, Paul, 154
Weil, Herbert, 169, 171
Weimann, Robert, 168
Welles, Orson, 165
Wells, Stanley, 55n, 57n, 61, 190–1
Wentersdorf, Karl P., 185
Werstine, Paul, 187n, 188, 191
West, Grace Starry, 175
West, Mae, 81
West, Rebecca, 53n
West, Thomas G., 164n
Wetherall, Jack, 60
W. H., Mr, 190

White, Thomas, 140
Whittaker, Herbert, 84n
Whittington, Thomas, 174
Wickham, Glynne, 178
Wilde, Oscar, 21
Wilkes, G. A., 188
Williams, Charles, 30
Williamson, Marilyn L., 170n
Wilson, F. P., 109–10
Wilson, John Dover, 49n, 107n, 182
Wilson, Robert, 176
Wine, M. L., 121, 123n, 129n
Winston, Mathew, 172
Wittgenstein, Ludwig, 21, 22, 23, 24, 25, 26, 27
Wixson, Douglas C., 171
Władysław IV Vasa, Crown Prince of Poland, 145, 146–7
Wolfit, Sir Donald, 81
Wood, Clive, 152
Woodhead, M. R., 176
Worcester, Edward Somerset, 4th Earl of, 142
Wotton, Sir Henry, 144
Wycherley, William, 82

Yang Zhouhan, 55
Yeats, W. B., 1, 29–30, 51
Yeobright, Clym, 95n
Young, W., 147n

Zeifman, Hersh, 23n, 25n
Zhu Shenghao, 55

The Quest for Shakespeare's Globe
JOHN ORRELL

New evidence about the size, the shape and the architectural nature of the Globe playhouse of Shakespeare's time, the most important theatre in English history. Professor Orrell's findings have implications beyond this particular theatre: they mark a clear advance in our hard knowledge of the theatre buildings of Shakespeare's time, to the point where reconstructions may be undertaken with confidence.

0 521 24751 9 **Hard covers**

The Children of Paul's
The Story of a Theatre Company, 1553-1608
REAVLEY GAIR

'... the story of the theatre company attached to St Paul's Cathedral ... neatly told by Professor Gair in this attractively produced volume ... Gair has a knack of making domestic events, in and out of the theatre, take on a living actuality, and his historical approach makes an excellent accompaniment to larger, wider histories of the Elizabethan scene.' *The Stage*

0 521 24360 2 **Hard covers**

The Shakespeare Revolution
Criticism and Performance in the Twentieth Century
J. L. STYAN

'This is an important survey ... for scholar, player and playgoer ... indeed for everyone ... who believes that a criticism based on a strong sense of the play as something incomplete until it is performed, seems likely to grow in importance.' *Theatre Bookshelf*

0 521 21193 X **Hard covers**
0 521 27328 5 **Paperback**

The Texts of King Lear and their Origins
Volume 1 Nicholas Okes and the First Quarto
PETER W. M. BLAYNEY

The first in a two-volume study which attempts to solve the problem of the relationship between the Quarto and Folio texts of *King Lear*. This volume reconstructs the working conditions in the printing house of Nicholas Okes, who printed the 1608 Quarto.
New Cambridge Shakespeare Studies and Supplementary Texts

0 521 22634 1 **Hard covers**

The Winter's Tale in Performance in England and America, 1611-1976
DENNIS BARTHOLOMEUSZ

This book reaches outside the scope of theatrical history to consider the critical tradition: how actors have influenced critics and vice versa.

'Dennis Bartholomeusz narrates and documents this history with skill and knowledge ... any competent reader of *The Winter's Tale* will find his sense of the play greatly extended by reading this book.' *The Times Higher Education Supplement*

0 521 24529 X **Hard covers**

Shakespeare's Rome
ROBERT S. MIOLA

Discusses Shakespeare's changing vision of Rome in the six works where the city serves as a setting: *The Rape of Lucrece, Titus Andronicus, Julius Caesar, Antony and Cleopatra, Coriolanus,* and *Cymbeline.* Dr Miola also re-examines Shakespeare's classical sources, by studying the Renaissance editions of the texts.

0 521 25307 1 **Hard covers**

CAMBRIDGE UNIVERSITY PRESS

120029